Habits of Industry

The Fred W. Morrison Series in Southern Studies

• Allen Tullos •

Habits of Industry

White Culture and the Transformation

of the Carolina Piedmont

The University of North Carolina Press

Chapel Hill and London

The paper in this book meets the guidelines for permanence
and durability of the Committee on Production Guidelines for
Book Longevity of the Council on Library Resources.

Printed in the United States of America

93 92 91 90 89   5 4 3 2 1

Library of Congress Cataloging-in-Publication Data

Tullos, Allen, 1950–
Habits of industry : white culture and the transformation of the
Carolina Piedmont / Allen Tullos.
    p.   cm. — (The Fred W. Morrison series in Southern studies)
Bibliography: p.
Includes index.
ISBN 0-8078-1838-0 (alk. paper). — ISBN 0-8078-4247-8
(pbk. : alk. paper)
    1. North Carolina—Industries—History. 2. North Carolina—
Economic conditions. 3. Family—North Carolina—History. 4. North
Carolina—Social conditions. 5. South Carolina—Industries—History.
6. South Carolina—Economic conditions. 7. Family—South Carolina—
History. 8. South Carolina—Social conditions. I. Title. II. Series.
HC107.N8T85   1989   88-36730
338.09756'5—dc19   CIP

Design by April Leidig-Higgins

For Dorothy and Rolf,
and for Cynthia

Contents

'Oh could we climb where Moses stood,
And view the Landscape o'er'
Not Father's bells—nor Factories
Could scare us any more!
                          —Emily Dickinson

Preface

Among many matters of fact and threads of narrative that have led me onto the meeting ground of history, biography, and regional development in the Carolina Piedmont of the American South, memory turns again and again around a cotton spinner's World War II nightmare.

In 1902 nine-year-old Bessie Buchanan, one of fourteen children, having never sat a day behind a school desk, learned to spin in the Erwin Mill in Durham, North Carolina. For a twelve-hour shift she was paid ten cents. Not until a half-century later would she retire from the spinning frames and bobbins at Erwin.

"The last strike they had over there," Buchanan told an interviewer in 1976, "I reckon it was in '41 or '42. They had a long strike of about eight or nine months. And I was laying here on the bed one night. And this girl who lived with me knew I was opposed to the union, but we never fell out about it. We never had argued about it. . . . I didn't push my feelings on nobody else.

"So I laid down that night and went to sleep. And it was just before World War II, and I dreamed that the Germans had built a wire fence around the whole world and everybody was in that wire fence. And I was out hollering, 'The Germans are coming! The Germans are coming!' [laughs]

"And I don't know why I had that dream or nothing about it. But in that dream, they got me. And they carried me up in an old barn where wheat had been in, and they put a white uniform on me. And they was going to shave my head. And there was two girls, and both of them was in white uniforms. And over here I could hear the awfulest mourning and hollering a-going on.

"And I said, 'What's the matter? Where are they at?'

"And said, 'They's in a lion pit.'

"They'd shave your hair off, and then they'd throw you over in that lion pit if you didn't come over and do what they wanted you to do and join the union.

"Then they come to me and while they was fixing me, I was still sitting up in a high chair. And while they was fixing me to cut my hair off, I says, 'Why are you all doing this to me? I never joined a union in my life, and I never had no part of it.'

"And one of the girls says, 'Could you prove that?'

"I said, 'Sure, I can prove it. Can't you take my word for it?'

"And she opened a door and said, 'You see that road out there?'

"I said, 'Yes.'

" 'There's a gang of men with these knives going this way, swords going that way, and if you can walk down that line and not get killed, I'll let you out of here.'

"Well, I didn't know how in the world I'd do it, but I prayed and prayed.

"And said, 'Now if you look back, they're going to kill you.'

"And so I just said, 'Lord, go with me.'

"And I went down that line, and I never heard so many people hollering at you and saying all kind of nasty things at you. And you could see the women on the outside just hollering at you. But I walked down that line, and I was not harmed, in my dream. And when I got out, I was the only person out.

"About that time, Mary waked me up. Said I was just hollering like everything. And I was scared to death. I ain't never found out why I had that dream about it. But I never have joined it, and I always felt like it was a vision that the Lord give me, not to take up or anything with it. . . .

"And I think about that dream every time I hear unions."[1]

Through a vivid association of labor unions with estrangement, Nazi imprisonment, and torture, Bessie Buchanan's "vision that the Lord give me" conveys a deep wariness felt toward the union movement by many Southern cotton-mill workers from the late nineteenth century until well into the twentieth. Amid biblically charged imagery suggestive of the Old Testament testing of the prophet and interpreter of dreams, Daniel, Buchanan is delivered through faith in God. Her salvation, in this regional culture deeply dyed by Upcountry Protestant fundamentalism, seems contingent upon antiunionism. But Bessie Buchanan's dream offers unacknowledged ambiguities that evade a single, simple interpretation. For among its figurative depictions of domination and dependence in the industrial milieu, her vision suggests that this Lord of deliverance wears a jealous and authoritarian face.

As she begins to tell her dream, Buchanan evokes the atmosphere of World War II and connects this era with the time of a long strike at Durham's Erwin Mills. She and her housemate, Mary, have determined not to let their opposing views about labor unions cause them to fall out of friendship with each other. Her self-restraint ("I didn't push my feelings on nobody else") intends domestic harmony. Her dream, however, is filled with tension and conflict.

The landscape of Bessie Buchanan's nightmare is a world fenced in by approaching Germans. Alone, she is shouting alarm, a voice in the wilderness. Buchanan is captured and taken to a barn where the storage of wheat (emblematic of life itself and of farming as a passing way of life) has given way to a kind of factory, a cold sweatshop of terror. Two "girls" dressed in uniform white put a white uniform on her, suggesting that they, seemingly with authority here, are not unlike her. They sit her in a barber's chair and prepare to shave her head, a conforming and desexing act with contemporary overtones of religious defilement. "Why do you bob your hair girls, it's not the Lord's command," sang Blind Alfred Reed and J. E. Mainer on hillbilly records of the late 1920s and early 1930s.[2] Bessie Buchanan must choose between being thrown in the pit or, more dreadful to her, joining the union.

When she insists upon her innocence of any labor union activity, the dream's movement shifts. She is not thrown into the pit. One of the young women in white now proposes a test. Opening a door, she points to a road lined with men wielding knives and swords. Buchanan must "prove" she has "never had no part" of a union by walking unharmed through this gauntlet and the surrounding crowd of women hollering abuse (like picketers awaiting strikebreakers). If she is untainted by unionism (now the white uniform suggests chasteness), she will be spared. She prays, asking the Lord to go with her. Whether he will or not depends upon her spotless testament. As she is awakened by her friend Mary, Bessie Buchanan finds herself as frightened and alone at the dream's end as she was when it began. For her the warning is clear "not to take up or anything" with unions. The vision, however, illuminates a more conflicted history.

Bessie Buchanan's dream reveals the strands of authority and feeling which, in this historical culture, tied household, workplace, and cultural ethos to the most personal and the most public relations of power. It recalls textile organizing campaigns launched and defeated and many seasons of union frustration in the Carolina Piedmont and throughout the South. Being in the habit of looking to family, kin, neighbors, and on-the-job workmates for mutual self-protection in communities where seldom were heard the voices of a sustained labor movement, farmers recently turned mill workers often saw the union as "foreign" to their experience, as un-American and atheistic, and as a threat to customary work arrangements and familial as well as paternalistic ties of employment.[3] How, given their historical situation, could they have seen otherwise? Industrial union traditions in this region were more novel than factory work itself. Until the 1930s, many, perhaps most, Southern textile workers had never spoken with an organizer. In the family wage system of the mills, workers' first concern lay with household survival. A family could quickly find itself without home or livelihood, or even blacklisted in the mills of neighboring towns, for being too friendly with persons who talked union.

As capitalist industrialization and agrarian collapse transformed the Carolina Piedmont during the last quarter of the nineteenth century, the merchants and mill owners who emerged profited from their knowledge of the seams of this regional culture. They knew, as second nature, the intimate intricacies of paternalistic labor relations. As the new mills went up, the new mill men sought workers from nearby agricultural labor networks.

Economically beleaguered farm families who turned to mill work saw few fat years and few opportunities for pressing the terms of their livelihood beyond the necessities of subsistence. Inside the mill villages, they shared in, as well as resisted, the climate of opinion, values, and structures of power dominated by the region's manufacturers and superintendents, town merchants, mainstream Protestant preachers, race-baiting politicians, chamber of commerce boosters selling cheap and docile labor, and the New South–era businessmen-publishers of local newspapers. As suggested by the presence of Bessie Buchanan's roommate, Mary, there were always workers insistent and outspoken enough to voice common discontents, to fight the pressures to speed up or stretch out, and to lead the occasional walkout and rare strike, sometimes with success. These dissident workers ranged from the most disorderly and profane to the most religiously devout. When economic times were toughest, when the levers and loyalties of paternalism faltered and became discredited—as when manufacturers in the 1920s cut wages, laid off workers, introduced new machinery, and imposed rationalized routines of work—conditions were ripest for moments of labor resistance and revolt that might be triggered by the most personal of incidents.[4] In the crushing of these moments, manufacturers could count on the support of the highest officials of state government and upon the state's police power.

By no means intended as a comprehensive history of the Carolina Piedmont, nor of the making of its working or ruling class, nor of its engineers and politicians, *Habits of Industry* moves among all of these histories—and across the lines of class and gender within the industrial milieu of white society—in search of motive, desire, social character, and relations of power. Throughout the book, each chapter of which takes a different but complementary form, I seek to integrate themes and particulars of biography and family history with the lineaments of the region's industrial emergence. *Habits of Industry* reckons with the formation of attitudes toward work, the shift from farm to factory, the transition from folk to working class, the writing of regional history, and the sources and shape of cultural authority.

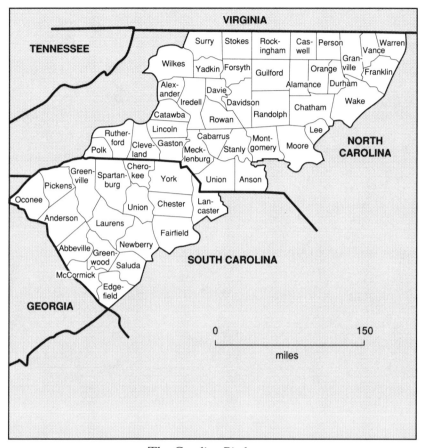

The Carolina Piedmont.

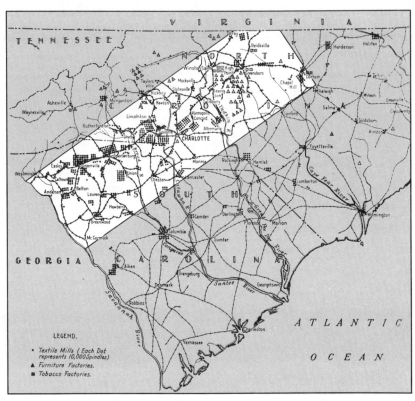

Industries of the Carolina Piedmont. (Reproduced from *Management and Administration*, May 1924)

Habits of Industry

Introduction

The Carolina Piedmont

Along the southern shoulder of the Piedmont Plateau that stretches from New York State into northern Alabama, the Carolina Piedmont spans the 250 miles from Danville, Virginia, to the western boundary of South Carolina where the Blue Ridge watershed slips into the Savannah River. As it extends across the clay hillsides and rock-bottomed river valleys of North and South Carolina, the Piedmont spreads, seventy-five to a hundred miles wide, from the Appalachian foothills to the geological fall line that announces, with a string of rapids, the Atlantic Coastal Plain below. Here and there the regularity of the region's rolling landforms is broken by stubborn mountain remnants known as monadnocks, most prominent in the Kings Mountain range, the Uwharries, and the South Mountains.

The Carolina Piedmont of the late twentieth century lies covered with landmark white oaks and ridges of mixed hardwood and pine that border pastures and patchwork farms; with steadily enlarging small cities strung regularly along the region's central thread, Interstate 85; with the windowless concrete slabs of modern manufactories ("on one floor, under one roof"); and with shopping malls anchored by Belk department stores, whose parking lots blend into the angular blades of suburban evangelical churches. Offering glimpses of the region's history, present-day cityscapes preserve the handsome, brick-and-timber, turn-of-the-century tobacco warehouses in Durham's central city, project the modular geometries of Research Triangle Park and the glaciated financial spires on Charlotte's Trade and Tryon streets, and hide the wooden-frame poverty of Greenville's alleys.

The Piedmont and Coastal Plain of North Carolina equally share nine-tenths of the state's fifty thousand square miles, while the Southern Appalachians claim the western edge. The South Carolina Piedmont extends across a third of that state's thirty thousand square miles. Except for a small strip of the Blue Ridge and the Chattooga Ridge in its northwest corner, nearly two-thirds of South Carolina lies below the fall line.

That the Piedmont Plateau fills a larger portion of North than of South Carolina has significantly affected the histories of these two states. That the backcountry boundaries of both were determined by Crown and colonial interests acting officially in the Low Country meant that the Carolina Piedmont, which extends naturally and culturally across state lines, has had no legitimate sovereignty or unified political clout. In this, the Carolina Piedmont can be compared with other regions of the South, such as the Southern Appalachians or the Black Belt.

The Piedmont, long the most closely settled region of the Carolinas, is also, characteristically, a region through which travelers are always passing toward destinations outside. Before the construction of I-85, U.S. Route 29 tied principal towns and secondary roads together. When cotton mills were still being built from two to four stories tall, with red brick walls, heavy timbers, and tall, paned windows that could be opened, Highway 29 and its tributaries enabled farm families to shift seasonally in and out of the factories or move to town altogether while maintaining ties with rural kin. U.S. 29 paved the way for some of the first hillbilly bands to earn their livings performing at a Spartanburg high school auditorium one night, at a Gastonia mill recreation center the next evening, and on a Charlotte radio station the following morning. It sped the flying squadrons who, with caravans of autos, sought to shut down the region's factories during the 1934 General Strike. U.S. 29 supported the beginnings of a trucking industry tying the Deep South, by way of the Piedmont, with the cities of the Midwest and the East Coast.

In 1932 the South's premier geographer, Rupert Vance, observed from his vantage point in Chapel Hill, North Carolina, that the "Piedmont may simply be taken as the pioneer fringe of an industrialism that is advancing upon the whole South. Those on the ground lack perspective while many people in the North fail to realize the size and importance of the industrial transformation under way."[1] By the time that Vance and his colleagues at the new Institute for Research in Social Science of the University of North Carolina began to take its measure, the momentum of the Piedmont's transformation had gathered force for a half-century. As Piedmont development became both more regionally distinctive and more tied to national trends and world economies, the next half-century continued to be characterized by startling changes, most visible along the routes of highways 29 and 85.

Piedmont landscape with farmboy on a mule, Granville County, N.C.,
1939. Photo by Marion Post, Odum Subregional Photographic Study.
(Courtesy of the Southern Historical Collection, University of
North Carolina)

The Piedmont and the South

"The Piedmont is another land," observed North Carolina journalist Jonathan Daniels in 1939. "It has," he continued, "always been a more serious
minded land. Somehow, the Episcopalians, though they are relatively few in
number, seem to have marked the East, not as a church but as a people. In
contrast, the Piedmont seems more directly to have grown from the stern
spirits of the Quakers of Guilford, the Moravians of Forsyth, the Calvinists of
Mecklenburg, the ubiquitous Baptists, and that practical Methodism from
which the Dukes emerged."[2]

To understand the Carolina Piedmont, one needs to know when to tell
about, and when to leave off telling about, the South. Although the Carolina
Piedmont has shared in all that is Southern, like other *regions* inside and
outside the *section* of the United States known as the South, it also has
experienced a distinctive past. Historians have tended to carry the scenes and

acts of plantation slavery and of Confederate nationalism to a Piedmont theater without looking to see what other dramas and players might already be occupying the stage. Some have seen the Piedmont's post-Reconstruction development as a reconsolidation or extension of planter rule, and mill-village paternalism as deriving singularly from the plantation ethos. The Piedmont's industrialization, however, broke from the broken world of the planters. And its capitalist paternalism finds antecedents not only in planter-slave relations, but also in deferential patterns and customs of the region's eighteenth-century Scotch-Irish, German, and English settlers.

The Piedmont became the heartland of an antebellum Southern yeomanry. This is not to say that there weren't self-sufficient farmers everywhere throughout the South, or that there were no planters in the Piedmont. But planters were less frequently found here and, in general, were not as wealthy as those of the Low Country, Tennessee Valley, Tidewater, Delta, and Black Belt. On the other hand, the spread of the staple economy and the temptations and incursions of the market in the antebellum Piedmont (particularly in the lower piedmonts of South Carolina and Georgia) were more evident than in the small farming areas of north Alabama, the Mississippi hills, and the Southern Appalachians. Piedmont yeomen were middling agriculturalists.

Distinctions between the Carolina Piedmont and other Southern (and Northern) regions begin in topography, climate, and natural ecology and extend across the range of historical experience and culture. "Between the Eastern and Western parts of this state," observed the editor of the *Raleigh Star* in 1810, "there is as great dissimilarity in the face of the country, productions, and means of subsistence as usually exists between different and widely separate nations."[3] Between eastern and western Carolina lay the middle ground of the Piedmont. A redundant landscape of farms and forests, interrupted by the occasional plantation, punctuated by crossroads stores, gristmills, and meetinghouses that lent their names to loose neighborhoods, the antebellum Piedmont developed a characteristic cultural geography that differed from the Deep South as much as it did from Appalachia's ridges and valleys.

The Piedmont's Transformation

While persons and events of the first four decades in the twentieth-century Carolina Piedmont are the central actors and subjects of *Habits of Industry*, they are best understood in the context of the region's longer history. The autobiographical recollections of elder Carolinians interviewed in the 1970s and 1980s touch the nineteenth century and sometimes earlier. The three scenes of chapter one, "A View of the Landscape," illustrate this book's thematic engagement of biography and history and call forth chapter two's historical overview.

Chapter two offers a summary interpretation of the Carolina Piedmont's settlement and its antebellum culture. Following the killing and displacement of native Indian populations, as the backwoods shifted from a land of hunters, trappers, and herders into one of farmers, Scotch-Irish, German, and English-descended families spread across the region, some bringing or acquiring African-American slaves. The assertive coming-of-age of this Upland South yeoman culture was announced from Kentucky to the Coastal Plains by the Great Revival of the early 1800s, an indigenous outpouring of theology, song, sermon, and camp meeting. Certainly there were evangelicals in the Tidewater and Carolina Low Country, but the movement's most numerous and most enthusiastic bands of believers were counted above the fall line.

Throughout the first half of the nineteenth century, and especially after the mid-1830s, world market demand for cotton and tobacco, and for slaves to tend these crops, resulted in a growing enticement to yeomen and a continual spreading of the staple crop, market economy around and within the Piedmont. Ultimately, many Piedmont farmers and small slaveholders joined the secessionist camp. Thousands of them fell among the South's Civil War dead.

Confederate defeat was followed by agrarian crisis, farmer protest, a brief agricultural heyday that in later memory often took on the glow of a "golden age," and years of sharecropping and rural collapse. Alert to new possibilities, and exploiting a particular combination of natural and cultural resources, a rising class of Piedmont merchants and manufacturers (such as the Belks, the Loves, the Dukes, and numerous others) climbed to wealth, power, and prominence during the late nineteenth and early twentieth centuries. Local economies became increasingly incorporated into regional, national, and international structures. The important parallels between industrialization in the Carolina Piedmont and that in other American regions, however, are not the subject of this book.

As part of a movement for regional development, the laying and linking of railroad lines, begun in the 1850s, recommenced in the 1870s, sending Carolina Piedmont cotton, yarn, and unfinished cotton goods north toward new markets. In return came boxcars filled with Yankee-crafted textile machinery, then Pullman cars filled with every kind of salesman and sample case. Water power for factory wheels and electric motors was wrung from the region's rivers by the capital and compulsion of Durham tobacco monopolist Buck Duke and the audacity of Duke engineer W. S. Lee.

An elected leadership ranging from North Carolina's genteel turn-of-the-century governor, Charles Brantley Aycock, to South Carolina's visceral duo of "Pitchfork" Ben Tillman and Coleman Livingston Blease, oversaw the channeling of political power into one-party, white man's rule. A false bargain, as Georgia writer Lillian Smith later called it, based upon a false consensus between Mr. Rich White Man and Mr. Poor White Man over the division of available "public work" (wage labor), excluded black workers from operating the machinery of the new cotton mills and tobacco factories.[4] On the mill hills of the Piedmont, a white farming folk found "public work" and became a working class. Paternalistic relations brought from agrarian households and rural neighborhoods felt the rationalizing efficiencies and intensifying pressures of manufacturers. Across the Victorian neighborhoods of Charlotte, Greenville, Durham, and Greensboro, among the planted oaks and elms, captains of Industry and the new middle class paraded on the latest stage of the region's economic history.

Chapter three traces three generations of the Love family of Gaston County, North Carolina, from the ranks of prosperous farmers into those of merchant capitalists and mill owners, culminating with the development of the nation's largest textile corporation, Burlington Industries. In the person of J. Spencer Love, the family's Presbyterian intensity and his own secularized, risk-taking competitiveness joined with Harvard Business School training and the economic stringencies of the depressed industry to lead a transformation of Southern textiles in the 1920s. Through the narrative of Icy Norman, a longtime worker in the mills of Love, the concluding section of the chapter uncovers the face of a vestigial but still symbolically potent paternalism.

Because the history of the region's transformation remains untold in sufficient biographical depth from a working-class perspective, chapters five, six, and seven follow families who moved from the Piedmont countryside to live and work for decades in factory towns. Drawing upon oral interviews, diary entries, textile trade journals, school scrapbooks, newspapers, and the writings of historians, chapter five tells of two generations of the League family in the Poe Mill of Greenville, South Carolina. In the lives of D. W., Lora, and Nigel League, the traditional morality of work collided with the accelerating demands of the industrial regime of the late 1920s and the 1930s. For weave-room overseer D. W. League, a stand of Christian conscience against the "stretchout" left him bewildered and broken. D. W.'s son, Nigel, was stirred by American dream and Protestant "call" to political office, before public tragedy brought an end to both. Through the local legend of Nigel League, Greenville mill workers projected their hopes and weighed the next generation's prospects. For Nigel's sister, Lora, the primary narrator of the chapter, ties to family and mill-village church sustained twenty-five years of tending the spooling machinery at Poe Mill.

Chapter six, subtitled "A Pilgrim's Progress," is the oral autobiography of Ethel Hilliard of Burlington, North Carolina. Gifted with a poet's ear for keen, multivalent language and a storyteller's long memory and skill of form, Ethel Hilliard tells a class and gender history in a daily detail that has affinities with allegory. Her escape from a hardscrabble childhood in the backwoods North Carolina mining town of Eldorado was followed by bitter years of struggle to sustain a family that seemed to grow larger "every time the moon changed." As she faced and finally faced down her husband's brutality; in her pranks; in her pleasure in scalloping bedspreads at J. Spencer Love's factory; and in her refuge in Holiness piano playing, Hilliard held to a near-inscrutable hope for her children. By chronicling her life and times and by commenting upon the faith she kept even though it compelled tortured years of marriage, Ethel Hilliard's autobiography maps the cultural landscape where habits of industry, the factory regime, fatherly authority, and motherly determination meet.

Few members of any community possess the narrative talents and candor of an Ethel Hilliard. Without compositing the telling fragments of several individual lives into a synthetic whole (a form of historical writing that has its place), the technique of interviewing often can elicit the autobiographies of those not usually identified as storytellers. Through the form of a transcribed, edited interview with former cotton-mill workers Grover and Alice Hardin of Greenville, South Carolina, chapter seven allows their diffident, understated voices to be heard in a jointly told narrative of survival. Preceding chapters have provided the necessary background for the Hardins' spare, evocative description of a life together raising three families on the tightest domestic economy. They recall the migration from farm to factory, the experiences of child labor, the hierarchies of power in the mill, and the debilitating routines of machine tending that left Grover with brown lung disease. Quietly and incrementally, the matter-of-fact tale of the Hardins, resonant with earlier voices and motifs, accumulates their lived evidence while reassessing the lives of factory laborers and the several dimensions of power in the industrial Piedmont.

"The whole vital problem which lies at the heart of the new industrial society," observed Harry Chase, urbane president of the University of North Carolina, in 1920, is "whether the Southern civilization of the future is to center about the machine or the man."[5] *Habits of Industry* concludes by examining the self-study of the Carolina Piedmont's industrial emergence as depicted in the work of the Institute for Research in Social Science (IRSS) at Chapel Hill. Under the avuncular leadership of one of Chase's first recruits to the university, the regional sociologist Howard W. Odum (founder of the IRSS), the history of the Piedmont's transformation and the advocacy of regionalism itself were harmonized into a conflict-free theory of social change and an uncritical allegiance to American nationalism. With a bit of hammering out by Odum and those contemporary and later writers most under his influence, the habits of Industry appeared as inevitable, manifest, progressive. Moments of desperate labor protest, such as those of the late 1920s and early 1930s, were interpreted as signs of the need to adjust Industry's machinery in the area of "labor relations," not as symptoms of an increasingly permanent structuring of inequalities.

The Metaphor of Family

"The family," Erich Fromm has written, "represents the spirit of the society into which the child enters."[6] In the Carolina Piedmont during the era of industrial emergence, no more important institution existed than the family for the socialization of children, the teaching of temperament, the delineation and affirmation of authority, and the lending of support during times of opportunity and crisis. The meaning of family in the Piedmont extended beyond the relations of spouses, parents, children, and siblings to include, depending upon circumstances, a variety of close and distant kin. The metaphor of family extended and complicated the social relations and expectations of many who shared experiences, if not blood. By focusing especially upon families with long tenure in the Piedmont's textile milieu, *Habits of Industry* sketches the formation of temperament and social character in households and explores the consequences of the family metaphor when it is carried onto the factory floor.[7] The spirit of the society into which white, working-class Piedmont children entered during the late nineteenth and early twentieth centuries was strongly colored by an authoritarian paternalism, by the work ethic, and by a strong desire to reproduce the familiar family.

"You can't tell me," says retired mill worker Mary Thompson of Charlotte, North Carolina, "that the way people's raised ain't the way they go. They might sometime get off from it a little bit, but they'll come back. The Bible says raise a child up the way it should go and it won't depart from it. And I believe that, because I seen too much of it."[8]

Early twentieth-century postcard view of Poe Mill, Greenville, S.C.
(Courtesy of the Greenville County Library)

When the mill-building fever of the last quarter of the nineteenth century took hold, manufacturers seized upon the labor of distressed farmers and the tradition of family work (and of large families) to fill the mill villages. Until the 1930s, a "family wage" commonly meant that children and adults all had to tend the factory machinery to earn a livelihood. Mill bosses understood that much of the job of enforcing discipline and industry among the youngest workers would be managed by the fathers and mothers in this family system. "Besides [being] under the company's jurisdiction," says Grover Hardin, who entered the mills of Greenville, South Carolina, as a child, "you was under your parents."

On contested territory within the mill, parental authority sometimes prevailed over the rules of superintendents and second hands. "Back years ago," recalls a former worker, "kids used to be brought in the mill to go to work. They'd make about ten cents a day. They'd get in there and start playing. You know how kids will do. And someone would go tell their daddy and the daddy would whip them.

"That's one thing about these people back then—they'd didn't let nobody else whip their children. If they did, somebody'd get their head cracked. You don't go around whipping other people's children. You go and tell their daddy, if they done something wrong. But you better watch out, he'll whip you. Back in them days, mill folk stuck together."[9]

The language that demanded children's obedience often sounded like that of the Old Testament. Fear and love mixed with ties of intense loyalty to family, kin, and home. "Because I said so," was reason enough. "We had to walk a chalk line," remembers Lora League Wright. "And I deeply appreciated it too. Cause it helped us to be better men and better women. I'm not boasting of our family but there's not any one of us ever been in any kind of trouble."

To a child, religion, stoic discipline, fatherly authority, and the mill hierarchy seemed to be cut from the same cloth. "I don't remember my father ever whipping me but one time," Lora League Wright continues. "I was about seven years old. And we went to Sunday School at two o'clock. And the overseer of the spinning, Mr. Walter, lived below us. And his daughter was sitting behind us and we were sitting on the second seat next to the front, cause my father had us sit right where he could keep an eye on us. And so she said something to me and I turned around then and stood up and heard my father, 'Ahem.' He was sitting in the choir. He blowed the horn, the coronet. And I heard him clear his throat and he pointed his finger. And I knew I was as good as whipped.

"And that's the only time. Except one time he slapped me when I was, I guess eight or nine years old, something like that. At that time, when we were that age, we didn't have the nice bathroom and toilet facilities that we have now. We had the chambers and combinettes. And so I brought one of the little ones in here to the combinette. So Papa, he always had a family prayer, he read the Bible and had a family prayer on Sunday morning. And so Papa said, 'Hurry up, Lora.'

"And I said, 'In a few minutes.' And when I passed him, why he give me one slap. But now that's all I can remember. But Mama said I was just naturally a very nervous person, nervous child. And I did not want to eat at the table with the rest of them. Papa corrected you if you needed correcting. When we was at the table, why he corrected you. And so, I think it just, you know, caused me to be nervous that way."[10]

For children who were born in the South's textile towns or came to them during infancy, the sounds and sights of the industrial landscape came to be joined and identified with the meaning of home itself. The deepest ties between parents and their children could be enmeshed with the factory environment. Parental care and a child's most carefree years recalled and anticipated the story that would one day lead up the streets to the familiar mill.

"And the first thing I remember," recalls retired weaver Geddes Dodson, born in 1904, "why, we was a-living at Inman, South Carolina. And the old mill, great big old mill about the size of Brandon Mill, was down thisaway and the streets run up that way. And I was a little bitty feller, and my mother'd make me a pallet out on the front porch. I was too little to get out and run around. But I remember that, and I lay [laughs] there on the pallet and listened to that old mill roar."[11]

The chain of authority in the mill was very different from the paternal chain of authority in the rural household and community, yet the paternalistic structure of the family buttressed and helped legitimize the authority that existed within the mill. In small, rural mills, workers were often related by blood or marriage to mill bosses. Father figures in both small and large factories extended down from owners (such as the Loves) through the all-male ranks of superintendents, department overseers (such as Lora League Wright's father, D. W. League), second hands, and machine fixers.

"I came to Plaid Mill [in Burlington, North Carolina] March 21, 1932," recalls retired weaver Betty Davidson, "and Mr. Copland, the superintendent, put me to work with the reference of my father, because he knew my father.

"He expected everybody to work just like he worked. One day he came through the mill and I had a pickwheel missing. So he got me down, said, 'Betty, you see that pickwheel's missing?' And he caught ahold of my arm and he didn't realize how big his hands was, and left the print of all his fingers on my arm. But he didn't aim to hurt me, he just did it.

"He was a hard-working man, and he wanted you to work hard. He expected you to work just like he did. He didn't expect any more out of you than he did. He kept busy, real busy."[12]

Whether a superintendent was a "hat-stomper" like Jim Copland who bullied and intimidated his "hands," or a milder sort who varied his methods of motivation, bosses who successfully commanded or won the loyalties of workers could always find employment. Such a superintendent "was just like the father of the whole shebang," says one former worker. "They all thought a lot of him if he was a decent sort of a fellow, and treated them right. When he took a job in another mill, he took his help with him."[13]

From the household to the workplace and from private to public lives, *Habits of Industry* considers the fatherly voices that sought to control the historical Piedmont's here and hereafter. In these voices of authority and in those counterposed to them, the power of speech and the will to impose consent or silence around family dinner tables, across merchants' ledger books, in pulpits and along pews, down weavers' alleys between rows of looms, and over oak desks at the offices of the region's manufacturers reveals much about the harnessing of the Carolina Piedmont's most important industrial force—its humanity.

Race and Region

Although this book is centered upon relations within white society, the Carolina Piedmont's industrial emergence also depended upon the cheap labor of the region's black population during the long Jim Crow era. For a subsistence pay of dimes and starch, table scraps and castoff clothes, black women took in the laundries and cleaned the houses not only of middle-class but also of many mill-hill families. Black men worked as construction laborers and were consigned to the most strenuous and hazardous of jobs, such as the firing of steam boilers. Black men and women undertook the dirtiest, dustiest, hottest, and heaviest tasks in the tobacco factories of the Reynolds family in Winston-Salem and of the Dukes in Durham. All but a relative handful of blacks were excluded from the Piedmont's textile mills and from the operation of tobacco-processing machinery until after World War II.[14]

Something of the relationship between the prototypical Piedmont mill owner and black labor is revealed in an incident from the life of manufacturer Simpson Bobo Tanner. In Gerald W. Johnson's adulatory biography of Tanner (1853–1924), a man "representative of the type," readers glimpse the rise of this puritanical "dynamo of energy" as he climbs from modest beginnings to the ownership of several cotton mills.

"Paternalistic to the last degree," Tanner, writes Johnson, "regulated not merely the working conditions, but the private lives of his operatives." At Tanner's Henrietta Mills in Rutherford County, North Carolina, company police enforced prohibitions against drinking, "rowdiness," and "sexual misbehavior." Tanner acted as ultimate judge. Although biographer Johnson finds his regime authoritarian by "modern" standards, he defends Tanner's rule as "discipline, not mere domination" by insisting that it was necessary for the transforming of rural whites into town dwellers and efficient factory "operatives."

Disorderly conduct meant prompt expulsion from Tanner's mill town. Gambling was forbidden. Although profanity was not to be tolerated, contemporaries who talked with Johnson delighted in recalling an exception to this rule. A wagon hauling a very heavy safe to the office sank hub-deep in a muddy road and the four-mule team simply quit. After all efforts to rouse the mules had failed, a large black muleteer stepped up to Tanner and said he could get them out if the boss would let him use his own methods. Told to go ahead, he proceeded to "gee" and "haw" the team into a straight line, then flew into lurid profanity, cursing the mules collectively, individually, up one side and down the other. "He swore," writes Johnson, "until the air was blue and crackling. And the mules, hearing the voice of mastery, with one accord sank belly to earth, surged into the collars and pulled the wagon out of the mud.

"'Hm-m-m,' said Tanner thoughtfully. 'Looks like they really needed cursing, doesn't it?' "[15]

Even as it chides the moralistic code of mill owners like Tanner, this scene embodies the prevailing racial arrangement and the idealized place of the white man, who stands high, dry, clean, and disdainful while the black muleteer (suggesting a creature half man and half mule) does the essential dirty work among the mudsills.[16] In just this way, white social standing rose upon an unacknowledged black history. The Tanner narrative suggests that much of what passed for progress in the Carolina Piedmont in the decades between Reconstruction and World War II, occasionally amid a blue and crackling air, depended upon "mere domination."

Habits of Industry

In thinking about the men, women, and children whose lives were deeply affected by the coming of industrialization to the Piedmont countryside, the venerable phrase, "habits of industry," has proven helpful. The oldest and most customary usage of "habits of industry" embraces the Protestant work ethic central to the ideology of industrializing America. If, as Daniel T. Rodgers argues, the "commitment to the moral primacy of work" waned in the North by the end of the nineteenth century, it showed no signs of slacking among the Baptists, Methodists, and Presbyterians of the Southern Piedmont.[17]

The daily and seasonal rounds of agriculture had inured generations of Piedmont farmers to long hours and hard labor. Pressed for their own self-sufficiency, farm families came to habits of industry through a necessity confirmed by evangelical Protestantism. When forced from the farms to the spindles and looms, they continued to work with all their might at whatever their hands found to do. Such was the faith of their fathers and mothers. Habits of industry soon included workers' shared knowledge of mechanical skills and mastery of tricks of the trade. The steadiest took satisfaction from humming looms and frames. "I'd a whole lot rather weave than eat pie when

Tobacco warehouses and factory, Durham, N.C., 1940. Photo by Arthur
Rothstein, Farm Security Administration. (Courtesy of the Southern
Historical Collection, University of North Carolina)

I'm hungry," went a familiar saying among weavers. Even the hardest daily
efforts and stoic endurance, however, guaranteed no lasting security against
landlords, lien merchants, and mill bosses.

Within the factory walls, workers had to accustom themselves to the deaf-
ening roar, to the humidified fog intended to lessen the breakage of spun
fibers and threads (called "ends"), and to the cloud of cotton dust drawn in
with every breath. These, too, became habits of industry, habits of an industrial environment geared to produce wealth at the least cost for mill owners.

"To show you how it was in the mills in those days," recalls a retired
spinner from Durham's Erwin Mill, "my father worked for years and years in
the weave room. It was a racket in there, a constant noise. And soaky hot and
wet. And lint a-flying everywhere, covering you all over.

"Just about every day that my father worked in there, my mother fixed his
dinner to carry. One of the things she'd make was a fried fruit pie, a turnover.
She called them 'poorboys in a blanket.'

"As a joke one time she baked him a poorboy with a wad of cotton stuffed
inside it instead of apples or pears. Mixed the cotton filling with a little

cinnamon and sugar and water. She put that pie with his other food and off Papa went, not knowing.

"That evening he came in just like he always did. Didn't say a word. Finally Mama couldn't stand it and asked him how he liked his dinner. He said it was just fine. So she told him about the cotton poorboy, and he wouldn't believe it. He'd eaten it and never even noticed. He just wouldn't believe she'd done that. But she had. I watched her."[18]

Carolina Piedmont farmers-turned-factory-workers were no pie eaters. On the farm they had been accustomed to working "from can 'til can't see," all the daylight hours. Laboring in the mills for fifty or sixty hours a week at wages pegged just above a farmer's subsistence, they strained to make ends meet.

Industry's Habits

"All work, even cotton-spinning is noble," wrote Thomas Carlyle in *Past and Present* (1843), in words that the most paternalistic of Southern factory owners—perhaps hosiery king Julian Shakespeare Carr—could have uttered: "work is alone noble." By capitalizing the final word of the phrase, *habits of Industry* expresses the liturgical zeal ("work is worship") that animated the ascending class of New South merchants and manufacturers in the Piedmont as they mastered businesses, bought and sold mills, altered river courses, built towns, enacted designs upon the region, and presumed to know best for the workers they called "our hands." A calculating religiosity of ledger books captured the Piedmont's nascent capitalists. Habits of industry directed toward the quest for profits and the acquisition of economic power became Industry's habits, embodying the assumptions, prerogatives, and practices of—to use another of Carlyle's phrases—Industry's Captains. In time, Industry's assurance of having its way and of having it publicly confirmed became one of the Piedmont's, and the South's, most secure habits.

· 1 ·

A View of the Landscape

Mill on the Haw

"That was in the summer time, when the water gets low," says Ethel Faucette (born just before the Christmas of 1897) as she remembers the first years of a lifetime's work in the Glencoe Cotton Mill. "There's a big old rock out there in Haw River they call Lily and—I forget the other one's name, but there's two of them. When you begin to see them two rocks, you'd know we was going to get a rest. Cause the water was getting low."

"Yeah," adds George Faucette, Ethel's husband, "they made up songs whenever the water'd get low. Get out in front of the mill under two big trees—they done cut the two trees down. Get out there in the shade and sing."

"Sometimes it was two or three times a week," says Ethel, "when it didn't rain. We had dry weather just like we have now. People say, 'Oh, I don't remember it.' Well, I remember it very well, for I was working in the mill, and I know'd when it'd shut down for low water."

The narratives of Ethel Faucette, her husband George, and their sons Don and Paul tell of three generations of life and work in the Glencoe mill village, located along the small and seasonally inconstant Haw River. Their memories lead back toward the turn of the century in historical fact, but they point even further back, glimpsing the region's late-nineteenth-century transformation and, at moments, even evoking the tentative antebellum beginnings of Carolina Piedmont manufacturing.

"We run by water then, had water wheels. That was the power that run the mill. And when the water'd get low, maybe they'd stop off for an hour or two. Well, there was a crowd that would get their instruments and get out there in front of the mill. They would sing and pick the guitar and the banjo. Different kinds of string music. And maybe they'd stand an hour or two and the water'd gain up, and they'd start the mill back up.

"And I did have a piece that one man wrote about the whole mill. I lost it somewhere. He made up a song about the whole mill, but I forget what it was, don't you, George?"

"What?"

"The song where, was it Walt Dickens—who was it made that song up about the mill? And it started at the first of it, where the cotton started in. From the breakers and the lap room and so on about the different kinds of work. He rhymed it up and made a great long song. But I can't remember, been so long ago."[1]

"I remember one time back in the Depression," says Don Faucette. "Water was low and sometimes the mill would stand. Once when I carried the dinner up there, Daddy was standing out there up to his hips, getting the mud out from the back of the dam so the water would come down the race so they could go back to work.

"I remember well when they run the mill by water. Cause we had lights at Glencoe and at nine o'clock the lights went out. The mill furnished your lights and they'd come on about six o'clock at night and stay on till nine and then come on again at five in the morning and go out about seven.

"You'd be sitting there studying and the lights would go down. One of us would say, 'An eel has hit the wheel.' In a minute, that eel would grind up and the lights would go back on. There used to be some good fishing too in the Haw River. Until they turned that dye and stuff loose in Greensboro."

"There was carps up there that weighed twenty-five pounds," says Don's brother Paul. "There was catfish, bream, bass, white perch. White perch is called crappie now. Blue gills, and oh, what did they call them with the red stomach? I don't remember. We used to fish there until they started turning that dye loose up the river. After that, we'd have to go out there and rake the fish off the gates to let the water keep the mill running."[2]

"My mother was Mary Elizabeth Marshall," says Ethel Marshall Faucette, "and my daddy, he just had initials, M. M. Marshall. He was a twin and they named his sister Alice and Granny wanted him named David and Grandpap wouldn't have it. So they just called him their "little man." And that's as much as he ever had. And he just signed his name M. M. Marshall. That's the way he signed. It went that-a-way as long as he lived. [laughs] And it's that-a-way in the cemetery."

"Man" Marshall was born and raised on a Carolina Piedmont farm. When

Mill workers at Glencoe, N.C., ca. 1900. Ethel Faucette's father is the bareheaded man in the top row. Note the groupings and postures by gender and age. (Courtesy of Ethel and George Faucette)

he died in 1939 at the age of seventy-two, he had held the superintendent's job at the Glencoe mill for forty years. Like her seven brothers and sisters, M. M. Marshall's daughter Ethel was working a ten-hour day in the Glencoe mill when she was more a child than an adult. She learned to operate the twisting and drawing-in machinery, earning $.85 a day when she began and $1.69 an hour by the time the mill shut down in 1954.

"Daddy had a little better wages, but we didn't," says Ethel about the children of "Man" Marshall. "We fared just like the rest of the help. He made us do, and do right.

"And when we come from that mill, we didn't sit at the table and talk about what the other fellow done down there—if we did we got our mouths mashed.

"He says, 'You leave the mill out of your conversation.' He didn't allow us to say a word about it."

The builders of the Glencoe mill and village, where the Faucette family worked and lived, were named Holt. The Holts, who had lived in the area since the mid-eighteenth century, were one of the Carolina Piedmont's pioneering and prominent manufacturing families from the 1830s until their interest in the textile industry began to wane in the 1920s. Michael Holt, father of mill pioneer Edwin (1807–84), was a prosperous merchant, farmer, and slaveholder. It was on the site of the family's power dam and gristmill that Edwin and his brother-in-law, William Carrigan, in 1837 built the first Holt cotton mill, a small operation with around five hundred spindles and no looms.

To propose the construction of a factory in the Carolina Piedmont in the 1830s required outlandish views. But Edwin Holt was persuaded by the success in that same decade of Henry Humphries' steam-powered Mount Hecla Mill in Greensboro and by the encouragement and support of prominent North Carolina jurist Thomas Ruffin, a longtime family friend. Holt's father bitterly opposed the project at first but lived to salute its profits.

Critical to the successful operation of antebellum Southern factories such as Edwin Holt's and Henry Humphries' was Yankee machinery and technical assistance. A Paterson, New Jersey, firm supplied Edwin Holt's first mill and sent a machinist who supervised the installation of equipment and remained for a year and a half to give instruction in its running and maintenance.[3]

As they did in other antebellum Carolina Piedmont factories, white girls and women from the immediate neighborhood made up most of the labor force at the Holt and Carrigan mill. In the five cotton mills operating in Alamance County in 1850, there were 155 women workers and 33 men. Revealing the low status of factory work and the pitiful regard given to women forced into it, a traveler through Alamance in the 1840s wrote that a mill job was generally seen as a "blessing," an unanticipated bit of good fortune, giving "employment and comfort to many poor girls who might otherwise be wretched."[4]

Throughout the antebellum era, yeoman farming embodied the ideal of domestic independence in the Carolina Piedmont. Not until the long agricultural collapse that, in the last quarter of the nineteenth century, began to uproot farmers from their traditional livelihood could mill owners recruit an increasing number of male "hands." As entire families moved to the villages, they often arrived with some sense of failure and with a strong determination to return to farming as soon as they could save enough money to buy the land. Neither factory wages nor agricultural conditions, however, favored a return to the land.

Antebellum manufacturer Edwin Holt cast an early eye to possible markets outside the county and even outside the Carolina Piedmont. In the 1850s an itinerant French dyer taught Holt and his son Thomas the process of dying yarn. Successful sales in the North of "Alamance Plaids," the South's first colored cotton cloth woven on power looms, assured the Holts' wider reputation and success.[5]

In 1849, in a display of his new status and orientation, E. M. Holt built his home, Locust Grove, from the design of a New York architect. Locust Grove, notes architectural historian Carl Lounsbury, "was the first known house constructed in Alamance County which owed nothing in its plan and arrangement to the local building practices. It was the first clear-cut example of popular architectural tastes supplanting the vernacular tradition and foreshadows similar developments in the last half of the nineteenth century."[6] In his business and his tastes, Holt looked to markets and influences beyond the Piedmont, a wider world that would not find full entry into the region until after the Civil War.

Holt mills prospered through the war years, producing cloth for the Confederates. Then, reaping the rewards of established pioneers, Edwin Holt and his progeny refurbished their old factories and built several new ones in the 1870s and 1880s, mills that made fortunes for several branches of the family. Because of their small sizes and inconvenient locations, though, they were eclipsed, near the century's end, by a new era in Carolina Piedmont manufacturing. The newest New South mills housed tens of thousands of spindles and hundreds of looms and sat alongside railroad spurs and trunklines.

Like Randolph County (to the southwest) with its Deep River and (still further west) Lincoln County with its many fast-running creeks, Alamance County and the Haw River offered tempting locations for the Carolina Piedmont's antebellum experiments with cotton factories. Like the Holt mills, the first generation of Carolina Piedmont cotton factories (a handful of tiny mills built between 1813 and 1830) emerged out of the region's tradition of home weaving and its experience with water power for the grinding of grain and cereals. These early cotton mills were begun in order to supply yarn for domestic weaving in the surrounding communities. Transported by wagon, bundles of coarse yarn were sold and bartered throughout the region and into the Southern Appalachians. The tiny antebellum factories were vastly outnumbered in a landscape dotted with gristmills and sawmills, centers of community life that stood along every good-sized creek.[7]

Unlike the major rivers of the Carolina Piedmont, which begin in the Appalachians and are fed over a wide watershed, the Haw, which furnished power to the Holt mills, rises in the Piedmont counties of Rockingham and Guilford and depends for its water level on local rainfall. The flow of this bedrock-bottomed stream varies dramatically from week to week and, as Ethel Faucette remembers, predictably from season to season. The power to drive the Piedmont's industrial emergence did not lie in the Haw or in the Deep River, but with mightier waters to the west, such as the Yadkin and the Catawba. Around the turn of the twentieth century, these rivers spun the turbines of a regional power network under the control of James B. ("Buck") Duke's new electrical company.

In 1880, about the time that the Glencoe mill, with its 3,000 spindles and 180 looms, began operation, several Carolina Piedmont mill builders had already begun to shift away from the beside-the-old-mill-stream mentality toward one of increasingly larger, beside-the-railroad factories relying on coal and, soon, electricity. In addition to the advantages offered by railroad access and cheap power, a search for available labor also appears to have promoted the location of new, large mills in areas of the Piedmont where the cotton farming crisis was felt most severely.[8]

When they built Glencoe, a three-story mill that was fifty feet wide and two hundred feet long, the Holts also built a mill village. Lined along two streets, more than three dozen two-story hall-and-parlor houses were solidly constructed of wood and drew upon a folk architectural form widespread among antebellum Piedmont farmers. Between the inside and outside walls the builders added a layer of insulating brick nogging. At the rear of these houses stood separate kitchen buildings, also in vernacular form. Rows of white oak, the Carolina Piedmont's signature tree, grew to shade the streets.[9]

In 1880 the six hundred mill workers in Alamance County accounted for 18 percent of North Carolina's entire textile work force. Forty years later, Alamance counted three thousand mill hands, but these comprised only 3.2 percent of North Carolina's ninety-four thousand textile workers.[10] When it closed in the mid-1950s, after decades of pounding out coarse fabrics, the Glencoe mill was tiny by contemporary standards, holding only four thousand spindles and two hundred looms.[11]

The modern textile manufacturing companies of the Carolina Piedmont left Glencoe and scores of similar mill villages behind, touchstones to an earlier era of localism. Once, they had helped shift the mainstream of a region's way of life. Then, having no railroad, sitting astride no major highway, losing the early advantages of their water-power sites, suffering the neglect of their owners, unable to recruit sufficient workers, and failing to modernize their machinery, the Glencoes were pushed into the eddies. As such towns lingered—places with names like Bynum, Orange Factory, and

Coleridge—the shapes and materials of their houses and the memories of their abiding residents recalled lost heydays.[12] The newer Piedmont spread away from the side roads and sought the major rail and U.S. highway axes.

"It was so far back when I told this," says Charles Murray, another of the handful of Glencoe holdouts. "But I did it as a joke. I'd hear people tell it. There's some fish in the river they used to call terkel. And the mill would send a wagon off and get terkel and they'd come back and pay you off. They'd give you a big terkel. And you'd go to the store and buy anything, and you'd give them a big terkel and they'd give you little terkels back."[13]

"People then just thought they was fortunate to be working," says Ethel and George Faucette's son Don, himself a textile worker in nearby Burlington. Born in 1925, Don remembers growing up in a Glencoe that seemed stunting and isolated. "To have food on the table and clothes on their back and a roof over their head, that's all that mattered. I mean, that's the reason I wanted to get me a car and get out, just like a bunch of us did. Old Ed King and Vann Kerr and all of us, we wanted to have something, you know. And we just felt like we couldn't have nothing staying over there at Glencoe.

"Momma and Daddy seemed like they was satisfied just as long as they'd get to town and all. Uncle Ed seemed like he was happy just as long as he could get over there to the beer joint and get him a beer on payday. Then he'd be waiting for next payday. I wanted more than that."

When the Glencoe mill shut down in the 1950s, most families moved away. The abandoned houses began to fall apart, conceding to vines and trees. A factory outlet remnant store opened in a section of the old mill building beside the Haw. Occasionally, squads of firemen from some more defensible town set, then practiced extinguishing, blazes in the empty houses. For a few days in the mid-1970s Glencoe stirred to life when a low-budget movie production company set up to shoot an antebellum scene in which Glencoe stood in for Graniteville, William Gregg's South Carolina textile town.

A hundred years after one of Edwin Holt's sons contracted for construction of the three-story, brick Glencoe mill on the Haw River, George and Ethel Marshall Faucette walked across the street from their house to draw drinking water from a well. In their eighties, living in a house without running water, their children grown and moved away, the Faucettes were among the last citizens of Glencoe. They managed on their monthly Social Security checks, receiving no pension for their lives of labor in the Holts' mill at the bottom of the hill.

"This was a pretty place," Ethel Faucette says, looking from her front

Ethel and George Faucette, Glencoe, N.C., 1979. Photo by Allen Tullos.

porch. "They kept it clean as could be. All this growth around here has growed up since the mill shut down.

"Every one of these houses stayed full of people. They had a big garden, they raised their hogs, they kept their cow—if they owned one—and their horse. And there wasn't no trouble here. They kept things cleaned up. You didn't smell no hog lots nor cow lots or nothing. They had to keep it cleaned up."

"Well, I'll tell you," says Zelma Murray, wife of Charles Murray, "It used to be that everybody that lived here were kinpeople. They were related to each other."

"Yeah," agrees Charles, "the superintendent, he was my uncle, he married my father's sister."

"Yes," says Zelma, "used to be, just about everybody around here [laughs] was related some way or another. It might not be close, but most of them were, you know, some kind of an uncle or aunt, or some kind of a cousin or something along that line."

In the early years of Glencoe Mill, organizers with the National Union of Textile Workers (NUTW) tried to unionize the mills along the Haw. October 1900 saw the Holts stifle a rising of Alamance County mill workers. With no tradition of unionism and little means of leverage, strikers faced lockouts, evictions, and intimidation amid the rural isolation of Glencoe and similar villages. The visible defeat of the NUTW in Alamance affirmed the authority of the Holts and gave mill owners a precedent in the industrializing region.[14]

Ethel Faucette remembers a few short-lived efforts at unionization during the years that her father was superintendent of Glencoe Mill. "Nobody wouldn't vote for the union. My dad didn't pay a bit more attention to it than he would a dog barking. I just remember them talking about it. We didn't never ask Daddy nothing about the mill because that was one thing he didn't allow. He said it wasn't none of our business—that's just what he'd say."

"And you better do just what he said, too," adds George Faucette.

"And we knowed it," says Ethel Marshall Faucette.

Water Power and Millwrights

"It is well worthy of the attention of capitalists desiring to locate in this vicinity," wrote George F. Swain in 1885 as he described a promising water-power site on the Haw River in Chatham County, twenty or so miles downstream from the Glencoe mill village. Swain's *Report on the Water-Power of the South Atlantic Watershed*, compiled as part of the tenth census of the United States, presented a detailed guide to the significant water-power sites in the Southeast. In addition to his own field studies, Swain relied upon reports of the Army Corps of Engineers, officers and engineers of various railroads, civil engineers, and such state officials as North Carolina's geologist, W. C. Kerr.

Swain wrote with urgency about the need to master the streams of the Carolina Piedmont, or, as he called it, the "middle division" of the Carolinas. Water not busy turning wheels and driving shafts was power lost, as was water that spilled over or around an existing mill dam. "The factory is run night and day," Swain complained of more than one mill dam, "and there is always waste of water."[15]

The Carolina Piedmont, as Swain beheld it, offered a vast region of waterfalls dispersed across lengthier, more numerous, and altogether more useful streams than those found, by contrast, in the New England textile districts. Rather than the concentrated river power of the twelve-mile stretch between Lowell and Lawrence, Massachusetts, the Piedmont offered a more variegated physiography, a geography capable of supporting a more decentralized mill region.

> The middle division is topographically very favorable for power. The fall of the streams is great, but as a whole tolerably uniform, and their volume moderately large. They cross the ledges of rock at large angles, forming many rapids, rifts, or falls in all parts of this region. These ledges, being composed of hard, durable, and impervious rocks, generally granite or similar rocks, insure the permanence of the powers, and afford everywhere good sites for dams. The shape of the river valleys is such as to render the utilization of the power in most cases easy. . . . The facilities for storing water are, on the whole, good.[16]

Sixty years before George Swain pointed out the suitability and distinctiveness of the Piedmont for manufacturing and compiled his lists of utilized and potential power sites on Carolina streams, Robert Mills prepared and published a remarkably detailed set of maps showing the locations of dozens of Upcountry water mills. A tradition of water-power use in the Carolina Piedmont was as old as the first Scotch-Irish and German settlers' mid-eighteenth-century need to grind grain. Mills's *Atlas of South Carolina* (1825) shows that, whether in Abbeville, Greenville, Spartanburg, Chester, or any other district above the fall line, creeks and rivers were dotted with gristmills and sawmills having names like Hammet Mill, Benson's Mill, Pollard's Mill, and Widow Picken's Mill. A variety of industries appears in Mills's *Atlas*: Benson's Iron Works and McCool Shoals Cotton Factory in the Greenville District; Jackson's Furnace and Hill's Old Iron Works in York; a limestone quarry, several furnaces, forges, and iron ore sites in northeast Spartanburg; and two cotton factories on the Tyger River. And there are other signs of small-scale enterprise: blacksmith shops, tanyards, rural taverns, and crossroads stores. Religious meetinghouses are marked and are as common as water mills.[17]

"I come from a line of people who were involved in the textile industry in Scotland," says Robert Roy Adams (born 1899) of Greenville, South Carolina. In 1923, after graduating from Furman, a Baptist college in Greenville, Adams joined the industrial engineering firm of J. E. Sirrine, designers of

Water power at the falls of the Reedy River, Greenville, S.C., ca. 1900.
(Courtesy of the Greenville County Library)

many Piedmont textile factories. He became a partner in the Sirrine Company in 1937 and spent much of his working life drawing the plans for Southern mill towns.[18] A third-generation engineer, he bridges the generations with a continuous narrative of work, of the activities of building. Even his mother appears primarily as a domestic manufacturer. In its descriptive detail of handicraft, of religious belief, of regional independence, Adams's telling of his family history makes clear the Carolina Piedmont's distinctiveness.

"My grandfather," says Adams, "was John Adams. He was raised in a textile town, Lennoxtown, about twelve miles out of Glasgow, Scotland. They had a textile printworks there. And he was an apprentice and got to be a millwright.

"When he was about twenty-six he married and came to the United States. That was in 1834. He landed at Charleston, and he met someone there who had some connection with a textile operation in Lincolnton, North Carolina. This man told him he could go up there and probably find work. So my grandfather went to Lincolnton from Charleston and worked up there with Vardry McBee. McBee was one of the early pioneers in Greenville who used to own nearly all of what is now the city of Greenville. He bought about eleven thousand acres of land about 1817, I believe it was, and then later on, around in the 1830s, he decided to build a textile plant down here on the Reedy River. And he persuaded my grandfather to come from Lincolnton down here to Greenville and supervise the construction of what became known as the Conestee Mill down on the Reedy River.

"Being a millwright and also knowing machinery and having had some experience in Scotland with plants over there, he could build the mills, select the machinery, and build the dam, and supervise the whole operation. He also built a paper mill for Mr. McBee down there around 1850 or '60. The paper mill is long since gone. Hardly anybody knows that a paper mill existed down there.

"My father was also a millwright. He built a number of flour mills in the Greenville County area, and he owned a flour mill. In 1877 he built one down on Gilder Creek. He was a surveyor and millwright and built mills. He built one down at Greenwood. He built one over at Spartanburg. These were just small flour mills. They did the grinding of wheat on a toll basis.

"The people who worked in the building of flour mills, a lot of them worked in building textile mills, too. My father was never involved in textile mills, but my grandfather, John Adams, was. And talk about religion, he was a staunch Presbyterian. My grandfather was the first ruling elder of the First Presbyterian Church here in Greenville. He originally lived down in the lower part of Greenville County around Fairview. The Fairview church was a very old Presbyterian church. And in 1848, when they wanted to organize the church here in Greenville, they asked him to come up, and he helped organize it and became their first ruling elder.

"He designed and built this little church at Conestee, where this cotton mill was. It was an eight-sided church. It's still down there, and now it's on the Register of Historic Places. And John Adams is the man that built that.

"My ancestors on the other side of the family were Taylors. You know Taylors, South Carolina? They came into that area just after the Revolutionary War. They came down from North Carolina with a group that came down from Virginia. That first ancestor was James Taylor. His son, Thomas Taylor, born in 1781, was just a child when they came in out there.

"My mother's father was Alfred Taylor, who developed Taylors, out here. He was born in 1823. By the time he died in 1912, he owned about seven hundred or eight hundred acres. He was a jack-of-all-trades. He had a flour mill and a grist mill out there on the Enoree River. Our family still owns ten acres of land where that old mill was. He grew rice, had a sugar operation, had a sawmill, had a cotton gin. He had a brickyard, was a farmer and a dentist. He actually did dental work. He had dental tools and he'd go throughout the area working on people's teeth.

"Grandfather Alfred Taylor was an ardent Baptist from way on back. He built the first Baptist church in Taylors, South Carolina. He actually built it with his own hands. They originally were members of the old Brushy Creek Baptist Church, which was organized in Greenville County here about 1795. My great-grandfather was one of the first members of that church. So my mother's side was strong Baptist. And she reared all the children Baptists, but my father always went to the Presbyterian church as long as he lived. He'd go to the Presbyterian church, and my mother would go to the Baptist church. And all the children were reared in the Baptist church, but as they grew older they more or less gravitated back to the Presbyterian church.

"Alfred Taylor farmed and did mill work and grew hogs and cattle and things of that sort. Those people were farmers primarily, and then they would go into grist mills because there was demand for the surrounding areas to have a place they could grind their flour, and also corn for meal. But those grist flour mills were all over. Over in Pickens County there was a flock of them. It didn't take more than about twenty-five horsepower to run one of those mills, and they could get that from a little water wheel, a fifteen- or twenty-foot fall in the creek. They could get that with a little small stream. But they weren't too closely related to textiles, because they were farmers and they continued that way of life.

"Back in those days you had to be independent, you know, because the only things they bought from outside were probably tea and coffee and things that they couldn't make themselves. Everything else they made themselves. They had sheep. They made their own wool and spun the yarn and wove their own cloth. My mother, Sarah Elvira Taylor, used to run a loom at their home there. She was a remarkable person.

"She was born in 1860. She remembered when my grandfather came back from the Civil War. My grandfather was in Virginia at the end of the Civil War, and he had to walk back to Taylors.

"After the war, times were very hard in the South, and my mother ran a loom and did all the home work up until the time she was married, in 1880. She would take the wool or cotton and had hand cards, and they'd card it into these little slivers, and then she'd take those slivers and spin them into yarn, and then they had a hand loom that she would make the cloth, and then they'd make the clothes out of the cloth.

"After she married, she continued to use these hand bats to bat material to use as filling for quilts. And she manufactured quilts up until fairly recent years. Had these quilting frames. They'd make these bats of cotton or wool and sew them between two pieces of cloth and make quilts out of them.

"My mother lived to be ninety-eight years old. She just died in 1959.

"My father was a farmer and a surveyor and a millwright and owned a flour mill. He supplemented his income with farming. He always owned a farm, because there wasn't much else to do up in this area at that time. The textiles began to develop in the 1880s and '90s, and then they really got going around 1900 or so."

No Idle Time

"Man is a working animal." John Belk speaks to me across his desk in the Belk stores headquarters building in Charlotte, North Carolina. It is a July day late in the twentieth century, but Belk's voice reaches with compelling authority from the mid-eighteenth-century arrival of his family in the Carolina Piedmont through the extraordinary rise of his father, William Henry Belk, a prototypical figure of New South transformation.

Gold-plated shovels lean against a far corner of the office. John Belk, chief operating officer of America's largest privately owned department store group, former mayor of Charlotte, sits with courteous impatience to be interviewed. Neither gilt shovels nor visitors with tape recorders get the Piedmont's work done.

"I don't know any family sayings," says John Belk. "I know a lot of family teachings. They believed in educating their children, Christianity, integrity, and treating your fellow man right and everybody working. They believed that mankind's a working animal and that everybody's supposed to work. You're not supposed to loaf. We were raised that way. We had certain chores on the farm. Started as clerks, check boys in the store at age eight or nine. There was no such thing as idle time."[19]

In 1888, John Belk's father, William Henry Belk (1862–1952) began the first of the family's stores with a mercantile business in the farmers' market town of Monroe, some twenty-five miles southeast of Charlotte. Of the scores of upstarts who carried a wagonload of work britches and household furnishings to a Carolina crossroads town and set up to "tend store" in the post-Reconstruction years, Henry Belk was the most successful. The legend of his dry goods' ascendance remains.

"When William Henry Belk came up here," offers a Charlotte furniture store owner and former city councilman, "he was just absolutely right off the farm in Union County. There's a million Belks down there. He was just another good ol' farm boy who started a little store down there in Monroe, and then just kinda moved over and started a second store here in Charlotte. Now they've got four or five hundred stores and are worth hundreds of millions of dollars."[20]

Such a man, writes Henry Belk's biographer, "born and reared in the very air that gave Andrew Jackson to the Democratic party," proved that "a poor country boy willing to work and use his brains might even yet become a great business leader with millions of dollars to command as he feels they could serve best."[21]

"Mr. Henry Belk is a great merchant and businessman," wrote a federal circuit court judge, one of many men who, when young, clerked in a Belk store.

> Beginning as an humble helper in a country store while the dark shadows of war and Reconstruction still hung like a pall over our Southland, at a monthly wage less than a skilled mechanic now demands for half a day's work and with nothing but his high character and the inspiration of a Godly mother to help him, he worked hard, made friends, and saved from his meager wages until he had accumulated a few hundred dollars. With this and a few hundred more that he was able to borrow, he bought a small stock of goods from a failing neighbor and launched into business for himself. From then on the record of his life reads like an Alger success story or a tale from the Arabian Nights. The little store in

Monroe grew and other stores were added. The simple merchandising of the country town became a complicated commercial system of nearly three hundred stores extending over the entire South. The pitiful savings of the hard-working clerk grew into many millions of dollars.

And what lesson can be gleaned from the life and labor of William Henry Belk? "Indisputable proof of the value of our system of free enterprise and a vivid demonstration of the copy book maxims of an earlier day."[22]

"Mankind is a working animal," says John Belk, "and the Scottish are a very industrious people." (In calling the family ancestors, the Wauchopes, Scottish rather than Scotch-Irish, Henry Belk would say, "They didn't mix much with the Irish while they were in Ireland.")[23]

"It's the same thing now," continues John Belk, "if you go to Africa. They don't work over there. They didn't change until the white man came."

Had the Belks' English and Scotch-Irish great-great-grandparents been planters down in the Waxhaw settlement of the Carolinas? "You can call an undertaker a planter," answers John Belk. "He lays you to rest.

"The Belks was just farmers," he continues. "They had some slaves, but nothing like the great big houses in *Gone with the Wind* or in the Mississippi Delta.

"They just raised cotton and the land was pretty poor down there. The Catawba Indians couldn't make a living out of it."

What is still known to local residents as the Waxhaws lies in present-day Union County, North Carolina, and Lancaster County, South Carolina. East of the Catawba River, between Camp Creek and Waxhaw Creek, "the land is rolling but not rugged and the surface was doubtless a vegetable mold for which the red clay made a good subsoil," writes Robert Meriwether. The district is "composed chiefly of the fan-like system of Cane Creek and its tributaries." Its name comes from the Waxhaw Indians who inhabited the area until, evidently, an epidemic of smallpox in 1740 killed most of the tribe's members. The Scotch-Irish, including John Belk's Wauchope ancestors, quickly moved down the Wagon Road from Pennsylvania to occupy the district.[24]

"Into this goodly country," recounted a Carolina Presbyterian historian in 1861, "these men, in most instances, no doubt, accompanied with their wives and children came to set up their tabernacle." In the Waxhaws, and to the southwest in what was known as Long Canes, a prairie-like landscape was cut by numerous streams and canebrakes. Along what they named Reedy River, Reedy Fork, and Cane Creek, settlers found that rich land could be identified by a remarkable growth of canes, with heights of twenty to thirty feet. In more ordinary soil, further from the watercourses, canes might never reach more than head high.[25]

Under the 1760s ministry of William Richardson, an Englishman educated at Glasgow, the Waxhaws became the Presbyterian center of the South Carolina backcountry. In the late eighteenth century the area lay at the heart of a Calvinist darkness that was censured and deplored in the journals of the Rev. Charles Woodmason, Anglican of Charleston, missionary from the Low Country.

The Waxhaw district was the birthplace of Andrew Jackson (1767) and the burying ground of his Irish father, who died (before ever seeing his son) one winter, oral tradition has it, after tearing his insides loose lifting a log. Longtime residents of the Waxhaws still tell how the neighbors who were carrying Andy's pap to the graveyard—drinking corn liquor for warmth as they walked beside a mule-drawn wagon—arrived for the burial to find that the body had fallen out somewhere along the way.[26]

In the mid-eighteenth century, the patriarch of the Waxhaw Belks, the Englishman John Belk (the great-great-grandfather of the merchant Henry Belk) acquired, by means of land grants, considerable holdings in and around the district. At the time of his death and the division of property among several children in 1804, Squire Belk held title to at least a thousand acres scattered throughout several North and South Carolina Piedmont counties. In the 1850s, Henry Belk's grandfather, Thomas (grandson of the original John), was known in Lancaster, South Carolina, as "the big man down in that part of the country." And although Thomas Belk lived nearer the sandy eastern side of Lancaster County than he did to the fertile cotton lands that lay near the Catawba River, the 1850 census shows that at age thirty-six he owned real estate valued at five thousand dollars and claimed title to twenty slaves, nine of them above the age of fifteen.[27]

On his mother's side of the family, Henry Belk was descended from Wauchopes (colloquialized as Walkup), strict Scotch-Irish Presbyterians who came into the Carolina Piedmont from the Valley of Virginia and Pennsylvania during the mid-eighteenth century. "There's much good in all churches," Henry Belk told his biographer in the late 1940s. "But I just like the Presbyterian brand best. It seems to me that Calvinism is the best developer of sound Christian character. I believe that it is likely, if a man follows it, to make him a strong moral force in his community. My mother was a strong Presbyterian and I guess that has a lot to do with the way I feel about the Presbyterian denomination."[28]

During the Civil War, Henry's father, Abel, whose weak lungs kept him out of the Confederate army, was mistaken for his father Thomas and drowned by raiding Yankee troops when he failed to tell the hiding place of the family's household treasures. With Emancipation and Rebel defeat, several Belk slaves ran away. Sarah Walkup Belk, Abel's widow, arranged work contracts with the five free blacks who remained on the farm.[29]

Although they found themselves land poor after the war, the Belks were never dirt poor. Sarah Belk furnished the tenants with horses, mules, and half the expenses of farm equipment. In return, she received half their crop. The other half was divided among the tenants and a white overseer who, in 1866, when Sarah Walkup Belk was thirty, became her second husband. In 1870 the family's combined real and personal estate totaled eleven hundred dollars.[30] As before the war, they fared better than most of their neighbors. Even by the ruined standards of Reconstruction wealth, however, the family could hardly be counted among the prosperous of Piedmont Carolina society.

Distinct class and Presbyterian advantages did remain for the Belks and Walkups. For as long as there had been Presbyterians in the Piedmont, there had been an insistence upon schooling almost as much as upon churching. "From our earliest history," wrote a mid-nineteenth-century chronicler of the Carolina Scotch-Irish, "the church and the school-house have gone together. As soon as rude dwellings could be erected . . . there was a rude Church to stand at some central point, and a rude school-house by its side. . . . To the more private school succeeded the academy, and then the college."[31]

Sarah Walkup had attended Carolina Female College in Ansonville, North Carolina, in the 1850s. At home in the 1860s and 1870s, she taught her children to read and write. When the family moved to Monroe in 1873, Sarah sent young Henry to Mecklenburg County to live with an uncle, Henry Clay Walkup (a medical doctor with a name reflective of the family's former Whig allegiance), whose home stood near a good school.

Henry Belk could have chosen to go to college. His mother had seen to it that he was prepared. Yet, as the oldest male of nine children (only four of whom lived to adulthood), Henry understood the expectation that he take his place as head of the Belk side of the family. That he did not continue his education became part of the modern legend of adversity overcome. That he succeeded at all was due to his mother, a fact that was ultimately embellished in the service of regional myth.

"Notwithstanding his lack of a collegiate education," observed U.S. senator Sam Ervin of North Carolina in 1958 to an assemblage of Piedmont businessmen at a commemorative dinner, "Henry Belk was well equipped to face the hard world of his day. For this he was indebted to the precept, the example, and the love of his great mother, Sarah Walkup Belk, who taught him habits of industry and thrift, and implanted indelibly in his mind and heart an unfailing integrity of thought and word and deed, an abiding love for good men and women of all sorts, a dedicated devotion to Calvinism as interpreted by the Southern Presbyterian Church, and an unshakeable Faith in God."[32]

In the masterful rhetoric of Senator Ervin (who shared his subjects' Up-country, Scotch-Irish, Calvinist lineage), Sarah Belk, faithful widow of the Old South and devoted mother of the New, becomes a sentimental figure of regional womanhood capable of inspiring the most dedicated labor.[33] Motherly love and love for "good men and women" are joined, in the formula of Ervin's speech, with Sarah Belk's faithfulness in teaching her son habits of industry, thrift, and integrity, and in implanting a zealous devotion to the Piedmont's Calvinist God—keeping the faith of the fathers.

The equipping of Henry Belk "to face the hard world of his day" led in 1876, when he was fourteen, to a clerk's job in the store of the leading merchant of Monroe, North Carolina. "I had been wanting to get into the store business so I could trade and traffic," he recalled near the end of his life. "So I went to see Mr. B. D. Heath and told him I wanted to learn the business." When the Union County commissioners chose Henry as the recipient of a scholarship to the university at Chapel Hill, he turned down the offer, persuaded by Heath that he was "cut out to run a store."

"The stores opened early in the morning to catch the first folks stirring about," Henry Belk remembered, "and they stayed opened as long as anybody was still stirring. There wasn't much time left a fellow except to eat and sleep." He commonly worked a seventy-hour week.[34]

The Seaboard Railroad, connecting Wilmington with Charlotte, reached Monroe (a town of about two thousand inhabitants) in 1874. In Charlotte, the recently built Air-Line Railroad tied the Deep South and the Carolina Piedmont to the cities of the East Coast. In the interiors of the states of the recent Confederacy, all along the new rail lines and links, farmers were growing unprecedented acres of cotton, some of them planting the crop for the first time, to bring for sale and shipment in market towns like Monroe. In Union County between 1870 and 1880, the number of bales of cotton grown yearly increased from 1,200 to 8,300.[35]

Even earning five dollars a month, as he did in the beginning, Henry Belk could be counted among only a few Union Countians whose jobs paid cash. His status as store clerk was enviable. "When a boy comes into town from a farm and starts working in a store," Henry recalled to his biographer, "he's used to long hours and hard work. He's afraid that if he doesn't make good, he'll have to go back to plowing."[36] If Henry, however, had not made good as a clerk, he would have gone, not back to the farm, but to Chapel Hill. He was not, as oral tradition would have it, just another good ol' boy. He was a boy with a foot up.

Henry Belk clerked in the Heath store for twelve years, learning to size up farmers seeking credit, learning what lines of shoes, cloth, hats, utensils, candy, and scarves would sell and at what prices. Then, at age twenty-six, with $750 in savings, another $500 borrowed from a longtime family friend, and a stock of merchandise bought cheaply from a bankrupt storekeeper, he began his own mercantile business in Monroe in 1888. In a play for public notice of the store (the parent to the Belk group of three hundred stores in the South by 1949), he called it the *New York Racket*. "I figured . . . everybody would think that sounded big. I figured it would help my trade."[37]

Among the Belk household gods, who included John Calvin, John Knox, Benjamin Franklin, and Robert E. Lee, now sat John Wanamaker. Belk had discovered this Philadelphia merchant, widely known for "cash and carry" merchandising, while on buying trips for B. D. Heath. When he began his Monroe store, Belk introduced Wanamaker methods to the Carolina Piedmont. He abandoned the practice of selling on credit and eliminated the custom of bartering. Avoiding the crop-lien nexus of advancing mules, tools, seed, and fertilizer to farmers for a mortgage on their crops, Belk sought penny margins on goods selling for the nickels, dimes, and quarters he painstakingly teased from the growing Piedmont railroad towns. Nor did he exchange yards of cloth or spools of thread for the farm women's eggs and butter. He marked his goods with a single price and sold for cash only. He advertised. He exchanged goods or refunded money to dissatisfied customers. He bought large quantities and undersold competitors.

The industry and frugality that trailed Henry Belk from the 1860s into the lean years of Reconstruction had become, by the 1880s, permanent features of a disciplined temperament engaged in a tightfisted miracle. After a few years in the Monroe store, Henry persuaded his brother John, who had studied medicine at New York University, to become his business partner. In 1895, the Belk brothers decided to open a store in Charlotte, the railroad and trading center of the Carolina Piedmont. Here they could sell not just to farmers in town for a Saturday afternoon, but to an increasing population of town residents who earned wages or drew salaries. John looked after the store in Monroe while Henry moved himself and the Belk wares into a downtown Charlotte building.[38]

For years, Henry Belk gave himself to methodical buying and selling, making his smaller profit margins and larger turnover work against less calculating merchants. In Charlotte his routine was much like it had been at Monroe. For twelve to fourteen hours a day, six days a week, he sold and oversaw the sale of goods, instructed and supervised clerks, and placed orders. At night he went to the living quarters above the store, checked his accounts, conceived new lures for the farming folk, mill hands, and town people, and composed hyperbolic advertising copy. Belk advertisements— with their bombastic nationalistic allusions, boldfaced proclamations of dozens of items that could be purchased for a single penny, and the motto of "The Cheapest Store on Earth"—filled the pages of Charlotte newspapers, were carried throughout the Piedmont on the sides of farmers' wagons, and were slung sandwich-board fashion over the backs of animals. Belk's knack for the magical whimsy of advertising bears out Randolph Bourne's observation that "instincts and impulses, in the puritan, are not miraculously cancelled, but have their full play."[39]

Each Sunday Henry Belk traveled by train to Monroe to visit his mother. His stores, of course, were closed on Sunday and he—and any aspiring clerks—never missed church services. For Henry Belk there were no dalliances, no dawdling, no courtships, no worldly entertainments, no vacation trips, no hunting or fishing, no drinking or dancing, year after year, for decades. Belk's conscience scowled over such popular amusements as picture shows, barrooms, traveling musicians, and play makers.

As world cotton demand surged forward in the first twenty years of the new century, bringing better times to Piedmont farmers and towns that had suffered through the depressed 1880s and much of the 1890s, the Belk brothers were positioned to profit. By 1913, they had established eleven Belk stores in the Carolina Piedmont. North and south of Charlotte, their new stores tended to follow the tracks of the Southern Railroad through Greensboro, Gastonia, Salisbury, and Concord, each significant in the developing textile and furniture industries. Towns with Belk stores near but not on the Southern, such as York and Statesville, were also factory towns.

The Charlotte and Monroe Belk stores became testing grounds for clerks who might eventually receive backing to open Belk branches in other Piedmont towns. Belk money also began to be invested in cotton mills, manufacturing enterprises, banks, businesses, and real estate.[40]

Through the new prosperity and constant expansion, Henry Belk held to his stringent habits and expected similar adherence from his employees, especially from any Christian man who intended to rise from clerk to manager or lesser partner in a Belk store. In the 1900s, beginning Belk clerks made six dollars a week. Check boys (youngsters who earned twenty-five

William Henry Belk. (Courtesy of the North Carolina Collection,
University of North Carolina)

cents a day) arrived to sweep the stores before seven in the morning, stayed
on the run all day carrying merchandise, and often accompanied the delivery
men at night.[41] Standing six feet and three inches tall, Belk was master of the
considerable territory he surveyed. He had, as a former clerk recalls, "little
patience with indolence."[42]

"The secret," John Belk says of his father, "was that he trusted his fellow
man. That's the religious background. A lot of people, if you talk to them,
especially in New York, how we do, they can't understand because they don't
trust anybody. They want a contract. Daddy never had any contracts with
anybody. His word was his bond. Whatever he said, that's what he did. And
he expected that of his fellow man. He knew how to pick honest people.
That's the reason he was so strong on religion. He gave everybody a dollar for
learning the catechism, cause he figured they'd be better if they learned it."

"When we were growing up," continues John Belk, "you had respect for your elders. You didn't talk back to them. Mother taught us, 'You have respect for what your father says.'

"They read the Bible at home daily and had prayer. Read aloud. Every Sunday we'd have to learn another verse. And their parents before them the same thing. I'd go stay with my grandmother and we'd read the Bible every night and in the morning at breakfast.

"Daddy couldn't carry a tune. He didn't believe in dancing. They had the Puritan viewpoint here. That's the way religious people were.

"We didn't go to dances until after we went to prep school. Daddy was against dancing. I was president of the Panhellenic Council at Davidson College when they had their first dance ever. Daddy was a trustee of Davidson. He said let him know so that he would miss that trustees' meeting because (he was in his late seventies) he wouldn't vote against his son."[43]

Timorous and uncomfortable around women, Henry Belk stood tall but uneasily in the millinery department of his own stores. Only after his mercantile business had produced a fortune and an empire did Henry Belk, in his fifties (1915), meet and marry Mary Irwin, Presbyterian daughter of a prominent Charlotte physician. Like an Old Testament patriarch, he turned to the raising of a family (five sons and a daughter) and to the training of his sons in their father's business. "I always said I wanted the same size family old Jacob had—twelve sons and two daughters. I didn't do quite half as well as old Jacob."[44]

"His hours were unlimited," says John Belk, son of this grandfatherly father. "That's one reason he was so long in getting married. He lived above the store for a long time. Work and religion—that's all he did. He'd go and see his mother on Sunday. He didn't get into politics. He built churches and stores."

In the puritan's renunciation of the world, the flesh, and the devil comes a paradoxical pleasure through the satisfaction taken in renunciation, in conspicuous humility, in the pleasure of acute self-control, and in the power to enforce these stern virtues and habits in others.[45] William Henry Belk embodied this sort of Piedmont puritanism. The new opportunities presented by the postbellum opening of the Carolina Piedmont to the modern capitalist economy gave men such as the Belks unprecedented channels for their single-visioned energies.

Men like the puritanical Belks had colored the temperament of the Carolina Piedmont since its Scotch-Irish settlement: stoic, calculating, ceaselessly working, ascetic stewards of a God who could not dance. Largely contained during the antebellum era by the geography of their interior location and the hegemony of the plantation districts, their rationality throve upon the postwar expansion of cotton and tobacco cash-crop agriculture, the accumulation of merchant capital, the linking of the Piedmont by rail with Northern markets, the building of towns, the construction of factories, and the availability of cheap, unorganized labor. Soon, the steadiest of these men of steady habits, the Presbyterians, were found in disproportionate numbers among the first ranks of the Carolina Piedmont's business class.[46] The city of Charlotte became their capitol.

"What has always fascinated me about Charlotte," wrote Harry Golden, editor of the *Carolina Israelite* and popular author of books about the Southern Jewish experience, "was that I was able to turn the stereotype inside out." Golden, who had grown up in New York City, settled in Charlotte during World War II and soon was "enthralled as I watched the Presbyterians, Methodists and Baptists chase the buck. The Protestants do have all the money, and they go at it with an intensity unknown anywhere else in the civilized world."[47]

"Man is a working animal," John Belk says to me for the third time in an hour as he rises from his desk in the Belk Building in Charlotte.

· 2 ·

The Customs of the Country

The lower part of the state was settled primarily by people from over in England, whereas the upper part of the state was settled primarily by Scotch-Irish that came down from North Carolina and Virginia. They were just different kinds of people, and there was usually somewhat of an antagonism between the two, not to the point of doing any fighting, but there was a certain amount of difficulty between them.
—Robert Roy Adams

Backcountry and Low Country

The farmer folk of the mid-eighteenth century who settled in the Waxhaws, along Little Lynch's River and on the banks of Fishing Creek near the boundary between North and South Carolina, had traveled thousands of miles and a generation or more from Northern Ireland, but they still knew how to confound an Anglican cleric. Charles Woodmason, who had left wife and child in England while he made and lost a fortune as a planter and merchant in Charleston, had, in later years, become the Reverend Mr. Woodmason, bearer of the legitimate church to the backcountry. Woodmason's journal records the meeting, in the late 1760s, of Low Country and Carolina Piedmont:

> I had appointed a Congregation to meet me at the Head of Hanging Rock Creek—Where I arrived on Tuesday Evening—Found the Houses filled with debauch'd, licentious fellows, and Scot Presbyterians who had hir'd these lawless Ruffians to insult me, which they did with Impunity—Telling me, they wanted no D——d Black Gown Sons of Bitches among them—and threatening to lay me behind the Fire, which they assuredly would have done had not some travellers alighted very opportunely, and taken me under protection. . . . Not long after, they hir'd a Band of rude fellows to come to Service who brought with them

57 Dogs (for I counted them) which in Time of Service they set fighting, and I was oblig'd to stop—In Time of Sermon they repeated it—and I was oblig'd to desist and dismiss the People. It is vain to take up or commit these lawless Ruffians—for they have nothing, and the Charge of sending of them to Charlestown, would take me a Year's Salary—We are without any Law, or Order—And as all the Magistrates are Presbyterians, I could not get a Warrant—If I got Warrants as the Constables are Presbyterians likewise, I could not get them serv'd—If serv'd, the Guard would let them escape—Both my Self and other Episcopals have made this experiment.[1]

Set against the high society of London and the emulative planters, merchants, and ladies of Charleston among whom Woodmason preferred to circulate, the Carolina backcountry folk appeared primitive, defiant, and depraved. Scotch-Irish Presbyterians, Baptists, Methodists, Quakers, Dunkers, nonbelievers, and Catawba Indians delighted in keeping him in an uproar during his six-year itinerancy. There were only a few friendly "Episcopals." Woodmason did, however, become the spokesman with Charleston for the South Carolina Regulators, a contingent of up-and-coming slaveholders intent on bringing enough law and order to the backcountry to make it safe for planting and property.[2]

Had Reverend Woodmason followed the Catawba River further upstream or turned northeastward into the Yadkin Valley or northwestward toward the Greenville and Spartanburg districts, he would have found similar settlements. White immigration by way of the Valley of Virginia, combined with the frontier resistance of the Cherokee, gave the first loosely aggregated "neighborhoods" in the North Carolina portion of the Piedmont region as much as a twenty-year start on those of South Carolina. Certainly there were distinct differences in wealth, social connections, and landholdings. There were more Germans here and Quakers over yonder. Throughout the region, however, a broad similarity existed among these early backwoods farm families as they pursued the relative independence of a household-centered, agricultural livelihood. And if a family felt too constricted, or too lorded-over by a belligerent or haughty neighbor, or found itself badly situated on the land, it could pick up and move onto an as-yet-unclaimed tract.

Throughout the upper South Carolina Piedmont, as the itinerant Woodmason found, the settlers were a headstrong, dissenting lot. He took note of the few books in the cabins of families who gave him lodging, disapproving of what he found: "the Assembly, Catechism, Watts' Hymns, Bunyan's *Pilgrim's Progress*, Whitefield's and Erskine's sermons." In these neighborhoods,

Woodmason discovered that his dependence upon the written rather than the spoken word made his preaching suspect. The insistence by backcountry congregations that prayers and sermons be performed "extempore," as evidence of inspiration, and not read as cold words on a page forced him to "repeat the Liturgy by Heart and to use no Book but the Bible, when I read the Lessons. I have the whole Service and all the Offices by my fingers Ends ... but cannot yet venture to give Extempore Discourses, though certainly could perform beyond any of these Poor Fools."[3]

The light, homemade, Sunday dress of backcountry farm women posed an irreverent distraction:

> How would the Polite People of London stare to see the Females (many very pretty) come to Service in their Shifts and a short petticoat only, barefooted and bare legged without caps or handkerchiefs—dress'd only in their Hair, Quite in a State of Nature for Nakedness is counted as Nothing—as they sleep altogether in Common in one Room, and shift and dress openly without Ceremony—The Men appear in Frocks and Shirts and long Trousers—No Shoes or stockings—But I should remember that I am talking of my Self, and Religious Matters, Not the Customs of the Country.[4]

During the last quarter of the eighteenth century, the farmsteaders and herders against whom Woodmason railed laid effective claim to the backcountry of the Carolinas. Here their ways, not his, became the customs of the country. And whether considered by features of nature or of culture, theirs was a world away from Charleston, the Low Country, and the Tidewater.

From Beaufort, South Carolina, to Elizabeth City, North Carolina, the Carolina coast was dominated by planters of primarily English descent (with scatterings of French Protestants, Scottish Highlanders, and Scotch-Irish) who worked slave labor on large tracts of land in the production of tobacco, cotton, rice, indigo, and naval stores. By the mid-eighteenth century, these Low Country plantation parishes contained black-majority populations. Tied to the British mercantile system, and increasingly to each other through bonds of marriage and family, the ranks of Carolina planters included ambitious local upstarts as well as transplanted sons of wealthy Virginia or English families in pursuit of new fortunes.

In the Albemarle area of northeastern North Carolina—where planter wealth never approached that of the Chesapeake to the north or that of the Carolina Low Country—tobacco had, by mid-eighteenth century, become the staple crop. Along the southeastern North Carolina coast, Albemarle and

South Carolina planters purchased land on and near the Cape Fear River and learned, from slaves, the cultivation of rice. They sapped vast tracts of longleaf pine forests for turpentine, pitch, and resin. Slave crews cut lumber. From the British naval stores industry, the name "Tarheels" stuck to North Carolinians.

The interior of the state's coastal plain, including the counties of Edgecombe, Pitt, Halifax, Greene, Martin, and Bertie, entered the plantation economy during the first decade of the nineteenth century, when the invention of the cotton gin allowed expansion of short-staple cotton cultivation in response to increasing international market demand. By the late antebellum era, this Tidewater-influenced area had become North Carolina's leading cotton producer. The hall-and-parlor farmhouses that once seemed sufficiently grand were superseded by "some of the most sumptuous mansions in antebellum North Carolina."[5]

Swamps, marshes, savannahs, and pine barrens at a hundred feet or less above sea level broke irregularly across the Carolina Coastal Plain. Social relations, trade, political power, and high church came together in Edenton, Wilmington, Beaufort, New Bern, Charleston, and, to the south, in Savannah. The small cities of the Carolina coast sat at the mouths of partially navigable rivers facing the Atlantic tide and the currents of English language, institutions, and tastes.

The South Carolina Low Country extended some sixty or seventy miles inland. Immediately beyond lay an area known in the colonial era as the backcountry. The backcountry, which was opened to white settlement from the coast after the Yamassee War of 1715–17, included the upper Coastal Plain, Sandhills, and the Upcountry. The Upcountry began at the fall line, the upper limit of boat travel to the interior, and reached to the eastern ridges of the Blue Ridge Mountains.[6]

Crossing the rivers and streams of the Carolinas at a distance between 100 and 150 miles from and running parallel to the Atlantic coastline is the belt of waterfalls and rapids known as the fall line. The fall line divides ancient residual Appalachian soils from a recently surfaced (measured in the eons of geological time) ocean bottom. Here navigation upriver from the coast is forced to halt. In North Carolina, the fall line historically separated "east" from "west"; in South Carolina it marked the beginning of the Upcountry. It was not until after the mid-nineteenth century that the region from the fall line northwestward to the foot of the Appalachians would come to be widely known as the "Piedmont."

In North Carolina, the Cape Fear is the only major river that flows directly into the Atlantic. About eighty miles inland, where waterfalls forced an end to

Cape Fear navigation, a group of Scottish Highlanders laid out a town in the 1740s that came to be known as Fayetteville. From the colonial era through the antebellum decades, Fayetteville served as the major locus of exchange between the eastern North Carolina Piedmont and the coast. Throughout these years, the Cape Fear never lacked for undercapitalized canal-building schemes, each one promising a path for water transport that, ultimately, never got very far.[7]

Near fall line sites on the rivers of the southeastern states, market towns similar to Fayetteville grew to handle interregional trade. Richmond, Raleigh, Camden, Columbia, Augusta, Macon, Columbus, Montgomery, and Tuscaloosa emerged in such locales, with several doing duty as state capitals, situated as they were in the middle ground between contentious Coastal Plain and Upcountry interests. "Antagonism between the inland settlers and the stabilized aristocracy of the coast had begun before the Revolution," note the writers of the *South Carolina Guide*. "The removal of the capital from Charleston to Columbia in 1786 was an effort to bring the two sections of the state into more amicable relations."[8] The legislature's choice, in 1801, of Columbia as the site for South Carolina College (later the University of South Carolina) was strongly supported by the old-guard planter ranks of Low Country Federalists, who saw the college as "a state-supported institution where a common education in the classics and a common network of friendships and rivalries" would help "draw prominent South Carolinians from all parts of the state toward common purposes."[9]

Almost all of the Carolina Piedmont lies west of a line, drawn by linguist Hans Kurath, separating the South's two major dialect groupings, the South Midland and Southern Coastal. As patterns of dialect developed after the era of eighteenth-century settlement, the speech of the Piedmont's white farmers retained the influence of Midlands English and Lowland Scottish dialects amid the occasional notes of Atlantic Coastal and African-American voices. Slaves made up only 10 percent of the Piedmont's population in the 1760s, and even by 1800 only two or three counties across the entire region had black populations of more than 30 percent. In the cultural geography of ethnicity and spoken language, as in the landscape, the Carolina Piedmont stood distinct from Low Country and Tidewater.[10]

At several stretches along the fall line, from the Carolinas into Georgia, a remnant of prehistoric seashore known as the Sandhills separates the Piedmont from the Atlantic Coastal Plain. In the mid-twentieth century, retirees and vacationers from throughout the United States transformed the crossroads towns of the Sandhills into comfortable golf communities, while farmers learned the secrets of cultivating fruit trees on its thirsty soil. In earlier generations, the Sandhills was legendary for its barrenness and for being home to scrub oak, jack pine, and the hovels of Carolina poor whites, a marginalized population who struggled on the least productive of lands. As she traveled by carriage from antebellum Charleston to her family's summer retreat in the Carolina Upcountry, diarist Mary Boykin Chesnut cast a haughty eye on these "sand tackies." In the first decade of the twentieth century, Dr. Charles W. Stiles of the U.S. Public Health Service discovered widespread hookworm infection among the Sandhillers, convincing himself and the philanthropy of John D. Rockefeller that here lay the explanation for Southern laziness and backwardness.[11]

Settling the Piedmont

The break between the Appalachian Blue Ridge chain and the westward edge of the Piedmont is sharp, with the elevation falling as much as three thousand feet across a dozen miles. Dropping southeasterly from the Blue Ridge with the Carolina Piedmont's transverse slope, hundreds of creeks and streams feed dozens of rivers, which merge into five major watersheds: the Yadkin–Pee Dee, Catawba-Wateree, Broad, Saluda, and Cape Fear. The Yadkin, Catawba, and Broad rivers carry Appalachian waters through the western half of the Carolina Piedmont. The Yadkin becomes the Pee Dee when it enters South Carolina; the Catawba, which rises near the Yadkin, becomes the Wateree, later merging with the Santee. The Broad River is formed from several streams uniting just above the South Carolina border. As the Broad moves across the Piedmont it is increased by the Pacolet, Enoree, and Saluda rivers before arriving at the city of Columbia. Eventually the Broad reaches the Santee and the Atlantic Ocean.[12]

"By neither soil nor climate," observes Robert Meriwether in his excellent description of the late-eighteenth-century Carolina Piedmont landscape, "was it well adapted to the staples of the day. Far worse than this were the difficulties in the way of transportation."

Each river made its exit from the piedmont by tumbling over a series of rocks; a dozen other shoals lay back of this point and navigation even with small boats was so tedious and dangerous that early settlers found pack train and wagon preferable. Land transportation in turn faced great obstacles, for roads paralleling the rivers crossed many creeks, some deep and nearly all with steep banks. The best routes were among the ridges between the rivers, but these ran at a distance from the desirable

Routes of settlement from the Great Wagon Road into the Carolina
Piedmont. (Reproduced from Clay et al., *North Carolina Atlas*)

land of the river bottoms. Thus the corn, wheat or cattle which the
piedmont could produce so well and which the rice plantations could
afford to buy must be carried or driven from one to three hundred miles
to market, and there sold in well-nigh hopeless competition with similar
products from the upper or lower pine belts from Pennsylvania. Therefore the piedmont remained in isolation—back country indeed—until
the slow coming of the canal, railroad, and cotton.[13]

The formidable distance, the lack of adequate wagon roads from the coast
into the Piedmont, the impassability of rivers, and the difficulties of move-

ment around the cascades and rapids of the fall line left Upcountry settlers largely to their own resources and arrangements in the root-hog-or-die era of the region's history.

From the 1730s throughout the eighteenth century, most settlers entered the Carolina Piedmont, not by trekking inland from the Low Country, but by following the Great Wagon Road that led down the Valley of Virginia from Pennsylvania. The first farmers along the banks of the Hyco, Eno, and Haw rivers in North Carolina were part of a Scotch-Irish migration that brought between 150,000 and 200,000 people from Ulster to America between 1720 and 1775. Depending upon the decade and their particular point of origin, these immigrants—about half of whom were indentures—were fleeing an oppressive system of rack-renting under local and absentee English land-lords, economic sanctions against the wool industry, a collapse in the linen trade, anti-Presbyterian laws and forced taxation to support the Anglican church, numerous bad crop years, famines, and the profiteering of corn speculators. They were drawn to America by news of land bounties pro-claimed in the advertisements of shipowners and by the letters of kin and friends who already had made the trip.[14]

To reach fertile, unoccupied land in the middle colonies after their arrival in Philadelphia, the major port of entry for the Scotch-Irish, the immigrants had to push beyond William Penn's coastal settlements and beyond the holdings of English, Welsh, and German Protestant immigrants. They settled first in the Cumberland Valley, and in Cumberland County, Pennsylvania, their "main cradle in the New World," the Ulsterites established namesake townships of Antrim, Armagh, Derry, Fermanagh, and Tyrone.

Avoiding the French and Indians beyond the Appalachians and the diffi-culties of the mountain crossing, the immigrants turned down the west side of the Valley of Virginia, opposite to the German groups that had preceded them. As the migration continued throughout the middle decades of the eighteenth century, Scotch-Irish traced the Wagon Road from Philadelphia through the valley and into the Carolinas. York, Chester, and Lancaster counties in South Carolina reflect the Pennsylvania background of their first citizens. Once into the Carolina Piedmont, the new settlers, contained no longer by the trough of the Great Valley, spread into the region between the fall line and the Blue Ridge.[15]

Before the influx of whites from the Wagon Road, well-traveled trading paths connecting the towns of such Siouan Indian peoples as the Catawba, Saponi, and Saura ran across the Piedmont from mountains to coast. Two schematic maps drawn by Indians, probably in the 1720s, suggest broad intertribal relations among southeastern Indians and a Charleston-centered market network into which white traders enticed the movement of such goods as herbs and deerskins from across the Piedmont to the Low Country.[16]

After the white occupation, the Catawbas turned to the handling of the deerskin trade with tribes further west. The Cherokee, after a period of openness in commercial contact that lasted until about 1750, withdrew into the mountains in an attempt to preserve the heart of their culture. They faced the ravages of smallpox and the exterminating intentions of settlers. Later they would contend with the wrath of the Scotch-Irish Piedmont Carolinian, Andrew Jackson, and ultimately with forced removal from the South.

As early as the 1760s, with Cherokee displacement from the South Carolina Piedmont, whites rushed in from two directions. Most came from the north via the Wagon Road as it ran between the Pee Dee (Yadkin) and Catawba rivers. These settlers entered the Waxhaws and expanded through what would become the counties of Lancaster, York, Chester, Fairfield, Union, Newberry, Abbeville, and Edgefield. Still more Scotch-Irish sailed directly from Ulster to Charleston and moved into the Upcountry in response to a South Carolina householder bounty that provided farming tools plus a hundred acres for each man and fifty acres for each woman and child. Drawn by the same offer, a few hundred Germans arrived at Charleston and struck out for the interior.[17]

Many of the immigrants who trekked into the Carolina backcountry brought few possessions other than clothing and some tools. They might be leading a horse or cow. Some hired themselves out to established farmers in order to raise the stake needed to make a claim on a farm. A small number remained landless tenants or laborers for life. And, "equally early in the process," observes Robert Meriwether, "came a somewhat more well-to-do farmer, his several horses carrying his family as well as his goods."[18] From the beginning of white settlement, the Piedmont was a farmer, rather than a planter, society. Yet the gradual "achievement of settled community life and the organization of churches," writes James Leyburn, historian of the Scotch-Irish, "tended to revive all those distinctions given by property, education, background and manners."[19] Although diluted by backwoods circumstances, class distinctions were obvious, as were the deferential relations of a traditional patriarchal society.

"Within the context of a subsistence or yeoman economy," observes Rachel Klein about the South Carolina backcountry, "some ambitious men were able to win sufficient profits to begin acquiring slaves." Other men arrived with an inheritance or a knack for shrewd trading. Klein notes that "many of the families which would emerge as the leading slaveowners and political figures of latter day Abbeville District [S.C.] were part of the same general migration from Augusta County, Virginia."[20] Among these migrants were some bearing the names of Calhoun, Anderson, and Pickens. "Where the origins of substantial Piedmont landowners have been traced to the middle Atlantic states," writes Douglas DeNatale, "they have proven to be substantial landowners and in many cases the proprietors of small manufacturing establishments before their move to North Carolina."[21] Although scarcely comparable in numbers or power to the elite of Beaufort, Charleston, or Wilmington, early Piedmont society had its ranks of propertied men.

While thousands of immigrants came directly into the Piedmont from Ulster, Germany, or England, others arrived after a series of moves down the Great Valley in search of available or cheaper land, such as that advertised by the agents of Lord Granville in North Carolina. By the beginning of the Revolutionary War, writes James Leyburn, "the North Carolina backcountry had at least sixty thousand settlers, while that of South Carolina had eighty-three thousand—almost four-fifths of the colony's white population." Some of these Upcountry newcomers made their way from the Carolina coast, but most were " 'transfers' from Pennsylvania, Maryland, and Virginia—a few Swiss and Welsh, large numbers of Germans, but more Scotch-Irish than all others put together." Sometimes entire communities made the migration.[22]

The distinctive regional society of the Carolina Piedmont was produced, as cultural geographer D. W. Meinig has written, "by peoples whose origins, social character, economic interests, and political concerns differed sharply from those of the older coastal societies."[23] The farther above the fall line that settlement took place in the Carolina Piedmont, the more strongly the bonds of kith and kin reached toward the Scotch-Irish and German culture of the Great Valley of Virginia and into Pennsylvania, rather than to the Tidewater. One immediate consequence of this development was a "profound geopolitical tension" within each of the Carolinas.

If the Great Wagon Road established the corridor of first effective white settlement into the Carolina Piedmont, the Scotch-Irish cast an enduring color upon the region's temperament. A mordantly tough, persistent, and relatively homogeneous body of English-speaking immigrants of predominantly Presbyterian antecedents, the Scotch-Irish, once they had killed or expelled the region's native population, became—by means of numbers, aggressiveness, and tenacity—the new natives.[24]

Adapting their own traditional agrarian practices and borrowing agricultural and architectural techniques from both German and English Upcountry immigrants, the Scotch-Irish spread a family farm, log-house, livestock, corn, and woodlands-pasture culture throughout the Piedmont and Southern Appalachians. This family farmstead, writes E. Estyn Evans, "surrounded by its extensive woodlands 'outfield,' was an Atlantic heritage, very different both from the village system of New England and from the plantation mansions of the southern tidewater."[25]

By 1790 thousands of Scotch-Irish had moved into Upcountry Georgia and, by the early nineteenth century, into the northern parts of Alabama and Mississippi. "In each colony the story was generally the same," concludes P. Richard Metcalf. "The pioneers spread throughout the forests, cleared what land they chose, fought bloody skirmishes with Indian occupants, and cared little for the claims of seaboard governments for jurisdiction or administration. When the colonial governments returned this disregard in the form of unbalanced representation, overtaxation, and failure to provide what the backcountry settlers believed were adequate defense measures against Indian depredations, the Scotch-Irish were not loath to take violent action, as evidenced by the march of the 'Paxton Boys' in Pennsylvania (1763) and the Carolina Regulator movement of 1768–1771."[26]

In the habit of providing for themselves, Upcountry settlers had little use for colonial or state governments beyond seeking their help in the destruction of Indian populations. And, although most of the Scotch-Irish settlers were strong partisans of independence during the Revolution, their interest lay in obtaining as much autonomy as possible, whether from the Crown's government or from a state authority that spoke for coastal planters and merchants. A characteristically bumptious letter dispatched from the backcountry of North Carolina during the summer of 1775 warns "the Coast, that they (the back Inhabitants) would not submit to any Stoppage of their Trade, and that if their ships were not suffered to proceed with the Produce of the Country, they would come down and burn all the Houses on the Coast, and put the People to the Sword."[27]

Upcountry Scotch-Irish, writes Metcalf, "evolved a folk society and customary law of their own." Associated with this way of life are most of the "classic American pioneerisms, from husking bee and corn whiskey to turkey shoot and shivaree." Yeoman settlers homesteaded two- to three-hundred-acre farms, often claiming ownership by right of possession and improvement. Metcalf notes that "while German families . . . tended to stay in a place once settled, many Scotch-Irish were continually on the move." Wherever they moved, they laid claim. Scotch-Irish leaders tended to be "militant moralists" among whom, in a few more generations, free enterprise would be "raised to the level of a theological dogma."[28]

The chief religious contribution of those "Puritans of the Middle and

Southern Colonies," the Scotch-Irish Presbyterians, suggests historian Leyburn, "aside from establishing churches wherever they went, lay in their identification of religion with character. The result," he continues, "was a definite rigidity of character," often a "stern severity that was as hard upon others as upon oneself. It was uncompromising; it could be bigoted and even merciless, for it might be quite unsoftened by human kindliness and grace. It tended to hold some individual responsible when things went wrong in general." Even where formal denominational ties were absent, the severe, frequently authoritarian spirit of Scotch-Irish Protestantism, as it engaged and fed the experience of militant backwoods independence, cast a lasting hue upon the social character and institutional legitimacy of Piedmont society.[29]

Accustomed to hard and tenacious living on the farms of Ulster, the Midlands of England, or the interior of Pennsylvania, the immigrants who filled the Carolina Piedmont and the Southern Upcountry turned a leathered face to nature, Indians, and government. "It became clear," writes Metcalf, "that the poverty-stricken new arrivals had little patience with proper forms of land patents or quit-rents and cared not at all for Indian claims to unceded lands. The Scotch-Irish made plain their feeling that 'it was against the laws of God and nature, that so much land be idle, while so many Christians wanted it to labor on, and to raise their bread.' "[30] They moved against idle land and rank nature with the same manifest hand they applied against the tribal heathen and the African-American slave. An antebellum shape-note hymn from *The Southern Harmony* proclaims a menacing gospel from the perspective of a civilized, privileged voice:

> Let the Indian, let the Negro,
> Let the rude barbarian see
> That divine and glorious conquest
> Once obtain'd on Calvary;
> Let the gospel,
> Loud resound from pole to pole.[31]

In groups of families and small communities, thousands of Germans made their way down the Great Valley and into the Carolinas between 1745 and 1775, establishing Lutheran and German Reformed settlements in the Yadkin and Catawba river valleys. Moravians purchased the Wachovia tract in the present-day county of Forsyth and organized the communitarian colony of Bethabara in 1753. As farmers and artisans, the Germans had a reputation for self-sufficiency by "their mode of living, their industrious habits, and their simplicity of manners, to all of which they had been accustomed in their Fatherland."[32]

The Germans mixed slowly with other settlers. In newly formed Orange County (1752), German Lutherans occupied the area immediately west of the Haw River and Scotch-Irish the east. "Had a traveller from Pennsylvania visited, about forty or fifty years ago," wrote the Wilmington Lutheran pastor Gotthardt Bernheim in 1872, "portions of the present counties of Alamance, Guilford, Davidson, Rowan, Cabarrus, Stanly, Iredell, Catawba, Lincoln and some others in the state of North Carolina, he might have believed himself to have unexpectedly come upon some part of the old Keystone State."[33]

Some German immigrants did enter South Carolina from the Yadkin and Catawba valleys, but the majority who had traveled from Pennsylvania and Virginia fastened upon the Old North State. With a reputation as "industrious, economical, and thrifty farmers, not afraid or ashamed of hard labor," the Piedmont Germans "were soon blessed with an abundance of everything, which the fertile soil and temperate climate of that portion of North Carolina could furnish them."[34]

Only gradually did the Carolina Piedmont lose the outward evidences of German habitation. By the end of the Civil War, the German language had all but passed into extinction in the region; Pastor Bernheim noted that a small number of elderly speakers remained, "but in a few more years the last vestige of Pennsylvania-German will be sought for in vain in this state, where once even many of the negro slaves of these Germans spoke no other language."[35] Late in the twentieth century, travelers across the Yadkin Valley could still find a German legacy, not only in the names on rural storefronts, roadside mailboxes, and in Lutheran churchyards, but in the architecture of houses and outbuildings.

Across the Piedmont, where scores of streams and branches inscribed a veined landscape of hills and valleys, river bottomland was most prized. Latecomers moved onto the plateaus or divides between the region's south-easterly flowing rivers. To avoid a continual fording of streams across this rising and rolling region, trails and wagon roads sought the well-drained high ground between watersheds.

Here and there, as with the small tract that lay between the two Buffalo creeks on the present site of Greensboro, North Carolina, were prairie-like stretches or "pine barrens." These small prairies, where buffalo had grazed, furnished open ranges for cattle. "No man of any respectability," wrote a contemporary, "ever thought of building or settling himself there with a family, because the soil was deemed too thin for cultivation." As open pasture, these occasional prairies served the farmers of surrounding settlements with grass and waist-high pea vines in summer and as a source for winter hay. Along the sides of the prairie patches stood densely covered glades of black-jack oak, maple, elm, and sweet gum. Once home to packs of wolves, "here, in these sequestered retreats ... the 'Black-Jack Lodges' of Freemasons frequently held their meetings during the war; and here the mowers, from Buffalo and Alamance, in the Dog-days, when oppressed with the heat and weary of toil, retired to rest awhile and drink their grog and whet their scythes, and crack their jokes."[36]

"This was the topography of the piedmont," observes Robert Meriwether, taking the eye of the pioneer, "infinitely complicated in detail, but simple in plan and impressive in the constantly recurring sweep of valley and ridge. Later generations were to see many of these hillsides cleared and abandoned, lonely as sand hill or pine barren, with all the larger streams reddened or yellowed by the clay poured into them. But the newcomer saw clear waters and the varied unbroken green of the great forest of oak, hickory and pine."[37]

Until depleted by heavily erosive forest-clearing and farming practices that, with each rainfall, turned streams to a muddy soup, the hill and plateau earth accumulating for centuries out of the hardwood humus of the upper Piedmont was almost as rich as the valley land of the lower Piedmont. Sometimes a thin layer of sand ran beneath the surface loam. The characteristic red and yellow Piedmont clay was formed from the weathering of underlying granite and gneiss. Not as fecund, flat, or easily cultivable as the plantation regions of the Mississippi Delta or Alabama Black Belt, the Piedmont contained good land for growing wheat, corn, barley, fruits, hay, and pasture grasses. With broader and flatter bottomland, somewhat hotter summer temperatures, a longer growing season, and closer access to markets, planters and farmers in the lower Piedmont of South Carolina turned earlier and more eagerly to the cultivation of cotton and the expansion of slavery than did residents of the upper Piedmont.

Patriarchs of the Piedmont

The most successful of the Piedmont's cultural fathers during the era of regional settlement are commemorated in small books of biographical sketches, usually written at the far edge of memory by family members of subsequent generations. An Old Testament–style tallying of property and numbering of heirs distinguish these sketchbooks, effectively suggesting that the measure of a man's wealth directly corresponds to the possession of certain virtues, high among which is a faithful application of the habits of industry. The typically foreshortened and compressed language (such as that in the following example) conveys a near-legendary tone.

"Colonel Alexander Mebane, the patriarch of the family," begins one Carolina chronicle written in the mid-nineteenth century,

> came from the north of Ireland and settled in Pennsylvania, where he remained several years, when he removed with his family to North Carolina and settled in the Hawfields, in Orange county. He was a man of good sense, upright, industrious and prudent in the management of his business affairs and soon acquired considerable wealth. He was commissioned Colonel and Justice of the Peace under the Regal government. He had twelve children, six sons and six daughters, all of whom, except one, married and settled and raised families in Orange county.[38]

Except for their role in the making of sons, the occasional note about transmission of dowries, or the rare sentimental testimonial, mothers and daughters can go unmentioned in these Piedmont patristics. Consider the sketch of Thomas Allison (ca. 1773–1844), tanner and Presbyterian elder, as memorialized in 1897 in the Scotch-Irish chronicles of Andrew Phelps McCormick:

> Allison had come to Iredell [County, N.C.], then Rowan, in 1773, an infant in arms. His parents starting from Philadelphia crossed the Potomac at Harper's Ferry, bringing themselves, their infant son, and all else they had, on two horses, settled on the South Yadkin in that year. Thomas received a cornfield, schoolhouse education, and at 18 years of age was bound to one Hovalter, a tanner to learn this trade. He was to receive from his master one suit of summer and one suit of winter homespun and a change of linen and of underclothes each year, and to get, when free, a suit of good clothes and fifty dollars in money, or a saddlehorse and outfit worth fifty dollars. When his time of service was out he had become so proficient in his trade that he easily arranged with his master, who wished to retire, to take the business. He died in 1844. He left an estate, wholly unencumbered with debt, consisting of 1200 acres of land around the manor-house we visited, 50 negro slaves, 30 horses, 100 head of cattle, 100 sheep, a large stock of hogs and full plantation outfit, and his business of tanner and harness-maker and vender, in full and healthy operation, to be continued by his son and by the grandson whose guests we were. The growth of the interstate commerce since the Civil War has dispensed with the general local use of the manufacturing trades, as it theretofore obtained, and the grandson of

the apprentice of Hovalter has closed his tanner's business on the South Yadkin.[39]

The McCormick family chronicle, which furnishes the example of the rise of tanner Thomas Allison, also provides a glimpse into the biographies of several leading men in the early history of Piedmont society, beginning with Andrew McCormick's great-great-grandfather, the "full-blooded Scotch-Irishman" Andrew McKenzie, and concluding with McCormick's grandfather, also named Andrew.

Attempting to claim lands his father had acquired in 1720, the family patriarch, Andrew McKenzie, emigrated from Ireland to New Jersey in 1760. Failing in this first effort, McKenzie received from Lord Granville's agent a grant of land in the North Carolina Piedmont along Third Creek. A prosperous brewer in Ireland, McKenzie followed the same occupation in North Carolina. He served in the Revolutionary War and afterward received two additional land grants from the state.

As it points out differences between Piedmont society and that of the plantation districts, a passage from the McCormick narrative reveals the contours of a local economy, an awareness of a regional way of life, and the existence of regular intercourse with commercial centers inside and outside the South. Also, true to its form, this family chronicle revolves around the inheritances between fathers and sons, their training, their work, and their accumulation of property—the measure of their independence. Particular Andrew McKenzies melt into an intergenerational paternal figure. As this excerpt ends, unencumbered female kin disappear: "[T]he sisters . . . had taken their respective journeys into a far country. . . . [H]e became the 'McKenzie.'"

His [Andrew McKenzie's] principal active business was growing grain and distilling spirits but in the absence of a sufficient volume of sound money to serve as a circulating medium, he had to accept in barter live stock and other movables in exchange for that portion of the product of his distilleries which supplied his local market. In this way his son, James, became trained as a dealer in domestic animals, horses, meat cattle, sheep, etc., which he drove to distant markets, the chief and nearest of which were Philadelphia and Charleston. . . . Andrew—my grandfather—seems to have been inducted into the active management of his father's home business at an early age. In his twenty-seventh year, 1798, he married Elizabeth (Betsy) Stevenson, and received with his wife a generous share of Mr. Stevenson's landed estate. By the year

1800, when James McKenzie died, the sisters had received the portion of goods that falleth to each child and had taken their respective journeys into a far country. The home business grew to be Andrew's. In a few years more he became the "McKenzie," his father still retaining the title to the home-place and a few slaves, and possibly—perhaps probably—an interest in the manufacture and sale of the "spirits" produced.

By gifts from his father and father-in-law, supplemented by the occasional purchase, Andrew McKenzie owned and cultivated, at one time, "more than one thousand acres of the then still virgin soil in that fine farming country." Operating four distilleries, he ran a constant wagon train of spirits to market in Charleston, bringing supplies in return.

In 1803 he built on his Stevenson farm what was in that day and in that section a palatial mansion-house, not as large or as grand as Washington's regal palace at Mount Vernon, or as Marshall's baronial academic castle at Buck Pond, in Kentucky, or, perhaps, as a number of the "great" houses in the coast plantation districts of North Carolina, but it was large and imposing for this Piedmont country in 1803.[40]

Piedmont Folk Culture

In the small, celebratory glimpses of prominent Piedmont families such as the Mebanes and McKenzies, at least historians have something tangible to ponder. For Piedmont white farm families, artisans, tenants, herders, laborers, and African-American slaves, the evidence of changing conditions, prospects, motives, and sensibilities remains piecemeal, oblique, and only recently sought. Except when their paths cross those of the writers of journals, or when they stand revealed in the records of church, or census, or county courthouse, or make brief appearances in a newspaper or petition of the day, the vast majority of the region's antebellum population remain seldom-glimpsed historical figures.[41] Yet because the region's industrial evolution emerged out of the transformation of the Piedmont's historical farming culture, at least a summary sense of that agrarian world is necessary.

Rural life in the antebellum Carolina Piedmont pivoted around the family farmstead and the limits of what cultural geographer John Stilgoe has called a "distinctively American space": the neighborhood, a community of vital social interests circumscribed by the distance (perhaps thirty-five miles by horse) of a day's travel and return. Among the rural communities in the Upland South, the interior of Pennsylvania, and much of antebellum mid-America, yeoman farmsteading was sustained by relations of kin and neighbor.[42]

In a region of farmstead neighborhoods, where household sufficiency came first, Carolina Piedmont farmers typically raised a few cows, hogs, and chickens along with a diversity of food crops. On the whole, throughout the antebellum era, farmers who owned at least fifty acres of cultivable land could produce this sufficiency.[43] Then, depending upon their ambition for more than subsistence, their situation on the land, available labor, access to markets beyond the Piedmont, and year-by-year price trends, they grew staples (chiefly cotton, but also tobacco in the upper North Carolina Piedmont) for sale.

Antebellum farming in the Carolina Piedmont, as Steven Hahn has concluded about the Georgia Upcountry, "renders somewhat artificial the neat categories of subsistence and commercial agriculture, pointing instead to an entire system of productive organization—paralleled elsewhere in early America—that combined features of each within an overriding logic of its own."[44] Farmer logic was powered by a commitment to personal independence, family self-sufficiency, and neighborly interdependence that varied, region by region, according to cultural and agricultural potentials, relations of social and economic power, and extraregional ties and forces.

In the Carolina Piedmont, the ideal of independence (what Lacy Ford has called "country-republicanism") measured the success of farmers by their ability "to control the economic affairs of their household." If farmers equated dependence with degradation, "ownership of productive property was the surest guarantee of personal independence."[45] In the pursuit and maintenance of independence, the farm household itself became the yeomanry's most important productive resource.

On the farmsteads of the Carolina Piedmont, a general division of labor by sex and age prevailed. Men (and boys in their teens) cut trees and cleared land, built cabins and barns, erected snake fences that kept out free-grazing livestock, hunted and trapped, and did most of the field labor. The actual herding of livestock was a male activity, although women might accompany their men to keep camp along the trails and cow pens that were strung from the Appalachian foothills to the market towns on the Atlantic coast. When families were small or especially hard-pressed, women sometimes plowed and did other heavy field tasks. There was less stigma attached to women's farm work the farther one lived from the plantation districts.

Most women's work on Piedmont farmsteads consisted of tending children, preparing and preserving food, washing and cleaning, perhaps helping

Marget Dixon A[ged]
34 yeres In Love we L[ived]
& In Love she Died
Life was required But
God Denied

Buffalo Presbyterian Church, Greensboro, N.C., ca. 1790. Carver
unknown, probably her husband. Photo by Daniel W. Patterson.

to plant, hoe, and harvest field crops, tending gardens, providing medical
care, and making clothes, coverlets, and quilts. The oldest and youngest
family members, male and female, were set to such tasks as spinning thread,
making baskets, gathering herbs, milking cows, and feeding chickens. "By
hard work and careful planning," Douglas DeNatale writes of life in the

six sons
two daughters
HERE LIES THE RE
MAINS OF HANAH
WATSON WHO departed
THIS LIFE AUGst 13th 1799 in the
74th year of her age

1
my soul come meditate the day
and think how near it stands
when thou must quit this house of day
and fly to unknown lands

2
and you mine eye look down and view
the hollow gaping tomb
this gloomy prison waits for you
whner the summons come

Beersheba Presbyterian Church, York County, S.C. Carved by Samuel
Watson, son of Hanah Watson. Photo by Daniel W. Patterson.

Carolina Piedmont, "a yeoman farm family in the antebellum period could hope for some improvement in their land status, and increased security in their household economy."[46]

The most important neighborhood institution of the early Piedmont, and the only one capable of transforming a loose aggregation of settlers into a congregation as well as a touchstone on the common landscape, was the church or meetinghouse. In telling of the building of an early meetinghouse, a family chronicle written in the 1850s suggests the web of history and social relations joined by the rural church:

> Samuel Clarke, whose sons appear to have been all decided Whigs, during the war, is said to have come originally from the north of Ireland, and belonged to the stock of Scotch-Irish Presbyterians. He came to North Carolina, with a young family, in the early settlement of the country, and located himself on Deep River, a few miles above Bell's mill. The family were all Presbyterians during the war, and for a number of years after. As there were some other Presbyterian families near enough to attend preaching at the same place, they built a log house for a place of public worship, about three miles from Bell's mill and known for a long time as Bell's meeting house.[47]

In this culture which merged religious and public spheres, meetinghouses served as neighborhood schoolrooms, singing schools, and sites for temperance discussions and political rallies. At the churches of evangelical Baptists and Methodists, even the hours of Sunday sermon would find a customary knot of men sociably gathered under the shade trees bordering the church grounds, swapping horses and stories and perhaps sampling the whiskey that, inside the meetinghouse walls a few feet away, a preacher was denouncing.

The community gristmill, often with attached store, provided the day-to-day nexus for trade and talk. Like the meetinghouse, the water-powered mill gave definition to the bounds of neighborhood. "My father's corn mill," North Carolinian Zebedee Mathews told a Federal Writers' Project interviewer in 1938, "was put in over a hundred years ago. It was built partly by the neighbors. There were no mills nearer than twenty-five miles from here. Pappy fixed his corn mill so it would grind wheat also. It would not take any of the husk out; it ground the whole grain. Biscuit made of it was black and people over the community called them 'Reuben's Blackbirds.' "[48]

Throughout the Piedmont and Upland South, farm families looked first to local handiwork for daily household goods, tools, and clothing. Nearly every home had its cards, spinning wheel, and loom. A 1794 survey of the South Atlantic backcountry maintained that "family manufactures in cotton are much greater in the four southeasternmost states [including North and South Carolina] than in the four eastern states." The 1810 census revealed that North Carolina's domestic textile production was larger than that of all New England.[49] "When I see a farmer appear in company genteely dressed in homespun," wrote the *Miner's and Farmer's Journal* of Charlotte in 1830, "I think of Solomon's description of a good wife. If the farmer's family wants new clothes, the industry of his wife supplies them."[50] Household inventories and wills reveal that spinning wheels and heir*looms* were common among families well into the nineteenth century.

"Sparseness of population," observed Reverend Bernheim from his familiarity with German settlements in the Carolina Piedmont, "compelled each family to manufacture their own articles of clothing and implements of husbandry; the loom, the anvil, the tannery and the shoe-shop became necessary adjuncts to almost every household. . . . Useful industry became every member of society at that time, and the hum of the spinning-wheel resounded in almost every dwelling."[51] In meeting necessity, farm families and specialized artisans produced objects of lasting beauty.

Piedmont artisans (perhaps 10 percent of white household heads by 1850) crafted a variety of wares for the region's farm families, while also tending to their own fields. Potters, for instance, were "part-time craftsmen who worked equally hard at farming, sawmilling, wagoning, and dozens of other occupations." Their craft, writes Charles Zug, "was perpetuated within the family or among neighbors by . . . tradition and on-the-job-training."[52] They dug the region's red, orange, and yellow clays, turning and burning jars, jugs, crocks, and churns with forms beautiful beyond their everyday usefulness for food preparation and storage. Smiths, millwrights, carpenters, cobblers, gravestone carvers, coopers, and furniture and wagon makers, some with full-time shops and apprentices, suggest the diversity of regional artisans.[53]

As their religion and work allowed—after, for instance, a neighborhood corn shucking or barn raising—Piedmont householders opened their homes to the dance music of fiddle and banjo. They selectively adapted secular ballads and lyrical tunes from British tradition, sometimes inventing new songs with local themes. Farmers, blacksmiths, carpenters, surveyors, itinerant music teachers, and preachers composed and published sheaves of religious songs in singing-school collections (such as William Walker of Spartanburg's *Southern Harmony*) that sold hundreds of thousands of copies in the quarter-century before the Civil War.[54]

Reflecting a combination of European folk building traditions adapted to local requirements by the Scotch-Irish and German-descended immigrants, Piedmont houses, outbuildings, and public structures were built by the region's farmers and carpenters. The "distinctive building tradition" that re-sulted, writes architectural historian Carl Lounsbury, "suggested marked differences in methods of construction, use of materials, and planning ar-rangements from the Anglo-American building traditions of the coastal plain."[55]

Although increasing prosperity was usually accompanied by an incorpora-tion of more stylish and less vernacular architectural features and forms, log-building techniques remained popular and widespread among Upcountry planters, yeomen, and tenants alike throughout the antebellum decades. "Solidly built and well finished log houses," writes Lounsbury, "such as those found in the western Piedmont dating from the early nineteenth century, demanded the specialized skills of a trained craftsman familiar with log building practices. Unlike certain sections of the coastal plain which had relegated log construction to use in inferior outbuildings and slave quarters after the first or second generation of settlement, most of the Piedmont maintained the use of it in domestic architecture through the Civil War." What distinguished the log houses of small planters from those of tenants were not construction techniques but the quality of craftsmanship and the degree of exterior and interior finishing. Not until the 1830s—and even then not uniformly—did wealthier Piedmont residents begin to break with tradi-tion and build more fashionably in wood frame from the Greek Revival pattern books published in Boston and New York.

Beyond the organization of neighborhoods around farmsteads, churches, mills, and crossroads stores, the formation of counties and the construction of courthouses and courthouse squares in "county seat" towns gave structure to secular authority and affirmed local autonomy even as it tied the locality within the larger rule and jurisdiction of the state. "For most men," writes Rhys Isaac in his discussion of late-eighteenth-century Virginia, "the primary mode of comprehending the organization of authority was through participa-tion in courthouse proceedings."[56] Inside and around the courthouse, as J. William Harris suggests in his study of the antebellum cotton-growing Geor-gia Piedmont, "rich and poor learned more about the law through observa-tion and conversation than any college could teach." As the courthouse became the geographic and political center of county organization, slave-owners (the wealthiest and most powerful members of the county) "suc-ceeded, most of the time, in getting poorer men to see themselves as part of a single white community." The courthouse helped effect a unity of white society through its several forums for oral culture, through the public dramas with their enforced rewards and penalties played out in sessions of open court, and in the everyday keeping of the records of property ownership and

Gristmill in Guilford County, N.C. (Courtesy of the North Carolina
Collection, University of North Carolina)

exchange. Courthouses and their surrounding grounds furnished meeting
rooms for clubs and societies, drilling sites for the militia, rallying spots for
politicians, and locations for trading in local goods and commodities.[57]

In the cash-scarce Carolina Piedmont, the exchanging of labor and goods
complemented individual family efforts at self-sufficiency. "However difficult it is to determine just how much a farmer set aside for sale," Hahn
suggests, "household and agricultural needs brought all into a complex of
trade relations distinguished largely by direct transactions between various
producers." Bartering and the buying and selling of household wares, farm
goods, and livestock commonly took place on courthouse squares or at
crossroads markets with fixed "trade days," events that remained popular in
areas of the Upland South far into the twentieth century, eventually appealing
as much to travelers and tourists in search of the quaint as to locals trafficking
in necessary supplies and narratives.[58]

Throughout the antebellum era, and especially during the Southwest
cotton boom of the 1830s, the Carolina Piedmont experienced significant
outmigration. The organization of neighborhoods and counties spread across
a wide Southern geography. As they moved further south and west, struggling
farm families seeking new lands and new chances contended with expansion-
minded planters. And although many families left the Upcountry, others

remained, becoming permanent residents of older, settled counties. "From birth to death," reports Robert Kenzer in his study of the spatial arrangements of kin and neighborhoods in Orange County, North Carolina, "most residents rarely found it necessary to leave the settlement's borders."[59] "Among the lower classes," writes Guion Johnson, "there was practically no traveling except to carry produce to market. It often happened that a person lived and died without ever having gone beyond the bounds of his native county."[60]

"A Mighty Waking Up"

With the flowering of camp-meeting revivalism throughout the Upland South during the early nineteenth century, the plain folk asserted their presence across a large territory. In the Great Revival's tent communities, with their nightly testifying, shouting, singing, and preaching, men, women, and children expressed the here and hereafter, the fears and hopes of their experience. In the broad arena of grace that the revival provided, the strenuous conviction of sin wrestled with the agency of free will.

Formed not "in reaction to the dominant culture," or as the "popular response to a mounting sense of social disorder" that Rhys Isaac describes for mid- to late-eighteenth-century Virginia, camp-meeting revivalism in the Upcountry grew from the righteous assurance that had killed and displaced Indian natives, had stung General Cornwallis at the hornet's nest of Kings Mountain, and would soon flex itself into Jacksonianism.[61] "Frontiersmen," writes Bernard Weisberger, "who often took land without asking and lifted their caps to nobody, were apt to lose interest altogether in a heaven whose gates were barred to all except a small aristocracy of 'saints.' "[62] In its spontaneous communities with their hundreds, often thousands, of campers, the revival embodied the cultural "settling in" of several generations.

"Towards the close of the year 1801," wrote a North Carolina Lutheran minister, eyewitness to the Great Revival's arrival in the Piedmont,

> there occurred a mighty waking up of religion among the English people in Guilford and Orange counties, which caused our German people to understand the true worth of the gospel. Both the pastors and their people were surprised, for it appeared exceedingly strange to those, who were well acquainted with the order of salvation, that true conversion should consist in such a way as declared by these people; that true faith should originate in such sermons, which caused such corporeal convul-

sions, such representations of the devil, death and hell; the fearful and awful expressions of lightning, thunder, hail, fire and brimstone against the sinner deprived many of their senses, and prostrated them in fainting fits.

As the like proceedings were upheld and defended by so many English preachers, and as many had declared that by means of such workings they had received the true and reliable witness of the pardon of their sins and of the new birth, many of us hesitated to contradict such proceedings ... but many good meaning persons defended them as scriptural.[63]

Although it soon spilled over into the Coastal Plain, the Great Revival's strength rose from the Appalachian fringe and the hills of the Piedmont. Its camp meetings were filled with families from the poor lands of Virginia's interior ridges and valleys, from the Carolina Piedmont's corn, wheat, and tobacco fields, from the hill country of Georgia and Alabama, and from the mountains of Tennessee and Kentucky. Visible with a startling suddenness, the phenomenon developed from years of religious tillage by scores of anonymous preachers, especially the circuit-riding Methodists.[64]

Writing in 1937, sociologist and historian Guion Johnson suggested what more recent historians have rediscovered: the Great Revival did not simply burst forth as a bolt of ecstatic energy charged by irrational backwoods prophets. It represented the fruition of seeds sown for decades. Johnson notes a visit to North Carolina by Methodist evangelical George Whitefield as early as 1739 and mentions his preaching to large crowds. She also points to mid-eighteenth-century encampments of hundreds of Separate Baptist men in North Carolina, as well as local revivals held by Methodist circuit riders and Presbyterian preachers. Francis Asbury, who became a chief advocate of camp meetings, toured the state on several trips before 1800. Through a schedule of local revivals and constant evangelism, the Methodists led the way to the outpouring collectively known as *the* revival.[65]

As the evangelical movement spread into the Carolina Piedmont in the early 1800s, it succeeded under the guidance of the Methodist itinerants, along with former Separate Baptists and dissenting, or New Side, Presbyterians. Several young Presbyterian ministers had helped initiate the earliest camp meetings in Kentucky. The small rural seminaries that trained these preachers were the legacy of Scotch-Irish Presbyterians from the middle colonies such as Gilbert and William Tennent.[66] Out of one of these "log colleges" came the best-known of the Great Revival preachers, James McGready, a native North Carolinian.

Camp-meeting revivalism entered the Carolina Piedmont sweating and shouting. It picked up multitudes of converts in the Upcountry, far fewer in the plantation districts. Opposition to evangelical revivalism came from the wealthier, long-settled areas of the South and from the most Calvinist of Baptist and Presbyterian ministers within the Upcountry. Whether preached by Baptists, Methodists, or dissenting Presbyterians, the as-yet-unincorporated theology of the evangelicals made the egalitarian offering of a home in heaven to any and all—including the slave population—who sought redemption and experienced deliverance.

When it came to enrolling converts and establishing church congregations among the rural settlers of the Southern Upcountry, Methodists and Baptists soon won the day from the Presbyterians, who, as a body, continued to insist upon formally educated clergy who preached a more Calvinist theology of emotional self-control. Affirming the voice of inspired calling, the evangelicals ordained their preachers largely from the ranks of the unschooled folk who filled the camp meetings' mourners benches.

Perhaps the most inquisitive contemporary observers of the camp meeting's arrival in the Carolina Piedmont were a handful of German Lutheran ministers who approached the phenomenon curious about what their Scotch-Irish neighbors were expressing. "There prevails now, for over a year," wrote the Lutheran Rev. Carl A. G. Storch near Salisbury, North Carolina, in 1803, "a something, I know not what to name it, and I should not like to say *Fanaticism*."

> Christians of every denomination assemble themselves in the forest, numbering four, six and sometimes ten thousand persons; they erect tents, sing, pray and preach, day and night, for five, six and eight days. I have been an eye-witness to scenes in such large assemblies, which I cannot explain. I beheld young and old, feeble and strong, white and black, in short, people of every age, position and circumstances, as though they were struck by lightning, speechless and motionless; and, when they had somewhat recovered, they could be heard shrieking bitterly, and supplicating God for mercy and grace.
>
> After they had thus spent three, and many even more, hours, they rose up, praised God, and commenced to pray in such a manner, as they never were wont to do, exhorting sinners to come to Jesus, etc. Many of those, who were thus exercised, were ungodly persons before, and we can now discover a remarkable change in them. Even deists have been brought to confess Christ in this way. Thus this thing continues even to this hour.

"Brownson," a shape-note hymn from William Hauser's *The Olive Leaf.*
(Religious songbook collection, Music Library, University of North
Carolina)

Opinions are various in regard to it; many, even ministers, denominate it the work of the devil; others again would explain it in a natural way, or in accordance with some physical law; whilst others look upon it as the work of God.[67]

Less inclined to withhold condemnation than the Reverends Henkel and Storch, orthodox historians of American religion for many years tended to view evangelical culture as the expression of a defensive and marginalized population of backwoods farmers. Repelled by the unfamiliar emotionality of the camp meeting or by the homemade roughness of Piedmont and Southern Appalachian farmsteads, observers have sounded much like the offspring of Rev. Charles Woodmason during his 1760s errand among the "lawless Ruffians" in the Carolina wilderness. A brief sampling of these writers illustrates a long and caricatured history written mainly by outsiders. Catherine Cleveland, whose *The Great Revival in the West* (1916) can be considered the first scholarly study of frontier revivalism, depicted Upcountry settlers as "men and women with no sense of moral responsibility." "Hard drinking and rough and degrading amusements," Cleveland wrote, "formed the only recreation of the lower class, and the lawless life of this element stamped many localities with a low moral tone."[68]

Historian of religion William Sweet's mid-twentieth-century assessment of camp-meeting revivalism essentially recounts views that appeared in Robert Davidson's 1847 *History of Kentucky Presbyterianism.* Judging the social benefits of the camp meetings to be reprehensible and the religious blessings as almost nonexistent, Sweet described "the vast crowds which assembled in the woods, in which the dissolute and the irreligious were always more numerous than the professing Christians and the serious minded. . . . There is abundance of evidence every camp meeting was largely attended by the dregs of frontier society."[69] As recently as the 1960s, historian Walter Posey concluded that the institution of the camp meeting was "ill conceived and poorly conducted," and thereby "fitted to the frontier character." "The [revival] preacher's lamentable ignorance and zeal far exceeded his culture or prudence, and he was willing to cater to depraved religious appetites."[70]

The more sympathetic assessment of the camp meeting and Upcountry religious culture, suggested by the early scholarship of Guion Johnson in the 1930s, was carried further in Charles Johnson's *The Frontier Camp Meeting: Religion's Harvest Time* (1955). Johnson reckoned with the class-bound prejudices of travelers from the Low Country and of college-educated ministers, as well as with the impressionistic bent of journalistic and fiction-writing scavengers in search of sensation. "In all the analyses," Johnson concludes, "there has rarely been a dispassionate attempt to appraise the worth of the backwoods revival."[71] In his representation of Upcountry evangelical culture, Johnson ties the Great Revival to its historical milieu, seeing it alongside house raisings, cornhuskings, militia musters, and Jacksonian-era political barbecues and stump speeches. Writing of "sociability in the tented grove," he places the camp meeting as a high holiday in the yearly routine of the yeoman family. The prospect of several days and nights of congregational preaching, praying, singing, and visiting was eagerly envisioned through the spring and summer months of plowing, planting, and tending crops.[72]

As scholarly appreciation for the diversity of historical Southern cultures has grown, recent writing on antebellum revivalism has emphasized pattern, internal direction, rationality, social purpose, and even a more egalitarian spirit (however momentary) across lines of sex, race, and class. Methodism is seen where madness was once taken for granted. Mind has appeared where meaninglessness was assumed—in the evangelical theology. Harmony, rather than crying in the wilderness, is heard in the camp-meeting spirituals.

In reexamining early nineteenth-century writings about the camp meeting, historian T. L. Agnew concluded that past critics, "decorous ministers and believers in the older denominations," were out to slander the meetings.[73] A similar reconsideration of revival evangelists prompted John Boles's comment that "in the scholarly mind the revivalist preacher often occupied a despised and ridiculed position. It would be fatuous to argue that the Southern ministers of the Baptist, Methodist, and Presbyterian churches, as a type, were genuinely sophisticated, rational, and erudite defenders of their faith. Even so, the ministers possessed these traits to a remarkable degree."[74]

As evangelical culture has traveled the road toward historical redemption, appreciation has grown for the camp-meeting spiritual, the innovative song form expressive of the theology and musicality of the antebellum, Upcountry farming culture. The spirituals emerged, not from the literary tradition of the English hymns, but out of oral tradition—including the hymnody of eighteenth-century New England Baptists, the folksongs of the British Isles, and the visionary imagery of new converts. The lively pace of many of the spirituals and their simple, repeated, emotionally compelling refrains distinguish them from older congregational forms such as metrical versions of the Psalms or, in the more liberal congregations, the hymns of Isaac Watts.

The spirituals were shaped to large group singing. An easily learned refrain and the use of "lining out" (the quick chanting by a song leader of the verse about to be sung by the congregation) eliminated the need for hymnbooks and allowed for more rhythmic movement, even dance, to combine with song.[75] And in their messages, the spirituals complemented the substance of the camp-meeting preaching, effectively popularizing the theology.

Camp-meeting spirituals spoke to the too-common tragedies experienced by nineteenth-century rural families: the frequent deaths of infants, of mothers in childbirth, of neighbors and kin taken by "contagion." A heaven of rest and reunion was promised to steadfast and toiling pilgrims. Endurance, persistence, and faith were exhorted in the imagery of travelers caught in life's storms and worldly wilderness.

We'll camp a little while in the wilderness
  In the wilderness, in the wilderness.
We'll camp a little while in the wilderness,
  And then we're going home.

Chorus:
And then we're going home,
And then we're going home.
We're all making ready
And then we're going home.

Oh fathers [mothers, sisters] are you ready?
  Ready, oh ready?
Oh fathers, are you ready?
  And then we're going home.

[Repeat chorus][76]

Deeply intertwined with the historical experience and aspirations of the Upcountry farmer culture, expressive of the most intense moments of biog-

Concordia Evangelical Lutheran Church, Rowan County, N.C. Drawing by
Henry Denny. (Courtesy of the North Carolina Collection, University of
North Carolina)

raphy, the images of camp-meeting spirituals and shape-note hymns, oft-
quoted biblical passages, formulaic sermons, and homely prayers embodied
and animated a worldview that echoed in the oral tradition and commanded
the allegiances of working-class whites well into the twentieth century. Later
expressive forms tuned themselves to the experiences of later generations,
such as the jubilatory evangelicalism of Holiness singers and instrumentalists
and the sentimentality of early hillbilly bands, building upon the emotional
vocabulary and narrative techniques sewn and harvested in the era of the
Great Revival.

Toward the Mainstream

In the early 1800s, the evangelicals of the South had often spoken out
against slavery. By the 1830s, however, as both slavery and evangelical religion spread into new Southern regions, the predominant religion of slaveholders had become either Baptist or Methodist. In a new rhetoric of accom-
modation, the evangelical denominations now asserted the view that, in
bondage, the heathen descendants of tribal Africans had a precious chance to

find eternal salvation. Even the enclaves of North Carolina Quakers lost the field in the proslavery climate; many migrated out of the Piedmont, while others acquiesced to the prevailing sentiments.

As the Carolina Piedmont filled with neighborhoods of farmsteads, revival enthusiasm became more quiescent and more concerned with the maintenance of churches and the growth of congregations. By the second decade of the nineteenth century, Methodist leaders were working to tame the "democratic excesses" of the camp meeting. In the pursuit of denominational respectability, the brush arbors and canopied forest clearings were outfitted with log tabernacles and wooden "tents" for annual "protracted meetings." Individual churches also constructed their own substantial buildings to hold revivals. "As some Methodists and Baptists became more affluent and more 'responsible,'" writes Dickson Bruce, "sectarian practices such as those of the camp meeting were no longer thought appropriate."[77] The transformation of the camp meeting accompanied the emergence of the Presbyterians, Baptists, and Methodists as established denominations within the Southern social order. All of these denominations had, by 1840, greatly increased their number of trained clergy, founded religious colleges, and were publishing journals.

"Social and economic pressures," writes J. William Harris, "had squelched early Baptist and Methodist opposition to slaveholding," with the result that any Southern reform impulses paralleling those of Protestant denominations in the North "had been channeled almost entirely into efforts to preach salvation."[78] With its energies turned to the moral ordering of settled communities and permanent congregations, church indignation pursued not slaveholders but backsliders, who, on pain of expulsion, were brought before congregations to confess to swearing, gambling, fighting, fornication, and drunkenness.[79] The making of whiskey as well as the making of worldly music, dancing, card playing, Sabbath breaking, attending plays, and the idle passing of time all served their turns as sins in the evangelical congregations above, and below, the fall line.

"Work for the Night Is Coming"

"Man is a working animal," litanizes John Belk, builder of mercantile stores and brick Presbyterian churches, across his family's two-and-a-half centuries of Piedmont experience. Wherever the spirit of Wesley, Calvin, and Luther took hold—among planter or yeoman congregations or among many who remained formally unchurched—the curse of toil as punishment for the fall from Eden explained a life of hard labor as surely as Ham's sin justified slavery.

From the pious of the Piedmont there came a body of "calling" narratives descriptive of the anxiety with which one awaited God's direction to preach, teach, practice law, keep store, or farm. The fear that individuals might "miss their calling" (the anxiety of James Lee Love, related in chapter three) could stir considerable self-doubt, especially if gender and social class allowed some choice of occupation. Into the twentieth century, and even among members of the emerging factory class, the tradition of a "calling" remained meaningful (see the history of the League family in chapter five). While the conception of calling could provide assurance of mind and sacrifice of self, driving its possessors toward unheard-of aspiration, it could also counsel quiescence, stoic labor, and anonymous endurance in the industrial routine. Or, if imposed upon by what was perceived as an immoral or overbearing use of authority, one's confidence of calling could provide the impetus for dead-set refusal.[80]

Nor was the possibility that claims of calling could be used in the hope of avoiding the arduous chores of farming lost to the regional imagination. A story that is still told in the rural Piedmont involves a young preacher who, after several years of fruitless and frustrating ministry, found himself questioned by a deacon as to why he ever believed he had been called to the pulpit. "I was out in the field one hot June day, behind my mule," he answered, "and I looked up and saw the letters 'P C' formed in the clouds. I knew that meant 'Preach Christ.'"

"Did you ever think," asked the deacon, "it might have meant 'Plow Corn'?"

Years of wearying, repetitious work, domestic frugality, sacrifice, neighborly aid, and luck enabled the survival of nineteenth-century Piedmont family farms through rounds of seasonal tasks and the constant daily grind: clearing land and spreading tables, raising houses, barns, corn, children, and livestock. Not everyone, however, willingly fell to.

A wry nineteenth-century ballad, familiar in the oral tradition of the Carolina Piedmont and throughout yeoman Middle America, makes a man's willingness to assume his share of farmstead work the prerequisite to marriage and acceptance into the community of householders:

The Young Man Who Wouldn't Hoe His Corn

There was a young man lived on Beaver's Creek,
He didn't make corn for to sell nor keep;

And for the reason I can't tell,
For this young man was always well.

He went to his corn field and looked in.
Shallot weeds were to his chin;
The weeds and grass so thick did grow
That he was afraid to venture his hoe.

The nearest house that he went to,
The girl he courted, I suppose,
She says to this young man in great scorn,
"Oh," she says, "young man, have you weeded out your corn?"

He answered her with this reply:
"No, kind miss, I've laid it by.
There is no use to strive in vain
When I know I shan't make nor a grain."

"What is the use for us to wed,
When you can't make your own bread?"
Saying, "All I am I expect to remain,
For a lazy man I shan't maintain."[81]

Every settlement knew which of its members "wouldn't hit a lick at a snake," just as it could point to a knot of Piedmont puritans who sought to enforce the rectitude of soberest high ground. Because yeoman survival depended upon hard and seasonal work, most of the members of this regional society who sought the frolics of banjo and fiddle (the "devil's box"), of circling dancers, or who fell under the glow of fruit brandy, did so only after they had "laid by" their necessary chores. Yet, an emphasis on the industry of Piedmonters should not overlook a highly visible contingent of grasshoppers.

"A tangle of contrary tendencies," suggests sociologist Kai Erikson, made up of contending virtues and vices and played out on "axes of variation," gives shape to a historical culture. "Whenever people devote a good deal of emotional energy to celebrating a certain virtue," writes Erikson, "or honoring a certain ideal, they are sure to give thought to its counterpart."[82] In the antebellum Piedmont and Appalachian South, the judgment carried by the proverbial phrase "thicker than fiddlers in hell" represented no idle threat.

The ascendant tone of settled communities, established churches, and courthouse government that rose throughout the antebellum era highlighted, by contrast, those discordant and contrary individuals (chiefly male) who lived near the boundaries of irreverent, philandering, irresponsible, drunken, sadistic, shirking, slothful, and deceitful possibility. One might be debauched

A Carolina Piedmont corn shucking, 1939. Photo by Marion Post, Odum
Subregional Photographic Study. (Courtesy of the Southern Historical
Collection, University of North Carolina)

on Saturday, converted at camp meeting, capable of several days' work from
sun to sun, then backslide to the liquor jug and fishing hole by the next
weekend. Even the most unassuming, industrious, and predictable neighbor
or next-of-kin could startle a community with a wild-haired act. What happened next depended upon a complex network of personal relations.

In the autumn of 1836, state senator Stephen Fox of Mecklenburg County
wrote to the Honorable Richard Spaight, governor of North Carolina, re-
questing a pardon for William Ranier, a farmer sentenced to hang for the
election-day murder of his good friend William Stilwell. Ranier, "when
sober," was "a hard-working, peaceable and honest man" who had lived a
"near neighbor to Stilwell for a considerable time." On this particular election day, however, the two men were drinking cider together (for "Ranier
drinks no spirit") when a quick trading of words led to a trading of blows that
left Stilwell dead. As there was "no intent of malice" evident in the incident,
the dead man's uncles and relatives, along with "many of the most respect-
able citizens," the prosecuting attorney, and the high sheriff, signed petitions
for Ranier's pardon. Although he balked at putting his own name on the

petition, even Stilwell's father felt that Ranier should not hang. Considering the circumstances and the sentiment, Governor Spaight pardoned Ranier.[83] Here, the bonds of neighborliness had been rallied; at other times kith and kin were left with a legacy of bad blood and enmity.

In seeking to understand the seemingly opposite poles of behavior possible within the range of a historical culture, Erikson suggests that "when individual persons or whole groups of people undergo what appear to be dramatic shifts in character, skidding across the entire spectrum of human experience from one extreme to another, it is only reasonable to suspect that the potential had been there all along—hidden away in the folds of the culture, perhaps, but an intrinsic element of the larger pattern nonetheless. Such shifts do not represent a drastic change of heart, not a total reversal of form, but a simple slide along one of the axes of variation characteristic of that social setting."[84] That an ordinarily genial, steady, and hardworking Piedmont farmer or mill worker could "fly off the handle" with fists or knife at the drop of a verbal slight from a family member, friend, or stranger, or in reaction to an overbearing command, reveals the deep fold of touchy independence spanning the historical transformation from white farming culture to industrial working-class culture.

Further along the spectrum from the consistently steady yeoman, who yielded to occasional temptation or impulsive act, stood individuals more chronically fractious, willful, or (like the young man who wouldn't hoe his corn) indifferent to the habits of everyday and seasonal labor. This potential was also carried into the industrializing Carolina Piedmont, embodied and eventually made into a profession, for instance, in the legendary life and the popular songs of mill hand turned rambling musician, Charlie Poole.[85]

Houses of the Fathers

In interviews conducted during the last few years of his life, the farmer, mechanic, surveyor's assistant, and gifted storyteller, Frail Joines (1914–82) of Wilkes County, North Carolina, recalled the arbitrary terror with which his father controlled family life on their small farmstead. Wilkes County, located in the Brushy Mountains at the northwestern boundary of the Carolina Piedmont, remained as rooted in the backwoods folk culture as in the cash-economy and machine-age South until late in the nineteenth century. Here an older ethic persisted, requiring, for instance, a young man to either "fight or run" when challenged by neighbor youths on the public roads of the settlement.[86]

"I was borned," says Frail Joines, "in the year nineteen and fourteen, the seventh day of August. When I was about six or seven years old, my daddy'd put me to plowing with a big team of horses, and logging; he'd take me out of school to log in the winter-time. He'd take contracts a-logging. And I drove the team. I was the team boy.

"When I was a-growing up—all of us kids was little—he was a good hand to get around and push us and get a great big crop put out. And then he'd either get hooked up and start making liquor, or he'd stay drunk. And it was left up to me to whip the other kids—and two or three of them older than I was—and make them work this crop out.

"We'd work all day and my mother'd work in the field, and cry, you know, with a bunch of kids, and then he'd come in and cuss her and accuse her of talking to other men and beat her up 'til us kids got big enough to fight him. After I got up any size he was afraid to try it because he knew I'd take a stick and knock him in the head if he jumped on my mother."

The agrarian world of household, neighbor, and kin saw brutality, physical and mental strain, and sacrifice underneath the golden images of harmony with which nostalgia has embraced the yeoman homestead. The bullying domestic acts, sprees of drunken disappearance, flights from crucial seasonal work, and drop-of-the-hat knife frolics were as much a part of male glories as the all-night tale-telling sessions set around mountainside campfires while fox dogs barked and gave chase through the deep woods.

W. J. Cash, who, in *The Mind of the South* (1941), addressed both the "hedonistic" and Puritanical potentials within the Piedmont farmer and saw them as a "split in the psyche of shamefaced whites," felt that these contrary ideals were like "two streams" that "could and would flow forward side by side and with a minimum of conflict."[87] Contrary to Cash's view, however, narratives like those of Frail Joines—and like those contained in scores of antebellum petitions delivered by farmer folk to Carolina governors and legislators—display a constant conflict between these potentials.

Frail Joines's recollections about Upcountry yeoman life depict the arbitrariness with which traditional fatherly authority could seek to enforce— physically if necessary—household compliance. Certainly not all families existed in this kind of day-to-day anxiety. Certainly, too, as Frail Joines remembers, there were farm women "who were not afraid of God, man, nor the devil." The dominant tradition, however, was embodied in a deeply planted, fatherly sovereignty that reached across lines of social class. At its rhetorical extreme, when joined with Protestant, fundamentalist religious sanction, the authoritarian potential of this social character found expression in ways such as that depicted in a scene from Fielding Burke's novel of mountain farmers and Carolina mill hands, *Call Home the Heart* (1932).

" 'How many wives you had, Uncle Hewey?' " asks a young farmer of one of the community's elders as they sit outside a church meetinghouse. The congregation is about to vote to cast from its membership, "in the name of the Lord," a woman who has fled kin, husband, and farm in an effort to break out of the perpetual cycles of drudgery, debt, and motherhood. Uncle Hewey brags:

> Eh? How many? Four. Four I had, an' I knew what to say to 'em. They'd let you know who wuz the man ef they's here today. There wuz Mattie Ann, who fell off a ladder the fust year an' died right off. A bit lazy, but I didn't let it hurt her. I saw she got about. An' Susan, she had yaller hair an' wuz right under my thumb. An' there wuz Emmy—Emmy—He struggled with memory and triumphed—Emmy Jane! She never put her foot out o' the house ef I jest lifted my little finger agin it. All fine women, with minds o' their own, an' I managed 'em. I knowed how.[88]

The claims of the blowhard Uncle Heweys of the Upcountry stood upon slow-to-change prerogatives, customary practices, and legal precedents. "In the patriarchal household economy," writes Steven Hahn of the antebellum Georgia Piedmont, "relations of legal and customary dependency, not equality, linked all to the male head." Women gave up their property rights upon marriage; they could not vote. "Children also stood juridically subordinate and were expected to live and labor on the homestead without remuneration until they started families of their own." In the most abject position stood the slaves, "permanent, propertyless dependents in a society that looked upon such a status with fear and contempt."[89] Paternalism or fatherly authority, ranging from the despotic to the well intended, in relations both familial and societal, constituted a deep legitimizing force within white Piedmont society from the time of backwoods settlement through the era of capitalist industrialization.

Countryside and Capitalist Transformation

Between the Coastal Plains and the Appalachians, in the middle ground occupied by the Piedmont, the growth and the extent of commercial agriculture depended upon a variety of conditions that included the natural limits of cotton or tobacco cultivation, availability of suitable land, sufficient household or slave labor to work the crops, access to fall line or coastal markets, international demand for staples, and the local strategies of particular farmers and planters. As a steady "geographic expansion of the slave South during the early nineteenth century broadened the base and strengthened the foundation of the slaveholding class," the backcountry of one generation, as Steven Hahn has observed, could become part of the Plantation Belt in the next.[90]

In the lower South Carolina Piedmont, as early as the 1780s, an expanding cotton belt attracted planters and tempted farmers into staple-crop cultivation. Increasing transatlantic demand for cotton to feed textile manufactories led to the discovery of a short-staple cotton plant that, unlike long-staple sea-island cotton, could be grown over the wide territory of the Southern interior. Eli Whitney's invention of the cotton gin on a plantation near Savannah in 1793 offered an easy means to separate the tightly clinging lint of short-fiber boll from its seed. Enterprising planters moved quickly to take advantage. Upcountry fortunes were made in the years between 1800 and 1830.[91]

Many yeoman farmers in the lower Piedmont were also attracted to the money that cotton produced. How much of their efforts should go toward domestic self-sufficiency and how much to cotton? How much of their acreage to wheat, oats, and corn? How much to cotton? The more that freeholders entered into commercial agriculture, the more specialized they became—and the more entangled in an economic web that threatened their cherished independence.[92]

The small-scale farming of cotton during these early years carried none of the stigma, or the reality, of dependence and indebtedness that would come in later generations. To the contrary. A contemporary state historian in Charleston argued that cotton's value to the "Up Country," in "its capacity to incite industry among the lower classes of people, and to fill the country with an independent, virtuous yeomanry is of the highest importance."[93] By this view, as cotton kept Piedmont farmers from the paths and habits of sloth it would also give them a staple that grew well on the region's soil, transported without spoilage, and, in those years, could be sold quite profitably.

Just as Steven Hahn discusses Georgia's upper Piedmont of yeoman farmers and its lower Piedmont dominated by planters, Lacy Ford, in his analysis of the expansion of cotton culture into the South Carolina Upcountry, emphasizes the importance of lower and upper subregions in the South Carolina Piedmont. The four lower Piedmont districts of South Carolina closest to the fall line (Edgefield, Abbeville, Fairfield, and Newberry) contained black majority populations by 1830, "similar in many ways to the plantation regions of the South Carolina Low-country and the Deep South black-belt." As commercial cotton agriculture expanded, three other lower Piedmont districts (Chester, Union, and Laurens) acquired black majorities during the 1840s. In contrast, South Carolina's upper Piedmont (Anderson, Pickens, Greenville, Spartanburg, York, and Lancaster districts) remained over 65 percent white in 1850 and "continued to be dominated by small farms throughout the antebellum period."[94]

When compared with South Carolina, early nineteenth-century North Carolina presented a more diverse picture of agricultural activity. In the longleaf pine region of eastern Carolina lay the turpentine belt. Near the coast, especially in New Hanover and Brunswick counties, rice was a plantation staple. In the northeast, wheat and corn were grown. With its silica-rich soil, the northern edge of the Carolina Piedmont, along the Virginia border, proved well suited for the growing of bright-leaf smoking tobacco. On the small farms of the Piedmont south of the tobacco belt, food crops predominated. In the mountain counties of the west, another area of small farms, the growing of grain and livestock for the domestic economy prevailed.[95] The farther up country one traveled in the Carolinas, the further one entered the world of the yeomanry.[96]

Throughout the antebellum era, the distance across the Piedmont, between the North Carolina state capitol in Raleigh (at the western edge of the Coastal Plain) and the mountainside farms of the Blue Ridge near the state's western boundary, measured separate social worlds. An 1836 petition, for instance, dispatched to North Carolina governor Richard Spaight from citizens of Burnsville, in the mountain county of Yancey, protested the severity of a hundred-dollar fine imposed on a local citizen for breach of peace by a traveling state judge, who was unacquainted with the mountains. Noting that the defendant, William Arrowood, is a "poor man with a large family depending on him alone for support," the petitioners acknowledge that Arrowood was drunk when provoked into a fight but attest that this was his first offense. The outlandish magistrate, one Judge Strange, concede the petitioners, was carrying out what he believed to be his duty, yet "he overlooked some considerations arising from our locality which should have had weight with him":

> We live in the mountain district where money is scarcer it is believed than in any other portion of our state and what would be a small fine in other places would be and is felt most sensebly [sic] here. It is believed too that erroneous opinions are entertained abroad as to our moral standing that we require heavy penalties and chains and prisons to civilize our half-barbarous mountaineers."[97]

It was among such antebellum mountain freeholders that antigovernment and antiplanter feeling burned most intensely, that antislavery societies found enclaves of sympathizers, and that Unionist loyalties of a mountain republican sort were common. The small farmers of western Virginia, eastern Kentucky, western North Carolina, eastern Tennessee, and the hills of northern Alabama, Georgia, and Mississippi entered into an economy of staple agriculture late and least fully.

Farmers in the North Carolina Piedmont, where there were no counties with a black majority, embraced the cotton culture much more slowly than did the inhabitants of the lower Piedmont of South Carolina. In 1810 cotton as a commodity was grown nowhere in the entire state. By 1830 it had become a significant crop in two areas of North Carolina: in the east, including Edgecombe, Bertie, Pitt, Martin, and Lenoir counties; and in the Piedmont or near-Piedmont counties of Mecklenburg, Iredell, Union, Anson, and Richmond.[98] Boom-and-bust times for cotton farming, in the upper Piedmont of South Carolina and throughout most of the North Carolina Piedmont, came after the Civil War. In 1850 South Carolina's Upcountry (primarily the lower Piedmont subregion) produced 5 percent of the South's cotton crop; the entire state of North Carolina produced 3 percent.[99]

The history of commercial agriculture's expansion to its Upcountry limits can be read in the patterns of soil erosion. When, from the mid-nineteenth century on, farmers of the hillier land turned to row-crop, cotton-staple agriculture, erosion became epidemic. "As the wave of settlement passed south and west," writes Albert E. Cowdrey, "and especially as cotton planting destroyed natural ground-cover without replacing it, erosion increased," a pattern that was "clearly the consequence of conventional southern frontier practice imposed upon a sloping and fragile region."[100]

Stanley W. Trimble's careful study of erosion in the Southern Piedmont from Virginia to Alabama ("one of the most severely eroded agricultural areas in the United States") points toward an increasing incidence of soil loss that reached its peak during the two generations following the Civil War.[101] "The antebellum period," Albert Cowdry adds, "saw the transition from very low natural levels of erosion to the very high ones of the Cotton Kingdom which would eventually strip the region of an estimated six cubic miles of topsoil."[102] The patterns of heaviest erosion occurred where Piedmont farmers were entangled in one-crop agriculture and where tenants slipped into an increasing dependency. The New South era would see thousands of these distressed farmers and their children move into the region's cotton-mill villages.

As the commercial economy expanded, in the North Carolina Piedmont as in the upper Piedmont of South Carolina, the small farm, not the plantation, dominated the landscape. In 1860 the average North Carolina Piedmont farm covered 278 acres, about 70 acres less than the state average and more than 150 acres less than average holdings in the Coastal Plains plantation districts. Ownership of land in the Piedmont was more widely distributed than in any other area of the state, with over half of the region's free population owning some acreage.

The Piedmont yeomanry, observes Carl Lounsbury, "usually worked their fields without the aid of slave labor—less than one-quarter of the Piedmont population was slave in 1860. In certain areas of the region such as the cotton counties in the south and the tobacco counties along the Virginia border, slavery became an integral part of the expanding staple economy, but in general few families owned slaves and those that did rarely possessed more than a half-dozen."[103] As late as the 1850s, over two-thirds of the farmers in the North Carolina Piedmont owned no slaves at all.[104]

Increasing involvement by farmers and planters in the commercial economy can be mapped by the rise of new types of houses on the Piedmont's landscape, houses influenced by outside fashion. "In the last decades before the Civil War," writes Lounsbury, "many farmers in flourishing agricultural sections erected more solid and spacious farmhouses which frequently displayed a concern for fashionable architectural detail and planning." The profitable expansion of tobacco production in Rockingham, Caswell, Person, Granville, and Warren counties was reflected in a transformation of house plans. Although, in number and in refinement, Piedmont plantation houses could not match those of the Low Country, Delta, or Black Belt, "during this flush time," continues Lounsbury, "planters in these counties erected two-story, single and double pile houses which were often finished with Greek Revival and Italianate details."[105]

The transformation can be seen, for instance, in the North Carolina county of Cabarrus. Here, farm houses dating from the last quarter of the eighteenth century were typically one-room log buildings with an attic and a mortared stone chimney. As late as 1840, the county's customary small farmhouse was a log-constructed single- or double-pen dwelling, although "wealthier farmers were more likely to use frame or brick construction." The Greek Revival style, with columns, entered Cabarrus in the 1840s and, although log construction was still part of the common landscape, more expensive houses were of frame. The change in the county's building practices occurred along with the agricultural shift. Half of Cabarrus's farmers grew cotton by 1850, more than three-quarters in 1860.[106]

Throughout much of the Carolina Piedmont, the agricultural boom of the

1850s, stimulated largely by world cotton demand, led to the building not just of new-fashioned houses for the prosperous, but to the development of rail links within and beyond the region, the subsequent growth of towns, the establishment of banks, the flourishing of artisanal industries that supported the agricultural economy, and a general sense of quickening activity. The new rail connections enabled Piedmont merchants to become cotton buyers themselves, a change that, in its implications for credit relations and capital accumulation, altered the nature of local commerce. From the ranks of merchants, planters, lawyers, and a handful of manufacturers emerged a class of money-minded men whose intentions ranged "from a simple eye for the main chance to grand dynastic ambitions."[107] While there was local wealth to be made in the Carolina Piedmont during the late antebellum years, the grander designs would wait until after the mid-1870s, when a new generation of capitalists could connect their paternalistic manner and industrial plans with the water-power resources and increasingly abundant and available labor force of distressed Upcountry white farmers. In the 1850s however, thanks to world market demand for their staple, farmers were enjoying relatively good times as they became increasingly reliant upon commercial agriculture.

The hopes of aspiring yeomen depended on a good piece of ground and the right mix of food crops with cotton production, the labor of many family members, the affordability of slaves, the ability to avoid extended indebtedness, frugal household management, and considerable luck. Yeoman fortunes also turned upon the maintenance of good relations with local planters and merchants who could provide credit, who owned gins and gristmills, who lent machinery, and who often marketed the small farmer's crop. By virtue of their wealth and influence, these leading men, (Ford calls them "local notables") of the antebellum Upcountry sat atop loose hierarchies of neighborhood relations. In the give-and-take of farmers' relations with the local notables, an etiquette of paternalistic deference and the entanglements of dependence contended with the yeoman ideal.

Local notables exercised considerable clout across a range of public activities from militia exercises and annual road maintenance to slave patrol duties. They sought out state politicians "to take up the cudgels for a certain cause in the state or national political arena." In turn, aspiring and successful politicians had to negotiate the "complex and ever changing network of local cliques" by becoming "thoroughly familiar with local habits and sentiments and sensitive to the whims of the many delicate egos involved."[108]

Political barbecues, hustings speeches, and stump debates that stirred enthusiastic Upcountry crowds in the style of camp meetings revolved like an intense, multipartnered dance among the voters, the local notables, and candidates. This seasonal dance enabled a democratic flirtation, even though the formal rules, electoral machinery, and officeholding itself were guarded by the propertied.

"Popular choice," writes Harris about the political process in the cotton-growing lower Piedmont near Augusta, Georgia, "gave politics . . . a democratic cast. At the same time the power of a relatively small elite guided and limited local democracy." In this antebellum society, "popular choice" itself meant a franchise already restricted to a minority of the adult population. Among this electorate, "some men could sway fifty votes; some, hundreds. Wealthy planters with many slaves had resources in labor and capital to help build support among neighbors: they could afford the clothing, fine horses, and summer barbecues to display liberality suitable in a leader; they could attend expensive academies and colleges to polish their oratory; they had the time to stump for votes and the money to treat the patrons of local 'groceries.'"[109]

Although the inhabitants of the Carolina Upcountry substantially outnumbered those of the Coastal Plain as early as 1800, the planters of the Coastal Plain maintained political control of their states by means of undemocratically apportioned legislatures. South Carolina's constitution of 1808, enacting what became a near-sacred "compromise" between Low Country rice and sea-island cotton planters and the Upcountry's leaders, gave outright control of the state senate to the plantation parishes and based representation in the house of representatives upon both population and taxable wealth (including slaveholdings). Throughout the antebellum era, the South Carolina legislature chose all the statewide officials as well as the state's presidential electors.[110]

In North Carolina, "there was a constant effort on the part of the yeomanry," writes Guion Johnson, "to take from the upper classes the control of public offices. They constantly demanded the popular election of justices of the peace, constables, and other petty office-holders, but these reforms did not come until after the Civil War."[111] As in South Carolina, the propertied controlled state government. In 1850, the percentage of North and South Carolina legislators who owned slaves (over 80 percent) was greater than in any other Southern legislature.[112]

Appealing to state unity in the face of perceived Northern bullying, meddling, and expansionism that intensified after 1830, the most skillful and successful of Southern politicos (the paragon being John C. Calhoun) reasoned publicly that the independence of both yeoman and planter, of Upcountry and Low Country, were bound together with the protection of property. A threat to slaveholding, it was argued, was not only a threat to the wealth of both large slaveholder and small farmer, but a threat to state sovereignty and personal freedom. Aggressive free-soil and abolitionist pressure must be resisted, even if resistance led to separation from the Union or a war for Southern independence. The political power of the planter class was offered as a shield to yeomen's property as well as slaveholders'.

"So long as the slaveholders made few demands on [the Upcountry]," write Elizabeth Fox-Genovese and Eugene Genovese, "their claims to being champions of local freedom and autonomy against all meddling outsiders appeared perfectly legitimate. Northern abolitionists and free-soilers appeared as outsiders who claimed the right to determine local institutions. Conversely, the provincialism of the upcountry held to a minimum demands on the slaveholders for extensive expenditure for an infrastructure capable of 'developing' the nonplantation areas."[113] When the 1840s became the 1850s, as much as the region's prosperous yeomen and local notables might resent the arrogance of fire-eating planters both within and outside of the Piedmont, they nourished an even more anxious suspicion and resentment of Yankee motives and actions.

And the War Came

"Ma was a Williams, born in Chatham County," recalled Mary Rumbley, a Carolina Piedmont textile worker in 1938, to Ida Moore, a member of the Federal Writers' Project. "Her Pa owned a little farm there before the Rebel War. His two sons was killed in that war and it seems plumb funny to me they had to go. Grandpa Williams never owned no slaves nor Grandpa Rumbley neither. Truth to tell, none of my folks never did. Like I asked my brother one day, 'Have you ever knowed of any niggers in this part of the state taking the name of Rumbley or Williams?' Just the same them uncles had to go and they both got killed."[114]

Because Confederate General Joseph E. Johnston surrendered to General William Tecumseh Sherman of the Union army one April day in 1865 on a farm known as the Bennett Place, the wooden hall-and-parlor house of James and Mary Bennett today stands reconstructed on its original Durham County, North Carolina, site. The houses of plain folk have rarely received such attention. The Rumbleys and the Bennetts were like thousands of other Carolina Piedmont yeoman families living on farms of a couple hundred acres or less. Through industry, sacrifice, frugality, and luck the Bennetts had risen in their lifetimes from the status of tenants to that of owners. Producing food crops and raising a few farm animals, the Bennetts also grew enough corn and wheat to sell a surplus for cash. Like the vast majority of Carolina Piedmont farmers, the Bennetts owned no slaves.[115] North Carolina, home to the Bennetts and Rumbleys, heartland of the yeoman culture, lost over forty thousand men in the Civil War—more than any other Southern state.[116]

Men regularly march to war, wearing the same uniform for different, even contrary, reasons. For the yeomen who fought the "rich man's war," it took Lincoln's call for troops, the threat to home, kin, and property that the feared Yankee invasion represented, and nightmares of a countryside filled with freed blacks, before they would make themselves into Rebel soldiers.

In South Carolina, where the upper Piedmont was the only yeoman-dominated portion of the state, the secessionists easily prevailed. The Unionists, under the leadership of Greenville's Benjamin F. Perry, were defeated badly in late 1860 in the selection of delegates to South Carolina's secession convention. During the war, South Carolina's "Dark Corner," in the mountainous northwest of Greenville County, became a refuge for Confederate deserters and a "center of hostility to the lowland government."[117]

When North Carolina planters began to urge secession, however, many yeomen, seeing little to gain for their own "local freedom and autonomy," resisted. When, in February 1861, Governor John Ellis urged the state's citizens to follow the lead of South Carolina out of the Union, the voters rejected the proposed formation of a secession convention. Predictably, the secessionist vote was stronger in the state's Coastal Plain than in the Piedmont or the mountains.

Few Carolinians questioned their states' right to secede from the Union, but many had wondered aloud for years about the wisdom of the strategy. Fort Sumter and Lincoln's response put an end to much of this internal debate. The fear of loss of their independence, the preservation of white supremacy, the protection of slavery, and the defense of undemocratic state governments were wound together into the ideals of state sovereignty, private property rights, and the protection of liberties. Support for the Confederacy was viewed as the manly, honorable, and righteous choice, in the Carolina Piedmont as in the Black Belt, Low Country, and Tidewater. In the Carolina Piedmont, secession was ultimately embraced by nearly all of the local notables much in the manner of the leading Whig Unionist of Randolph County, North Carolina, planter-industrialist Jonathan Worth, who exhorted his Piedmont friends and neighbors: "Let us fight like men for our firesides."[118]

· 3 ·

Labor of Loves

For I will have you learn soon that the two abominations are sloth and idle thinking, the two virtues are work and the fear of God.
—Simon McEachern, in Faulkner's *Light in August*

The Loves and Rhynes of Gaston

The carefully tapered brown beard of Robert Calvin Grier Love came free from its braiding and from its everyday covering for Sabbath meeting. The descendants of Seceder Presbyterians were an austere lot, but they indulged a bit of strutting on Sunday. In the years after the Civil War in Gaston County, North Carolina, full, flowing beards were common. Beards that began among the war's privations lengthened in defeat and in the postwar season of ruin and scarcity, a visible sign of memory and manly bond. Beards begun of necessity or on a dare or as a joke of initiation now held the memory of dead enemies and buried brothers, missing arms and muddy bivouacs. To shave meant putting a clean face on those memories, on the bitterness and the loss.

Grier Love was hardly twenty years old in 1861. Two of his brothers died in the war, a third came home with nerves shattered at Gettysburg. Grier saw little, if any, shooting, serving as captain of Gaston County's home guard and, near the war's end, with Confederate troops in eastern North Carolina. Grier Love was never a Southern fire-eater. Nor did he join the Ku Klux Klan, although several kinsmen did. He didn't belong to the Masons, or to any other secret fraternal order. He was not, observes his son James Lee Love (1861–1950), "a club-able man at all."

> He was not a social man . . . and from sixteen years of age on he was a very busy man in work and business.
>
> His early religious training had increased his native disposition to

dutifulness, to industry, to sincerity, to frankness (he was too outspoken to be a "popular" man), to his home life.

He was not a "convivial" man. He was the only absolute "tee-totaler" I've ever happened to know. My mother was not a "tee-totaler," having been brought up in a home where there was a "still-house" and where there was no objection to whiskey and brandy and wine temperately used. But my father's opposition to liquor was, all his life, passionate; and, in his later years, although not an officer in the town of Gastonia, he was more feared by the "bootleggers" than any other man in town.

In my childhood my mother used to make homemade blackberry wine; but, I think, latterly, Father wouldn't allow that.[1]

At six feet and two hundred pounds, "robust, broad of shoulder and deep of chest," Grier Love had the physical proportions to go with his stature as a fourth-generation Presbyterian elder in the Love lineage. Grier had been named for his parents' minister, Robert Calvin Grier, later the first president of Erskine College at Due West, South Carolina. Erskine, begun in 1839 to produce the schooled clergy demanded by Presbyterians, was named for Ebenezer Erskine, founder of the Seceders in Scotland in the 1730s.

William Love, Grier Love's great-grandfather, had come to the Catawba River Valley and York County, South Carolina, in the 1760s as part of the Scotch-Irish migration. His son, William, had fought on the Patriot side in the American Revolution and emerged a lieutenant. Grier's father, Andrew, was, in the words of Grier's son James Lee Love, "a well-to-do small farmer—a Scotch Presbyterian of the strictest sect."[2] Andrew Love was one of Gaston County's leaders. He had surveyed the boundary and served as a member of the commission that fixed the line when Gaston was created out of Lincoln County in 1846. He had served as justice of the peace and as chairman of the first county court.

In the Love family chronicles, even in the remarkably sensitive and detailed reminiscences of Grier Love written by his son Lee, almost nothing is said about the family's early female members. Isabella Swansea, bride of the first William Love, is remembered only for introducing large brown eyes into the typically red-haired and fair-complected features of the Love line. Mary Wilson, who married Andrew Love in Gaston County in 1832, is recalled only as being "of sturdy Presbyterian stock"—sturdy enough to bear eight children.

"All were thrifty," writes Lee Love, "and Andrew had farms and cattle and horses and slaves to bestow in his will drawn and executed in 1856."[3] Upon his father's death, Grier, age fifteen, inherited a two-hundred-acre farm and two slaves no older than himself. Older brother Samuel, who lived on his own farm in the same neighborhood, a couple of miles down the road toward Pisgah Church, helped Grier to get his start. Samuel died from battle wounds at Richmond in 1862.

On his farm, Fairview, Grier and his slaves cut the timber, sawed the logs, and through the neighborhood tradition of a house-raising built a white, weather-boarded, hall-and-parlor style dwelling, probably in the year 1859. In 1860 Grier Love married Susan Elizabeth Rhyne. He was nineteen, she twenty. James Lee Love was born a few weeks before the Civil War's opening shots.

Lee Love's written account of his father's young manhood in the "critical decade of the 1860s" reads much like that of an Old Testament culture hero. Grier Love was nineteen when he married Susan Rhyne. Four children were born to them in a decade of Civil War and Reconstruction hardship. With crops and livestock Grier maintained his growing family and saved money from the surplus. He was able to enlarge his house and to buy a few "conveniences" such as a cookstove and a hand-driven sewing machine. "New ground" was cleared as needed to increase the farm yield. A careful husbanding throughout the year included the application of composts and manures to the fields, which added to the soil's fertility. Although there apparently was no nearby spot for fishing, Grier Love and his neighbors hunted on horseback for partridges, driving coveys of the birds into an extended wing net.[4]

Susan Rhyne's family home stood ten miles from Grier's. She represented the fifth generation of Rhynes, who had come, in the mid-eighteenth century, from near the Swiss border of southern Germany and settled with other Germans on the Catawba River's South Fork. The Rhynes of North Carolina were successful farmers, millers, and merchants. Susan Rhyne's family was wealthier than Grier Love's, although apparently not of the status of planters.

Of his mother's father, Moses Rhyne (1812–88), Lee Love writes:

> Moses H. Rhyne was a kindly, jolly, and lovable man, with hearty appreciation of all friendliness and fellowship—slow to anger and ready to laugh—generous to slaves and in all relations of charity and church. He sent his children to the best schools he could find—at home, in Greensboro, and at Mount Pleasant. He taught them industry, fidelity, courtesy, justice, public spirit, and all neighborly kindness. All of them loved him devotedly; and not one of them failed him in the course of their long lives of industrious service.[5]

The Rhyne crossroads store in the village of Woodlawn had long been a familiar gathering place. It was home to the successful movement to form Gaston County from the lower half of Lincoln County. Rhynes and Loves had been among the leaders of this campaign. With several relatives and partners, Moses H. Rhyne had built Gaston County's second cotton mill, the Pinhook, in 1850. From the 1870s through the early 1900s, Susan's brothers undertook the construction of mill after mill in Gaston, Lincoln, and Mecklenburg counties.

The Rhyne family sent their daughter Susan to a boarding school and then to Edgeworth Seminary in Greensboro. Upon the death of her mother, Margaret Hoffman Rhyne (1818–59), Susan left Edgeworth to take care of her father's household, which included five brothers and a sister.

"Moses H. Rhyne," continues Lee Love, "was a man of action, or progressive spirit, of industry, and of high Christian character."

He was a lifelong member of the Lutheran Chapel Church, near Gastonia, and was buried there. He was well-to-do according to the standards of that day; and although he was a partner in merchandising and manufacturing he gave his time to farming. His home was on the road now joining Mt. Holly with McAdensville, in Gaston County; and about four miles southwest from Mt. Holly, which was then called Woodlawn. His dwelling was a two story wooden house, which he replaced about 1869 with an eight room brick building, today occupied by his grandchildren. He married twice: first a Hoffman, then a Springs. His first wife bore seven children of whom Daniel E. Rhyne was the sixth. His second wife bore six children. Moses H. Rhyne's "hobby" was gold mining, in the small mines that were very simply worked for little gains in several quarters of Gaston County. The gold was taken to the U.S. mint at Charlotte for coining.[6]

In formulaic language, Moses Rhyne is shaped to a catalog of virtues while wife and children appear as testaments to property and progeny—attributes of manliness. As with the account of Grier Love in the 1860s, there is a juxtaposition of birthing and the production of income. Generic wives bear children, gold is mined and coined.

Lee Love suggests that Grier Love and Susan Rhyne may have met at a singing school in one of the community churches. Throughout the nineteenth century, the singing school was a popular social and religious institution. A singing master, native to the area, circulated throughout the year from church to church teaching the rudiments of music by an easily learned system of notation. The schools were well attended by young and old, male and female. "Only hymn tunes were taught," writes Lee Love, "always, nearly, using the so-called 'square notes'—the 'do, ra, me, fa, sol, la, ti, do' system. I have seen the old singing books, and used them in such singing schools which I attended myself about 1874, taught by a Mr. Collins, whose sole occupation (besides his farm in Mecklenburg County) was in the conduct of such schools." That the shaped notation was, in the 1870s, already seen as provincial and old-fashioned among the genteel is suggested by Lee Love's memory of a singing school he attended as a child in which several young women, home from boarding school, made a strong effort to substitute songbooks with standard round notes.[7]

If Grier Love did attend the singing schools, it was somewhat out of character with his stated preference for the Presbyterian psalmody. He preferred to sing only in church or, rarely, at work—and never other than religious songs. "I doubt if he could sing anything else—having no tolerance for 'fiddling,' dancing, or the songs that go with social festivities." Susan Rhyne had learned to play the piano at Edgeworth Seminary. When she set up housekeeping with Grier Love at Fairview she brought the piano along, although it was heard "with increasing rarity" in the following years.[8]

The site of Fairview, the farm of Grier and Susan Love, today lies within the city of Gastonia, alongside a section of the Southern Railway. In the 1860s it stood in the rural countryside of Gaston County, in the Catawba River Valley of the Carolina Piedmont. A half-mile separated the Loves from their nearest neighbor. Two more families lived within a mile; kin were as close as two miles. Farther neighbors, folk seen at church but rarely throughout the week, were scattered within three miles. Down every road stood a church—Baptist, Methodist, Lutheran, or Presbyterian.[9]

At the heart of nineteenth-century Carolina Piedmont culture beat the rhythm of Upcountry Protestantism. "The major part of my father's education," writes Lee Love, "must have been gotten from Presbyterian sermons." Produced at Davidson College (a few miles north of Charlotte) and at Erskine College, ministers trained in the Seceder faith (later Associate Reformed) represented "a strict, Scottish, Psalm singing, devout, consecrated, presbyterian body, among whom card playing, dancing, and fiddling were regarded as direct doors to perdition. Sunday was called 'Sabbath,' and was rigidly observed according to the scriptures. No Massachusetts, Plymouth Rock, or other Puritans could out-Puritan them."[10]

As a boy, in the family pew, Lee Love sat through Sabbath after Sabbath of stony preaching. His usually barefooted feet bound for that one day of the week by shoes that always seemed too small, Lee felt as if he "were standing on live fire coals." Able neither to sleep nor to pay attention to the sermon, he was made to sit absolutely still.

> [T]he adjacency of my Father prevented sleep. He had a thumb or finger which was potent for digging into my ribs, and he could quickly discern if I showed symptoms of sleepiness.
>
> What impressions can a child get of a sermon or worship under those conditions? I can't say for I have forgotten all of them except the discomforts. I was given a dreadful theology which made me fear to disobey or misbehave in church. I do remember it included a Hell of actual "fire and brimstone" . . . where all evildoers were sure to be sent for eternal torment. A fearsome practice in that Hell was that if you got thirsty in this "burning lake" and called for water, the Devil would pour melted lead down your throat.
>
> God was a "Fearful God." I don't remember anything about His mercy and compassion and forgiveness.[11]

The Presbyterian churches attended by the Love family, churches like Bethany and Pisgah, stood plain and wooden with astringent rectangular geometries containing rows of pine benches that faced sturdy pulpits. An aisle running down the middle of the church separated women to the preacher's left from men to his right. In the 1870s, a few former slaves, sitting in a "railed off" section near the rear, still attended these church services with their former masters. No musical instruments were allowed and only congregational, never solo, singing was permitted. The inspired psalms of David rather than human-framed hymns were sung. Relief between the two long Sunday sermons came from a picnic dinner spread outdoors and shared among the congregation's families.[12]

As purposefully plain as these Presbyterian churches were, Piedmont Baptist and Methodist churches were plainer still, and cruder in construction. In the cemeteries of the Presbyterian churches, the gravestones spoke of the relative prosperity of parishioners—again, when compared with nearby Baptist and Methodist churchyards that had only fieldstones, rarely decorated and often uninscribed, as markers. Presbyterian stones gave opportunity to several stonecarvers in the region who carefully shaped and often inscribed the grave markers with geometric designs and religious motifs.[13]

"Fearsome through Voice and Look"

"Train up a child in the way he should go," the Presbyterian preachers at Bethel and Pisgah repeated, "and when he is old, he will not depart from it."[14] Lee Love got only one whipping from his father. It happened when the family lived at Fairview. The cause went unremembered, but not the "serious talking to" in the buggy shed and the several swats across the shoulders with a switch.

> I do not remember that he ever "whipped" any of the other children. He was always decided and firm, and fearsome enough through voice and look to keep all of us under control. We never dared to talk back to him, in any way, shape, or manner. We feared to do so; and when he told us to do anything, we did it, as nearly as we could just as he wanted it done. We knew that he was a close inspector, and would always discover any disobedience of orders, and visit the offender in tones of reproof that made us tremble. Physically, he was always a powerful man; but he was just, and kindly; and we knew that he was always right—we respected his judgment and good sense and good will, far more than we feared him—and we feared him, too.[15]

The biblical God-the-Father of love and compassion was also a God and Father of punishments to be feared and of accounts that one day must be settled to His satisfaction: "The LORD, the LORD God, merciful and gracious, longsuffering and abundant in goodness and truth, keeping mercy for thousands, forgiving iniquity and transgression and sin, visiting the iniquity of the fathers upon the children, and upon the children's children, unto the third and to the fourth generation."[16] "Tones of reproof," in Lee Love's words, "that made us tremble." These fearful tones color the region's social character and reverberate into the twentieth century's industrial transformation. They are the tones that chill Bessie Buchanan's nightmare (see the preface) and echo in the authoritarian mill-owner voices of a long era's labor relations.

"Duty and Industry the Sole Guides"

Grier Love learned surveying from his father and his brother Samuel. Apparently he was taught by his mother and father to read and write.

> My Father's formal education was very meager. I know not what books, except the Bible, were in his father's house. But I am sure there could

have been very few; and these few limited to Bunyan's *Pilgrim's Progress*, and books of a religious character. I doubt if there were any histories or biographies. The only books I can surely recall as in my father's house during my childhood were: (1) Bunyan's *Pilgrim's Progress*, which I read through two or three times before I was ten; (2) a book with a green cloth cover containing the lives of Columbus, Washington, and Franklin—all brief sketches—which I also repeatedly read; (3) a book on physiology which I read in part at least, but remember no more about; (5) *The Secrets of the Convent and Confessional*, a religious story written as anti-Roman Catholic propaganda, which I read diligently; (6) a book which I dimly recall containing a series of small allegorical religious pictures (engravings) with reading descriptive matter. I seem to recall something about a "Rake's Progress"—showing pictorially a "Rake's" descent from respectability to ruin—but am not sure it was in this book. . . .

The only one of the above books which I think my Father purchased was no. 5. I think he probably got the others from his own Father's collection. There were a dozen or so other books in my father's house during my childhood and youth; but I cannot recall any of them. They were probably, mostly, books of religious dogma, sermons, tracts, or the like—church assembly reports, etc.[17]

Once, Grier Love found a copy of Charles Lamb's *Tales from Shakespeare* that his son had hidden for secret reading. He immediately tore it up.[18] "My Father," Lee Love writes, "was as much opposed to poetry as to novels and to music. I should have been reprimanded severely, if not punished, had I been caught by him reading a book of poetry—a chance which I escaped because I never saw a book of poetry in those days; unless it may have been once a casual glance at a collection of poems in a book by Robert Burns. If there was any other poetry than Robert Burns's in that community I have no recollection of it."[19]

In Grier Love's youth there were few newspapers in the Piedmont. His father, Andrew, subscribed to a Presbyterian paper, which James Lee Love knew as *The Associate Reformed Presbyterian*, published at Erskine College. Grier Love also subscribed to the *North Carolina Presbyterian*, published in Fayetteville, and *The Southern Home* and the *Charlotte Democrat*, both published in Charlotte. *The Southern Home*, a magazine of sectional chauvinism and nostalgia, was edited by General D. H. Hill, lately and gallantly of the Lost Cause.[20]

Like most of their neighbors, Grier and Susan Love rarely traveled very far from their farmstead. Occasionally, Grier made trips to Charlotte and

Lincolnton, North Carolina, or to York and Chester, South Carolina, carrying wheat, corn, cotton, bacon, and other crops for barter. He would bring back coffee and sugar and items not grown on the farm. He would trade for cotton yarn for the home loom and for calico and dress material.

Four miles northeast of Fairview was Dallas, the county seat. With its post office, two doctors, and a few stores, Dallas was the metropolis of Gaston County, retaining its importance until, in the 1870s, it refused to let the Air-Line Railroad enter its boundaries. Where the railroad went around the town, Gastonia sprang up, soon "to cast a heavy shade over old Dallas." The rise of Gastonia in the late nineteenth century and the decline of Dallas fits a familiar pattern in the New South. All along the postbellum railroad lines, especially the Air-Line (later the Southern), new towns grew to capitalize on the trade in cotton. Trading towns of the antebellum era that, by choice or chance, were not located near a railroad typically declined.[21]

As a boy at Fairview, Lee Love learned to card wool and cotton for the family spinning wheel. He also learned to spin. But, he writes, "by the time I grew old enough to have acquired sufficient skill to be useful, these honorable and ancient industries were dis-carded in my home; because the Yankees had learned how to do all such things cheaper by machinery and they sold us their productions." For a few years during and after the war, the Love family kept up their work on the loom, spinning wheel, and cards. The nearby Pinhook factory sold five-pound bales of cotton thread and yard-wide, plain cotton sheeting. Like many Carolina Piedmont families well into the nineteenth century, the Loves kept a flock of sheep, which were sheared yearly for their wool. As there was no nearby woolen mill, blankets and cloth were carded, spun, and woven at home or else "bought from some neighbors where womenfolks were industrious enough to furnish a surplus to be sold."[22]

A varied handicraft tradition was one constituent of the Piedmont's farmer culture. Shoes were made locally from leather tanned in nearby tanyards. Quilts pieced at home became the central focus of women's sewing parties that sped the arduous process of attaching the tops to prepared cotton batting. The Carolina potteries were at their peak in uniting utilitarian functions with pleasing forms made from native clays. Basketmaking, toolmaking, blacksmithing, bricklaying and carpentry skills were found among many households.

At Grier and Susan Love's Fairview farm, Grier, with some help, had built not only the house but a detached kitchen, well house, smokehouse, corncrib, buggy shed, stable, barn and wagon bed, hog pen, and ash hopper. The house itself consisted of two rooms: a main living room (about twenty by twenty-five feet), which was entered from the front porch, and a bedroom. The living room was ceiled and walled with dressed, notched pine boards. It contained a fireplace and three windows. A back door opened out toward the kitchen. In the center of the east wall of this room, opposite the fireplace, was the door to the house's other room. This room, the bedroom for all the family, was as wide as the house and about twelve feet long. There was little furniture. Bedsteads were made by a neighbor. This same neighbor, a Mr. Bloomfield of Dallas, Lee Love recalls, "made all the household furniture I ever heard about."[23]

When it came to making up their beds, families preferred a goose-feather bed upon a straw tick. Less desirable, but common, was a mattress of chicken feathers. Poorer families slept on straw or shuck beds. Although the Love family had some experience with chicken-feather beds, most of their nights, and certainly those of the Rhynes, were spent on goose feathers.

"Susan always had a colored woman to help with the cooking," writes Lee Love, "but she did an astonishing amount of work herself." Love extends a comparison of his mother's industry with that of black "helpers" into a sermon on unceasing work:

> Mother was the best, and swiftest, cook I ever knew. A Negro woman in the kitchen with her was a hindrance instead of a helper. She could rarely endure their slowness and awkward ways. "E'en down to old age" it was the same with her. Her unfailing industry, good sense, and lifelong devotion to duty were an equal match for Grier Love—in every respect. Idleness, at any time, was unnatural to them, an anathema. They grew up in pioneer, puritan homes where idleness was sin, and they never gave up nor ceased to practice the habits they formed under the conditions of their youth which were emphasized by the war.[24]

In the winter of 1870–71, Grier and Susan Love and their four children moved to Woodlawn (renamed Mt. Holly in 1874), a village that had emerged before 1800 by virtue of its location near a ford of the Catawba River. While at Fairview, Love had managed to save, borrow, and be entrusted by several farmer neighbors with a few hundred dollars. Certainly Love's opportunities had also improved since his marriage into the Rhyne family. He was able to acquire his brother-in-law Abel Rhyne's half-interest in the family's old crossroads store. Soon he added the half-interest held for some thirty years by his wife's father, Moses. Grier Love also bought a house and a farm that contained fine Catawba bottomland.

Grier Love had never had a bank account. In the 1870s, there was little cash in the rural Piedmont. The few limited banks of the region were found in towns such as Charlotte. An earnest, honest, industrious man with his eye on his business and his hand on his tools, Grier Love clearly held the respect and trust of neighbors in both Fairview and Woodlawn. "His word is his bond," a manly pledge that served in lieu of written contract, popularly expressed the trustworthiness of community leaders like Love. Grier Love served many of his neighbors as banker, taking on the small sums of friends and paying them 6 percent interest. Situated as a storekeeper, he stood at the nexus of whatever little cash changed hands in eastern Gaston County and western Mecklenburg.

No man for idle conversation, Grier Love moved quietly from duty to duty, always busy except on the Sabbath. "I never heard him relate a story of any sort," says his son. "He wore good clothes and kept himself well groomed in quiet subdued patterns. He required these things in his home and of his family. No ostentation or flaunting of superiority was tolerable with him. He was not sentimental—on the surface—and strangers might think him lacking in warmth and affection; but his emotions were vivid and too strong to allow any relaxation of control."[25]

The Rhyne—now Love—store sat beside the crossroads where two back-woods trails led to the Catawba River, only a mile away. Along the north-south trail in the 1870s still came the occasional droves of fifty or so mules and horses from Tennessee on their way for sale in Charlotte. Drivers, usually no more than two at a time, often spent the night in the Love house while their animals occupied the barnyard. When the Wilmington, Charlotte and Rutherford Railroad was built in the 1850s, its route crossed Woodlawn. The horse trails began to be superseded by the orientation to train travel. At the time that the railroad was built, a second store, one not owned by the Rhynes, was placed at the train station, reflecting new prospects from the world outside the Upcountry's boundaries.[26]

Although the move from Fairview to Woodlawn was no more than ten miles, the observant Lee Love saw a great difference between the two communities. At Fairview, farmers cultivated their own land with a minimum of hired black workers. "All the boys and men of the family worked on the farms and did nothing else; there were no tenant farmers, and no class of white men or families who did not own their land and worked as hired men for others—and there were very few Negroes about that section."[27] Fairview belonged to the yeoman world.

At Woodlawn, around the fertile river bottomlands, there had been more slaveholding, and landowners in the postwar period frequently supervised tenant farmers: "There was a distinct class of white tenant farmers and of

white men who did not own land and whose sons hired out to farm for
landowners." Even at Woodlawn there were a few white, small-farm owners,
but these did not predominate as they did at Fairview. "In the seventies,"
Love notes, "the gentlemen farmers worked diligently themselves, mostly—
the recovery since the war had not been completed." "Altogether," writes
Love, "Woodlawn was a community a good many years in advance of the
whole rural, widely scattered community at Fairview." Lee felt out of place
among the genteel of Woodlawn:

> At and about Woodlawn were a few "educated" people—like the family
> of General Hill, who didn't remain long—and others like the Daven-
> ports, the Nims's, the Shipps, the Rutledges, the Rhynes, and others,
> who had been, and were, of a more intelligent and a better bred class
> than anybody in the Fairview community—where all had been "rustics"
> apparently for generations.
>
> The people—and others like the Rankins at and near Woodlawn—I
> have named were of a distinctly higher breeding and social standing—
> values and exhibited better manners, and would appear to all anywhere;
> for they had "been about," had travelled and mingled more or less with
> the best the state contained. But the war had left every one of them in a
> condition of semi-poverty—nothing left but their farms; so that all social
> life seemed dead; and never was revived.
>
> I did not understand these things then, of course—I was conscious of
> the difference in the people, but that consciousness only made me more
> shy, for I knew nothing about their world; I never was dressed as I felt
> "at home" in their nice houses—whose more or less stately furniture
> always silenced and awed me, on the rare occasions when I got inside
> their homes. Their well laid out yards with fences, walks, and rows of
> box-wood and somewhat, then, neglected shrubbery, which was about
> all of their homes I ever saw, suggested to me a magnificence that was
> unknown and fearsome to me.[28]

Grier Love had married up in the world. Now, with his store, better farm,
and, in 1873, his new water-powered cotton gin (built by local craftsmen),
the habits of industry were beginning to pay larger dividends. Grier Love's
country store, says his son, was "the most popular place in the county." This
was the heyday of the crossroads merchant, soon to be superseded by the
larger and more diverse stores and mercantile operations in the emerging
railroad trading and factory towns. Grier Love would also make this leap. But
for a few years, at Woodlawn, he stocked his store with the basics requested
by farmers, continued to learn the methods of business, and accumulated

capital with an eye for expansion.[29] He bought cotton and, in addition, ran a water-powered gin and press.

The barter system remained strong in these years. Farm produce, especially items like meat, fruit, berries, milk, and eggs, could be exchanged for store goods. "A merchant who had good sense in selecting his goods, and good feeling and fairness in selling them, was a man beloved and useful," writes Lee Love.[30] Before merchants like William Henry Belk brought the "one-price" system of labeling store merchandise into the Piedmont, town and country storekeepers regularly dickered with customers. They would mark goods with a code indicating their cost to themselves and the store clerks. Grier Love used the ten letters of the words "white sugar," representing the numbers one through nine and zero, or "naught" as it was called. A cost price, in letters, was written on the goods and under it, in numbers, was the announced selling price. Lee Love writes: "To the consumer who never would buy until the salesman had given her a reduction from his asking price, the clerk would ask the top price marked on the goods. To the regular and reasonable customer the clerk had another fair price generally below the marked sales price."[31]

The storekeeper's success depended upon a careful sense of just how much of each item to stock, when to stock, and when and how much credit to extend to farmers who were increasingly planting more cotton. Financially successful Piedmont merchants also tended to be, like Grier Love, energetic, ascetic, frugal, methodical, and in the habit of working long hours—men like Henry Belk or Grier Love's clerk, his brother-in-law Daniel Efird Rhyne. Clerking was a form of apprenticeship from which one might make the jump to store owner, businessman, or mill partner.

D. E. Rhyne (1852–1933) had grown up on Moses and Mary Rhyne's farm, where "his training in industry began early and was pushed progressively as he grew older: at planting, hoeing, ploughing, gathering, and storing crops of corn, wheat, rye, sugar-cane, oats, fruit, honey, cotton, and caring for farm animals, with milking, churning, chopping at the woodpile, bringing in firewood for the hearth, mending fences, keeping ditches open, and clearing off new ground for the farm." In 1872, at age twenty, after a few years of schooling—"a privilege enjoyed by very few young people before 1880"— D. E. entered Grier Love's Woodlawn store at a salary of forty dollars a month plus room and board in the Love home.[32]

Devoted to work, the lifelong bachelor D. E. Rhyne proved an ideal clerk. "Success found him as reticent and self-effacing as ever—as industrious, silent, and efficient, without brag bluster or showiness." After two years in Grier Love's store, D. E. had accumulated a thousand dollars. In 1874 he invested this money with his brother Abel P. Rhyne (1844–1932), who had $19,000, in the Mt. Holly Cotton Mill. This was Gaston County's first postwar cotton mill and the fourth mill built in the county since the pioneering one was constructed in 1846.[33]

With single-minded purpose, a bit of capital, and a strong market demand for their goods, the Rhyne brothers were on their way to a fortune in the cotton-mill business. Later, D. E. became a partner (with Grier Love and Grier's son Edgar) in the first mill to make fine combed yarns from long-staple sea-island cotton—the quality yarns that would make Gaston County famous in the textile trade. "During the second half of the 1920s, and until the great crash of 1932, D. E. Rhyne was the leading promoter of new cotton mills, and the most uniformly prosperous cotton manufacturer in Piedmont Carolina." Rhyne held stock in seventeen mills when he died in 1933. He owned three mills entirely, twenty-one parcels of real estate, and stock in three banks. By the low assessed valuations of 1933, Rhyne's property was worth over $500,000, but the "total face valuation," notes Love, was much greater than this.[34]

Although Lee Love clerked in his father's store as a teen, he never enjoyed it. He would rather slip out the back door and hide in the large dry-goods boxes to read the *New York Ledger*, *Godey's Lady's Book*, or other forbidden "trash." By and by, his father would notice his absence and call loudly and angrily. Lee would return, attend to customers, and hope that Grier Love would forget the anger and the absence. Provoked once too often, Grier ordered his son to leave home. Lee didn't go far. Hiding under the front porch, he waited for dark and then went back into the house and up to his bedroom. By the next morning "the storm had passed":

I was penitent enough but nothing was said. I had not learned the grace of a proper apology for a misdemeanor. "Silence was consent" and actions were apologies—words were always used in our house in minimum degree, except for orders, directions, reproofs, needs and wants. Praise was always conspicuous by its absence and "self-praise was half scandal." Sentiment, affection, caresses were unspoken and unshared. Duty and industry were the sole audible and visible guides and incentives to speech and action. Life was robbed of all its sweetness at home and abroad.

Puritanism has much glory to its credit; and the balance must be, on the whole, in favor of Puritanism, but it is hard on the young, hard on everybody, and has had many mistaken applications, and is responsible for much unnecessary and provoking and profitless suffering. In its way, its evil side is akin to what we read of in the religious persecutions of the old Spanish Inquisition. For a wholesome development under a guided liberty, it substitutes a cramping and unhealthy restraint by power exerted on the individual from the outside.[35]

Scenes of the Piedmont Countryside

Among the most detailed and expansive of James Lee Love's manuscript accounts of Gaston County life in the last quarter of the nineteenth century are his observations on those seasonal and special occasions in which farm neighbors helped each other with large or urgent jobs. Love takes careful note and offers meticulous descriptions of molasses makings, corn shuckings, log rollings, house-raisings, wheat threshings, and quiltings. Offering information rather than stories, he describes the settings of these workdays, the tools used, and the methods of work. A glow of nostalgia accompanies the reminiscences, written forty years after the actual events, and turns the heaviest labors into "festive occasions."

Love's descriptions of the neighborly sharing of work in the nineteenth-century Piedmont farming culture present the images of a white society comfortable within its own social and class arrangements. Yet never do the "well-to-do" Davenports and Rankins, "of distinctly higher breeding and social standing," hunker with the smallholders and tenants to shuck piles of corn, eyes and hands searching for the red ear that won the finder a drink of moonshine. Perhaps they joined in occasionally, just as they might have turned up on the edge of a square dance crowd or for a few moments at a camp meeting. Lee Love doesn't say. Certainly, Grier Love neither danced nor tolerated the presence of liquor.

Love's backward glance from 1921 captures a rosy memory, compressing and coloring the onerous, exhausting, day-to-day world of nineteenth-century Carolina Piedmont farm life:

> When the corn was all shucked the supper would be ready. The latter was served out of doors, usually, for kitchens were too small, in the moonlight. Indeed the big chicken pot pie with its wealth of dumplings had to be cooked out of doors in the wash kettle—no ordinary kitchen utensil was big enough. There were no stoves then, and all the cooking had to be done over open wood fires. The women, therefore, had as hard a task, and a more disagreeable one in preparing the feast, as the men who shucked the corn.

But the big feast was a joy; a neighborly good deed had been done in shucking his corn; and thus the country life was made happier by such mutual co-operation.[36]

Or the competition of log rolling:

The men enjoyed the rivalry of lifting against each other. In piling the logs a handspike was pushed under the log—a handspike at each end of a light log, and additional handspikes between when the log was heavy. The man at one end of the handspike had to lift against the one at the other end. Here was a chance to show strength and skill in lifting in competition. It was made the most of. Sometimes for a very heavy log, there had to be two men at each end of a handspike. Sometimes a sturdy herculean form would challenge two men to battle the other end of his handspike.[37]

When Lee Love writes of the restraint, discipline, and emotional control present in his father's house, painful feeling informs his recollection. When he writes about the black and white laborers on the farm, he knows them playfully and too simply as an embodiment of his longing. "They were genuine, and care-free, and much happier than I was," Love remembers. His words suggest an unawareness of the everyday lives and temperament of these agrarian workers.[38]

There were no "nasty" books, so far as I knew, circulating privately among young people, in the communities where I dwelt. There were the usual "dirty" stories and "nasty" practices—but there were no books about them. I was as eager as any other boy, I suppose, to hear "shady"—and even repulsive—stories circulating among the black people, and white people, too, of the laboring class—the people you worked in the field with. But such stories were very few—not from lack of demand for them, but from the mental poverty of the story tellers. A young man named Miller, of an Irish Catholic family, worked for a year or two for my father. We hoed and plowed together. I used to beg him to tell me a story. He was clever; he would keep me busy to keep up with him in the rows hoeing corn in the hope of getting a story out of him. He could tell very few—about all I could get was "Once upon a time," etc.— he would string this out row after row. But he was pleasant, full of fun, and a clean young man who never taught me anything dirty. I'll have to say, also, for the colored men I worked with, that they, too, were clean, so far as I was concerned, and so far as I knew them. I remember one short, thick-set, coal black fellow that I worked with many a day, on the farm,

whom I should be delighted to see again. He was a good worker, jolly—
with the broadest smile and heartiest laugh; but I can't recall his name.

I've no doubt my father used proper discretion in selecting the men
whom he put to work with me.[39]

As he came of age, a "proper discretion" demanded that Lee Love put away
the "mental poverty" and the childish play of childlike people. As he entered
the transformed world of his father, his tentative attraction to and acquaintance with the "rough" classes became increasingly more "indistinct" and
"forbidden."

Of course I was too young to go to parties when we lived at Fairview if
there had been any young people's parties—which I remember nothing
about, and doubt the possibility of—to go to. In the years at Woodlawn I
heard occasionally of young people's parties—where they had "square
dances" and games—but I cannot recall ever attending one.

. . . I have indistinct recollection of witnessing some rough country
dances among people of the tenant and laboring class. A violin ("fiddle")
or a banjo, or both, furnished the music; with someone "patting his
hands," either together or on his knees, accompanied by stamping his
foot on the floor to "beat the time" for the dancers—who danced only
"square" dances. Such dances afforded vigorous action—the men did
not merely walk through the "figures"—they danced energetically, "cutting the pigeon wing," or executing the "double shuffle," and other
supposedly graceful and rhythmic steps. The sound of the feet on the
floor made a din which could be heard outside much further than the
music.

I seem always to have had a longing to imitate a skillful performer on a
musical instrument. A fiddle was somehow out of the question; so, I
surreptitiously acquired a banjo and, for almost a week, practiced on it at
night in the store, where Tom Love and I slept as a safeguard against the
burglars who had previously broken in at night. The store was about
sixty yards from our house. My practice came suddenly to an end one
night when I heard my father's voice outside saying, "Lee, you stop that
right off, and take that banjo back to Monroe Hovis tomorrow." Henry
Hovis was one of his farm hands, a white man; and Henry's son Monroe
was a good banjo player and from him I had acquired the forbidden
instrument.[40]

In his retrospective account, Lee Love recalls a scene representative of
another, related parting of the ways—the excitement stirred by the arrival of a

threshing machine and its attendants, especially for children (see Ethel
Hilliard's account in chapter six). The scene was one of those neighborhood
gatherings in which men and women shared seasonal tasks.

Threshing time was different. Some person in the community—
perhaps living miles away—owned a threshing machine. In our case, my
grandfather Rhyne, twelve miles away, owned the machine that did
most, if not all, the threshing in my neighborhood. Hamlin Garland has
described the whole performance beautifully in his book *A Son of the
Middle Border*. The threshing machine, the power and all, as he describes it at the same date, sixties, in Wisconsin, were the same in
Gaston County.

It was feast day for the children, and we looked forward to the coming
of the threshers and enjoyed their stay as much as the modern child
thrills at the circus. It was the only circus we knew.

There was only one difference I noted between Hamlin Garland's
threshers and ours. His announced their approach to the farm by the
clarion call of a strong lunged man. Our threshers announced their
coming by the long, flying, winding notes of a long, slender metal horn,
which, to my fancy couldn't have been excelled in splendor by the Angel
Gabriel's trumpet. We were listening for it. We knew the threshers were
at the next farm, and about when they would get through there. Following soon after the horn's announcing notes the lumbering noisy, dusty—
oh how dusty the whole outfit was—and the men's grimy, wet, dusty
shirts and faces—would appear coming out of the woods half a mile
away.[41]

As it happened, Lee Love's Grandfather Rhyne, owner of the threshing
machine, was also the cotton-factory owner Rhyne. When the patterns of
family and neighborhood work soon were adapted to the purposes of manufacturing, of Industry, in the Carolina Piedmont, Rhyne's "grimy, wet, dusty"
neighbors, their daughters and sons, listened for the morning whistle at the
Rhyne and Love mills.

Awaiting the Call

Until he went away to Chapel Hill and the University of North Carolina,
James Lee Love saw little that appealed to him for a life's work. That he had a
choice testifies to his family's rising status, and to the improving fortunes and
growing number of merchants, manufacturers, and men of the "professions"

in the Carolina Piedmont. By age seventeen, Love had encountered a variety of farmers, craftsmen, preachers, doctors, dentists, millers, masons, and horse traders. He had known one editor but no lawyers. And he had glimpsed cotton manufacturing:

> I had been in the office of Uncle Caleb Lineberger, manager of the old, pre–Civil War Woodlawn Cotton Mills, and I had seen its spinning machines and looms at work. I had been inside the cotton mills of my uncles, Abel P. Rhyne and Daniel E. Rhyne. Those were real eye-openers and opportunities for me, but somehow, I cannot explain why, they never roused in me any interest as a life-work, or even as a tempo-rary job. And later, in 1887, when my father built the first cotton mill of the long series of mills afterwards established in the town of Gastonia, I was not in the least tempted to give up my teaching and join him.[42]

What, then, was Lee Love to do? His father apparently wanted him to become a minister:

> I had not joined the church, and shrank from doing so through the shyness and fear to talk with the preacher or the elders about religion or my feelings and I also was possessed with the Presbyterian doctrine of "effectual calling."
>
> I believed ministers should be called of God to preach and that unless, somehow, you felt and knew you had that call, you should never think of preaching. This was only one of many other deep things of life I did not understand—and perhaps, still do not understand.
>
> Of course, I often thought of the ministry but I never got any call to it, hence, never seriously considered it. While I was always serious and earnest and tried to be truthful and decent and honest, the ministry never took hold of me at any time. . . .
>
> Who knows whether or not I have "missed my calling" through mistaken notions of what it is that we must listen to as constituting our call?
>
> The two things my father offered, the farm and the store, surely never gave me anything I then could discern to be a call.[43]

"A Mighty Throbbing Engine"

At a time in which there were no public high schools in North Carolina and only a few "graded schools" in the largest towns, education remained a resource within the reach of only a few white families. In Presbyterian fashion, Grier and Susan Love devoted themselves to providing for all the education their children could hold. If there were no schools in the community—around Fairview, for instance—then the children went to live with relatives who lived near to schools.

Grier Love built the first wood-frame schoolhouse in Gaston County in 1873, furnished it, and recruited an experienced teacher, a Davidson College graduate. In 1878 Lee Love went to Kings Mountain High School, one of only a handful of private boarding schools in the state. In December 1880, he entered the university at Chapel Hill. A year later, Grier Love sold his Woodlawn property and moved the family to Kings Mountain so that the family's other children could live at home and attend school.[44]

In two more years, Grier and Susan Love moved again—this time back to the growing town of Gastonia, which was beginning to spread along the new railroad line that ran near their former Fairview home. Gastonia had been chartered in 1877. In Gastonia, among many friends, Grier Love carried on a very successful merchandising business. He also remained active in Presbyterian matters, holding elderships in three area churches and helping to establish the First Presbyterian Church of Gastonia.[45]

Reaching toward a more profitable and larger enterprise, in 1887 Grier Love, town merchant and buyer and seller of cotton to area mills, quit the mercantile business and helped to begin the Gastonia Cotton Manufacturing Company. Love and a handful of Gastonia businessmen, none of whom had manufacturing experience, organized the mill—the first in Gastonia—with a capitalization of $150,000 (see discussion of G. W. Ragan in chapter four). Grier Love was president and manager. As superintendent, the new mill men selected George Gray (1851–1912). Gray's story is remarkable. The son of working-class parents who had tended machinery for years in the Pinhook Mill, George Gray began working at Pinhook when he was nine and had learned all the operations of a cotton factory within the next decade. Talented, industrious, and obedient, Gray caught the eye of Pinhook owners and was awarded the superintendent's job at age twenty-one.

In the 1880s, skilled superintendents were still rare in the Piedmont. What few there were had either come from New England or had acquired their training in the region's few antebellum mills. That George Gray was the key to the successful operation of Love's Gastonia factory is acknowledged by Lee Love. Gray, says Love, "was ready to superintend the new Gastonia enterprise on terms not hitherto offered to any employee—he was also a stockholder." Grier Love and the Gastonia mill's other organizers enabled Gray to buy five thousand dollars worth (fifty shares) of stock in the new mill.

Over the next twenty years, Gray helped to start many Gaston County mills (including the Loray mill in cooperation with Grier Love's son John). Lee Love writes of Gray that "he was able to do more than any other man" in making Gaston the South's leading textile county.[46]

The Gastonia mill prospered, making cotton yarns available for sale by brokers in New York. Grier Love remained in charge until his death in 1907. The Gastonia Cotton Manufacturing Company was, by its success and through the training of workers and the generation of capital, the "mother plant" of other mills in the young city. In 1924, under the direction of James Lee Love and his son, J. Spencer Love, a portion of this mill's machinery was moved to Burlington, North Carolina, to help form the pioneer plant in what would eventually become the largest U.S. textile corporation, Burlington Mills.

In giving his reasons why the Gastonia mill deserves commemoration in Gaston County's history, Lee Love concludes that the success of the mill stopped the building of distilleries and focused individual resources and workers into the building of more cotton mills—so many mills that Gaston County became the leading county, measured by spindledge, in the South.

Love's mention of distilleries suggests one alternative path that the county —and other areas of the Piedmont—might have followed. In Gaston County immediately after the Civil War, there were only three small, water-driven cotton mills, and none in the adjoining counties. "A young generation," writes Love, "coming into action and seeking outlets and profitable ways to make a living" turned to distilling, "an industry that needed only a small capital investment to begin with and furnished a large immediate return."[47] By the 1880s Gaston County had the largest number of licensed distilleries and produced the most alcohol of any county in North Carolina. Although Grier Love was a bitter enemy of drink and Lee Love's uncle, Laban Rhyne, was a U.S. revenue officer, the distillers, operating alongside the creek banks of the countryside, for a time had the upper hand. Love's comments give evidence that the movement for temperance, leading to the eventual disappearance of legal distilleries, found its strongest adherents among the emerging "town class" and its established churches.

The Gastonia mill—the "old mill," as it came to be known—was also significant, Lee Love believed, because it was the first mill built not by a family, but by "a group of citizens working together." As such, it represents the arrival of a spirit of capitalist enterprise in which civic boosterism and town building became inseparable from money-making. In dozens of towns along the recently laid railroads, the fortunes, future, and moral tone of the

Piedmont were being publicly shaped by the interests of a rising business class.[48]

In the last years of his life, Grier Love slowed his pace considerably. Despite their acquired wealth, he and his "thrifty and devoted wife" continued to live "as frugally as when he had started on his business career at Woodlawn." Other Loves—John, Edgar, and Robert—had been set on the family's way in manufacturing. Lee Love was teaching mathematics at Harvard, and the most industrious Love of all, Lee's son Spencer, was having a New England childhood. Now and then, on short winter vacations, Grier Love and his "self-effacing and industrious helpmeet" made visits to the orange groves and hotels on Florida's Indian River and once, in 1904, to Palm Beach.[49]

When Grier Love died in 1907, Gastonia's businesses closed their doors for a day, as did the Gastonia Cotton Manufacturing Company and Avon Mills. "In his battle for what he believed to be best," read the obituary from the Record of Gastonia's First Presbyterian Church, "he served at one and the same time as a mighty, throbbing engine, and as a powerful restraining brake." The funeral was attended by "perhaps the largest body of the best and most representative citizens from all parts of Gaston and neighboring counties, that ever attended a funeral in Gastonia."[50]

Cornelia and James Spencer Love

At Chapel Hill in the early 1880s, Grier Love's son Lee's search for his calling finally led him to the study and teaching of mathematics. He seemed to have found his way among his fellow students at the university, for he was elected president of the class of 1884—a class in which twenty men received B.A. degrees. The effects of the Civil War were evident in the institution's depleted resources for educating and in the extent to which the war "robbed us who came to Chapel Hill of adequate preparation for college." Indeed, "it deprived most of the youth of our generation of the chances of education of any sort, beyond the merest rudiments of the 'Three R's.'"[51] The reopening of the university after the war had been delayed until 1875, when Kemp P. Battle and Cornelia Phillips Spencer (mother of Lee Love's wife-to-be, June Spencer) waged a campaign with the state legislature.

In a speech made for the fiftieth anniversary of his graduating class, Lee Love reflects upon 1884 as a time of deep poverty, turbulence, and depression in the South. There was little capital to begin any sort of industry except

June Spencer Love and Cornelia Spencer Love, 1899. (J. Spencer Love
Papers, Southern Historical Collection, University of North Carolina)

the building of cotton gins. Despite this, Love saw 1884 as "the turning
point" in the postwar recovery. For him, the election of Grover Cleveland
meant that "for the first time we had a friendly, fair minded man in the White
House." "We, of the class of 1884," recalls Love, "went out into a world of
unprecedented opportunities. It did not appear so to us. Far from it."

Lee Love went on from Chapel Hill, with his bride and his undergraduate
degree, to Johns Hopkins and, in 1889, to Harvard on a mathematics fellowship. He received his Harvard M.A. in 1890 and from that year until 1911
was instructor, then professor, of mathematics at Harvard. For a time he
headed the Lawrence Scientific School.[52]

Both of Lee and June Spencer Love's children, Cornelia Spencer (b.
1892) and James Spencer (b. 1896) were born while the couple was living in

James Lee Love, late 1880s. (J. Spencer Love Papers, Southern Historical Collection, University of North Carolina)

Cambridge. The children grew up there and attended public schools. Several times the Love family returned to Gastonia to visit Grier and Susan. Cornelia Spencer Love recalls a "wonderful trip" back to Chapel Hill when her father attended his graduating class's twenty-five-year reunion in 1909:

"In those days, the commencement balls were very important, they were great social events. And here was I, a little Yankee girl, just seventeen, knowing how to dance and loving it but not knowing anybody at all . . . and I just had the time of my life. I enjoyed it thoroughly. The dances were held in the Commons, on the edge of the campus. Off the campus because you couldn't have dancing on campus in those days.

"The Methodists and Baptists were strong in the land. They totally disapproved of dancing. Girls weren't supposed to do it and they were always pointing out the wicked University. The Presbyterians were just as bad. My mother was a Presbyterian. She thoroughly approved of my dancing. My brother and I went to dancing school, but she never danced a step in her life and she felt that she was too old to learn. It was greatly disapproved in the state; but it went on in spite of it."[53]

After attending Radcliffe (where she received her B.S. in 1914) and the New York State Library School (1915–17), Cornelia Love returned to Chapel Hill, pulled by connections of kin and region and at the request of Louis Round Wilson, moving force of the university library. From 1917 until 1948, she served as head of the orders department. With the Love family living in Cambridge, there had never been any doubt that Cornelia would attend Radcliffe and her brother, Spencer, would go to Harvard. The commitment of the Love and Spencer families to education once again guided a decision about residence. Lee Love had turned down the offer of the presidency of Tulane University in order that their children might enjoy the advantages of Boston.

Between 1894 and her death in 1908, Cornelia Phillips Spencer, stalwart of North Carolina education, lived in the Loves' Cambridge household, helping to teach her grandchildren reading, writing, and geography. Grandmother Spencer would read Cooper, Scott, and Dickens aloud to young Cornelia while the child sewed. "I never sat there doing nothing. She taught me how to sew, to embroider and insisted that I be employed while she was reading." Both Cornelia and her brother Spencer attended the Boston Latin School, and both children went to dancing school and took music lessons. "My mother was a very good Presbyterian," Cornelia Love says. "She didn't let me sew on Sunday or play games. There was 'Biblical Authors'—we could play that.

"When I was ten, my mother wanted me to start piano lessons, so she wrote to my Grandpa Love and told him of that and that we didn't have a piano. He wrote back and said that he would give me a piano if I would learn to make biscuits and sew a button on my brother's trousers. So, I had to send him a symbolic button sewed on and he gave my mother *carte blanche* to get any piano she wanted.

"My brother [Spencer] was very, very gifted in a musical way. He had true pitch. You could strike any note and he could tell you what it was. If he heard a tune, he could play it with accompaniment. The only lessons that he ever had were given to him by me. Now what I could teach him was to read music.

"His playing was always a delight to us. He would sit down at the piano after dinner. He loved things like the 'Desert Song,' and Sigmund Romberg and the 'Showboat,' the popular things, that sort of music. He could play it.

"There wasn't anything apparent to me that Spencer was anything more than a bright little boy. My mother once said that he was the brightest little boy she had ever taught except for one of the Winstons. She had had a little school when she was living in Chapel Hill. Well, you could just discount that as parental.

"We were very congenial. We did things together after he got to be four-teen or fifteen. We would go to a show in Boston at Keith's Orpheum. I remember going one afternoon with him and there were a pair of comedians in straw hats who came out and sang 'When You Wore a Tulip and I Wore a Big Red Rose.' Years later I would say to Spencer when he was at the piano, 'Play "When You Wore a Tulip." ' "

Spencer began school at age five, then skipped a grade or two. Due to his youth, he was kept out one year between high school and entering Harvard. He spent that year at a manual training school, then entered Harvard at age seventeen. He made good but not excellent grades, took extra courses, and completed the undergraduate curriculum in three years. Wanting to graduate with his class, he took an additional year of classes in the newly opened Harvard Business School. Then came World War I.

Cornelia Spencer Love arrived in Chapel Hill in 1917 to begin her work in the university library. She had originally intended to be a secretary, but while studying at Radcliffe and working a part-time job at Episcopal Theological Seminary Library in Cambridge, she met Edith Fuller, niece of Margaret Fuller and head librarian at the seminary. Fuller persuaded Cornelia toward a more ambitious plan.

Cultural and family traditions remained strong forces in Cornelia's life. She, for instance, was not involved in the suffrage movement. "No," she says, "I was tainted by my grandmother's thinking.

"She [Cornelia Phillips Spencer] was so keen for women's education and did a great deal to bring it about. Otherwise, that dormitory wouldn't have been named for her at Greensboro and the one at Chapel Hill. She knew the leaders, the McIvers, Vances. She knew those men that started the women's education. She wrote letters. That was her power, the power of her pen. And she would write in the newspapers. She had this column in the *Presbyterian Standard* for young girls. In that way, she did wield a lot of power. But she did not believe that women should have the vote. I guess that her reasons have been justified.

"She felt that women would vote more or less as their husbands did, that they wouldn't strike out on any new paths. She felt that they had their mission in life, that they had lots of influence but that they did not exert it by the vote."

J. Spencer Love in the Army Quartermaster Corps during World War I.
(J. Spencer Love Papers, Southern Historical Collection, University of
North Carolina)

"The Day Spencer Love Came to Town"

From Harvard, Spencer Love went first to the U.S. Army Officers' Training School at Plattsburg, New York. He was commissioned a first lieutenant
in the fall of 1917 and then was off to Fort Dix. With a group of unassigned
officers Love was sent temporarily to divisional and camp headquarters,
where his organizational abilities caught the eye of superior officers. He was
assigned the task of replanning headquarters administrative procedures.
General Hugh McRae carried Love overseas with the 78th Division's headquarters staff. Soon Spencer Love became the youngest major in the Expedi-
tionary Forces.[54]

Cornelia Love remembers: "Oh, I'll tell you how I first realized that he was
something unusual. He had finished at Camp Dix and was a first lieutenant
and was waiting to be sent overseas. A friend of his, who had to be away for a

while, asked him to do the work that he had been doing, just temporarily, for a few weeks. The work that he asked him to do was in the Quartermaster's Department, the planning and administration. Well, my brother proved to be so good at that, he was kept in it and was sent overseas, was made a captain almost right off. He was made a major before he was twenty-one years old. He never did combat, but he was always with the planning. Then I realized that he must have some extraordinary talent and ability for the Army to have recognized that and kept him doing this and that and the other thing."

Service in the Quartermaster Corps, with the opportunity to manage men and equipment on a large scale, added a final, and critical, term of preparation for the business Spencer Love was about to undertake. In 1919 he went South, visited the family's "Old Mill" at Gastonia, and, at his father's suggestion, first assisted then took over from his uncle, Robert Love, the management of the mill. With Lee Love's moral support and financial credit, Spencer purchased the controlling interest in the Old Mill from his uncle.[55]

After the first year's operation under Spencer Love, the Gastonia mill's profits amounted to nearly half its indebtedness. The second year, however, due to a postwar slump, proved disastrous. In addition, hard use had badly worn the Old Mill machinery and buildings. Love decided his best course would be to sell the increasingly valuable mill property, which lay within the city of Gastonia, and search for a new location in which he could enter wholeheartedly into the weaving of cloth.[56] Several Carolina Piedmont towns offered enticements, but the chamber of commerce of Burlington, North Carolina, made the best proposal, agreeing to underwrite a stock sale of $250,000.

The initial issuance of stock in the new Burlington Mill was $480,000: $250,000 to the local investors for cash and $230,000 to Spencer Love. Lee Love writes: "I believe we had the good luck to pay off our personal notes, as well as all mill notes, before we moved the plant, or very soon after, to Burlington in 1924. And, in addition to the plant equipment for which we received $180,000 in common stock of the Burlington Mills, we invested for the company $40,000 in cash."[57]

Reid Maynard (b. 1896), a Piedmont native who became one of Alamance County's major hosiery manufacturers (and president of the American Hosiery Manufacturers Association), graduated from the University of North Carolina in 1919 and took a job clerking at the First National Bank of Burlington that same year. He remembers the condition of the town's mills in the 1920s and the arrival of Spencer Love.

"It was the Holts and the Williamsons who had run the old plain cotton mills. And they had let them go down. They were at a low ebb, a lot of them closed, some of them bankrupt, the others just took their money out and quit.

"There was the Sellars Hosiery Mill, the Standard Hosiery Mill, owned by John Shoffner. The Glen Raven Mill owned by the Gants. Aurora Cotton Mill, owned by the Holts. Ossippee owned by the Williamsons. Just a few families. There wasn't any broad stock, there was just family.

"There are still some family mills. Glen Raven—the Gants still own that mill. You couldn't buy stock in it for love nor money. And, of course, the Holts went out and the Williamsons closed them out or done something. They had plenty of things on the side, none of those people died poor, they were well fixed, but the old mills, they just give them up.

"That was the day Spencer Love came to town. Spencer came here in 1923. His father, you know, taught math at Harvard and Spencer was a Harvard graduate. He was in the army. He was the youngest major. He and I was two weeks different in age, but he was a major when I wasn't even a decent private.

"He came home and worked to get in the textile business. He and his daddy bought this old run-down cotton mill in Gastonia. I don't know what got him to Burlington. The Chamber of Commerce, I think, went after him, and Love moved—closed down that old cotton mill he had in Gastonia—and moved the machinery down here in some building. He put that in for a certain amount of money, value. Then they got out and sold stock here for him for I don't know how many thousands of dollars. From that Love started here in Alamance."[58]

The new mill began with a single-story brick building built in a cornfield, two hundred employees, some 150 looms, and ten thousand spindles. Anticipating expansion, Spencer Love put a wooden wall at one end of the building that could easily be knocked out. With its long tradition of textile manufacture, depressed Alamance County easily provided experienced workers for low wages.[59]

As Love's Burlington Mill searched for a successful product, it made flag cloth, buntings, cotton scrims, curtain fabrics, and diaper cloth. It tried coarse cotton dress cloth in the style of Alamance Plaid which E. M. Holt had made famous in his antebellum mills. Nothing seemed to sell. In desperation, Love finally hit upon a shiny fabric made with a mixture of cotton and "poor man's silk"—newly discovered rayon.

As Reid Maynard explains, "He saw that rayon would sell. It would make good cloth. The yarn was sorry, didn't run good, but he kept working on it. He got good men in the plants. He worked with Dupont. Dupont was making the yarn and they'd come down here and take his suggestions—try this and that—try to improve the yarn, and they did. At the same time he cashed in on it 'cause he was ahead of everybody else in that thing. All these other old boys were staying with cotton and cotton had gone to pot. Cotton goods. Gingham used to be the great thing back in those days. You'd make ginghams which was a light cotton cloth all women wore dresses out of. One size yarn or another and various sundry colors. But when you got rayon coming in it was slick, different whirl, and it went like—you couldn't make enough of that cloth."

Slick, flashy bedspreads made of "artificial silk" appealed to a new popular market. Rayon cloth cost about one-third the price of silk. Love's bedspreads sold well even though the first ones had a seam running down the middle, the result of having to weave on looms that were only forty inches wide and then sew two pieces of fabric together. Soon these looms were replaced by wider ones, and the difficulties of weaving the contrary rayon fibers diminished as Love and his workers became more familiar with its special problems. Love ran his first rayon in 1924, some 106 pounds. Ten years later Burlington Mills was the largest weaver of rayon in the United States.[60]

"At the same time," recalled hosiery manufacturer Maynard, "rayon was just coming in. Nobody would fool with it. It was hell to run. But Love was sold on it, and he worked it, from one little mill to another. Then he began buying—all these mills around here were bankrupt and all. He would get nothing much but the building, grounds and houses. Bought new machinery. He raised enough money locally to start one mill after another—there must have been five or six of them.

"He worked. I used to go to the mountains with him—he had a home up at Linville—in the summer. Play golf on Saturday and Sunday. And worked like a dog. Hard stripped for money, financing everything through a factor. But he did a job with it.

"A factor will loan you money on your inventory. You get a certified inventory by a auditor; for instance, you got a million dollars worth of inventory. They'll advance you some two, three, four hundred thousand dollars on that. As you sell it, you got to pay them back. In six weeks, two months, you redo the thing and you keep a cash flow in there. They charge you like the dickens. But if it's possible, they guarantee your accounts, furnish your money, tell you who you can sell it to, you know. In other words, you ask them, they approve your credit because they own that thing.

"Spencer Love worked with Minehart, Griff and Company in New York. I worked with them when I first started. Spencer knew their top men and he'd have them down here, taking them to Linville, playing golf and showing them this, that and the other. Keeping his credit up so he could get money. Had all the money borrowed from banks he could get."

With the success of the rayon bedspreads, expansion of Burlington Mills proceeded strategically. The parent company would form a new corporation, subscribe for a minimum amount of stock, purchase a bankrupt mill in a Carolina Piedmont town by selling mortgage bonds to town investors, make a down payment on machinery, provide a bit of working capital, and take, in exchange, stock in the new mill. The parent would supply yarn on credit to the new mill and cash for the payroll; it would also market the new mill's product, for a fee. Spencer Love organized at least thirty mills by this method.[61]

As the textile depression continued through the 1920s and as other mills were collapsing, Love managed to keep his company growing. Love drove himself and those who worked for him relentlessly and with the single purpose of showing a profit for his company. He competed fiercely. He enforced cheap wages on Burlington Mill workers and was vehemently anti-union. All of the old Love habits of industry were present in Spencer.

"Every inch a true Southerner," wrote a reporter for the trade magazine *American Fabrics*, "he is also a Puritan who does not smoke and drinks only to avoid an issue." Love worked eleven- to twelve-hour days and was singularly concerned with business. He "eats, lives, and breathes his business; . . . everything he does or thinks about seems to stem from it. He is interested in schools and colleges because they train for business; he is interested in the government because of its effect on business." Love spared only a little time for affairs away from work, and when he did he seems to have approached social relations as conquests or as a pretense for doing a little more business.[62]

Love was among the first businessmen to introduce modernized corporate organization to Piedmont textiles. He brought the technical tools of cost accounting and efficiency analysis into his mills, never adopted the institutions of village "welfare work," scattered factories throughout the region in order to make union organizing more difficult, and integrated his company's production and advertising into the constantly changing style demanded of national and international textile marketing.

Insight into Spencer Love's strategy is offered in a 1929 letter that he wrote to the *Southern Textile Bulletin*. The *Bulletin* had asked its mill-owner readers to reply to the question: "What's the Matter with the Cotton Manufacturing Industry?" Most replies complained of the ruinous practice of overproduction due to night operation—"mass production without mass consumption," as one mill owner put it. Love's answer revealed the advanced position of rationalization he had assumed. Already lean and tightly watchful of cost efficiencies, strongly committed to independent initiative on sales (in 1929 he took his company's sales out of the hands of commission houses), intent on keeping inventories low and flexible enough to adjust to buyers' changing demands, Love wrote:

Your query, "What's the Matter with the Cotton Manufacturing Industry?" can in my opinion best be answered by the fact that during the war and the prosperity immediately thereafter a great many individuals and concerns became well established in the cotton mill business by means of exorbitant profits, who really lacked either the knowledge or the inherent suitability or efficiency to be successful under normal conditions. Until these people are eliminated and the concerns which they represent pass out of existence or into more able hands, which is a process gradually taking place, I feel we are going to continue to have very close margins in our industry. A comparison of the cotton textile industry with other more prosperous industries today indicates that the other industries have either liquidated similar conditions already or have never had them, due to newness or other differences in fundamentals.

The particular facts and developments which individuals and concerns such as described above are least apt to appreciate are:

1. In the East and in certain sections of the Piedmont district it is almost impossible to compete successfully with mills in sections further South on poundage and production of staples because of the labor cost differences.

2. Much more rapid changes of fashions, improvements in machinery and fabrics, and increased style consciousness of the public result in: (a) Obsolescence of machinery, which formerly was only a negligible item, becoming a very important factor and in many instances one that should be rated as much or more than 10 percent per annum. (b) The necessity of new methods of cost accounting caused by these rapid changes and in the mixing of rayon and other fibres with cotton fabrics adding to the complexity of manufacture. (c) Greatly increased danger in making up stocks of unsold merchandise. (d) Need of much more close attention to selling and distribution policies.[63]

As fundamentally as the textile industry was fixed upon machinery and labor and upon the infinitely tedious spinning and weaving of threads and shaping of fabrics, success also depended upon the whimsy of fashion and the craft of image making. While Spencer Love drove himself and the people who worked for him like machines, he carefully cultivated and projected images of high style. He liked his Cadillac to be the latest model and his wife to wear expensive jewelry. In later years, he regularly played tennis in Palm Beach and cruised the Mediterranean accompanied by family and stacks of business papers.

"Spencer was a funny guy," recalls Reid Maynard. "He lived in nice homes. He lived in one of the Holt's homes right here on the corner. Paid three hundred dollars a month rent. And everybody in Burlington thought he was crazy: 'How's this guy going to afford that?' Nobody else paid over twenty-five dollars. He finally owned a home here, but most of the time he rented one of these old big houses, and lived well.

"He made a go out of this thing. Made the town, no doubt about that. And in the 1930s Burlington never had a depression. We never had things close down. You have to give Spencer Love credit for a lot of that."

With practical steps, Love elaborated his expression of style into an identity for Burlington Mills. One important move was the opening of a New York sales office in 1929. Now Love could escape the control of commission houses and have his own salesmen approach retail stores, mail order outlets, and home-furnishings manufacturers directly. Between the mid-1930s and 1942, Burlington Mills evolved a registered trademark and turned to trade and popular advertising in order to shape and stimulate demand for its own line of products.[64]

Another carefully cultivated expression of Burlington Mills's public identity was the image it maintained within the industry and within the Piedmont as a progressive company. Reviewing Love's strategies in a 1962 retrospective article, a writer for the *Charlotte Observer* noted that Love "spent more than his competitors for modernization and he sought to keep his plant's wage scale just above those of others. He thus fended off both unions and strikes in almost all of his plants, ranging from South Africa to California."[65]

Workers who knew Burlington Mills and Love best sometimes saw through the public image to the hand that moved the company. "There have been several attempts to get unionized," says Edward Harrington, a retired weaver who worked for many years in Burlington Mills, "but I don't think they've ever done it. I believe that old man Spencer Love said at one time that if they ever got a union in, he'd lock the doors and throw away the key. I don't know whether he said it or not, but sounds about like him."[66]

Throughout the Depression, Burlington Mills continued to expand, acquiring new plants and talented, well-trained management. Love might acquire a single plant or entire company primarily to obtain the men who ran them. An era of consolidation ended in 1937 when Burlington listed itself on the New York Stock Exchange. Then began a phase of diversification, beginning with an entrance into the making of hosiery. In May 1940, the first nylon stockings were sold, causing a revolution in the entire hosiery industry. Determined to control the quality and availability of yarn, Love oversaw Burlington's move into spun rayons in 1940; in turn, this led to the company's strength in fiber blending.

"Abortive vertical and successful horizontal integration produced a significant change in management," wrote Harvard Business School professor David D. D. Rogers as he reviewed Burlington Mills's history. "The president might have grown up in one area (as J. Spencer Love did in manmades), and that meant other areas had to be left to others—the Bill Klopmans (manmade gray goods), the Herb Kaisers (hosiery), the Hutchinson brothers (wool) and the Ely Callaways (worsteds). William Klopman with his passion for selling rayon gray goods already had helped Burlington increase its sales all through the Depression. And J. C. Cowan lent the company his great strength in people and manufacturing."[67]

By the end of World War II, Love's intricately constructed textile empire had deeply and profitably enmeshed itself in military production. Love himself ran the Textile, Clothing and Leather Bureau of the War Production Board. In 1944 Burlington Industries made its first move into foreign operations. The advantages of friendly government-business relations had been evident to Love for years. He would stress this corporate "team" view strongly in the coming years, even as he crushed any union sentiment in Burlington Mills.

"I personally feel," he wrote Burlington executive J. C. Cowan in 1948, "that we are going to have more and more planning and regulation. . . . Capitalism without controls can eventually destroy itself and lead to despotism by a privileged few almost as surely as other systems will."[68] Capitalism's controls, however, felt Love, must remain in the hands of enlightened capitalists.

"Right Much of a Taskmaster"

Likely the old patriarch, Grier Love, would have snorted at some of his grandson's ways: his three marriages and reputation as a womanizer; his working on the Sabbath as if it were any other day; his numerous homes and apartments in New York, North Carolina, and Florida. Had Grier Love looked closer, however, he would have seen that the habits of industry were undiminished.

"Love was a slight, wiry, youthful-looking man," wrote a reporter for the *Charlotte Observer*. "He stood about five feet, ten inches and kept his weight in the neighborhood of 143 pounds. He had to stay physically fit, working a seven-day week and traveling an average of 2,300 miles a week by plane and train, dictating and reading reports as he went."[69]

"Spencer Love's greatest asset," said the family's longtime friend, Gastonia banker and textile manufacturer A. G. Myers, "was his belief in hard work. He had a brilliant mind. He played a little, but not enough to interfere with business." Myers said this early in 1962, shortly after Spencer Love, at age sixty-five, collapsed and died of a heart attack while playing tennis at his Palm Beach, Florida, home.[70]

"Tennis and bridge were, in themselves, a business with the hard-driving textile tycoon," continued the *Observer* reporter in an obituary feature. "He had no patience with sloppiness and indolence in any pursuit, business, recreation or hobby."

"He was known in the industry as right much of a task master," said Myers. "He didn't believe in keeping a man who didn't perform satisfactorily. But he felt this necessary in order to protect the great investment of the stockholders and the large number of jobs at stake."

Even men who knew the hardest of physical work were awed by Spencer Love's compulsive and conspicuous display of labor. L. Worth Harris (b. 1908), the founder of Harris Motor Lines of Charlotte, North Carolina, had made the long climb out of the working class to become the owner of his own fleet of freight-hauling trucks. Harris's father had died when the boy was young, and his mother had operated a boarding house to support herself and her three children. "Hard work'll never hurt anyone," Harris heard her say many times. "And it was really difficult," says Harris, "for us to ever get her to quit working."[71]

As a teen, Harris worked at Palmetto Brick Sales Corporation hauling brick. In the 1920s, he bought used trucks and took other jobs, finally getting into the growing freight business between Charlotte and New York City. As Harris Motor Lines grew, it took on freight from such Piedmont textile mills as Celanese and Burlington Industries.

"Yes sir," recalls Harris, "I had the pleasure of meeting Mr. Spencer Love, their top man, one of the smartest men I think I've ever known. Played a little golf with him later on in Florida when he had a home in Florida that he spent a little time in. But that's the hardest working man I've ever seen.

"The first time I met him, actually, was in Florida. A real good friend of mine was a friend of his and asked me to play golf with him one day, and I said

J. Spencer Love at Burlington Industries, 1940s. (J. Spencer Love Papers, Southern Historical Collection, University of North Carolina)

I'd love to. I'd been wanting to meet him, I'd heard so much about him. So my friend said, 'Well, I'll let you drive the cart. He can ride with you.'

"He had a little pad and a pencil, and we were talking and I saw he wasn't paying a bit of attention to what I was saying. He was making notes all during the golf match, and of course I had a nice conversation. Then, later on, this friend of mine invited me to take a little trip with Love one Sunday on his yacht. He had a couple of secretaries on board ship, but that's about it. He let his guests have a good time, but he worked all during the time. A really hard worker."

Images of Love's habits and demands came through to workers in Burlington Mills. "He didn't care nothing about a bossman," says retired weaver Harry Adams. "He'd let him go just like that. He was a very swift-moving man. He was all business."[72]

"I never did know him personally," says Edward Harrington, "but I've seen him."

"He come through over there at Ossipee Mill one time," continues Harrington, "and I didn't know who he was. I was sitting down smoking a cigarette. He passed by me and looked at me, said, 'Well, what are you doing sitting there?' I said, 'I'm smoking my cigarette.' We had the privilege to go over to the smoking area and smoke. I was sitting in the smoking area smoking my cigarette. He didn't mean nothing to me. He's just a man, like I am. He's dead now. Of course, he didn't carry nothing with him either. He had all that money, and he didn't carry it with him either."

After two marriages which, as the *Charlotte Observer* reporter put it, "drifted apart over the years while he concentrated upon building his textile empire," Spencer Love married a third time, to Martha Eskridge of Shelby, North Carolina. And this "was the type of merger Love was accustomed to achieving." Eskridge had met Love when she was a Woman's Army Corps officer in Washington, D.C., during World War II. Love was serving as director of the Textile, Clothing and Leather Bureau.

"The story goes," continues the *Observer*, "that the late O. Max Gardner, former governor of North Carolina then practicing law in Washington, told the third Mrs. Love there was a secret to being happy with her husband: 'Learn his business,' he said. 'Learn everything about it, so you can discuss it with him and help him when needed.' They had four children as by-products of their happy marriage."[73]

In 1953 a journalist for *American Fabrics* wrote:

Mrs. Love is not immune to the treatment. The Loves may have aisle seats in the fourth row for "Wonderful Town" and may be all dressed for the theatre; but suppose the conversation with the man from the office brought along for dinner unexpectedly takes an interesting turn ten minutes before curtain time. That's easily arranged, as always with the utmost courtesy and consideration—one of the sons or some other qualified individual is asked to substitute at the theatre. Surely, Mrs. Love won't mind, especially since Mr. Love will join her right after the first act. His actual arrival at the theatre may depend on the number of acts, but he is pretty certain to get there before the finale. That's what happens when you are impelled by a merciless, relentless, driving force that knows no abatement.[74]

"Are You *All* Mr. Loves?"

"Management is so well arranged financially, physically and educationally-wise, that they can take that worker and brainwash him," says Harry Adams, a retired weaver from Burlington, North Carolina. "They'll take him in there and just show him that they are in such shape that they can't do no better. And they're fixed to buy other mills all at the same time. We've felt sorry for Burlington Industries here two or three times. They made you think they were on the verge of taking up collection for them."[75]

Spencer Love moved easily from ballroom to boardroom to weave room. The workers in Burlington Mills during the 1920s and 1930s moved between farm and factory town. To them, Love showed a face that appealed to the old bonds of paternalism.[76] His actions, however, took account of labor as one among several factors needing a swift, efficient, and firm hand.

Icy Norman (b. 1911) came to work at the tiny cluster of factory buildings on Piedmont Heights in 1929. Her father had died on the family's Wilkes County, North Carolina, farm a few months earlier, and Icy and her two married brothers, Dewey and Barney, sought mill work to support themselves, their mother, and their youngest sister. At first Icy and her brothers found work at a mill in Lynchburg, Virginia, but Depression conditions kept that mill from regular operation. It would run a week, then stand idle for two weeks. When the mill stood, workers had no income. Icy's mother suggested that the family ought to use their idle time to scour the area for other jobs. Soon they turned up at the door of Spencer Love's mill in Burlington. Icy worked there for the next forty-seven years.

Mary Murphy, a researcher with the Southern Oral History Program's Piedmont Industrialization Project, met Icy Norman in 1979 and interviewed her on several occasions. The following pages present my edited excerpt from the tape-recorded Murphy-Norman interviews. Against the background of family archives and published histories, company press releases, trade publication feature stories, and newspaper reminiscences, Icy Norman's words offer a worker's epilogue to the chronicle of J. Spencer Love.[77]

"Mama told Dewey and Barney, 'We can't live here like this. You don't know, the thing may shut down for good. We're going to go hunt you all a job.'

"We got in my daddy's T-Model. While the mill stood, we was on the road hunting jobs. We went everywhere. The Depression was starting. Mills was closing down. So you just couldn't get a job. Every freight train that you seen pass was loaded down with people going from town to town, hobo-ing.

Icy Norman holding a photograph of her mother, 1984. Photo by Mary Murphy.

"We tried here and there, and Mama said, 'Being we're this close, let's just go on to Durham and see Don.' That was Mama's oldest boy by her first [husband]. Him and his wife lived out on the Raleigh road. So we went down there and spent the night.

"Mama was talking to Don and said, 'We've been everywhere, and they can't find a job.'

"Don says, 'Well, I might could get them on there at the Golden Belt.' That was a hosiery mill. 'Next week I'll see what I can do. Mama, while you're this close, don't go home tomorrow.' That was Sunday. Says, 'Don't go home Sunday. Go up to Burlington. Somebody told me that they was hiring help. They're tearing out the cotton and putting in rayon. You might get on up there.'

"Mama says, 'Well, we ain't tried there. We have to go back that way anyway to go back to Lynchburg.' You see, we had to go through Haw River and Danville and then to Lynchburg.

"And so we come. Back then, they didn't have no fence. There was a little old bitty mill; it was a little old wooden mill, two rooms, and they had everything in it. What they had, they had a few frames of spinning, and they had two slashers, and then they had I forget how many dobby-headed looms. It wasn't many. And then they had spooling, and they had spinning. It was all in that little two-room building.

"We drove up, and Dewey and Barney got out. You know, anybody could go in, any time day or night that they wanted to. There was a little old bitty machine shop; it wasn't as big as this porch. I can just see that little old shop now. And they didn't have but two hands a-working in it. So Barney asked that man, 'Can you tell us how to find Mr. Copland?'

"He says, 'Yeah, he's right down yonder on that first. . . . There ain't but two slashers. You can't miss him. One of them's broke down, and he's down there helping us get that slasher going.'

"They went down there. He had his sleeves rolled up, and was greasy as a hog from his elbows on down. He seen Barney and Dewey and just had a fit. He says, 'Well, where in the world is your mama and my little girl?' My daddy worked for him there in Schoolfield, and he'd come every Sunday evening and spend the evening with my daddy after he got to the place he couldn't work. He thought the world of my daddy.

"Dewey says, 'They're out there in the car.'

"Boy, here he come. He grabbed up a piece of old cloth, and here's the way he was coming, just like this, a-wiping off. He come out there, and he was just tickled to death. He told Mama, he says, 'Well, I promised, the last time I seen Mr. Norman—I take it that he's gone.'

"And Mama said, 'Yes.'

"And he says, 'I promised Mr. Norman that if you ever needed any help and I could give you all a job, that I wanted you to come to me. I reckon that's why you all have come, ain't you?'

"Mama says, 'Yes, we've been everywhere hunting a job.'

"He says, 'Well, you don't have to hunt no farther. You've got a job. I can put Dewey and Barney to work tomorrow, but I can't put my little girl to work under three or four weeks.'

"So Mama says, 'No, if you can't put Icy to work, we'll not come.'

"So he says, 'They can go to work tomorrow. I need them.'

"And she says, 'No, if you ain't got nothing for Icy to do, we'll come back when you can give her a job.'

"He says, 'Well, you come back, and don't make it over three or four weeks.'

"You see, Barney and Dewey knowed everything in the mill. They could do anything; they could spin; they could doff; they could fix; they could do anything. And me, I was helpless; I didn't know nothing. I filled batteries in the Lynchburg Cotton Mill. That was in the weave room, filling batteries. I knowed how to do that, but see, they didn't have nobody doing that here.

"We come back and he told Mama that he was ready for me to go to work. He says, 'When can you move?'

"Mama says, 'Well, if you'll give Icy a job, we can move any time.'

"So he called up a moving van.

"I was so green, I didn't ask Mr. Copland would I make any money. And come to find out, anybody that didn't know nothing had to go in and learn the job. Learn for nothing. If you learnt the job and they was satisfied with you, they'd give you a job."

"Me and Barney and Dewey went to work Monday morning. That was the twentieth day of September, 1929. Barney and Dewey went to making money right off.

"Old Man Smith carried me over there and put me with Essie Gammons. He told her, 'You teach her everything about handling the yarn, how to tie it up, how to find the ends.'

"Well, you know, she was on piecework. She was making every penny. I could understand that. I could understand it. She wouldn't let me open a pack of yarn. She wouldn't let me touch that yarn. All she'd let me do, she let me take the full spools off and put the empty ones on. She never let me try to put up one end.

Well, about the middle of the week, Mr. Smith and Dewey McBride [a foreman] came over there. Mr. Smith says, 'Mr. Copland says to give you that little winder, that forty-three-end winder over there. Come on.'

"I thought to myself, 'I'm going out the other door.' It scared me to death. Went over there. Dewey McBride he weighed it up. They was in ten-pound packages. And it was five skeins in a hank. They called them a hank. You'd pull a hank out and shake it out and you had five skeins there. Dewey marked me up ten pounds. I said, 'There ain't no need to mark that up.'

"He says, 'Why? They give you a job.'

"I says, 'I can't help it. I don't know a thing about that.' Old Man Jim, he looked at me. He says, 'What's the matter?'

"I says, 'Well, you want me to tell the truth, don't you? I don't know nothing about that. I've never fetched one of them packs. I've never opened a pack. I've never pulled a skein out. I've never put a skein on. I don't know how to cut the tie bands. I don't know which way the tie bands go.'

"Old Man Smith, I can see him. He had a wad of tobacco in his mouth. He yanked his old hat off. He throwed it down. He spit in it, jumped on it. He was just cussing up a storm.

"Jim Copland come up. I was sitting there crying. I was scared to death. He sat down, he put his arm around me, 'Honey, what's the matter?'

"I says, 'They give me that pack of yarn and told me to go to work. Mr. Copland, I don't know nothing about it. I'm going home.'

"He says, 'No you ain't going home. I give you a job and you going to work on that job.'

"I says, 'You ain't give me nothing for I don't know nothing about it.'

"He says, 'Didn't that girl teach you?'

"I looked at him. I says, 'You want me to tell the truth? My daddy always told me to tell the truth if it hurt me.'

"He says, 'Yeah. I want you to tell the truth. I'll believe what you'll tell me.'

"I told him, I says, 'All she ever let me done, she let me take the full spools off and put the empty ones on. She never let me cut a tie band, she never let me touch that yarn. Mr. Copland, I don't know nothing about it.' I was just a-boo-hooing. Tears was just rolling. And he was trying to get me up.

"Mr. Copland says, 'Now, honey, I give you this winder. You're going to make a good hand.'

"He rolled his sleeves up and helped me get one side of yarn on. He went down to the next one, Ethel Glenn, now Ethel Smith. Her sister was working on another frame. He told both of them, 'If you see she can't find an end, you go down there and help her.'

"So it went on. I'd go home and I'd cry all night long. I'd get up the next morning and my eyes swelled shut. Mama just talked to me. She was so patient. So it went on.

"I was getting paid for what little I done. I think I made a quarter one day and one day I made fifteen cents. Anyway, I didn't draw but a dollar. And I just cried. All of them girls, they was on piecework, they'd make anywhere from twelve, fourteen, fifteen dollars a week. I knowed I never could. So I'd just cry about it.

"One day Mr. Love, he come by and he sit down. He says, 'Well, little girl, how you doing?' When he first sit down, I didn't know who he was. I didn't know he owned that mill. Him and his daddy, you know. He was goodlooking. He was young then. He says, 'You look like you been crying.'

"I sat down and I says, 'You know I hate this place.' And I started crying.

"He put his arm around my neck. He says, 'Don't cry. We all have to go through this.'

"I says, 'Yeah. I got a mama and a little sister to take care of. I ain't making nothing.'

"He says, 'You know one thing. Them's the ones that make the best hands. You'll catch on to it.' "

"Well, Ethel and her sister, I really did like them. If I got messed up, both of them would help, they'd have their side a-running. Well, they wouldn't have nothing to do until it run out and they'd start putting on more. They'd come down there and they'd help me. They'd help me find my ends. And they'd show me.

"Finally I got to the place I'd keep my side up pretty good. The first big check—it wasn't a check, it was money in a little envelope—I drawed five dollars. I thought, well that's better than drawing a dollar. I went home but I was still crying. So I was so disheartened.

"Mama says, 'It's all going to work out, the Lord's going to help you. He's going to be with you. I have prayed that the Lord's going to help you.'

"I says, 'I ain't getting no help now.' Back then I was a sinner, you know. My poor mama, she was a good Christian woman, her and my daddy both. So I kept on working.

"So one day it seemed just like something spoke to me, 'You can do it. Get in there and do it.' Just as plain. I thought, I says, 'Well, there's all of them girls working making good money. If they can do it, I can, too.'

"I went to work and I worked like fighting fire. I got so I could put the yarn on real good. It would go just a-flying. First things you know I run two packs of yarn that day. I was so tickled because I hadn't been running sometimes a half a pack a day. Dewey McBride says, 'You getting a little better, ain't you?' I didn't say nothing. I went on there, ripped that old pack open and I went to putting it on. I went to tying it up. Well, I got them all going. Ethel come down there, she says, 'Bless your heart. You're getting better, ain't you? I noticed on the board you're hitting about two packs.'

"I says, 'What?' I didn't let on. I knowed I run two packs. I says, 'I didn't even look at that old board.'

"She says, 'Honey, you ought to look at it every day.'

"I says, 'I did. I'm so downhearted. I hate this place.'

"She says, 'Don't feel that way about it. You doing good.' She and her sister would brag on me. So I run two that day. I run two more packs. I said, 'I'm running two packs a day.' Next day I worked just as hard as I could work. Next day I run my two packs. I went down to the scales and I said, 'Dewey, I want another pack of yarn.'

"He says, 'WHAT!' just like that.

"I says, 'I want another pack of yarn.'

"He says, 'What have you done with that other one, put it in the waste can?'

"I says, 'No. I run every skein of it.' He give me another pack and I run half of it. That was two packs and a half. Well, it was a little bit better than the other two days. I kept on going but I never would go on over and look at the production sheet.

"Here come Mr. Love and his daddy. They sit down there and got to talking. Spence says, 'Honey, come over here. I want my daddy to talk to you.'

"I drawed up. I knowed he owned the mill, him and Spence together. But I'd been talking to Spence but I didn't know that was his name. I just talked plain to him. Come to find out him and his daddy owned that mill. You could have pushed me over with a feather when I found it out. I went over there, his daddy slid down on the box. He says, 'I want you to sit down right here.'

"I sat down right between them. He got to talking, he says, 'Spence has been telling me what a hard time you had. Honey, don't feel bad about it. Everybody has to learn.' When he said 'Spence' then I knowed they was the ones that owned the mill. I could have went through that box.

"He says, 'He had to learn.'

"I looked up at him and I says, 'Are you *all* Mr. Loves? Lord mercy, here I've been talking to your boy telling him all my troubles and crying. Telling him how bad I hated my job. And he owned the mill. I apologize. But I do hate it.'

"He says, 'Little girl, you're doing fine. Mr. Copland is real proud of you.'

"I says, 'Mr. Copland's been knowing me ever since I was a baby.'

"Him and his daddy sat there and talked to me. Every time they'd come through the mill—we'd have boxes back here at the back of us to put our yarn in—they'd sit down there. They'd say, 'Come here, I want to talk to you a little bit.' If they hadn't encouraged me like they did—and Mr. Copland—I wouldn't have stayed in that mill as long as water would have got hot. I hated it. And on payday, them men, especially on second shift and a lot of them on daytime, they'd slip out, I don't know where they'd get it, they'd bring the stuff in there and get started drinking and they wouldn't know one end from another.

"I stayed on with them. A lot of people would try to get me to quit when the work was slack and go other places. I wouldn't do it. I stayed right on with them. I know work was getting so bad, Spence Love came down there and he look like he was so down and out. I said, 'Mr. Love, you look like you're mighty low this morning.'

"He says, 'I am. I am just on rock bottom. I don't know which way to do for the best. I'm going to have to close this place down.'

"I says, 'Well, there's always a brighter day coming. My mama told me that when I come here, and I told you how I hated this place. But I really love to work here now. It will be a brighter day.'

"He says, 'You really think so?'

"I says, 'Yes. It will be a brighter day. I'll stick with you through thick and thin. If you sink, I'll go down with you.' I laughed and he got to laughing.

"He says, 'You just beat all I've ever seen.' Then it wasn't too long until that strike, they walked out.

"Well, I think they was out, a week or two weeks. Some of them signed for the union and some of them didn't. I never signed it. Time and again since then they'd be out at the gate trying to get people to sign.

"I just heard so much about the union, I thought, 'I don't know whether it would pay or not.' I read the paper about the people being for months and months on strike. I just didn't believe in it. If you was working and was making money all that times you was out on strike, you would come out to the end a whole lot better than you would be laying out maybe three or four months at a time. So I never did sign it. So I stayed with the Burlington Mill. I did everything they ever asked me to do. I always got along with every boss man. I seen different bosses. In other words, I seen overseers, bosses, and second hands go and come. I always got along with every one of them. I never did have one say a short word to me because I always went and done what they would tell me to do. I do my work as near right as I know how."

"I ran one of those Universal winders. Run rayon, run nylon. I sure did love to run that little old Universal. I know one time they moved my winder over against the wall down there to give room to put in these nylon warp mills. Spence Love, he had been dead, I guess, two years. He was playing golf or something and had a heart attack and died. So it was about two years after he died that his wife and another lady come through the mill. They was looking around, come on down. I had my back towards them. I went to turn around, I was doffing my cones off, went to turn around. She come over and grabbed me and hugged me. She says, 'Honey, you are still with us, ain't you?'

"I says, 'Well, Mrs. Love.'

"She says, 'I don't see nobody I know. They're all new. I'm so glad to see you. You sure have been a faithful person. You have been faithful to the Burlington Mill.'

"I says, 'Yes, Mrs. Love, I give my whole entire best part of my life to the Burlington Mill.'

"She just hugged me and she says, 'I'm so glad to see you.' After she left, a lot of them come running over there. They'd say, 'Do you know her?'

"I says, 'I've been knowing her for forty-some years.'

"They said, 'I seen her grab you and hug you.' "

"When I retired, they fixed a dinner. On Wednesday. Milton come told me, says, 'Icy, they're going to take you to Greensboro tomorrow.'

"I says, 'What for, Milton?'

"He says, 'They're going to interview you at the main big office.'

"I says, 'I ain't going.'

"He says, 'Oh, yes you are. They're going to leave at eight o'clock in the morning. You come in dressed. You go have your hair fixed. They'll pay for it. I want you to look real pretty. The personnel man and Lloyd'—Lloyd was my boss man then—and Jimmy Jordan—that was the super—'they're going with you.'

"Well, I got my hair fixed and went in dressed the next morning. And they took me up there to that main office. They carried me all over that thing. I met everybody. Each floor had a different color carpet, different design, different furniture. I went clean to the top. You know what they had in the top? They had the prettiest white rug. It was a beautiful thing. Beautiful furniture. Everything was white.

"I says, 'They went all the way out with this, didn't they?' This girl that took us a tour. She was the sweetest thing.

"She says, 'Do you know what this room is, Icy?'

"I says, 'No, but it is something. Them other rooms is something.' That was the prettiest place I ever seen.

"She says, 'This is where the big shots come. This is where they have their meetings when they gather from New York.'

"I says, 'What?'

"She says, 'You going to meet all of them.'

"I says, 'No I ain't either. I'm going home.'

"Personnel man laughed and said, 'You won't go home until I take you home.'

"First thing you know, all them big shots from New York, twenty-five of them. There was poor little me, scrootched up with all them men. They got to talking to me, asking me questions. They asked me how long I'd been with the company. Some of them says, 'That's amazing. She's the oldest hand the Burlington Mill has got anywhere.' I'd been with the company longer, that's what I mean. They talked, they took pictures. Well, they asked me everything in the book. Sort of like you ask me, questions. I'd answer them. They says, 'You know one thing, you might not believe it, but if you ever come to New York I want you to come to the main office. You will have a welcome mat for you. You just really don't know how Spence Love has remarked about you. Did you know your name is on top in the main office in New York?'

"I says, 'Huh?'

"He says, 'That's right. We knowed you by Spence talking about you. I am so proud to meet you.' So then we went down to dinner. There I had dinner with all that bunch of men. I really enjoyed it. It was a whole day of it. We talked, I got to talking to them. I felt I knowed them all my life. We sit there at the table and we talked. They was taking down everything that was said.

"After dinner we went back up into another room. Then we went into the studio. They made pictures. They made all kind of pictures. They made pictures with me with some of them, pictures by myself.

"They says, 'You know, this will be showed on TV.'

"I says, 'You mean that's going to be showed on TV?'

"Them people from New York says, 'Sure, we can't let that go by without showing it on TV. I don't know when it will be, but we'll notify you. It will be on the "Sixty Minutes" program.'

" 'You know one thing,' one of them says. 'You are one hand that Spence Love said you went through thick and thin with them. You have made the Burlington Industries. Your part and your faithfulness to the Burlington Industries, you have got a part in all the mills that the Burlington Mills owns.' "

"And so I swung with them for forty-seven years. I retired in June of 1976. If I'd worked on until January I could have gotten in on the big profit sharing plan they got now. I begged them to let me work on but they wouldn't.

"See, if you're there so many years after a certain year and retire at sixty-five, you get $12,500. They knew that was in the making. They could have let me work on until January and I would have got that.

"I said, 'Just let me work one more year. Just let me work from now until next April. Then I'll have all my debts paid off.'

"The man says, 'I wish we could.'

"That kind of hurt me. Of course, I got my little dab of profit sharing. It wasn't much. I got it. But still that wasn't the main. I could really have used that money.

"I felt like if anybody was entitled to it, I was, because I put my whole life there. My young life, and I growed up there. I feel like I was part in the making of Burlington Industries, because I come there and stayed with them. I went with them through thick and thin.

"When I retired it was like leaving my family, because I felt like they was all my family. I was just with them day in and day out. They felt like my family. So that was the way it was. Every time I go back up there I feel like I'm going back home.

"I go back once in a while. Lots of time I'll take a notion to bake them a pound cake and take up there. I go about lunch time. Then I go around and talk to all of them.

"I went back up there about a month or two after I retired. Roy says, 'Icy, please go over there and creel that up for me. You know, I ain't run one yard all day long.'

"I says, 'Roy, you know better.'

"He says, 'I ain't.' "

· 4 ·

A History of Industry

"The Time for Prosperity Is at Hand"

Residents and observers of the Carolinas in 1870s and 1880s assumed
that the future, like the past, lay with farming. "Know as we do,"
affirmed a Charlotte newspaperman in August 1869, "that upon the
cultivation of our soil and the strong arms of our farmers depends the future
prosperity and general advancement of our country."[1] In market towns
throughout the Piedmont, the yeoman ideal was extolled and catered to by
local editors and their merchant advertisers:

> The crowded appearance of our streets yesterday convinced us that
> the fall trade had in reality commenced. From the time the sun first
> gilded the eastern horizon with his golden rays, till far up in the day,
> wagons could be seen wending their way into the city from every direc-
> tion, laden with cotton, flour, oats, wheat and other produce, and by ten
> o'clock that portion of Trade Street known as "Cotton-town" was liter-
> ally jammed with vehicles. Cotton, the principal article offered, though
> not bringing as good a price as it was a few weeks since, still commands
> remunerative figures, and we cannot but think it will again reach thirty
> cents a pound.
>
> Our grocery merchants keep busy, and from the way bags, bales and
> bundles pass from the stores to the wagons, will have to replenish their
> stock long ere the season is over.[2]

Prospects for railroad links that would fully open the Piedmont to the
world of trading and trafficking were harmonized by town editors with the
needs of a region of diversified farmers: "We assume that the time for their
prosperity is at hand. The world of the Railroad will soon commence, and
they will have a good market for every thing we raise, from a bushel of wheat
to an onion."[3] With the coming of the railroad, however, Piedmont farming

moved toward one-crop dependence upon either cotton or tobacco. Disastrous years lay ahead for farmers who, linked by merchants and landlords into the international cotton market or pressed to take the tobacco monopolists' price, were forced in unprecedented numbers into tenancy and off the land.

"The effect of a railroad in developing a country," the *Charlotte Observer* argued in 1875, "is shown by the increased productions lying on the line of the A. T. and O. Railroad, running on the dividing ridge between the Yadkin and Catawba rivers, without so much as crossing a stream of water for thirty miles. . . . Many farmers about Centre and Mooresville, who made from three to eight bales of cotton before the war, are now making forty to fifty."[4] Despite their increased production and dependence upon cotton, however, farmers discovered that prosperity seldom came by the bale.

From a wartime high of nearly a dollar a pound, cotton prices, reflecting demand, slid precipitously into the 1870s, stagnated, then collapsed in the depressed 1890s. For the seventies, cotton averaged twelve cents, for the eighties, nine cents. By 1890 the price stood at seven cents, and by mid-decade, at the height of the Populist revolt, it fell as low as a nickel a pound. Renewed world cotton and tobacco demand in the first two decades of the twentieth century provided the South's farmers with an era that some would remember too glowingly and come to expect as normal when the boom years of World War I gave way to the depressed 1920s and 1930s.[5] Independence and the self-sufficient farming ideal gave way to the fear and the reality of debt and dependence as tens of thousands of rural folk became part of an industrial working class.

The histories of the rise and spread of Southern sharecropping, the economic ascendance of town merchants, the appearance and fall of the Farmers' Alliance and the Populists, the political disfranchisement of poor farmers of both races, and the labor market consequences of the South's high fertility rates are now familiar and need not be repeated here.[6] My concern is to catch something of the social character, the temperament, of the captains of Industry who sought to place their designs upon the Carolina Piedmont during this New South era.

In the Carolina Piedmont of the 1870s and 1880s, merchants' control of farmers' crops and credit and the increasing dependence upon cotton or tobacco single-crop agriculture made possible (as David Carlton has observed about South Carolina) "the accumulation of capital by a new class of potential entrepreneurs, in a portion of the state which was well endowed with water power and had a heritage of small-scale manufacturing." As trade shifted away from coastal ports and factors, it was "being reconcentrated at several score small centers, where merchants gathered to take advantage of transportation and communication facilities, and where farmers came to sell their cotton, obtain their provisions, and arrange their financing."[7]

A combination of natural and social ingredients (including the suitability of soils for extensive monoculture, market demand for staples, population growth, a fluctuating regional labor market, the accumulation of merchant capital, habits of industry, political power, and so on) led to the particular shape of the Carolina Piedmont's mercantile and industrial emergence. In other historical regions of the South—for instance, the Delta or the Tidewater—varying combinations of natural resources and social forces produced distinctions and gave definition. In the Carolinas, the significance of the new arrangement is evident in the increasing use, and the changing meaning, of the word *Piedmont* in the postbellum era.

"We Are among a Hard-working People"

From the mid-eighteenth century, when *Piedmont* was first applied to American geography from its original Italian usage (descriptive of the region at the foot of the Alps), it encompassed the vast piedmont plateau of the eastern United States. "Between the South Mountains and the higher chain of the endless mountains," wrote an observer in 1755, "is the most considerable quantity of valuable land that the English are possest of; and runs through New Jersey, Pennsylvania, Maryland and Virginia. It has yet obtained no general name, but may properly be called Piedmont from its situation."[8]

Within the South, throughout the antebellum period, *Piedmont* was not a familiar designation. In his excellent *Atlas of South Carolina* (1825), for instance, Robert Mills describes the state's Piedmont region, emphasizes its agricultural potential, but does not use the word:

> The country between the last division and the foot of the mountains is about eighty or ninety miles wide, and possesses a pretty uniform character. It is of primitive formation and rests on granite and gneiss rocks. The surface is generally clay, covered with a rich soil, sometimes mixed with sand and gravel. The region is hilly, and in many parts too rolling for cultivation, without washing. . . . It is capable of great improvement in its agriculture, and of supporting a very dense population. It is much the thickest settled part of the state.[9]

Writing in *The North Carolina Reader* (1851) as a traveling observer of a state and its people, C. H. Wiley pauses at Hillsborough, the Orange County seat, to consider the striking distinctiveness of the "Upland regions of North Carolina" from the territory he has just crossed:

> We have now left the swamps, the level lands and broad sheets of water, the sand-hills and pine forests, behind us; we have got among forests of oak and hickory, into a country undulating with hills and valleys, and chequered with creeks and bountifully supplied with springs. Population is becoming more dense, mechanics and laborers are more numerous, and the land more universally cultivated. . . .

> We are, in fact, among a hard-working people; and all about us are signs of their industry, patience and economy. The sloping hills are yellow with the ripening wheat; and in the vales and bottoms the green grass waves in the summer breeze. There are no idlers—there is no appearance of waste or extravagance; but, on the contrary, the whole of the large population seems to be making enough to support themselves and to educate their children, and a little to spare. . . .

> A single laborer, with an ox, a horse, plough and wagon, can, on a few acres, live independently and comfortably; and the lands are divided among a multitude of small farmers of this sort.

> They form a race of people different from any we have yet seen; these small freeholders, composing the larger portion of the population, are a people peculiar to the upland districts of North Carolina. You will find them a sedate, sober, virtuous race. . . .

> They are at the same time extremely frugal and industrious, and yet very kind and neighborly; they give long credits to each other, seldom sue, and are as seldom sued; labor with their own hands and hold themselves the equal of the proudest of the human race. . . .

> There is a general absence of levity among them; they are a grave, and moral, and thinking people. . . .

> Now in the region through which we are passing . . . we find that the hope and dread of things beyond the grave, more than the fear of law or the love of worldly honors, influence the actions and dealings of men; and we observe that there is little taste for enjoyments purely sensual.[10]

Among residents of the antebellum Virginia Tidewater and Carolina coast, the Piedmont, when it was mentioned at all in print, fell into the Low Country frame of reference held by official Southern society: "the next breadth of country, known in several of the states as the Piedmont district, . . . more salubrious in its atmosphere."[11]

One deeply etched image of the Southern Piedmont, as a region given over

to the harmony of small farms and nature's bounty, persisted in the form of
the myth of the Garden, even during the years in which tenant farmers
multiplied in number, streams ran red from eroded fields, railroads cut
through the forests, and cotton factories blew their before-day whistles:

> Among the foothills, vales and spurs of the Blue Ridge Mountains,
> better known as the "Piedmont Region," is to be found the greatest
> variety of natural food for the opossum, raccoon, rabbit and squirrel. In
> the dense forests that cover the rivulets of the deep ravines with arching
> boughs or shelter the banks of the larger streams, and along the hedge-
> rows of the cultivated fields, abound the wild summer grapes, the crab
> apple, the winter grape that hangs upon the vine until far into the spring,
> the berry, persimmon, gooseberry and dogwood berry, together with the
> toothsome paw-paw and the large variety of wild nuts. And all of this
> makes the Piedmont Region the natural paradise of the nocturnal hunts-
> man.[12]

These romantic evocations appeared during an era in which the region's
industrial boosters were laying miles of railroad track in pursuit of an altogether different cornucopia.

With the construction of postbellum railroad links connecting the Carolina
Piedmont directly to the North, printed references to the region, which had
originally fit comfortably in the traditional associations with nature and farming, were altered by the energies and designs of capitalists, engineers, and
publicists from Danville to Atlanta. In their hands and by means of their
publicity, *Piedmont* came to mean primarily the industrializing Carolina Piedmont, whose area duplicated that encompassed by the electric lines of
"Buck" Duke's generating company, or—in the largest Southern view—what
geographer Rupert Vance called the "Piedmont Crescent of Industry"
stretching across the Carolinas and Georgia to the Birmingham steel district.
The modern sense of the Carolina Piedmont began with the coming of the
Air-Line Railway in the 1870s.

An essay, "The Piedmont Country of the Carolinas and Georgia," published by a Greenville, South Carolina, real-estate agency in June 1873, is
typical for its time in its ebullient self-advertisement. Readers are told of the
coming of the railroad, which will drastically shape and reshape the region.
The promotional tract connects the Piedmont as a region with a prosperous,
lily-white future assured by the Northern-built road. It promises marketplace
success for farmers and manufacturers, the restoration of "good government," and unequivocal benefits conferred by integration within a national
trade network:

The Atlanta and Richmond Air-Line Railway, traversing the Piedmont country of the Carolinas and Georgia, is now complete as far south
as Greenville, . . . a central point between Charlotte, North Carolina
and Atlanta, Georgia. In a few more months the trains will be running
through to Atlanta.

This great railroad, completing the direct line from New York to New
Orleans, is tapped at various points by rail, running out from the large
cities on the Southern Atlantic Coast. This Piedmont country is now
within eighteen hours run of these sea ports.

The value of this great highway to the people of the United States
cannot be overestimated. Its immediate political effect will be to restore
good government to the Southern Atlantic States, in the practical development of unsurpassed agricultural and manufacturing resources. . . .

As the resources of this Piedmont country—heretofore unknown
abroad—are developed by means of this great road, built by Northern
capital, so the deficiency of labor will be supplied by intelligent white
labor from Europe and the North.[13]

Towns, merchants, and manufacturers grew and prospered from the completion of the "great railroad," but the results for farmers were not so clear.
As for the anticipated immigrants, they neither arrived in significant numbers
nor stayed very long in the low-wage region. With the coming of the Air-
Line, the Carolina Piedmont acquired the core of its modern definition.

"The 'Piedmont Region' of the Carolinas"

At the end of the Civil War, the railroads of both North and South Carolina
lay in sorry shape. North Carolina tracks showed more the effects of heavy
use and minimal maintenance than of hostile action, while South Carolina's,
first worn out with Confederate service, had been torn up later by Sherman's
troops. For stretches of thirty to fifty miles to the east, north, and west, Union
soldiers destroyed the four rail lines serving the state capital and hub city of
Columbia.

The rebuilding of the Carolinas' railroads began slowly. The war had
wrecked state finances. There were efforts to loot railroads and efforts to use
them as political prizes. Absentee ownership and speculation flourished
throughout the late 1860s and early 1870s, although Northern capitalists
found more promising investments in other regions of the United States.
Railroad historian John Stover has observed that while rail mileage in the

North and West more than doubled in the first eight years after the Civil War, Southern railroad mileage expanded by only a third.[14]

Before the completion of the Air-Line Railroad in late 1873, the Piedmont areas of North and South Carolina were tied by rail not to each other, but to towns in the direction of the Atlantic Coast. In North Carolina, a 223-mile crescent, the route of the North Carolina Railroad, was built by state stock subscription between 1851 and 1856. Oriented toward Fayetteville, New Bern, and Wilmington, the NCRR extended west from Goldsboro to Raleigh, then toward Greensboro and Charlotte. Approved by the planter-dominated state legislature, the NCRR was intended to pull trade toward the coast and away from the backcountry wagon roads into Virginia and South Carolina.

In much the same way that the NCRR began to stimulate the growth of that state's Piedmont market towns during the late antebellum years, the completion of the Greenville and Columbia Railroad in 1853 helped draw Upcountry South Carolina farmers and merchants in to a town—Greenville—that had served primarily as a Low Country planter summer resort. When the G & C was rebuilt in 1872, a writer for the *Greenville Enterprise* noted that "for many miles around, especially in the direction of Laurens, Anderson and Pickens, the cotton producers seek Greenville as a place for a market . . . growing larger and more important every year. . . . It will thus be seen that ours is no mean city."[15]

Between 1865 and 1875, railroad mileage increased in North Carolina by 372 miles, to a total of 1,356, and in South Carolina by 328 miles, for a total of 1,335. The location, rather than the length, of these new tracks was critical for the industrial emergence of the Piedmont. The Air-Line Railway tied the older NCRR with other Piedmont towns all the way to Atlanta in the southwest and northward through Danville, Virginia, to the cities of the East Coast. Across the spine of the Air-Line, short connecting lines extended into the Appalachians and toward the Atlantic. The coastal cities of Charleston, Wilmington, and Savannah suffered as trade moved with increasing volume in a new geographical orientation reflecting the power of new political and economic centers. Piedmont newspapers cheered the regular "consummation" of connections among the region's towns. The new awareness of a Carolina Piedmont region began to be shared and shaped in the early 1870s by an emerging business class whose towns were zippered together by the Air-Line.[16] Johnstone Jones of the *Charlotte Observer* editorialized:

> As long as railroads last, Charlotte, Spartanburg and Greenville will be intimately connected in business relations; and, to a large extent, in social relations. Whatever therefore tends to strengthen and multiply the

bonds of mutual interest and friendship between the places, is worthy of closest attention and highest efforts.

The people of western North Carolina and upper South Carolina are nearly allied in blood and kinship. An imaginary state line divides us, but we have a common interest, the same historical associations, and much the same destiny in the future.

Let the two sections strive to cultivate as far as possible amenities of life that will tend to increase the ties that now bind us together. "Let us swear an eternal friendship."[17]

Another editorial in the *Observer* exhorted participation in an upcoming Fair of the Carolinas:

Were the great natural advantages of western North Carolina and upper South Carolina known abroad, the value of land in those regions of the country would be greatly enhanced. The main reason why this beautiful, rich and noble piedmont country is not sought by the emigrant is because little is known beyond our own borders of its great fertility, its varied production, its vast buried mineral wealth, and the surpassing loveliness of its valleys and streams, its hills and mountains; to say nothing of its water power and railroad facilities, its abundance of timber, and cheapness of provisions. One of the very best means of showing the important facts relative to the resources of our country, is through the medium of annual fairs.

It is, therefore, to the interest of every citizen of this region of the country, who has his country's or his own interest at heart, to do all in his power to insure a full and faithful exhibition of the splendid resources of western North Carolina and upper South Carolina. These two sections, though divided by a state line, comprise the "Piedmont Region" of the Carolinas, and are united in all their industrial or agricultural interests. They are both equally interested in the Fair of the Carolinas.[18]

As construction of the Air-Line was completed to each town along the route, railroad officials, merchants, bankers, lawyers, mill men, and mayors traveled back and forth across one another's state boundaries in special rail cars named after the influential politicians and railroad officials in their midst. It was a time of backslapping and boasting, of toasting and memorializing, of celebrating and prophesying. The fierce intertown rivalries lay in the future. Aware of the similarities that they saw out the coach windows and in each other, these leading citizens turned familiar territory into both regional revelation and advertisement.

"It was wisdom that pointed out this great route through the beautiful piedmont regions of the Carolinas and of Georgia, along the base of the Blue Ridge," wrote a newspaper correspondent aboard the Air-Line's first train between Spartanburg and Charlotte. Ultimately, the Future London of the South (Charlotte) and the Queen City of the Empire State (Atlanta) would be connected, enabling towns along the way "to be united henceforth and forever, and to march hereafter shoulder to shoulder on the high road to prosperity." The correspondent continued:

> At precisely 3:20 PM, we entered the corporate limits of Spartanburg, admidst the ringing of the bell of the "B. Y. Sage," and the firing of cannon, and cheering of the crowd of citizens that lined the side of the road. A large concourse of citizens were gathered at the depot to greet the first train on the Air-Line; fair hands made haste to decorate, with evergreens and flowers, the engine which had the distinguished honor of being the first to enter Spartanburg from Charlotte; and mutual congratulations were showered around amid joyous smiles and hearty handshaking.[19]

Behind the construction of the Air-Line stood the Southern Railway Security Company. Behind the Southern Railway Security Company stood Tom Scott and his cronies of the Pennsylvania Railroad, seeking control of Southern rail traffic. "Charlotte today is in the iron grasp of railroad monopolists," complained the editor of the *Observer* in 1873. "Every route leading out of our city to the great markets of the North and South, is under the control of the Southern Security Company."[20]

Unlike the small-time swindlers, promoters, and ringmen who flourished in the late 1860s in several Southern states, including North Carolina and South Carolina, the Southern Security entrepreneurs sought monopoly and legitimate profits by annexing short local and state-owned lines into their private systems. Their experiments were stopped short by the panic of 1873, but they signaled what lay down the track of the South's railroad future. Not until after 1880 did the Air-Line, reorganized and in the hands of the Clyde Syndicate, begin to show profits and expand along with the industrializing region.[21] By the turn of the century it became the major trunk line of the Northern-owned Southern Railway.

Running parallel to the mountains and the fall line, the Air-Line lay at the core of the Carolina Piedmont. Its route lay near the heart of the region's old settlements of Scotch-Irish, English, and German farm families. Like earlier movements of people into and across the region, this trunk line's traffic was gathered and dispersed all along the core. No single Carolina Piedmont town stood in a position of dominance, although Charlotte was eager to claim the role.

In the year of the Air-Line's arrival, Charlotte town promoters crowed over their tributary rail links and, counting everything from tiny woodworking shops to John Wilkes's iron foundry, claimed thirty-five "manufactories": "The centre of five railroads, with a prospect of others—the commercial emporium of a magnificent scope of country—the principal city of the Piedmont regions of the Carolinas, Charlotte must daily increase not only in commercial importance but also in an industrial point of view."[22] As Charlotte grew, so did the importance of the points of view of its leading men in commerce and industry.

The ascending influence of commerce extended to Piedmont towns all along the new railroad. The town merchant as well as the city merchandiser assumed central roles in the lives and market transactions of the region's farmers. "The Air Line Railroad has brought a new and extensive trade to the city of Charlotte," acknowledged the *Lincoln Progress*. "Many merchants of Union, Spartanburg and York counties in South Carolina are purchasing their goods in Charlotte and selling their cotton at that point."[23]

"The completion of the Richmond and Danville Air Line railroad in the early seventies," reflected a Greenville historian around the turn of the century, "gave new courage to the hearts and minds of our people and made Greenville the best mart for trade in the upper-part of the state. . . . The growth of our city, in population, in the decade from 1870 to 1880 was greater in ratio than in any other decade of her history."[24]

Among those celebrating the arrival of the first Air-Line train to their city was Greenville mayor H. P. Hammett, who addressed a gathering of Carolina elite before joining them for refreshments at the City Club. "The section of the country along its entire line," proclaimed Hammett, "possesses all the natural advantages and all the elements necessary to make a country rich, prosperous and great, to be found in any part of the civilized world. . . . The traveller passing through it cannot fail to be impressed with its beauty and advantages, and the capitalist must see that it is one of the very best fields for investment."[25]

Hammett knew how to take his own advice. In the mid-1870s he built the Piedmont Cotton Mill and the village of Piedmont about ten miles south of Greenville along the Saluda River and the Greenville and Columbia Railroad.[26] The G & C, of which Hammett had once served as president, tied into the Air-Line. As state legislator, railroad promoter, mayor of Greenville,

PIEDMONT MFG CO. PIEDMONT, S. C.

Piedmont Manufacturing Company, Greenville, S.C. *Inset*: Henry P.
Hammett. (Courtesy of the Greenville County Library)

and builder of the Piedmont Mill, Hammett (1822–91) showed a compre-
hension of regional industrial development not equalled until the arrival of
engineer-propagandist D. A. Tompkins and the Carolina Piedmont's grand
engineer of power and capital, James B. Duke.

A native of Greenville County, Hammett grew up on a prosperous farm,
and attended common schools, after which he taught school for a few years
and then clerked in a general merchandise store in the town of Hamburg.
Through his marriage to Jane Bates, Hammett joined a family with antebellum manufacturing experience in the region. His wife's father, William Bates,
was one of several Rhode Islanders who fled the New England textile depression and came South before 1820. Bates took his knowledge of cotton
machinery to mills on South Carolina's Tyger River and to Lincolnton, North
Carolina, an early center of small manufactures in the Piedmont. In 1833 he
bought a site on Rocky Creek in South Carolina's Greenville District and
built a wooden factory holding a thousand spindles. The factory and settlement were soon known as Batesville. "Bunches" of Batesville yarn were
bartered locally by wagon. The mill was a success, and Bates enlarged it
several times prior to the Civil War. H. P. Hammett was a commercial and
financial agent for the Batesville mill for fourteen years.[27]

During the Civil War, Hammett rose to the rank of colonel, serving the
Confederacy as a quartermaster in Charleston. Due to illness, he returned to

Greenville in 1864 as a tax assessor. Combined with his antebellum training in manufacturing, Hammett's wartime experience paid peacetime dividends, a common pattern in the rise of Southern industrialists following both the Civil War and World War I.

By 1870 Hammett was ready to enter the mill business on his own, and on a larger scale than was possible in a town like Batesville, which had no railroad connection. On a fine water-power site, the location of antebellum gristmills, he laid the cornerstone of the Piedmont Manufacturing Company in February 1874. He brought several families of experienced mill workers from Augusta, Georgia, to teach other workers drawn from nearby farms. "I do not admit," wrote Hammett in an 1883 letter to the *Atlanta Constitution*, "that the Northern people are any better material out of which to make cotton manufacturers and operatives than our own, and especially in the 'Piedmont belt,' of the South."[28] On 15 March 1876, the Piedmont Mill's machinery— of the most modern Northern make—was put to the production of thirty-six-inch, three-yards-to-the-pound sheeting for export to China.

The Piedmont Manufacturing Company was capitalized at $200,000, with the major portion of the stock taken by Hammett, a handful of coinvestors from Greenville and Charleston, the Northern manufacturer of the textile equipment (Whitin Machine Works), and the New York-Baltimore commission firm of Woodward and Baldwin.[29] "Mr. Hammett," wrote D. A. Tompkins in 1899, "may be said to have inaugurated a renaissance of cotton milling in the South. For, while there was a general renewal of the industry throughout the country, after the abolition of slavery, it was on the old lines, and with more or less old machinery. The Piedmont Mill was designed, built and equipped after strictly modern plans."[30]

Hammett's Piedmont Mill proved a success. Several thousand spindles and over a hundred looms were added in 1877. By 1883, with 25,796 spindles and 554 looms, the Piedmont had become South Carolina's largest mill. Hammett built Piedmont Mill Number Two in 1888, Number Three in 1889. By 1900, the Piedmont complex ran 61,000 spindles and about 2,000 looms. It was no longer the largest mill in the state, but it had demonstrated the possibilities of the large-scale mill building characteristic of the New South era.

"The wonderful success of Piedmont," wrote a Greenville historian in 1903, "was the incentive to building Pelzer, Clifton, Pacolet and many of the magnificent mills in this section which were built in 1882."[31] Significant, too, for the emerging Carolina Piedmont manufacturing region were the dozens of men trained in Hammett's Piedmont Mill who became superintendents in mills throughout the Carolinas and Georgia. Hundreds of workers who first learned machine operating and repair skills at the Piedmont Mill moved into and out of other mills, teaching workers just arrived from the farm.

"The Enterprising and the Hard"

The Carolina Piedmont in the last quarter of the nineteenth century hung ripe and toothsome for men with such names as Hammett, Holt, Lineberger, Cannon, Gray, Springs, Love, Reynolds, and Duke. The devastation of the Civil War had irreparably ruptured both the plantation and yeoman ways of life, broken the ability of the Low Country planters to keep the Piedmont from increased trading and trafficking with the North, and raised the prospects of manufacturing in this region of abundant water power and increasingly more abundant, cheap, white labor. The men who took advantage of this wide-open, rough-and-tumble situation represented a puritanical collection of capitalists that had never before stood in a position to set the pace and standards for Southern society. The New South was driven by men of a different temperament, centered in a different region than the Old South.

Certainly, a number of descendants of the antebellum planter class could be counted among the Carolina Piedmont's industrializing elite—men like engineer and New South booster D. A. Tompkins and manufacturer Leroy Springs.[32] Yet a "planter," in the Piedmont, had just as often been a merchant, physician, lawyer, mill owner, or trader. Hardin Reynolds (1810–82), for instance, sole heir of Abraham and Mary Reynolds, was a successful tobacco grower, manufacturer, and merchant. He increased his slaveholdings from nine to eighty-eight slaves between 1840 and 1863. In the late 1820s, Hardin and his father began to buy small lots of tobacco from neighbors and manufacture chewing-tobacco twists. Carrying the pressed twists by wagon through the backcountry was easier than the usual practice of rolling hogsheads of tobacco leaves over trails to markets more than a week's journey away. Like moonshine, chewing tobacco was a more compact product made from an Upcountry crop. Slaves labored over each step from tilling to pressing. The Reynoldses peddled all the chewing tobacco they could haul within the boundaries of the Carolina Piedmont.

Hardin Reynolds, observes Nannie May Tilley, historian of the family and of the tobacco industry, "utilized every opportunity for profit. . . . Though he lived his life in a landlocked area largely devoid of prime farm land, he nevertheless developed an estate of more than significant proportions. He was a proud and successful man who left an indelible mark on his older children and instilled into them a tremendous drive to succeed in business."[33] The best-known of Hardin Reynolds's children was R. J. (Richard Joshua), who during the last quarter of the nineteenth century built a tobacco company in Winston, North Carolina, that even Buck Duke's American Tobacco Company was unable to swallow up or drive out of business.

Among the emerging Piedmont elite were representatives from the small, antebellum cotton-mill owner-manager class, men such as the Holts, Hammetts, and Linebergers.[34] "The continuity between the industrialist stratum of antebellum and postbellum days," Eugene Genovese has written, "does not prove that the war had little effect; on the contrary, it suggests that the war, or rather the defeat of the South, created some of the preconditions for the liberation of the industrialists and of industrialism."[35]

Present, too, among the Piedmont's New South–era capitalists were several merchant-businessmen from the Low Country such as Ellison Smyth and Francis Pelzer, whose Charleston families had seen prosperous times but who now came to seek the unorthodox prospects in Upcountry manufacturing.[36] Here and there were also men from lowly origins who made spectacular successes: Duke, Cannon, Gray. Most numerous, however, seemed to be the businessmen and manufacturers who emerged from the ranks of yeoman farming by way of mercantile interests. Every bustling town had them, men themselves not long away from the furrows: Montgomery, Orr, Hanes, Ragan, Stowe, Belk.[37]

Taken all together, these rising men, whom W. J. Cash called "the army of the enterprising and the hard," were as much a part of the Southern Piedmont as were the rolling hills, waterfalls, and agrarian culture. They were not, however, as Cash has written, "mainly . . . such men as belonged . . . within the broader limits of the old ruling class, the progeny of the plantation."[38] The fathers of the modern Piedmont emerged across a broader spectrum than Cash would have it, coming not only from plantation backgrounds, but also, and especially, from the Upcountry's characteristic ranks —the sons of successful farmers and rising merchants.

The pioneer capitalists of the New South Piedmont need to be understood not only in terms of the changing social and economic relations within Southern regions and within the terms of the expanding industrial capitalism of the United States in the last quarter of the nineteenth century, but also in terms of temperament, ambition, and desire. Here, in the regional application of what Erich Fromm described as social character or Raymond Williams has discussed in terms of a society's structure of feeling, historians and biographers, when they have tackled the issue at all, have tended toward hagiography.

In reconstructing the historical temperament of the Carolina Piedmont's

emerging elite, Fromm's discussion of the "productive-exploitative character" proves quite helpful.[39] "The concept of the productive-exploitative
individual," writes Fromm, "implies someone who builds something that is an
imaginative response to new opportunities which the majority do not use.
The productive-exploitative syndrome characterizes the 'new men' who are
like small-scale robber barons in their character." Fromm's insight into the
character of these "new men" allows for at least a preliminary discussion, in
terms of cultural temperament and social character, of the insights of historians such as Eugene Genovese, Elizabeth Fox-Genovese, C. Vann Woodward,
Steven Hahn, David Carlton, and Lacy Ford as to the characteristically
ambitious, agressive, and exploitative behavior of the New South's emerging
business and manufacturing class.

The antebellum forerunners of these New South capitalists, men like
Piedmont manufacturing pioneer E. M. Holt and Henry Hammett's father-
in-law, William Bates, found themselves constrained by the Carolina Piedmont's relative isolation and its hegemonic relationship with the plantation
South. For the most part, they had to content themselves with being "big
men" in small antebellum communities and neighborhoods—consider the
Presbyterian Belks in the Waxhaw District, or the brewer Alexander Mc-
Kenzie. Certainly, too, the moral economy of the antebellum yeoman culture helped to hem in the potential for full exploitation of "neighbor" by
"neighbor."

The steady habits that typified the ranks of the Carolina Piedmont's antebellum yeomanry suggest what Fromm calls the "productive-hoarding" character of emerging middle-class groups. The traditional pattern of self-ex-
ploitative household labor, which produced the margin of success and
surplus possible on yeoman farms in the Piedmont, required slow hard work
and good fortune. By carefully managing, saving, and improvising, self-
sufficient farm families could count on a subsistence plus a small surplus
from their yearly labor on diversified crops. At critical times of the year and at
certain stages of life, self-sufficiency and independent work joined with
cooperative efforts. Personal responsibility to neighbors, kin, church, and
community bound yeoman families together and offered some protection
against bullying or domineering individuals. Yeoman-to-yeoman relations,
with their ideal of mutuality, constituted one tradition that accompanied the
migration from farm to cotton mill. Traditional paternalism, with its inherent
dominant-dependent relations, constituted another. The factory and mill
village met these traditional relations with an unencumbered industrial capitalism. In the changed postbellum circumstances, conditions were ripest for
Fromm's productive-exploitative individuals (rather than the more cautious,

community-based, safety-first farmers) to assert themselves and apply their obsessional and accumulative industriousness to the turning of wheels and profits.[40]

"In the changing, developing society," Fromm observes, "the entrepreneur is the new man who can be considered the village 'progressive.' But he is this only in a certain historical perspective of intensifying the class difference in the village and destroying its traditional structure." Consider, for instance, the rise of Bobo Tanner, Grier Love, or William Henry Belk. In the Carolina Piedmont, during the last quarter of the nineteenth century, the "new men" pushed their way out of the traditional neighborhood structure, out of the folk restraints, and set the tone of paternalistic capitalism that would dominate the region's affairs into the following century.[41]

A Romance of Industry

To read the legends of the fathers of the modern Piedmont is to read again and again the same story of the habits of industry turned single-mindedly toward the making of mills and money. "Gaston's [Gaston County's] prominence as a textile manufacturing center," wrote the *Gastonia Gazette* in a 1965 retrospective series entitled "Textile Pioneers," "is a monument to men of foresight like the late George W. Ragan, who died here June 9, 1936, and whose life and career would become a romance of industry if committed to book form."[42] "As a youth," the *Gazette* continued, Ragan's life "was very similar to those of practically all who were reared on small farms at that period. He was healthy, vigorous and very active, and performed in a careful, manly way those tasks that usually fell to the small boy on the farm."

Born in 1846, Ragan was the son of Scotch-Irish parents. Too young to join the Confederate army until the last year of the war, he served in the Seventy-first Regiment in eastern North Carolina, then, with the Southern surrender, returned to the family home. "He did not spare himself," Ragan's biographer tells us, "but went at his work with zeal, and performed all kinds of labor common to farm life without large means, from the lightest task to splitting rails." Soon, his father turned the management of the farm over to young Ragan.

In 1873 George Ragan "entered the mercantile business, and for nineteen years conducted his affairs successfully at South Point, Lowell, McAdenville and Gastonia." Along with R. C. G. Love, George Gray, and several other pioneers, Ragan was one of the organizers and original stockholders in Gastonia's first cotton mill (1888). A year later he helped create the First

National Bank of Gastonia. "Giving his undivided time and attention to the work he had in hand," Ragan built additional mills, pioneered in the Southern manufacture of fine yarns and became the largest holder of real estate in Gastonia. After "long years of honest toil," Ragan, a Presbyterian elder, lifelong Democrat, one-time mayor of Gastonia, and generous contributor to staunchly Presbyterian Davidson College, died at age eighty-nine.

And, there was Abel C. Lineberger, who, "like others of his time, did not for a moment sit down in sullenness and despair, but, without benefit of UNRRA or Marshall Plans, set to work with nothing but his bare hands to build out of the rubble of Reconstruction a new South that could stand on its own feet and ask favors from nobody."

"We of this favored age," wrote an anonymous Lineberger eulogist in 1948, "will never be able to appreciate the hard scrabble of poverty through which the men and women of that time labored their way to accomplish one of the world's historical miracles, but we can see the busy industries that dot the red hills of the Piedmont and the shining rails and broad highways that link them with the great market places—all standing as monuments to a courage and determination that have yet to be matched."[43]

And then there was Charles Cannon:

> Mr. Cannon's success was due to the trading and merchandising ability which was his original gift of genius, and to two attributes of character. One was absolute integrity, the other the will to give all he had to his work. . . . Mr. Cannon built up his reputation of hard work, so hard that it was his only interest.[44]

And George Gray:

> Gray was a dynamo of nervous energy. . . . He lived his life on tiptoes. An objective once in his mind, he drove at it incessantly. He went to his mills at 5:30 on summer mornings, and at 6 o'clock in winter, and was the last man to leave.
>
> Gray regimented his life—his rising and retiring were on the dot, he drank water at certain times during the day, if he said 'wait two minutes' he meant exactly that. But his eye twinkled, and people liked to call him by his first name. He insisted upon having associates he could rely on.[45]

And the tobacco and textile Hanes brothers:

> The story is told that when the Hanes boys were growing up and came to the house for their mid-day meal from working on the plantation, their mother would say, "Now you boys rest until dinner's ready. And while you're resting, go out and chop some wood."

Daniel Augustus Tompkins. (Courtesy of the North Carolina Collection,
University of North Carolina)

P. H. Hanes' industry and habit of rising early won him the nickmane
of "Early Bird," which was also to become the name of his most popular
brand of tobacco.[46]

And there was Daniel Augustus (D. A.) Tompkins. "He is a type of tens of
thousands of men, young and middle-aged," wrote *Manufacturers' Record*
editor R. H. Edmonds, "who, after 1865, went out of the South because of
the poverty and woe and wretchedness and lack of opportunity."

These men have been great leaders in the upbuilding of the North and
West. Fortunately for these sections, but unfortunately for the South,
nearly all of them continue their work beyond the borderline of the

South. Tompkins, on the contrary, had no sooner mastered the situation, and demonstrated in the North and in Germany the power of his brain to initiate and the strength of his will to carry forward to completion great enterprises, than he determined to give to Southern upbuilding all the strength of body and mind he possessed. . . . He returned and became a great leader whose influence has been more potent for good than that of any dozen men in political or public life combined.[47]

For these upbuilders and pioneers of the industrial Piedmont—men who "lived life on tiptoe"—habits of industry defined the meaning of their lives and became Industry's habits. Consider the biography of Gus Tompkins.

"I Had a Bent for Industrial Development"

"I was a child of the Old South," Daniel Augustus Tompkins (1851–1914) always said. Yet beneath the son's public courtesies and gentlemanly mantle, one doubts whether Tompkins's physician-planter father would have recognized the full-grown man—the engineer, industrial capitalist, and Piedmont propagandist. Even during his youth, when he lived on the Tompkins's two thousand acres in Edgefield County, South Carolina, Gus Tompkins is remembered as being less interested in the management of agriculture, slaves, and land than in what he could find and make in the carpentry and blacksmith shops.

"In the carpenter shop my brother worked on everything from fixing an old clock to making a complete wagon," recalled A. S. Tompkins. "He was fond of helping make the water wheels and trunks for our father's grist mill, a difficult task, and took great interest in the mill, working on the dam when needing repairs. I well remember when he took a notion to make a croquet set, balls, mallets, etc., and wore me out turning the old lathe for him."[48]

During the war years, while Gus Tompkins's father served with the Confederate army, his mother, Hannah Virginia Smyly Tompkins, supervised the growing of the crops. According to A. S. Tompkins, Virginia dominated her husband "by superior will power and executive ability." Of Scotch-Irish descent, a Baptist, "industrious and rigidly economical," she "wasted nothing, not even time; for she was always an early riser."[49]

Like many of the Scotch-Irish who came to the Carolina Piedmont in the mid-eighteenth century, the Smylys had migrated from County Antrim, Ireland. Virginia's father (D. A. Tompkins's grandfather), James Smyly, apprenticed himself as a worker in wood and iron in South Carolina's Edgefield

District. He later went to Columbia and bound himself to a master mechanic in order to learn to make fine carriages, gigs, and sulkies. He moved back to the Upcountry after serving in the War of 1812 and married into a German farming family.

James Smyly built and repaired wagons. As his shops grew, he apprenticed young white men to work in them and began to acquire land and slaves to grow cotton. He built and operated a large store and an inn on a stage road. Smyly's inn was typical for the Piedmont region, serving the considerable traffic from the mountains and surrounding countryside. "All sorts of people stopped here," writes A. S. Tompkins, "from judges to hog drivers":

> His lot was often filled with droves of mules, horses, hogs, and even turkeys, driven through the country from the Mountains, and beyond enroute to Augusta and Hamburg. The German settlers in the neighborhood would bring in great loads of corn and fodder, which he always purchased along with chickens and eggs and other provisions, paying for them mostly in goods from the store and would use the provender and provisions in feeding the passing consumers.

"His business increased rapidly," continues the family history, "the store was torn down and a new larger and neater one was erected, his shops were all the while kept going and he could usually be found in there at work." Late in his life, Smyly became a large cotton planter, but he continued to produce all the provisions needed on his plantation.[50]

In addition to his carriage shops, store, inn, and loom house, Smyly at the time of his death had acquired over two thousand acres of land and perhaps a hundred slaves. Since his wife had died a few years earlier, he left his estate to his children, one of whom, Virginia, had married a prominent Edgefield physician, Dr. DeWitt Clinton Tompkins. Young Gus Tompkins grew up with the image of his grandfather—the energetic antebellum manufacturer, trader, craftsman, and planter—as the model for success. Gus's brother, A. S. Tompkins, imagined what James Smyly would have done with the opportunities of the postbellum era: "Had he lived in this age with his industry and ability as a manufacturer, he would doubtless have reached the top of all that can be accomplished with steam and electricity."[51] Certainly, Grandfather Smyly would have recognized himself in his grandson Gus and in his daughter Virginia.

While her physician husband was away at war, Virginia Smyly Tompkins oversaw the family's slaves' production and storage of 130 bales of cotton. These bales, which were sold for the high prices of 1864–66, enabled the Tompkinses to clear a number of large debts and escape total ruin. The family was solvent, but there was no money to spare for such a postbellum luxury as college for the sons. Immediately after the war, Gus Tompkins, then in his midteens, convinced county officials to award him a contract to rebuild a couple of bridges in Edgefield. He used black labor to cut bridgework timber from the family's land and made enough money on this job to cover his first college expenses at the University of South Carolina.[52]

Tompkins arrived in Columbia in 1867 at age sixteen. He was a healthy young man, although, from a cause that remains unclear, he had already lost the sight in his left eye. At the state university he studied geology and natural philosophy with Joseph LeConte and math and engineering with General E. P. Alexander, former chief engineer of Robert E. Lee's army. It was Alexander who urged Tompkins into an even sharper break with the ways of the Old South. "I had a bent for industrial development," Tompkins would recall, "and he was the first person I had ever met who had any sympathy with my aspirations; and he, as a graduate of West Point, had been an important constructing engineer before and during the war. In talking over with me my hopes and expectations, he advised me to seek a trade also while studying to be an engineer. He recommended to me the Rensselaer Polytechnic Institute, at Troy, New York."[53]

Tompkins was to succeed heroically by Rensselaer's measure. In later years, classmates remembered his seriousness of purpose, his strong opinions, his ascetic habits, his gentlemanly authority. They elected him Grand Marshall, the highest student office.

At Rensselaer, as at USC, the practical, the useful, the means of getting ahead—these mattered most to Gus. "I am glad you are studying Botany," wrote family friend Eliza Mims from South Carolina, "if it has made you learn to love flowers. I thought of sending you some in a letter at one time but was afraid you were about flowers like you say you are about music—'don't-object-to-it.'"[54]

Tompkins's parents could provide little money to support his Rensselaer education, so throughout his stay in Troy, New York, he worked night and weekend jobs and full time in the summers. One summer he met Alexander Holley:

> He was a young engineer [recalled Tompkins] who was introducing the Bessemer process into this country. Youthful as I was, I recognized in him a man of ability. I did considerable work for him tracing drawings during my vacations. He also gave me work to do in my room while I was attending the institute. Through his influence, too, I secured work

during my spare time at 'Poly' in the John A. Griswold and Co.'s Steel Works of Troy, where I took a course of apprentice and machine shop.[55]

Alexander Holley, engineer and industrialist, introducer of the Bessemer steel process into the United States, was one of the founders, in 1880, of the American Society of Mechanical Engineers. Emerging out of the craft traditions of the shop-culture elite, Holley became a prime mover in the professionalization of engineering. After General Alexander at the University of South Carolina, Holley stood as another father to the young Tompkins, an example of a different type of man than the South had seen.[56]

For a year after Tompkins's graduation from Rensselaer (1873), Holley employed him in Brooklyn as confidential secretary and draftsman. He then helped Tompkins get an apprenticeship at the Bethlehem Iron Works under the management of John Fritz, one of the country's foremost steel makers. Tompkins's beginning pay was seventy-five dollars a month. "His career at Bethlehem," writes Tompkins's biographer George Taylor Winston, "was a continuous illustration of his favorite theory that genius is mostly application. While other employees were taking a day off for county fairs, or Fourth of July celebrations, Tompkins was at work."[57]

During his stay in Brooklyn while working for Holley, Tompkins had met and become engaged to Harriet Brigham, a schoolteacher of genteel background. He visited Brigham and her mother regularly on Sundays and, when he moved to Bethlehem, kept up an exchange of letters, with occasional visits to Brooklyn. The correspondence, begun in 1874, ended with Harriet Brigham's death in 1884.

The letters that remain from this friendship reveal primarily Tompkins's absorption in his work at John Fritz's ironworks and his single-minded practice of the habits of industry, often in acts of conspicuous display that would have pleased Benjamin Franklin:

> I have a feeling that I ought to persist in being absolutely punctual at my work until I shall have something to identify me with the Works. For instance since I have been here I have been working a good deal on the designs of some new engines which Mr. Fritz speaks of building and if he should conclude to build them, having had most to do with the design, I would naturally be depended upon to keep everything straight and that dependence would make for me a sort of tie. I want to have it so that when I am away they will miss me. It seems to me the best way to get a start in that direction is by punctuality and a willingness always to accept those responsibilities. To come so as to reach you by dinner time

would require only an hour and a half, and it seems almost foolish not to take it, but it is the impression upon Mr. Fritz's mind of going at all that I wish to avoid.[58]

As if to deny his actual words, a tone of pleasure, of puritanical self-satisfaction, colors Tompkins's account of the social isolation that routinely filled his away-from-work hours during the passing weeks:

> The week evenings seem to slip imperceptibly by me and before I know it Sunday is at hand with no letter on its way to you. With getting home at six o'clock, then bathing, dressing, and eating supper, and going to bed rather early to be able to rise at five and a half A.M. it leaves little time to perform the errands and duties of housekeeping incumbant upon a forlorn bachelor, that it is almost impossible to accomplish anything outside the works. You have no idea what a pest it is to me to see after the washer woman and have buttons put on my clothes, even tho' such things are done only when absolutely necessary.[59]

Tompkins remained at the Bethlehem Iron Works for nearly a decade, learning the skills of both shop craftsman and engineer. He might have stayed in Pennsylvania had there been room and enthusiasm enough in the ironworks' management to allow his advance—and had he not come to view the Upland South as having great prospects for manufacturers once the political situation had "settled down." Had he had the money, Tompkins would have entered the iron and steel industry in north Alabama or east Tennessee. Instead, being dependent upon salary, savings, and the beginnings of a few small investments, he waited and worked impatiently.

In March 1883 Tompkins accepted an offer from Westinghouse Machine Company to become their agent in the Carolinas, selling and installing steam engines and machinery. Westinghouse furnished the engines and guaranteed Tompkins $1,200 a year plus 15 percent commission on sales. This was a business opportunity that required Tompkins's skills but little start-up capital. His headquarters was to be Charlotte, North Carolina, population seven thousand.[60]

Stirring with new railroad connections that attracted merchants, farmers, and factories, Charlotte was the sort of place where a newcomer could take a room in a boardinghouse and list his profession in the city directory as "capitalist." From the perspective of D. A. Tompkins, however, a man who had now spent many years keeping pace with the changes of Yankee heavy industry, Charlotte appeared not so much a land of promise as a tiresome backwater: "I find the evenings here intolerably dull—I have made few acquaintances and southern people are particularly shy of strangers, and I think I have now so much the air of a northern man that they are afraid that I will make some of the money that they might make. N.C. is a very quiet state at any rate, and the people partake of the same character."[61]

In 1884, Harriet Brigham died. Tompkins, then in his early thirties, seems to have found in the death of his longtime fiancée a reason to resist intimate friendships with women for the remainder of his life. More and more he became engaged with the machinery of New South development. A single vision grew from Tompkins's mechanical knack, his long labor, and his identification of industrial success with the Piedmont and with the South's redemption from the legacies of slavery and military defeat.

Throughout the 1880s, Tompkins sold engines for Westinghouse. He also undertook a partnership to build cottonseed-oil mills. By the 1890s he had accumulated enough capital and contacts to engage for the design and construction of cotton factories. He purchased the newspaper that soon was named the *Charlotte Observer*. "The only thing I wanted the paper for," Tompkins later reflected, "was to preach the doctrines of industrial development and the reasons for it."[62] Within a few years he held controlling interest in three Carolina Piedmont newspapers.

Eventually Tompkins came to be chief owner of three cotton mills and director of another eight. By 1907 he claimed to have built, for clients of his machine shop, more than 250 cottonseed-oil mills and more than a hundred cotton factories. Typically, he would single out a likely man in a Piedmont town, make his acquaintance, then propose the construction of a cotton mill. Tompkins would design and erect the factory, convince the machinery makers in Massachusetts or Rhode Island to take stock, and help promote investment in the mill among the town's prosperous and up-and-coming citizens.[63] "In those days," recalled R. H. Edmonds, founder of the *Manufacturers' Record*, "it seems that Tompkins could have nearly, if not quite, equaled Edison in his ability to work twenty hours a day and sleep four. I have sometimes wondered if during that period he really knew a home, except the sleeping car, and even in a sleeping car he must have been too busy planning and working to have grudgingly yielded up many hours to sleep."[64]

As one of the most outspoken men in the Carolina Piedmont's industrial pantheon, Tompkins, as C. Vann Woodward has pointed out, was "supremely articulate and fired with a zeal to proselytize his unregenerate countrymen" as to the transforming power of laissez-faire capitalism.[65] "His speeches and pamphlets," writes Tompkins's biographer, "on good roads, broad tires, road building and repairs, farm and factory, cottonseed and its products, beef and dairy cattle, trade schools, early education, building and loan associations,

Textile machinery class at Parker High School, Greenville, S.C., 1920s.
Photo by Dowling. (Courtesy of the Greenville County Library)

and similar subjects were scattered broadcast, and produced throughout the Carolinas a pregnant spirit of progress and a harvest of industrial establishments."[66] Seeking the widest possible influence, Tompkins wrote articles for his own newspapers and for the *Manufacturers' Record*. He set his name as author to a partially ghost-written series of books on cotton mills and their profitability and to an inspirational history of Charlotte and its surrounding county of Mecklenburg.[67]

Tompkins signed on eagerly and served diligently both the National Association of Manufacturers and the National Civic Federation in efforts to block any federal legislation that would limit or prohibit child labor. In his view, children should be set to work as young as possible. "It's as easy to teach a boy to love work with the result of capability," observed Tompkins, "as it is to let him drift into habits of idleness with the result of incapability."[68]

"As long as men are greedy men there will be need ultimately of some law to set a limit to the overwork of children," Tompkins observed in a 1906 address to the National Civic Federation meeting in New York. "And also," he quickly added, "as long as there are tenderhearted women, there will be sentiments that are liable to injure children, as the tender mother so often spoils the child. I believe there are just about as many children spoiled by indulgence as there are by overwork." [Laughter and applause.]

A Voice: "More."

Mr. Tompkins: "A gentleman here says more, and I agree with him perfectly."[69]

As a prominent foe of the "habits of idleness" and as an industrial patriarch with wide contacts and great respect among Southern employers, Gus Tompkins received many letters from inquiring and hopeful fathers, much like the following from the editor of the *Baptist Courier*, A. J. S. Thomas:

> I have a son, twenty years of age, good habits, industrious, quick, polite, who I believe you could use in your work. . . . He has some head for machinery, and has some liking for that kind of work. I thought that perhaps he would soon develop into a useful man in the sale of it and knowing your interest in young men I have decided to write to you on the subject. The boy attended Clemson College and the Virginia Polytechnic for several years but got in the notion to go to work, and he has been at it and doing hard work at that. . . .
>
> If you can help me to make a man out of this my only boy I shall very much appreciate it. . . . Boys who are willing to work need looking after for they will make men if we help them.[70]

With regard to the national movement to slacken the eleven- or twelve-hour day for factory workers, Tompkins cautioned that "it must be well considered to what uses the surplus time will be put. To those without proper education, without developed tastes for reading and other profitable use of spare time, any excess of spare time is calculated to be absolutely injurious." When it came to wages, as with time, one must be careful not to give workers more than they knew how to use: "An important factor in the matter of wages is how much can a wage earner take care of with advantage to his family. It would seem not only useless to pay $200.00 a month to a man whose family and himself live as well if not better on $75.00. It has often happened that big wages ruined a man with drink and profligacy and made his family miserable and unhappy. Most negroes are of such temperament—wages beyond a reasonable good living are injurious rather than advantageous."[71]

From the mid-1890s, Tompkins stood as the driving force behind the successful movement to build textile schools in association with Clemson College in South Carolina and North Carolina State College in Raleigh. By design, from their beginnings, these textile schools were very closely allied; indeed, their purpose was to supply technical workers, engineers, and managers to the Carolina Piedmont's manufacturers. The region's mill owners donated resources for construction and machinery for teaching; they lobbied the state legislators and dominated the boards of trustees.

Tompkins's designs upon regional education were joined with clear intentions as to the control of New South industrial workers. "The education which fitted the control and direction of slaves," he wrote to his brother, A. S., "does not fit the control and direction of free white labor. The free white labor is all right if it be educated, and the education is all right if it be thoroughly adapted to free white labor and modern conditions of scientific farming, and to modern conditions of industrial pursuits."[72] "Are the people of this section fitted for factory management?," Tompkins asked the crowd gathered for the dedication of Clemson's textile school. "I answer, Yes."

"The Piedmont region," Tompkins continued, "leads in cotton manufacture. The coming generation wants nothing but opportunity, and this opportunity is chiefly a matter of education of the right kind."[73]

More than anyone before him, D. A. Tompkins conceived and articulated the modern image of the Carolina Piedmont as an industrial region, distinctive yet incorporated within the national economic order. He pressed his regional view unceasingly for decades, up and down the railroad tracks that ran through his headquarters city of Charlotte, the city he came to view as the keystone to the region:

> The Piedmont region seems to be the centre of the new industrial South. The city of Charlotte is the centre of the Piedmont region; and the new conditions are most emphasized in the matter of Charlotte's growth. If, as has been done in the past, Charlotte is initiative and progressive in the development of the resources of the surrounding country, if she continues friendly to her neighbors and interested in their developments, there is no reason that we should not have a city here such as never before has been built in the South Atlantic States. We have a situation most favorable for the building of a city, being one day's ride from Atlanta, one from Richmond, one from Washington. There ought to be a commercial centre for the great Piedmont manufacturing section, and Charlotte ought to be that commercial centre.[74]

Tompkins's politics at any time were those that best maximized manufacturers' profits and promoted government by propertied white men. With his own increasing wealth over the years, he moved from the ranks of Cleveland Democrats to embrace the Republicans and cast his ballot for Taft. "The Republican party," he wrote a friend in 1908, "is more in sympathy with the essential elements of modern prosperity than the Democrats."[75] When the American Cotton Manufacturers' Association proposed Tompkins as minister to China during the Taft administration (ultimately, the job went to a more *bona fide* Republican), scores of letters from Southern mill owners endorsed his nomination and testified to the wide support his views had among this fraternity.[76]

"About three years ago," wrote Tompkins to a friend late in 1912, "I had a nervous breakdown, and I have not been regularly in the working harness since."[77]

> Since I have been sick I have had occasion to reflect upon the multitudinous phases that exist in the nervous system of the human body, and the multitudinous ways in which these may get out of order. A life that is strenuous, but not the best balanced for exercise and recreation, is liable to lead to a sort of general break-down of the nervous system. . . .
>
> The probabilities are that at the Battle of Waterloo, Napoleon's energies and vital forces had been simply overstrained and therefore he lost the Battle of Waterloo. While he was on the Island of St. Helena, his vital energies seemed to be low. He was many times peevish and fretful. This is nothing but a general breakdown of one of the phases of the whole nervous system, due to overwork and over exertion, and not sleeping enough and not rest enough. . . .
>
> The weariness of the body may become incapable of taking care of the activities of the mind, and the mind becomes therefore crippled, and I guess it cannot get its ideas executed. It seems to me the remedy is wholly nature's remedy. . . . The greatest difficulty is for the man himself to get his own consent, or otherwise be able to pull himself loose from all his life ties, his life activities, and return to the simple life away from civilization. . . .
>
> The feeling of many a man is that this is such a revolution he might as well continue the old way and die—rather than enter upon restraint and lengthen out a useless life.[78]

Daniel Augustus Tompkins was laid to rest in Charlotte in October 1914.

Buck Duke, Master Builder

"There are three things I will never understand," Washington Duke is reported to have said, in the most legendary utterance of the Piedmont's oral tradition, "electricity, the Holy Ghost, and my son Buck." During the 1870s, George Washington Duke (1820–1905), a crafty, hardscrabble, Methodist yeoman farmer, had turned his family's home production of smoking tobacco into a modest factory operation whose sixty black workers daily filled tens of thousands of small cotton bags labeled "Pro Bono Publico." His success in the steam-powered factory near the railroad in the booming town of Durham, North Carolina, was hard earned and ample enough for him.

The elder Duke's mind balked when, in the mid-1880s, the youngest of his three sons, James Buchanan "Buck" Duke, gambling the family's wealth, prepared to move to New York City. There, by means of titillating advertising, the purchase of favored rights to the newly developed Bonsack cigarette machine, and no-holds-barred competition, young Buck proposed to do in tobacco what John D. Rockefeller had done in oil. By 1907 Duke's American Tobacco Company, by then worth some $500,000,000, had monopolized the tobacco industry from farm to final product. Prices of raw materials were controlled and rivals crushed. Machine-made cigarettes had been turned into a national desire.[79]

Buck Duke set aside a portion of his enormous and constantly increasing fortune for investment in Carolina Piedmont textile manufacturing, then, in 1905, he incorporated the Southern (later renamed Duke) Power Company with an eye to generating electrical power to industrialize the entire region. More than any single individual, James Buchanan "Buck" Duke (1856–1925)—tobacco monopolist, master builder of Duke Power, and homegrown robber baron—put his design upon the Carolina Piedmont's development, integrating hidebound industriousness, utilitarian ruthlessness, and fierce practicality with the risk-taking audacity made possible with the instruments of advertising, accumulated capital, and electricity.

"He had a wonderful power of making decisions," recalled W. S. Lee, the man whom Buck Duke selected to be chief engineer of his power company. "Generally," said Lee, "he had gone into the matter thoroughly, had the points fixed in his mind and was sure of his ground. He merely thought faster, more accurately, and grasped the points of a situation more quickly than most men. And once he had decided, he acted promptly."[80] Duke's decision making was speeded by his conversion of situations and prospects into dollars. "Mr. Duke had a great mind for figures," recalls a former foreman who worked on the earliest of Duke's hydroelectric dams on the Catawba River. "We would think about these plants in terms of kilowatts. Mr. Duke would think about them in terms of how many dollars that power would bring in." "Buy good automobiles and good men, buy good anything," said Buck Duke. "They pay profits."[81]

For the engineers drawn to Duke's power project—men such as Lee, David Nabow, Charles Burkholder, John Fox, and dozens of others who joined and stayed with the company for the remainder of their working lives—the attractions, challenges, and possibilities for technical achievement were extraordinary. With the zeal of missionaries and the enthusiasm of boys set to single-minded play, these engineers transformed the Carolina Piedmont's vast water power into an electric grid, leaving the issues of economic politics and power to Mr. Duke.

"It's been an amazing thing to me," recalls Herman Wolf, a child of the Carolina Piedmont who in 1916, at age twenty, went to work for Duke and eventually became an assistant vice president in the company. Along the way, Wolf also became the holder of a dozen patents for electrical equipment. "Here was a boy," he says of himself, "with very little knowledge, who's been able to do and work with all these things. It was fascinating. When I was manager of operations, I had a whole power company to experiment with."[82]

In the case of chief engineer W. S. Lee (1872–1934), who later became president of Duke Power, a boyhood fascination with water-driven toys, which he set turning on the creeks of his family's Carolina Piedmont farm, propelled him through engineer's training at the South Carolina Military Academy (The Citadel). Still hearing "the flutter wheels calling," Lee, who designed the earliest hydroelectric plans for the Catawba River Valley, had his maps, charts, and estimates ready in 1904 when Buck Duke was considering the formation of a power company.[83]

"I worked just as hard on that idea as if I had had unlimited capital at my command," recalled Lee. "I surveyed every yard of the Catawba River, and had my plans worked out in minute detail before I knew how the thing was going to be financed. It had even occurred to me that I might never realize anything out of it. But what interested me more than anything else was the practicability of the thing." When Buck Duke asked Lee about the cost, "I told him about eight million dollars. I thought that was about the biggest amount I had ever heard of, but it seemed to attract him."[84]

With Duke's underwriting and Lee's drawings, dams were constructed on the Catawba and a sales campaign was begun to build and electrify Piedmont cotton mills. Mill owners, doubting the potential of electrical power in industry, frequently required considerable reassurance before they would allow the strange new force into their factories. To help convince manufacturers, Duke money was invested in several new Piedmont mills. Scores of aspiring cotton-mill men took up the encouragement of Duke's sales force and the cheap rates and erected new factories along the routes of the power transmission lines.

By 1922 Buck Duke's power company, headquartered in Charlotte, had built ten hydroelectric plants and four steam plants, which supplied 93 percent of the total amount of electricity used in the Carolina Piedmont.

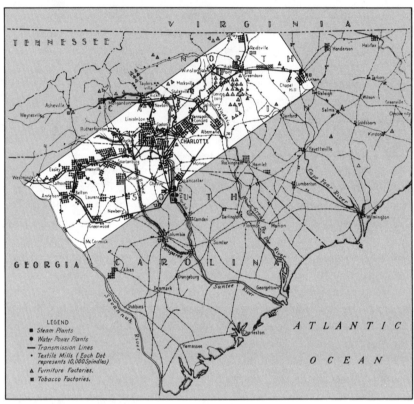

The Carolina Piedmont, showing steam plants, water power plants,
transmission lines, textile mills, furniture factories, and tobacco factories.
(Reproduced from *Management and Administration*, June 1924)

Nearly all of this electricity (90 percent) went to industrial users. Seventy-five
percent of Duke's output furnished power for textile manufacturing, 15
percent went to furniture and tobacco factories, and the remaining 10 percent was purchased by the region's towns. Household and farmstead use of
electricity—not part of Duke and Lee's original plan—was promoted slowly.
Duke Power, by 1930, was the largest power company in the South.[85]

In December 1924, James B. Duke set aside forty million dollars' worth of
power company, tobacco, and textile-mill stock to establish the Duke Endowment. Annual income of the Endowment was to be divided so that about one-
third would go to Duke University, the name given to transformed Trinity
College, a Methodist institution in Durham that Washington Duke had
rescued in 1892. Other, much smaller, yearly monies would go to the Presbyterians' Davidson College in Charlotte; to Furman University, a Baptist

James Buchanan "Buck" Duke. (Courtesy of the North Carolina
Collection, University of North Carolina)

school in Greenville, South Carolina; and to Johnson C. Smith University, a
black institution in Charlotte. Nearly another third of the Endowment's
yearly income was directed to aid for hospitals in the Carolinas. In addition,
the Methodist Church in North Carolina was to receive 12 percent of the
Endowment's annual income.

Duke philanthropy had begun at least as far back as old Washington Duke,
a Methodist steward who practiced and taught his children tithing. "In a time
when the Southern churches still kept the new social gospel at arm's length
and concentrated on the actions and responsibilities of individuals," writes
Duke biographer Robert Durden, "the old doctrine of stewardship remained
alive. Those who possessed wealth had the dual responsibility, according to

the teachings of the church, of both using and giving it wisely."[86] "I have selected Duke University as one of the principal objects of this trust," wrote Buck Duke in the Endowment's papers of indenture, "because I recognize that education, when conducted along sane and practical, as opposed to dogmatic and theoretical lines, is, next to religion, the greatest civilizing influence."[87]

With the establishment of the Duke Endowment, James Buchanan Duke had kept the faith of his father, just as, in replacing the name of Trinity with that of Duke, he incorporated and absorbed the lives and labors of thousands of anonymous Carolina Piedmont workers in Duke tobacco factories and textile mills and along the path of Duke power lines. From the mastery of the streams and rivers of the region's natural world to the education of preachers in Duke University's divinity school, Buck Duke sought his immortality through the transformation of the Carolina Piedmont. Dynamo and lightning rod, he fused the Holy Ghost world of his father with that of the electric, profit-chasing forces of modern America.

The puzzle that Washington Duke had once proposed about the young Buck received no satisfactory answer until one day late in the twentieth century, when a renegade Catholic priest stood in the regal, stony nave of towering, Canterbury-fashioned Duke Chapel, erected near the center of the Duke University campus, and observed: "You would think Mr. Duke had killed God and buried him standing up."[88]

"The Piedmont Carolinas"

"Gentlemen of the Rotary Club and fellow citizens of Piedmont Carolinas," began Charlotte businessman G. W. Freeman in a 1927 speech. "I am proud of my Piedmont citizenship—and why shouldn't I be? This is a go-getter section, peopled by men who are go-getters."[89]

Proudly, Freeman recited some of the facts and figures that the Duke Power Company had recently assembled in its little book, *Piedmont Carolinas: Where Wealth Awaits You.* "You all know," he said, "that one of the miracle spots of the country is the tremendously wealthy section around Grand Central Station in New York City. During the last 20 years, the value of that section has increased 631 per cent. During that same period the wealth of this section down here has increased 660 per cent."

"Another index of the go-getter qualities I meet down here," Freeman continued, "is per capita wealth." By Duke Power calculations, in the five richest states of the Union per-capita wealth had increased by 35 percent

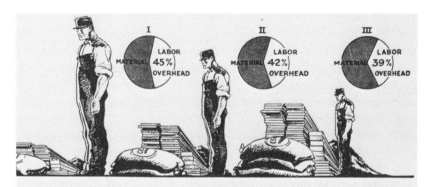

WHERE CONDITIONS FAVOR
STABILITY OF EARNINGS

"THE greatest stability in earnings is found in industries where raw material represents the largest part of the cost of finished goods."

That statement was made by one of America's business leaders, and is amply proved by the surer, more stable earnings of corporations that have migrated to Piedmont Carolinas.

Here, for identical operations turning out identical classes of products, labor and overhead represent 39% of the cost of the finished goods as against 42% to 45% in other sections of the country. Examine the figures on the above charts.

Chart No. I shows the figures for a group of factories, in an old, congested, highly industrialized section of the country. Chart No. II represents a group of factories in a small city area enjoying conditions unusually favorable to low cost production.

Chart No. III represents conditions in one of the *least* favorable sections of Piedmont Carolinas.

This chart may safely be taken as a *conservative* ratio figure against your own relative costs.

Labor That Produces

High wages are profitable where they result in high production. That is the secret of these favorable labor-costs.

Workmen are active, willing and cooperative. Of old native stock, they are untouched by unrest and un-American ideas. Low cost of living and high output keep costs at a satisfactory figure, yet insure high "real wages". There is more left over from the pay envelope at the end of the week than where money wages are higher but living costs are also higher.

If you want complete facts, raw material sources, wage tables, etc., send for the booklet illustrated above. It gives you all the data you need. Your request, addressed to Industrial Department, Room 719, Mercantile Bldg., Charlotte, N. C., will receive prompt and courteous attention.

Where Life Is Pleasant

You will enjoy the neighborly, friendly spirit of Piedmont Carolinas. You will enjoy the sunshiny days, the cool summer nights, the short, mild winters.

If you are a golf enthusiast you know the world-famous courses at Aiken and Pinehurst and Asheville—all a few short hours away.

You doubtless will be amazed by the mountain and seashore regions with their wonderful hotels and recreational facilities.

DUKE POWER
COMPANY

SOUTHERN PUBLIC UTILITIES COMPANY AND OTHER ALLIED INTERESTS

Duke Power Company advertisement from the Piedmont Carolinas' Campaign. (Reproduced from the *Southern Textile Bulletin*, 4 October 1928)

over the preceding ten years; for the Piedmont Carolinas, the increase had been three times as great. And Freeman went on through a catalog of indexes that fell pleasingly on the ears of the white gentlemen of Charlotte Rotary.

Freeman's purpose and that of the Duke Power Company, which supplied electricity throughout the region, was to enlist these go-getter businessmen and manufacturers in a project of regional advertisement. Known as the Piedmont Carolinas' Movement, this campaign built upon the rhetorical tradition of men like H. P. Hammett and D. A. Tompkins. Its ambition and potential grew around the structure set in place by Buck Duke. "How can we make this section better known?," speaker Freeman asked the Rotarians.

> Nobody ever asks where the city of Rochester is located. Rochester is known—known as the home of Eastman Kodaks, as the home of V. & E. filing cabinets, Blue Label Ketchup, and ninety other nationally famous products.
>
> But if we turn to the known and advertised products of Piedmont Carolinas, gentlemen—what do we find? Twenty-three advertisers and of these, Cannon towels are advertised under a New York City, Worth Street, address. . . .
>
> The Duke Power Company, as you know, is advertising this region as a great industrial section with a great industrial future.
>
> But when the American public buys the products of your brains, your handiwork, your energy and capital, does it know it?
>
> You spin yarn. You weave cloth. You make hosiery and underwear and blankets and furniture and bricks and clay products—but who knows it? . . .
>
> Here, gentlemen, is a . . . symbol [that] can be used to direct the eyes of the world toward Piedmont Carolinas. (The speaker displayed a handsome symbol, with the words "Product of Piedmont Carolinas.") . . .
>
> Suppose every Piedmont underwear manufacturer used this symbol on his product. . . . Suppose the Chatham Blanket Company used it on its goods.
>
> Vicks salve, Camel cigarettes, Cannon towels. . . . Suppose the furniture makers of High Point and Thomasville come in on this plan.
>
> Make your packing cases carry the message. . . .
>
> When you advertise in the trade papers, in the newspapers, and in the magazines include this symbol. Tell the world that you live and work in God's own country and that you're not ashamed of it.
>
> Now, gentlemen, you are enthusiastic about this method you can

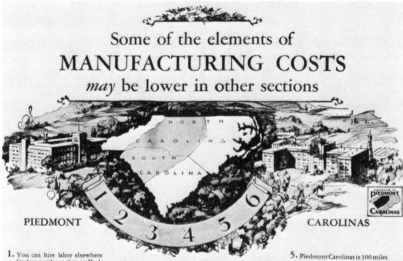

Duke Power Company advertisement from the Piedmont Carolinas' Campaign. (Reproduced from the *Southern Textile Bulletin*, 2 February 1928)

follow to cash in on the great advertising program of the Duke Power Company. You can see the advantage in identifying your company with this section that is getting to be known as a region that delivers a big and honest dollar's value for its merchandise.

Between 1927 and 1929, Duke Power promoted the industrializing Carolina Piedmont with speeches throughout the region by such men as Freeman and with a national advertising campaign in such publications as the *Saturday Evening Post, Nation's Business, World's Work, Review of Reviews, Time,* and the *Wall Street Journal.* At a time when tenancy engulfed nearly 50 percent of Carolina farmers, and when thousands of families had already fled the land looking for work of any kind, Duke Power dangled these displaced and desperate folk before prospective manufacturers within and outside the region.[90]

"Greater than any resource of Piedmont Carolinas," read the ad copy, "is the character of its men and women. That is what has made the industrial development possible and attracted a host of manufacturers."[91]

> Willing, intelligent white male labor is available in a steady supply. . . .
> And all, men and women, are 99% native born, Americans of old pioneer stock—keen, teachable and ambitious to work and get ahead.
> . . .
> A population marked by racial purity and unusually high character.

At a time when the region's manufacturers were placing workers under the most intensive pressures yet seen in the Piedmont, pressures that would result in labor resentment and short-lived revolt, Duke Power advertised:

> Willing labor, unhampered by any artificial restrictions on output; native born of old pioneer stock and not imbued by un-American ideas or ideals. . . .
> Labor in the building trades is constantly being recruited from the agricultural field and delivers an honest day's work.[92]

And, at a time when the cost of a miminum standard of living for a family with three children in Charlotte was $1,438, while the average wage of a Carolina mill worker (working between fifty-five and sixty hours a week) was $624 a year, Duke Power's copy writers boasted:

> Legislation, both state and local, is sane, reasonable and encouraging to industry. . . .
> Nearly 82% of the people of the Carolinas live on farms and in communities of under 250 population. . . . Small town life is an underly-

ing cause of the stable, productive industrial conditions you find here. There are no slums, no breeding places of unrest. It makes for a wholesome point of view. . . .

The birth rate of the Carolinas is the highest in the United States. Already a second generation of textile workers has come along, and in many older textile centers a third generation has grown up.

Upon the auction block of distressed farmers and farm labor, the go-getters of the Carolina Piedmont and increasing numbers of investors from outside the South restructured the region's economy between the 1880s and the 1930s. Habits of industry that were turned to the pursuit of profits and to the accumulation of economic power animated an ascending class of merchants and manufacturers as they took charge of the region and presumed to know best for the workers they called "our hands." In the Victorian ginger-bread neighborhoods and first streetcar suburbs of Charlotte, Greenville, Durham, and Greensboro, the captains of Piedmont industry resided along-side their cities' leading doctors and lawyers, just up the sunny side of the street from the most striving members of the new middle class. On the mill hills of the these same cities, the white farming folk who sought "public work" became a working class.

· 5 ·

The League Family of Poe Mill

"If I Were Building a Mill"

In 1922, D. W. League, a weave room overseer at the F. W. Poe Manufacturing Company in Greenville, South Carolina, won the twenty-five-dollar first prize in the *Southern Textile Bulletin*'s "If I Were Building a Mill" contest. Along with the winning entry, the *Bulletin* printed League's photograph and a brief letter from him expressing gratitude for the distinction. Dozens of overseers, second hands, and loom fixers from cotton mills throughout the South had mailed in the best designs they could imagine for layouts of openers, cards, spinning frames, spoolers, looms, power plants, and so on. The contest was judged by four experienced and successful superintendents and three of the South's best-known textile engineers.[1]

In form, D. W. League's entry appeared much like those of other contestants which the *Bulletin* printed over the course of several weeks. With varying specificity, they divided the manufacturing process into sequential departments, listing and itemizing the equipment. Their sentences, short and sparse, ticked off shopping lists of machinery. More than the others, though, League employed up-to-date adjectives: "The picker room should be equipped with automatic feed system. . . . Cone winders should be of latest type. . . . I would equip with the best humidifier on the market with automatic regulators in carding, spinning, weaving and cloth rooms."

The rules of the contest did not open to a consideration of the men, women, and children who would run the machinery, but D. W. League bent the format slightly, writing: "The mill village should be of a modern type with special attention given to sanitary, lighting, social, and spiritual features." The contest's runner-up, W. V. Jones of Goldsboro, North Carolina, wrote of the mill village as simply another productive unit of the factory: "The village and houses would be in keeping with the plant, convenient, modern and comfortable, with individuality and based upon 2.5 operatives per home."[2]

League's entry may have appealed to the judges because of his expression of confidence in the future. At a time when the textile industry—especially the manufacturing of the coarser quality of cloth that characterized Southern production—was suffering in a post–World War I slump, League proposed building a mill in which an improved grade of worker would produce a fancier line of goods for a market educated to pay quality prices. "My reason for making this class of goods," wrote League, "is (1) The trade is being gradually educated to use the finer quality of merchandise, . . . [and] (b) The help of the South is being educated up to the place where a mill of this type can be both successfully and economically operated." League's words point to two of the manufacturers' strategies to enlighten the "trade" and improve the "help": increased advertising and specialized technical schooling.

Contestants in the mill-building contest, men like D. W. League, had grown up in the Carolina Piedmont's cotton factory towns. After years of the hardest effort and self-discipline, of night school, correspondence courses, and good fortune, they had worked their way up to skilled mill jobs a notch or two above those of production workers. Through job hierarchies, through the sponsorship of fraternal organizations such as those for overseers or mechanics, and through conventions like the ones held by the Southern Textile Association, manufacturers cultivated these men, extending to them an equivocal hand of friendship. Inherent in this factory system was a chain of male authority that ran from owner to superintendent to department over-seers, second hands, and machinery fixers. An experienced overseer like D. W. League inevitably influenced the speed and quality of "his" weavers' work as well as their orderliness, efficiency, and demeanor. In the 1920s and 1930s, management's intensifying demands for profitability spread down-ward through the mill hierarchy and bore especially hard upon the customary relations of overseers and workers.

As an augury of actual construction, the *Southern Textile Bulletin*'s mill-building contest proved unrealistic. While many mills rose on the pages of the *Bulletin* in one month during 1922, fewer and fewer were built in the Caro-lina Piedmont as the decade wore on. Even as New England was losing the interregional spindledge war, Piedmont manufacturers increasingly were be-coming enemies to themselves. Struggling to keep their companies afloat on the laissez-faire flood of production that they had helped to create, they created a panic with competitive price cutting, wage cutting, layoffs of long-time workers, and the installation of new equipment. They ran night shifts to stretch costs across greater units of production, filling their warehouses but finding few buyers. Caught among commission house merchants, the mar-ket, and each other, many mill men led the parade of businesses into the Great Depression.

In the Carolina Piedmont, the 1920s and 1930s were years of increasingly rationalized textile production amid a deepening human disaster for those who worked for factory wages. There are at least as many ways to enter this industrial milieu as there were entries in the mill-building contest. I have chosen to pick up the thread of D. W. League's prize-winning plan and follow it into an interpretation of family history, workers' aspirations, and manufacturers' intentions in this era of technological speedup in the Piedmont's mills.

"Over and Over and Over and Over"

The biographies of D. W. League, his son Nigel, and his daughter Lora League Wright evoke the conditions of an era for Carolina Piedmont factory workers. This is not to say that the Leagues were a typical mill-village family. In the extremes of their personal crises, their life histories reveal the tumult and crisis in the region's industry and among the region's white working class.[3]

D. W. League put his imagined mill on paper for the *Southern Textile Bulletin* in 1922. Within little more than a decade, all that he had praised— the modern, the latest, the most automatic, even the machinery of education—had proved more a nemesis than a blessing to his family. His own solitary defiance of the intensification of industrial work left him cast aside, bewildered, literally heartbroken.

At the center of this family narrative is the story of Nigel League— intensely industrious and disciplined, ambitious and idealistic—who aspired to leap in a single lifetime the distance between the Poe Mill weave room and the South Carolina governor's chair. Through his quest and his tragedy, Greenville workers weighed the prospects for their own, and their children's, hopes and deliverance. In Nigel League's driven pursuit of Protestant "calling" and American dream, desire and work ethic met the limits of class, individual, and historical possibility.

The working life of Lora League Wright, daughter of D. W. League and sister to Nigel, was one of endurance in the industrial regime. She recalls years of daily routine in Poe Mill as well as particular times of crisis—such as the arrival of new technology and the imposition of the stretchout. While Nigel League pursued a messianic "calling," his sister's self-abnegating persistence drew strength from and sustained a web of family responsibility and a female circle of friends within the mill-village church.

Lora League Wright remained in the Poe Mill spool room for twenty-five years. "Just the same thing, over and over and over and over," she remem-

Commodore Butler and Melvina Robert "Bobbie" League and family, Poe Mill village, Greenville, S.C., ca. 1899. *Left to right*: Thomas Jackson, Butler, Bobbie (holding baby Holland), Daniel William, Atticus Wrightman, Margaret Beulah, Mary Eliza, Annie Marie, Florence Irene. (Courtesy of Shirley League Whitmire)

bers. Although missing most of the fingers on her right hand, she was chosen to play piano in the Poe Mill Baptist Church. Suffering from chronic heart problems, she was one of the handful of workers who kept her machine-tending job when the installation of high-speed spoolers prompted the firing of many workers in her department. Ultimately, exhaustion and nervous stress forced her to quit the mill.

"Men Were the Head of the Home"

D. W. League was born in December 1880 near the town of Simpsonville in Greenville County, South Carolina. His parents were farmers who grew cotton and corn as their cash crops. The Leagues did not own their farm but, in the 1880s, were in the process of buying it. In 1895 D. W.'s father, whose full name was Commodore Butler League, heard about the new cotton mill that F. W. Poe was building just outside the city limits of Greenville. Seeing an opportunity to earn rare cash that could be applied to the farm's mortgage, Commodore League moved his family to Poe Mill village and took a job there as a carpenter. His wife, Melvina, took in boarders at the six-room, company-owned house. The Leagues had eight children. Neither husband nor wife worked in Poe Mill, but their children did, beginning as early as age ten. Their wages went into the family coffers.

Around 1900 Commodore and Melvina League paid for and returned to live on their farm. They had gotten what they wanted from Poe Mill. About the same time, their son D. W., now a weaver in the mill, married Mary Odum. By Lora League Wright's account, her father met Mary Odum at Baptist church services, although they may have already known each other from work. "At that time," Lora recalls, "we didn't have a church in the community and they had services in a four-room house, number sixteen, First Avenue. So that's how they met because my mother's mother lived across the street and she kept boarders. And so Papa would come to the—it was what they had for a church." Besides church and work, there were few proper places for young men and women to meet and be seen together.

Mary League worked in the warp room and, like her husband, D. W., belonged to Poe Baptist Church. The couple set up housekeeping in Poe Mill village, where the first of their sixteen children, Ralph, was born in 1902. Lora League Wright, my principal oral source for the family's history, was born in December 1903. She and her husband, Edward Wright, were still living in Poe village when I met and began to interview them in the summer of 1979.

D. W. League started weaving at age fourteen. In a few years he learned to repair looms and moved into a fixer's job. Later he was promoted to second hand, then, about 1915, to overseer of the Number One and Number Two weave rooms. A few months after her marriage, Mary Odum League left the mill. "She didn't work but four months," recalls Lora. "That's all she worked. After she got pregnant, why my father, he encouraged her to stay home."

Like many mill-village women who had once lived on farms, Mary League knew how to cultivate a large backyard garden and how to preserve its harvest. "There's lots of yards that's washed away now," says Lora League Wright, "it's been so many years. But my mother had a big garden. My father had to work late hours, you see, and he didn't have gardening time. But my mother was raised in the country too. Her parents moved to the mill when she was fifteen or sixteen years old. She was a good gardener.

"We helped in the garden," Lora continues. "If we was disobedient about something, we had to work in the garden on Saturday afternoon when the other children were free to play. That was one way we were corrected."

As a child, Lora took on a job common among eldest daughters—the care of siblings. "My mother," says Lora, "taught all of us to have our responsibilities. And my twin sister, she didn't like to take care of babies and so she'd pinch them and make them cry. She'd rather cook or make dishes or wash or something like that. She'd rather be doing some household chore than to be taking care of the babies—that's just not her calling. I remember first taking care of Bessie—she was born in 1907. She cried for me. And Alton, my brother, why I carried him till he was six years old. He could walk, but if I was around he wanted Lora to carry him." Hefting and resting so many successive baby brothers and sisters on her hip during her growing years left Lora "a little bit smaller on my left side than on my right."[4]

On her pedal Singer sewing machine, Mary League made most of the family's clothing. She did the laundry using a tub and washboard. The Leagues owned a cow that they kept on company-owned pasture. They also raised and butchered a couple of hogs every year in the company-built hogpen. The availability of garden space, pastures, and pens provided by the company weighed heavily when workers were considering which mill to work in—especially in the years before the textile depression of the 1920s.

The League family kept its ties to the country through regular trips to the Simpsonville farm and visits to Poe village by D. W. League's parents, who always brought gifts of food such as sweet potatoes and homemade molasses. In a pocket-sized "diary," written in a neat, fine hand, D. W. League noted his purchases and major activities for 1917 (his diaries for other years have been lost). This daybook allows a glimpse of some of the ways in which the Leagues, like other families in mill villages throughout the Piedmont, held to habits of agrarian life even as they worked factory jobs.

Two of League's diary entries for August 1917, for instance, show the family's use of herbal medicine and traditional healers: "Ralph, Nigel and I went this PM to J. D. Hamson to get some Ratsbaine for to make me some tea to build up my Health"; and later, "Went over to City View to get Mrs. Kelley to come and treat the baby for thrash."[5]

"Our Grandmother League," says Shirley League Whitmire (Lora League's sister, b. 1915), "was a great hand at making the medicines for the family. Salves and ointments and liquids. She would gather herbs from the woods and cook them and make medicines. I have three cousins who were brought up in our grandmother's home after we had left, and they'll tell me now different remedies she used. They'd go with her to gather herbs. I've forgotten most of them. Of course, sassafras tea was used in the spring when people were sluggish; it would give them energy. Cherry bark made good cough syrup. There was also devil's shoestring and yellow root and lots of others that I've forgotten."

D. W. League, 1922. This photo was published in the *Southern Textile Bulletin* along with League's prize-winning essay. (Reproduced from the *Southern Textile Bulletin*, 22 June 1922)

D. W. League's faith in education as a means of deliverance came second to his dyed-in-the-wool Baptist beliefs. He served for years as Sunday school superintendent and as a deacon at Poe Baptist Church. Poe Baptist and Poe Methodist, the village churches, were built and their ministers largely paid by Poe Mill. League kept note of his weekly attendance at church events. He accompanied the Baptist minister to neighboring towns for revivals, special services, and shape-note singings. In their home, the Leagues held daily Bible readings and offered prayer before all meals. The children were brought up to attend church regularly and participate actively.

"I'm sure that you have learned," says Shirley League Whitmire, "that in that time, men were the head of the home. At the table Mother sat next to Father. He was at the head, she on his left. The smaller children sat next to her and on around until you got to my oldest brother on my father's right. We always ate on time and everybody knew that their place was at the table.

"When he sat down, he looked around to see that everybody was there, everybody was in place and everything was quiet. Then after our blessing, he would help his plate and pass the food on around. Everything was passed to our father first and then to Mother and then on around. If you didn't get your helping when it went around, it would be just too bad. With such a large family, you might not get it later.

"If you took anything on your plate, you had to eat it all. That was a rule. And when you finished, there was nothing ever left on your plate. You just grew up knowing that. I didn't ever know how that rule was started. And you had to take a little of everything that was on the table.

"We had good substantial meals, not fancy, breakfast, dinner, and supper. You didn't hear of salads back then. You had vegetables, meat, and for bread you had biscuits for breakfast and biscuits and cornbread for dinner. We drank a lot of milk and water. No tea. In summer on special occasions we had lemonade.

"My father did the grocery buying. The older girls would make out the grocery list. They'd go to the pantry and check all the items and then give the list to our father. He'd go to the company store.

"He bought large quantities: a hundred-pound tub of lard, a hundred pounds of flour, cornmeal, sugar, and Irish potatoes. Salmon by the case. And at that time you had people going through the village selling blackberries, apples, and peaches—farmers from the country.

"Our father took an interest in everything that went on in the home. Sewing, cooking, ironing, washing. . . . You'd know that Papa was going to check to see if all that was going on. But Mother had everything well organized.

"Father was a very stern, firm disciplinarian," continues Shirley Whitmire. "You grew up knowing that you were to mind and to respect our mother and father and their authority. And if they were not at home, you had to mind the older children who were left in charge. If you didn't, you got a whipping when Father got home. Our father was so very stern that we always tried to mind so he wouldn't have to do anything.

"Father had a leather strap, with a hook on it—a round ring on the end made out of the strap material, and it had a certain place it hung on a nail in our kitchen. We all tried to avoid that leather strap, even if our mother used it.

"If Mother or Father ever told us to do anything, they didn't explain why. We just knew that they had a reason and a good reason.

"We were told that if we got a whipping in school, we'd have one to follow after we got home. We had to sit still, face the front and behave in church too.

"If we did any little thing that a person in the community thought that our mother and daddy didn't approve of, sometimes before we got home they already knew it. Because they'd go tell on us. They'd say, 'Dan League doesn't allow his children to do things like that.'

"Do you remember hearing people talk about the Charleston dance? I was in elementary school when that came out. Once Eunice and Francis were dancing the Charleston on the front porch at home. Some of the people in the village passed by and then went and told Papa in the mill. They got a whipping when he got home. We were not allowed to go to movies or dance. Other families in the village were strict, but not as strict as ours.

"Any kind of entertainment that was on a high level, our father was interested in. All the girls were singers in church, Lora played organ and piano. Father played the tuba and was a member of the Greenville Shrine Band. He kept the tuba at home and sometimes he would play it while we sang, songs like Stephen Foster's. Nigel [Shirley and Lora's brother] played the trumpet and was a member of the Parker High School orchestra. He also played the fiddle but he would never play for a dance. Father was strictly against dancing. But when John Phillip Sousa would come to play at the Textile Hall, Papa would buy tickets for all the older children."

Beginning with the oldest son, Ralph, the League children usually started work in the mill at age twelve. But until they were eighteen or nineteen years old, they worked only during the summers. Their earnings went largely to pay tuition and purchase school supplies in the Greenville city school system. Poe Mill village did not have a school that went beyond the fifth grade until the creation of the Parker School District in the early 1920s.

D. W. League insisted that his children finish high school before working full time in the mill. This was unusual, even in an overseer's family, at a time when the wages of all family members were needed. (In 1917, D. W. League earned forty-five cents an hour for a fifty-five- to sixty-hour week, compared with a Poe Mill production worker's usual ten cents an hour.)[6] Education, he believed, was the chief means of deliverance for mill folk. Nine League children had graduated from high school by 1931, the year of D. W.'s death.

In 1922 Greenville's textile manufacturers, whose mills were concentrated just outside the city limits, acted together to create the Parker School District exclusively for the enrollment of mill workers' children. Development of the Parker District took advantage of South Carolina's recently adopted "601 law," in which the state agreed to provide six months of a teacher's salary if the local school district would pay the remaining one to three months. The fourteen textile communities that formed the Parker District (named after Thomas F. Parker, president of Monaghan Mill and a strong supporter of YMCA welfare work) contained some nine million dollars of taxable property—greater than that of any other school district in the state. In 1926 its twelve square miles were home to 25,000 workers and their families; 5,700 students were enrolled in its twenty schools. The district was supported by a self-imposed tax on mill property and was controlled by a committee representing the mills' managements. The jewel of the district's schools was Parker High (designed by the Greenville textile engineering firm of J. B. Sirrine), which graduated its first class of thirty-one students in May 1925. Parker District's schools supplied the Greenville mills with literate young workers, some of whom were already trained to run and repair mill machinery.[7] The district schools, particularly Parker High, turned as wheels within the larger industrial wheel. " 'Book larnin,' " wrote a reporter, "is not unduly stressed in Parker district. More emphasis is placed upon fitting the student for some trade."[8]

"Back of the activities of the Parker School District," observed a writer for the trade publication *Textile World*, "is primarily a desire to fight the lethargy which is probably the most unfortunate feature of our modern industrial life." As for L. P. Hollis, the energetic and innovative superintendent of the district, "he is trying to infuse into his school district an impulse which, for want of a better term, we shall call industrial consciousness." Hollis "is aware" that the modern temptations of "a Ford car, movies and a radio do not compensate for the loss of the thrill which comes from doing a good job."[9]

Lora, Lorene, Ralph, Thelma, Bessie, Eunice, and Francis

Lora League and her twin sister, Lorene, first worked in Poe Mill during the summer of their twelfth year. They worked there each succeeding summer until they began full-time mill work after graduation from high school. Lorene learned to spin, the customary beginning task for girls. Because Lora had lost parts of three fingers in a wood-chopping accident, she could not work as a spinner. "I learned to put up ends but I could not clean rollers with my right hand because of my fingers being off.

"It was a rule," Lora continues, "that you couldn't go to the spooler room until you were fourteen years old. They said until then you weren't tall enough to take the full spool and put it on the shelf on the top of the frame. But they made an exception for me. I'd have to crawl up on the trough that the yarn was in to put the full spools on top."

Children of Mary Odum and D. W. League, Poe Mill village, Greenville, S.C., ca. 1918. *Left to right*: Eunice, Lorene, Francis, Ralph, Thelma, Bessie, Shirley, Lora (holding baby Mary), Alton, Nigel. (Courtesy of Shirley League Whitmire)

Money that the League children made during the summers in the mill was turned over to their father. "The father was head of the household," says Shirley. "You worked and brought the money home to him until you reached the age of twenty-one. Then you'd pay so much a week as board."

Of the other League children who came of age in Poe Mill village, Lora recalls that Ralph, Thelma, and Bessie worked for a while for the company store. When Ralph married he left the Poe village and became a salesman with a coffee company in Charlotte. Lorene married and moved to Spartanburg; there she left the mill to raise a family. "Thelma was a good weaver but the weave room was hot and her feet were very sensitive to the heat. She lost lots of time because her feet would blister so. She quit the mill and went to Spartanburg and went into training for a nurse. She married and had a family too." Lora's sister Eunice graduated from Parker High, worked in the cloth room of Poe Mill and at a couple of other Greenville mills, eventually marrying and settling in at Judson Mill village. Lora's brother Francis, after finishing at Parker High, tried playing semipro baseball in California. He married twice and remained on the West Coast, working with the Borax Company.

"When Lorene finished high school," adds Shirley, "she wanted to be a nurse. But back when our Grandmother Bobbie League was growing up, it was not considered good for a woman to go into nursing. So Papa said to Grandmother Bobbie, 'Lorene wants to go into training, Mother.' She said, 'Oh, Daniel, don't let her go into training. Just bad women go into training.' So he didn't let Lorene become a nurse.

"Well, when Thelma quit the mill she went over to the school of nursing at Spartanburg General Hospital. She didn't tell my father she had gone in training. She was afraid to tell him. She was not married; she had worked long enough and was old enough to pay board, but she was still under his supervision. Needed his permission.

"Finally, one weekend when she came to visit, she told Papa that she was in training. And he was real happy. It had been a few years, and he had changed his mind a bit. He had always wanted to be a doctor. His great-grandfather on his mother's side had been a doctor. And Thelma and Papa would talk about her nurse's training. But they still hadn't told Grandmother Bobbie.

"So one day Papa got Grandmother and carried her to Spartanburg to see her great-grandson, Lorene's child. And they went to the hospital and Grandmother told it, 'I saw this young girl come swishing down the hall with those starched aprons on and somebody said, "How are you, Grandmother?" And I looked and there was that Thelma!' Of course she was mad for a while, but she got over it and was real proud of her."

Nigel League

Nigel Aberdeen League was born in 1909, the seventh of the sixteen children of Mary and D. W. The family always pronounced his name Nij-el (rhymes with "vigil"). "I have a niece," says Lora, "they named one of their boys for him and that's where I learned it was *supposed* to be Nī-gel. It's in the Bible. And that emphasis is on the *N-i*.[10]

"Now Nigel's ambition," continues Lora, "was to be a lawyer and go from lawyer to governor of the state. He had high aspirations. He was just so different from the rest of us children. Growing up, he seemed like he knew what he wanted, and that's what he worked for.

"He'd get a dictionary out and study it like you would the Bible. He wanted to learn everything that he could so he would be well equipped to do what his ambition was.

"He loved music. He had a trumpet. When he would go to Grandmother's, he would go on the train from Greenville to Mauldin, and then he walked three miles. When he would get on top of the hill where you could see Grandmother's house, he'd start blowing that trumpet and everybody around knew that it was Nigel."

Lora and Nigel's sister Shirley recalls that Nigel had another ambition besides that of politician. "He'd say, 'Now I'm going to be a mortician too, but that's just going to be a sideline.'

"His Latin teacher in high school, who later taught me, told me one time, 'Shirley, I'd want the children to draw pictures for me.' She'd frame them and put them on the wall. 'Every time I asked Nigel to draw me a picture, he'd draw one of a man in a casket. And I'd say, "Nigel League, don't you ever draw me another picture like that. Draw something else." And he'd draw the United States flag.' She told him the only thing wrong with his flag was that it was too stiff. It didn't look like it was waving."

As a youngster, Nigel took on several extra jobs for pay. Using Red Devil Lye and Gold Dust Washing Powders, he scrubbed the wooden floors of houses in Poe Mill village. "Nigel did that and the other boys did that," recalls Shirley. "The girls didn't do anything like that because we had chores to do at home." Nigel bought a windup projector and, apparently with his father's permission, showed silent films in the family's upstairs bedroom. "He'd charge so much money and everybody would sit on the bed and watch the movie. Everybody'd be real quiet—there was that discipline that come in."

While in high school, Nigel held a part-time job with a Greenville mortuary. "Nigel helped them in the embalming process," remembers Shirley. "And he would bring embalming fluid home. And Mama raised chickens. When the little chicks, dibbies they called them, would die, Mama would give them to Nigel. He'd save kitchen matchboxes and would bury the dibbies in them. And if people had dead kittens or a cat would get run over, he'd bury them in shoe boxes. He would conduct the funerals in the cow stalls in the barn. He'd be the mortician and the preacher. He preached from the Bible and followed the pattern that we'd learned from going to funerals ourselves. And we children were the mourners and our backyard was the cemetery."

Lora remembers another of Nigel's enterprises. "When he was in high school, on weekends, see they [the mill] paid off on Friday, he would get the materials to make hot dogs, and take them . . . now, that wasn't my father's idea of him doing that. When he learned he was doing that, Nigel had to quit because Papa told him he was taking the people away from their work. They'd go buy their hot dogs and come and go back to work. He would sell hot dogs to the people in the plant. That's how he started to making his money. Papa put it in the bank for him. Course, all he had when he went to the university was sixty or seventy-something dollars."

Nigel was a cheerleader at Parker High. "He put so much of his strength into what he was doing," says Lora, "that sometimes they said he would pass our leading cheers." In 1925, with a presentation of Henry Grady's speech, "The New South," Nigel won the right to represent Parker High in the South Carolina high school declamation competition. The year of his graduation, he won the state contest with Henry Ward Beecher's "The American Flag." He was also, in 1925, one of six South Carolina winners in the annual American Chemical Society high school essay contest, promoted nationally for the chemical industry by F. P. Garvan. For his essay, "Chemistry in Evidence of Life," Nigel won a certificate and twenty dollars in gold.[11]

Teenagers in the Parker School District had only the slightest chance of finishing high school in the 1920s. Economic pressures and cultural expectations pushed fifteen- and sixteen-year-olds into the mill. Schooling beyond the sixth grade might cause children to "rise above their raising," becoming, in effect, strangers to their friends and families.

In 1925 nearly six thousand children were enrolled in the Parker District schools. That year's high school graduating class had thirty-one members. More remarkably, sixteen of these (fourteen boys and two girls) planned to attend college.[12] Manufacturers and boosters trumpeted these few graduates as evidence that Parker District "is not educating its students to the mill, but to the colleges ahead." "To them," concluded a Greenville newspaper editorial in 1925, "has been opened the whole field of learning and the accumulated wisdom of the universe, the privilege to throw off the shackles of ignorance and superstition, the opportunity to become in every sense the leaders of the state."[13]

In 1926, Nigel League sought his opportunity. With a little money saved from summer jobs in Poe Mill, he entered the state university at Columbia. Outside of classroom hours, he pieced together an assortment of part-time and full-time jobs. He delivered both the morning and evening newspapers, waited tables at a boarding house in return for his meals, sometimes worked the third shift in a duck mill, and held a night janitor's job around the offices of the South Carolina state government. Nigel joined the National Guard for the dollar it paid for each attendance at drill.

D. W. League worried over Nigel's going away to college not only unsaved, but uncommitted to becoming a minister. "My father told him," recalls his sister Lora, " 'Nigel, I feel that God's calling you to be a preacher.' So he said, 'Well, Papa, if I felt it, I would. But I haven't felt the call.' " At the university, Nigel joined the Baptist church. But increasingly, he felt his "call" to be politics.

"Nigel seemed to be a friend of everybody that he came in contact with,"

Nigel League and Myrtle Staley, 1931. (Courtesy of Shirley
League Whitmire)

says Lora. "People older than him would come and talk about their problems.
When he came home to visit while he was in college, he'd go off to slop the
hogs and you'd see people start gathering around him. He'd go home with a
family and come in late at night."

On campus, Nigel was president of the junior class and a member of Blue
Key and Kappa Sigma Kappa honorary fraternities and the social fraternity
Sigma Phi Epsilon. He was an officer of the Clariosophic Literary Society,
circulation manager of the campus newspaper, the *Gamecock*, and a member
of the debating team for two years. As a sophomore, in 1928, Nigel announced his candidacy for governor of South Carolina in the *1948* elections.

His twenty-year intention was carried throughout the country by the Associated Press wire services and featured on the front page of the *New York Times*.[14]

After graduation, Nigel went directly to law school at Cumberland University in Lebanon, Tennessee. He took his law degree, passed the South Carolina bar exam, and opened a practice in Greenville. A close friend, Hubert Nolen, convinced Nigel to declare himself a candidate for a seat in the state house of representatives in the 1932 election. And somewhere along the way, he had secretly married a young woman he met in Columbia, Myrtle Staley. According to both Lora and Shirley, Nigel kept the marriage a secret because he wanted to be in a position to support Myrtle before they set up housekeeping.

"This Change That Had Come About"

In 1928, while Nigel was at the University of South Carolina, his father, D. W. League, continued to be the overseer of weaving at Poe Mill. Nigel's sister Lora, recently married to Edward Wright, was working in the Poe Mill spool room. In November a new superintendent ordered overseer League to increase the weavers' workload from twenty looms to forty looms. Lora and Edward recall what happened:

"They wanted him to stretch out his help and he said, 'N-o, no.' Because he knew what his people were capable of doing and he didn't want to make slaves out of them.

"The children of Israel, why, they were slaves to the Egyptians. Papa didn't want that said of him.

"So the super said, 'Mr. League, if you won't do what I want you to do, somebody else will.' Papa was out of his job.

"It was a new superintendent," Lora continues. "I don't know where he got his idea. He wasn't superintendent here long. The big shot, head man, president, general manager let go of him. Workers would complain. He left as a result."

D. W. League quit his job out of Christian principle and took the consequences in stoic, solitary fashion. "He wouldn't talk to nobody about it except his wife," says Lora. "He didn't want to hurt others," adds Edward.

Resistance to stretchouts, speedups, "curtailments" (layoffs), and wage cuts sparked some 175 strikes in Carolina Piedmont mills from the late 1920s through the mid-1930s.[15] In several instances, what were called "leaderless strikes" (without union involvement) resulted in temporary improvements in

working conditions. In the case of D. W. League and the Poe Mill weaving
department, Edward and Lora Wright recall that workers' complaints eventually forced the dismissal of the new superintendent. League's stand of
conscience, which cost him his job, points to the overwhelming pressures
applied to Piedmont cotton-mill workers during the depressed, shakeout
years of the post–World War I textile industry. Since the beginning of the
New South mill-building era in the 1870s, the give-and-take of paternalism,
as it shifted with labor and textile-market conditions, had sometimes moder-
ated—especially in the earlier years—the pace and intensity of regimentation
in the Carolina Piedmont's factories. As the market conditions for Piedmont
textiles turned cutthroat in the 1920s, and as the pool of white male labor
grew with the worsening plight of farmers, even the gestures of paternalism
gave way to an owner-worker relationship based on unmediated and ever
more alienated wage labor.

D. W. League drew upon the moral resources and authority of the biblical
tradition that guided his life. He felt that the Israelites' compulsory labor in
Egyptian bondage validated his refusal to make "slaves" of the Poe Mill
workers. His moral and manly responsibility to "his" weavers left no other
course. Ultimately, as most forcefully demonstrated during the Loray Mill
strike in Gastonia in 1929, the prerogatives of Piedmont mill owners were
supported by municipal and state police power. The issue turned on a
fundamental assumption of individual property rights. The established view,
derived from eighteenth-century republican, freeholder, and free-will prin-
ciples, held that the worker was "free" to refuse or to accept the wages and
conditions put forward by the manufacturer. Again and again, would-be
union organizers had to face the conventional laissez-faire wisdom that a
factory belonged to its owner to do what he wanted with. Even today, "You
don't have to work here" remains a familiar refrain in Piedmont factory
towns.

Certainly, too, there was a biblical interpretation contrary to the one D. W.
League held. "Now Mr. Striker," reads a letter to the *Greenville News* in
September 1929, "get your hearts right with God." The correspondent
quotes several variations on the ancient, oppressive theme: "Servants, be
subject to your masters with all fear; not only to the good and the gentle, but
also to the froward. For this is thankworthy, if a man for conscience toward
God endure grief, suffering wrongfully."[16] Having heard the superintendent's imperatives, yet seeing clearly his own duties to his weavers, D. W.
League found that he could neither acknowledge the legitimate authority of
this latest step of industrial capitalism nor summon the personal or collective
resources necessary to fend it off.[17]

League left Poe Mill for an overseer's job in Chesnee, forty miles away. Then, only a few months later, the Chesnee mill owners decided to install some new looms. "We were in church one Sunday morning," Shirley remembers, "during the preaching service. I can see the picture in my mind right now. The superintendent of the mill, a Mr. Jones, came up to my father and my father went out and talked with him and came back in and sat down. Then after we went home, he didn't even talk about it where we children could hear it. That afternoon my mother told the older sister that was at home at that time, Eunice, and she whispered it around to we younger children. We learned that our father had quit his job because Mr. Jones wanted him to come in to the mill that day. The equipment had come in on Sunday and he wanted those looms put down right then. And Father told him that he did not work on Sunday."

"He said that this was profaning the Sabbath, the Lord's Day and a day of rest," adds Lora.

"And," says Shirley, "the superintendent said, 'You'll work for me today or you won't have a job.' And he said, 'I don't have a job.'

"After we left there," continues Shirley, "we moved to Judson Mill at Greenville in October of 1930. Mr. Marlow Hughes had worked as a section hand under our father at Poe Mill. And he, like father, had worked his way up. He was overseer of weaving. Father went to him and he gave him work as a weaver. Then, Mr. Hughes got a job as superintendent in three mills in Anderson: Lad-Lassie, Toxaway, and Oakmont. These three mills were all under one head. Mr. Hughes asked Father to come as overseer of weaving at Lad-Lassie. The mill had stood for three years. When they re-opened it, the machinery was in bad condition. And of course the work was hard to run.

"That was when they began working two shifts of twelve hours each. Father was responsible for both shifts and so he was working a big part of twenty-four hours. But he did not work on Sundays. After twelve o'clock on Sunday night he would go back. And he always came home for mealtimes.

"Soon father realized that he could not continue to work this way and keep his health. He talked with Mr. Hughes. Mr. Hughes's and our family lived side by side and I remember seeing Papa and him sitting outside in the car talking together. It was on a weekend. And then, as usual, our dad talked to our mother and it would be handed on down through the family. Just kind of in a whisper, never talked out loud or at the table. It was handed down to we children by our older sisters and brothers that Papa had quit work there.

"Papa said, 'I have a farm and I'm going to move to my farm. I want you to know that I'm going to work a notice.'[18]

"And Mr. Hughes said, 'Mr. League, I can't continue to do this either. I can't hold up under it. I have a farm near Taylors and I'm ready to move too. But I don't think my family will go with me to the farm.'

"Pa said, 'Mr. Hughes, the only advice I can give you is to build a house and tell your family that's where you're going to move to and they're welcome to come with you. And if they go with you, all right. And if they don't, that will be their own decision.'

"So Mr. Hughes worked a notice too. Later we learned that he had built a home and his family had moved with him. They didn't go back to the mill. Later he got a job with Steel Heddle in Greenville as a traveling salesman. Then he had an auto accident and was not able to work."

With Mary and the five youngest children, D. W. left Anderson in March 1931 for the family farm. "He was under great strain," says Lora. "He had just got so confused, till he wanted to get quiet. He worried himself to death."

"It bothered him a great deal," Shirley remembers, "this change that had come about. People were not given the consideration that they had been before. You were pushed as a worker. More work was put on you. More looms. More than you could run."

"At the time of our father's death," Shirley continues, "he was cutting corn tops. He would go down so far on the stalk and cut the top. Those would be put in what they called a hand. They would be tied up with the leaves of corn—that was what they called fodder. It would be partially green and would be hung to dry on the part of the corn stalk that was left. Then he would take the fodder up in a wagon or in a small Ford truck he had bought. He'd take it up in the early part of the day when the moisture was still on it to keep it from cracking or breaking. He'd take that to the barn and put it in the loft. That's what you'd feed the cattle, horses and mules on.

"So father was cutting fodder. And he came in for lunch. Our sister Lorene was visiting. She and Mother were making tomato catsup. Mother had planted tomatoes in the watermelon patch after the watermelons had grown off.

"After lunch he lay down on the floor in the hall and took a nap. Then he got up and went back to the barn and got his knife to go and cut corn tops again. And he got severe pain in his chest. He came back to the house and said, 'Mary, I'm real sick. Will you fix me a glass of soda water?'

"He got worse and Mother sent to Simpsonville for the doctor. When we younger children got off the bus about a mile from the house that afternoon we could hear our father. It was a terrible, mournful sound. And two of our cousins who lived down the road with Grandmother went with us up to the house.

"When we got to the house, our father was sitting in a chair in the hall. Our mother and sister were there and neighbors had come in. He was still in severe pain.

"Dr. Richardson came and his diagnosis was the same as Dr. Smith's. I heard our father say, 'Now, Dr. Richardson, I would like you to tell me my condition and what my future is. What chance I have of living. If I can't live, I would like for you to tell me.' Both doctors told him that there was no possible chance for him to live. He passed away about 12:30 that night, the eighth of September. He was fifty-one years old."

Mary League and the children moved in with Lora's twin sister, Lorene, and her family in Spartanburg. "Lorene had two young boys," says Lora, "and she wanted Mama to look after them while she worked. So Mother did. We all helped with groceries and clothing for the children until they married or finished high school."

"Victim of His Own Enthusiasm"

D. W. League's death, in the late summer of 1931, came only months before his son Nigel announced his candidacy for the state legislature. "When Nigel was running," Edward Wright says, "they used to have about nineteen or twenty speaking events in the county. At every mill they'd have a speaking one night. And Nigel walked all over Greenville County. He didn't have a car and he wouldn't ask anybody to carry him. Unless somebody came by and picked him up, he walked. From one speaking to another."

Nigel League was a factory boy who had made good. His success and his promise embodied the hopes of many Greenville mill hands for their children. Nigel waged a campaign on behalf of mill workers, yet other than pledging to work for lower taxes, for an eight-hour day and the betterment of "my people," his appeal relied mainly on the customary strength of "friends and neighbors" identification, unaccompanied by any substantive criticism of the mill system or any populist-style platform. Going into the final week of the primary, the charismatic Nigel, at age twenty-four, had become the favorite and was expected to lead the field.[19]

On the night of 22 August, an exhausted Nigel League and nearly three dozen other candidates came to a speaking at Simpsonville attended by hundreds of voters. As a Greenville paper reported the event: "League arose to speak after 34 candidates had presented their pleas for suffrage, and with red-faced exertion and in a speech vibrant with emotion, he called upon his auditors to elect him for his purpose to lower taxes, favor an eight-hour working law for the mills, consolidate useless state bureaus and work for the betterment of 'my people.' He spoke with such violence that once or twice his voice broke into screeches."[20]

"They begged him not to speak that night," recalls Lora League Wright, Nigel's sister. "He was exhausted. But he spoke. And he put out so much energy when he would be speaking, exhausted so much energy. When he finished, his last sentence was, 'Be ye faithful unto death.' And he was gone that quick. He turned around and fell."

To read the Greenville newspaper coverage of Nigel League's death and funeral is to see how one family's tragedy compelled a popular urge for explanation and justification. One reporter wrote:

> There was a widespread gasp of horror, and then the throng pushed its way around to the front of the station where the victim of his own enthusiasm lay.
>
> Six or seven minutes after he had pleaded from the platform of the railway station in a hoarse, throbbing voice, "In the name of good government, give me a seat in the South Carolina legislature," he lay lifeless on the crude bier of a freight truck while the concourse of people, sobered by the pall of tragic realization, milled about quietly in an effort to view the still body.
>
> Tom V. Ingle, another house candidate, who a few minutes previously had jibed his fellow political aspirant good-naturedly, stood by the im-mobile body, his cheeks wet with tears. Ingle, who called himself "a cotton mill boy," frequently has told friends throughout the campaign that he was fathering the political ambitions of the other "cotton mill boy," who, sincerely and seriously, thought of himself as a rising Moses to lead his people out of the wilderness of unemployment and its conse-quent suffering.

Mixed in with sentimentality, sensationalism, and pathos of the newspaper accounts is the suggestion that Nigel, the "victim of his own enthusiasm," had sought an impossible labor of deliverance for the mill families. The imagery of enslavement reappears here, recalling D. W. League's refusal to stretch out the Poe Mill weave room. Nigel's death touched all those Greenville mill families whose best hopes for their children imagined a way out of the mill. Testimony to these shared hopes could be seen in Nigel League's funeral, held at Bethel Methodist Church near the family farm—an extraordinary gathering in the rural Piedmont. Five hundred people filled the flower-bedecked sanctuary, and another 2,500 listened to the services over loud-speakers set up outside.

Nigel League Dies At Campaign Meet As Crowd Looks On

Candidate Dies

Youth Drops After Finishing Speech At Simpsonville Station

THRONG GASPS WHEN TRAGEDY IS REALIZED

Meeting Immediately Adjourned By Chairman— Other Campaign Plans

Nigel A. League, 24, of Greenville, ended his whirlwind campaign for a seat in the house of representatives b e f o r e 3,000 Simpsonville voters shortly before 9 o'clock last night heeding the Biblical injunction: "Be thou faithful unto death."

Six or seven minutes after he had pleaded from the platform of railway station in a hoarse, throbbing voice, "in the name of good government, give me a seat in the South Carolina legislature," he lay lifeless on the crude bier of a frieght truck while the concourse of people, sobered by the pall of tragic realization, milled about quietly in an effort to view the still body.

VOICE WAS IMPAIRED

He arose to speak after 34 candidates had presented their pleas for suffrage, and with red-faced exertion and in a speech vibrant with emotion, he called upon his auditors to elect him for his purpose to lower taxes, favor an eight-hour working law for the mills, consolidate useless state bureaus and work for the betterment of "my people." He spoke with such violence that once or twice his voice broke into screeches.

The young candidate finished,

NIGEL A. LEAGUE, candidate for the house of representatives, as he looked a few years ago at Parker high school, who died during a political meeting at Simpsonville last night. Mr. League only recently had returned to Greenville after having spent five years in obtaining a higher education. His death was mourned by his political opponents as well as by the friends he had made throughout the section.

League Worked Way Up Through Early Hardships

Born At Poe Mill, Worked In Mill And Later For

Newspaper clipping about the death of Nigel League. (Courtesy of the Greenville County Library)

Funeral of Nigel League. Photo by Dowling. (Courtesy of Shirley League Whitmire)

"Every single move of this young man's life should be written and read throughout the country," said the Rev. J. Dean Crain, pastor of the Pendleton Street Baptist Church of Greenville. . . .

"This young man brought character and goodness into politics," he declared. . . .

"He reminds us of Joseph, who went from difficulty to difficulty, from pit to pit, yet who, at 30, was in control of Egypt. Mr. League, like Joseph, was true to God."

Before beginning the short sermon, the speaker read the service for the dead. As he came to the scriptural "In my Father's house are many mansions," the minds of some of the minister's auditors went back to the strenuous campaign for election to the general assembly the young man made before he was mortally stricken.

"I go to prepare a place for you," the speaker intoned. "I will go to prepare a better place for you," the youthful candidate had told numerous mill employees during his short-lived public career.

A dozen former schoolmates of the young man, all young women who are attending or have attended the Parker High School, sang three religious selections during the service.[21]

In retrospective accounts composed years after Nigel League's death, Greenville's journalists settled for the individualistic feature story of the self-made man instead of pursuing an exploration of what the story of Nigel's life meant in the community of mill families. Rather than address the limits of class possibility, a less troublesome image settled into place: "League's consuming ambition," wrote one columnist as late as 1940, "to make a place for himself had caused him to literally drive himself to death from work."[22]

A Little Hard Work Never Killed Anybody

In 1927 Lora League, daughter of D. W. and Mary Odum League and sister of Nigel League, married Edward Wright, a worker at Poe Mill, the son of mill-worker parents, and a Baptist. Ed was born in the mill village of Aragon, Georgia, in 1905.

Lora and Ed were married in the parsonage of the Poe Baptist Church. "I joined the church when I was fourteen. I was brought up in the church. So we started our married life in the church. I wouldn't marry any boy that wasn't a Christian."[23]

Lora and Ed met in the mill. "I'd doff and pour up yarn to her in the spooler room."

"He tried to go with me three years and a half before I'd give him a date. And we went together lacking one day of being four months, when we married. But I knew about him and he knew about me.

"My father didn't want me to marry because my health wasn't good. So I was twenty-three and just lacked a few days of being twenty-three and a half. Edward wanted to ask for me and I said, 'No, I'm a woman of my own, but I would like for you to tell my father that we're going to get married.'

"So when Edward came down, my father had company on the front porch and I told one of the children, I says, 'Go out there and tell Papa that I want to see him a few minutes, please.' So he came.

"And Edward said, 'Mr. League, Lora and myself have decided to get married. I would like your consent.'

"Papa said, 'Well, you don't have it.' He said, 'She is morally good but she cannot be a wife to you.' Because the doctors had told me that they didn't think that I could ever become a mother.

"You see, I had a fall when I was eight years old. We were down at Grandmother League's for a week in the summertime. Papa had a cousin that lived over the hill to the right of Grandmother. So I had carried the baby with me out in the yard and I was swinging on a rope swing tied to the limb of a tree. The cousins went in to dinner and I told them, 'No, I don't care for any.' And I was swinging. Well, the swing broke under the plank and I sat flat down, like that. They didn't used to carry children to the doctor, you see, way back in those years. And so the uterus, or the womb, was upside down and growed to the rectum. And the muscles—the tubes had growed to my intestines and the muscles of my backbone. And when I would have my monthly period—I guess you know that women have monthly periods—it was just like having pains to give birth to a child. I suffered from the time I started until I had surgery when I was twenty-nine.

"And of course I'd already told Edward that before I told him I'd marry him. Because I was engaged one time before and I told the boy that I didn't know whether I could become a mother. And so he acted smart and I just shifted him off. But I felt like I owed it to him.

"So then Papa, he went on and said several things. Papa said, 'You're not getting a wife, Edward, because her health's not good.'

"Edward said, 'Mr. League, I'd rather have her and know that she'd be sick as long as she lived than have to do without her.'

"I don't know why Papa called him big boy, but he said, 'Big boy, you remember that.' And just pointed his finger at him. He says, 'You have my permission.'

"And when Edward and myself married, the next morning—we went to Spartanburg on our honeymoon; my twin sister wouldn't listen to us going to a hotel. She wanted us to stay at her house for our first night, and so we did.

"The next morning, why we didn't get up and eat breakfast with her and her husband. We got up somewhere around nine-thirty or ten o'clock. But when we set down to the table for breakfast, why I was used to my mother or father returning thanks—my father always, except when he was absent. But I kept waiting and Edward said, 'What are you waiting for?'

"And I said, 'I thought you was going to return thanks.'

"And he said, 'If you'll return thanks this morning, I will from now on. I don't know how.' And so I returned thanks.

"We've had the Lord's blessing on our food ever since then. Sometimes he calls on me. But when I get my breakfast on the table, I come in here and get my Bible and his Bible and a devotional book and I carry it to the kitchen. As a general rule, I read the scripture. Now sometimes he'll read it, but not often. He wants me to read it. And then he prays. Then at night we read our Bibles separate to ourself, but then we have our family prayer, we pray out loud."

"And that's the way to keep your married life in harmony. Because you see the woman is reared by different parents to the man and maybe they're not accustomed to the same things in life. And you have to learn to live with one another. But after you take those vows, that you will, why it takes the help of God."

Lora's social and spiritual life has always centered around Poe Baptist Church, and especially a female community within the church. She pleasures in remembering the times she was chosen for service. When Lora was eleven, for instance, the regular piano player was absent from a Poe Baptist event. The preacher asked the gathered congregation, "Is there anyone here who can play?" Her girlfriends volunteered, "Lora can play." And, using her left hand and her partially dismembered right, Lora struck up "Work for the Night Is Coming." It was the beginning of much church playing.

"I've been teaching Sunday school since I was seventeen years old," Lora says. "I taught children at first. My father was a Sunday school superintendent and he was having a study course for adults. And I was seventeen years old and I asked him to let me go to the study course, and he did. And I made a hundred on my exam.

"Two weeks after the papers were corrected and everything, my father said, 'Lora, I want to see you a few minutes.' And I didn't know what in the world I had done. I couldn't think of a thing. But anyway, he says, 'Lora, I feel like that God wants to use you as a Sunday school teacher. Would you try?'

"And I said, 'Yes Papa, if you feel like God's calling me to teach it.'

"Later, I had to give up teaching for a while because of my health. The first Sunday I went back to Sunday school, well, when I come out of the classroom, Mr. Taylor, the superintendent, said, 'Mrs. Wright, there's some young ladies want to speak to you out in the auditorium.'

"I said, 'What do they want?'

"He said, 'Well, you go out there and they'll tell you what they want.'

"And so I went out there and I saw three young women that I knew. I said, 'Are you the young ladies that want to see me?'

"They said, 'Yes we are.'

"I didn't have any idea what they wanted. So I said, 'Well, here I am.'

"And they said, 'We don't have a Sunday school teacher and we'd like to have you for our teacher.'

"I said, 'Oh, I don't know a thing in the world about teaching adults.' So I set there and they looked at me and I looked at them. We looked back and forth at one another. And I said, 'I tell you what I'll do. I'll pray with you a week and give you an answer next Sunday.'

"They said, 'We'll be glad to pray with you but we've already elected you this morning.' And so I served six years in there, and I had two light heart attacks and I had to give them up. And then I went to the TEL class, that stands for Timothy, Eunice, and Lois. That's the elderly mothers and ladies. They elected me as their secretary. I was their secretary just a short time and they elected me president, and then they elected me as teacher of the class. And I served with the help of God—I give him all the praise and the glory of it—for twenty-five years. And the doctor asked me to resign because of my heart condition."

"A Many of a Knot"

In 1933 or 1934 a major change invaded the spool room at Poe Mill, where Lora worked. "They put in what they call the Barber-Colman spoolers and warpers. And I worked on the Barber-Colman spoolers. They were speeded up and you had to work pretty fast. You had to work faster [than on the older spoolers]. You'd be tired to death. . . . Yes, really, you would."

The introduction of the Barber-Colman automatic spooler and high-speed warper was one of the most important technological innovations in the American textile industry in the years between World Wars I and II.[24] In the sequence of processes in a mill, spooling and warping come just after spinning and before weaving. In the spooling and warping process, numerous short threads are combined continuously into fewer long ones, then wound side by side, by the hundreds and then thousands of threads, onto huge rollers called beams.

The new system speeded the process of warp preparation while it significantly reduced the number of workers previously required in this area of the mill. A Bureau of Labor Statistics study of mechanical changes in the cotton textile industry from 1910 to 1936 concluded that, of all departments in the mill, "the largest productivity increase was made possible in the spooling and warping department" due to the introduction of the Barber-Colman equipment. "The possible decrease in man-hour requirements for this department in 1936, as against 1910, ranged from 54.5 percent in carded-filling sateen to 63.9 percent in combed broadcloth."[25]

Lora League met her future husband, Edward Wright, in the spool room. Eventually Ed became a fixer of the Barber-Colman equipment at Poe Mill, but he had begun work as a spinning doffer, bringing the warp yarn spun on bobbins that contained two or three thousand yards and "pouring" these bobbins into the troughs beneath Lora's spooling frame. Before the introduction of automatic spoolers, Lora creeled (loaded) the bobbins of yarn onto the

Advertisement for Barber-Colman automatic spoolers and high-speed warpers. (Reproduced from the *Southern Textile Bulletin*, 15 January 1925)

frame and, using a mechanical hand-knotter strapped around her left hand, tied the ends of bobbin yarn to be wound onto large spools. One spool held six to ten bobbins of yarn. One frame wound several dozen spools at a time. Lora walked along the sides of two frames looking for broken threads, creeling bobbins and doffing (unloading) full spools. While she used her right hand to hold and change bobbins and spools, the flip of her left thumb against the small trigger on the mechanical knotter tied loose ends together. In time the knotter's trigger wore a permanent indentation across her thumbnail. "I worked that knotter ever since I was twelve years old until they put in the Barber-Colman automatic spoolers. Law me, I've tied a many, a many, a many, a many of a knot.

"When I first went to work, the woman that taught me how to spool showed me how to make gloves to protect my fingers on those old type spoolers. You had to wrap your fingers, especially when it was rainy weather, to keep them from being cut by the moving metal when you went to clean the lint off or stop the spoolers.

"Back then we worked eleven hours a day. But we had some time to rest. When we would catch up, spool all the yarn that was there, we'd rest and wait for more yarn. Sometimes it'd be half an hour till they doffed the yarn off of the spinning frame. Once or twice a day, the yarn boy would take a blowing machine and come and blow the lint off the spoolers. Sometimes that would take thirty minutes.

"It was a dusty job, but now I can't say that the dust affected me or anybody in the spooler or spinning room. Now in the carding room, I was talking with a Mr. Bain this morning that had worked in the card room and he had brown lung. There was a lot more dust down there in the carding room.

"Sixteen years ago when I had a full physical in the hospital, Dr. Williams said that I have a touch of emphysema. And now, I don't know that it was caused from that at all. I just couldn't say. Because I was short of breath, but I don't know that it was caused from that. Because, see, I hadn't worked since 1939, and that was in 1963."

With the introduction of the Barber-Colman automatic equipment, the mill "hands" who remained to operate it took a further step—in an already narrowed space—toward becoming unskilled machine tenders. The new-style spooler (sometimes called a winder) resembled the old one in many ways. It consisted of a frame with a series of several dozen swinging metal arms mounted along its sides. Instead of winding yarn from bobbins onto spools, however, each of the arms supported a starter or "cheese" core, named for the hoop-cheese shape of the completed yarn "package." Bobbins were wound onto the cores at a rate of twelve hundred yards per minute, compared with two hundred yards per minute on the old spoolers.[26] Spooler tenders like Lora were paid by the cheese.

Mounted on the top of the spooler frame was a single large mechanical arm known as the traveler, the disciplinarian of the new system. The traveler moved automatically along a track that carried it around the frame on a precisely timed journey. The traveler tied together cheese ends (threads) and bobbin ends; took up slack yarn in order to prevent kinks; ejected empty bobbins and positioned the new ones; measured the size of each cheese as it was filled; and stopped winding as the cheese reached its maximum diameter.

The spooler tender's job now became one of staying ahead of the traveler, putting full bobbins into place at the rate of twenty a minute, putting the bobbin end (thread) into position for the traveler to tie it to the cheese, and replacing full cheeses with empty cores. The spooler tender took the full cheeses off the spooler frame and placed them on a cart which was pushed by a warper tender into the warp room.

In warping, three to four hundred cheeses were spun off simultaneously, side by side, onto a cylindrical beam. The Barber-Colman high-speed warper performed this job at the rate of 350 to 900 yards per minute, depending on the size and type of yarn, replacing the old warper speed of about fifty yards per minute.[27] Or, in other words, "after the spools [cheeses] are filled they are taken to the warpers and placed in the warper creel which is a V-shaped frame holding about four hundred spools. A thread from each spool runs through proper combs and thread detectors to a large spool known as a beam. The threads are wound on this beam in a sheet."[28]

From the perspective of the machinery manufacturers, their engineers, and their publicists, the new spooling and warping system had arrived just in time to give the "far-sighted mill man . . . every possible advantage during the period of keen competition which seems to be ahead of the textile industry." Barber-Colman engineer B. A. Peterson pointed out that:

In a Southern mill whose spooling and warping machinery is fairly modern and in good condition the advantages obtained by the installation of Barber-Colman spoolers and warpers briefly consist of

A saving of one-half of the hands employed.

A saving in mill village expense.

A saving of one-half the spooling and warping cost.

A saving of one-quarter to one-half the yarn in process.

A saving of one-half the floor space.

A saving of one-tenth the weavers' wages or its equivalent. [The reduction in kinking resulted in less breakage and knotting at the loom.]
A saving of weave room expense.
An increase in weave room production.[29]

In a speech to the Birmingham meeting of the Southern Textile Association in 1927, Fred Still, superintendent of the Victor Plant at Greer, South Carolina, observed how difficult it was "to get spooler girls who will observe sufficient care to insure elimination of kinks," but that with the Barber-Colman system "the human element is eliminated and our tests show about 90 percent less spooler kinks." He also noted that "when the cheeses are full the spooler automatically throws them back, refusing to wind additional yarn. This feature is highly desirable, eliminating the human element of judging when to take off the cheeses."[30]

Following the lead of such men as engineer Peterson and superintendent Still, up-to-date mill owners shifted the responsibility for "the elimination of the human element" away from themselves and onto such ostensibly neutral forces as market competition and technological innovation. In the midst of a textile depression, with a large and growing number of unemployed, manufacturers' discussions of change centered not on the condition of workers, but on how to achieve rapid innovation: "We had a little trouble to get the girls accustomed to the winders after leaving the spoolers, but I do not think it was any different than we always have when we try to introduce new ideas or new machinery."[31]

"On the old spoolers," says Edward Wright, "they had thirty-nine spooler hands. When they put in the Barber-Colman spoolers, they didn't use but six. That was thirty-three hands they cut out."

Because of her speed, her compliant attitude, and her nearly twenty years' faithful service, Lora Wright was one of the workers kept by Poe Mill to run the new spoolers. She stood the pace for six years before her health broke in 1939. She received no pension from the mill. Ed Wright was moved into the less stressful job of spooler fixer. He retired in 1970, also without a pension.

"Well, you see," Lora says, "the traveler would come around and it would pick up the thread of the bobbin."

"Took it about three or four minutes to get around," adds Edward.

"And I had to fill up the pockets above nine troughs with full bobbins," says Lora. "The traveler would tie the bobbin ends to the ends from the cheese. And I would also take off full cheeses and put the starters on. Then the traveler would come around and it would tie up.

Lora League Wright at her home in the Poe Mill village, Greenville, S.C.,
1979. Photo by Allen Tullos.

"Just the same thing, over and over and over and over. But if you felt good,
why you didn't mind, it wasn't monotonous. You didn't mind at all. But if you
wasn't feeling up to par, why sometimes it did get aggravating."

"And them cheese, you'd better get your hands out of the way," Edward
says. "It comes off of that drum and hits you, it'd take the skin off. It'd burn
and take the skin off."

"But really," says Lora, "we didn't have to work as hard on the old spoolers
as we did on the Barber-Colman spoolers. Because it just didn't require it."

"You had to work faster on the Barber-Colman."

"You did," agrees Lora. "Now sometimes I would get all of my ends put up,
ready, all of this ready for the traveler to come around and then maybe I could
rest two or three minutes, or five minutes. I could go get me a drink of water
and I'd come back. And then sometimes . . . it was just according to how the
work run, whether the thread was good and stout. Then the work would run
better. But if the threads were not stout, why then they would break back,
break back.

"We had about fifteen minutes to eat lunch. And they would give you the
privilege of going to the rest room.

"Your shoulders and arms would get tired. And sometimes your back would be a little bit tired. Because I'd be reaching up to take off those cheese and to put the starters on. All that reaching up.

"I don't know whether it affected me or not, but I know that I had trouble with my heart. But I was a heart patient even before, but nothing like until after I retired.

"I had to retire because of my nerves. And then I just didn't have strength and I had these weak spells.

"I tell you, it was a strain to work on these spoolers. Because that traveler run around about every three minutes."

· 6 ·

Ethel Hilliard: A Pilgrim's Progress

I used to talk in my sleep. Oh law, I used to get out and pull. My mammy visited us one time and I got up one night and pulled the bed way out in the floor and her in it. She said, "You fool you!" Yeah, I just pulled.

We was down there in Frogtown at Cumnock. And she come down there in a blaze of dust. She was in the bed. And I just got up a-walking. I just pulled the bed way out in the floor.

—Ethel Hilliard

No one whom I interviewed in the Carolina Piedmont more eloquently, meticulously, and painfully mapped the cultural landscape where habits of industry, the factory regime, fatherly authority, and motherly determination met than did Ethel Hilliard of Burlington, North Carolina. This chapter is her oral autobiography. With a poet's ear for language and a storyteller's long memory, acknowledged by her mill-village neighbors as the person "you be sure to talk with if you want to know how things were," Ethel Hilliard narrates a class and gender history through the telling detail of the everyday. From the poverty of a backwoods mining town, to a brief sojourn in an Ohio shoe factory, to years passed in J. Spencer Love's Piedmont Heights textile mill, Hilliard chronicles a long life of hard physical labor, the raising of many children, a tortured marriage, and her family's year-by-year survival. As she ranges from the harrowing to the hilarious, Ethel Hilliard's excruciating self-scrutiny illuminates her life and times, suggesting, almost allegorically, the contours of temperament and moral choice that were faced by many in her generation of white, working-class, Piedmont women.[1]

"They Had to Work like Men"

But one thing back then, I know the first car. Do you remember a Johnson in Death Valley, that rich man? He was the one that was putting money out to run that Russell Mine up there. Mr. Bunker, he managed it and they would come over there in a car. You could hear that thing for a mile before it got to you. It looked like a buggy with two lights and everybody was running to the road to see it. That was the first car I ever seen. We just thought a thing like that was something. And it was too.

Then, I think the first airplane that I'd seen was when we lived in Cumnock, cause their gas give out and it landed in the field down below us. It looked like that Lindbergh. My husband went down there. I didn't. I was busy.

And I remember before there was any radios, we was in Goldston. There's a man had one and you had to listen at it with earphones. But I, to tell you the truth, I get to talking about it, I feel like I'm getting old. I will be eighty in November [1979].

I was born there in Eldorado, North Carolina—Montgomery County—a little mining town, in 1899. It had three gold mines and a copper lead. But one time, while I was little, Eldorado had a millinery shop, they had a drug store, they had a doctor there, they had a shoe shop, tanyard. But it just got to going down. And the doctor moved out. They went out of that business where they sold hats. And it just went down till there was just a wide place in the road, it's about all there is. But that's pretty land around there.

When my daddy married my momma, my grandparents was dead. All I know about them—my momma's people, the Safleys, lived in Stanly County, and my daddy's, the Harrises, where I was raised they'd always been there. I never heard tell of them living nowhere else but Montgomery County.

They called my daddy Uncle Leonard. Then there was a nephew they named after him. They called him Little Leonard. I reckon all the Harrises are bound to be kin some way or another through there. My sister married a Russell, and I married a Hilliard, and he was the second Hilliard I ever heard tell of. Now, I've said, the woods is full of them. And them Russells—she had nine children and I had ten. She lost two or three of hers but I ain't lost but one of mine. But I tell you I've been lucky not to.

Corella was my mother's name. They called her Aunt Rella. Aunt Rella and Uncle Leonard.

There come a cyclone through Eldorado one time. And I reckon that's the only one that ever did. But next morning them Mullinexes down there missed their chickens, heard the rooster crowing way down on Buck Mountain, toward Troy. It blowed that rooster plumb down there on that mountain. They got a big tower down there, it's a high thing. My mammy went over there and climbed it plumb to the top. I think she put her name up there or something. And she was getting old too.

She come down here and she wore her bonnet. Come down here, went over to the airport and got in that plane and rode like nobody's business, and I wouldn't a-got in it. Oh, she was just happy as a lark, and weren't scared a bit in the world. I don't know how many rounds he took her. I believe he charged about a dollar a trip around, the riding people over there. I didn't think she'd do it but she did.

My mother did a lot of work. She never stopped. Her folks had a lot of land over there and farmed. But they had to work like men after Grandpa died. There weren't nothing there but women and one boy. And Uncle Charlie weren't big enough to do nothing. He was a baby. There was Grandma and Momma and Aunt Lou, Aunt Lizzie and Aunt Addie.

Grandpa was in the [Civil] War. He got a minié ball under his shoulders that they never took out. That's what killed him.

I never knowed one of them to be sick and I ain't joking. I told them that at Duke Hospital and they couldn't believe it. They said they weren't joking. I said, "I'm not either."

They said, "Well, what killed them?"

I said, "He had that under his shoulder blade that killed him and her cousin drunk cider he had put in a tin tub and that killed him. And my mammy worked herself to death."

Momma used to cut and bind wheat—I've bound wheat too—and she used to plow before she married. I tried it one time and the old horse wouldn't go for me. And I couldn't hold the plow in the ground. She didn't mind taking a saw and going up a tree and trimming it. They kept cows, made syrup, had to live on their own over there. But I reckon they *did* want to get away. I reckon they wanted homes of their own.

My daddy was a right smart older than Momma. I don't know how much, maybe thirty years. They met going to associations, Primitive Baptist. My daddy was a Methodist but back then everybody went to everybody's church. He'd go over there to their associations and meetings in Stanly County. He got acquainted with all of them, go there and eat, you know, and I reckon he got stuck on her. He was a good man and her parents knowed it. Her people thought so much of my daddy.

My momma was a good woman and she was smart and worked hard. But I've often wondered why she would marry an old man. She was a pretty woman when she was young. Why her hair, she'd just sit down on it. Black, great long hair. And prettiest blue eyes—Elizabeth Taylor didn't have nothing on them. I've wondered many times why she married an old man with a crowd of younguns. She did like another man and they liked to have got married. She's told me about it. I don't know why they didn't. I believe he died.

My daddy was married twice. He had seven children by the first wife and two by the last, by my momma. Me and my sister Lola was all she had, but she raised them other children. Lola's still living up there yet, ain't never left there.

One of the neighbor women got sick with typhoid fever and they said she couldn't get well. They lived in Pekin, down below Troy. She begged for Mammy to take her children and keep them and look after them. She had two boys. One was a little baby the same age as me. My momma weren't no kin to this woman but was there waiting on her. The woman knowed how Momma was and that she'd take care of them. And she raised them two with us till they was eight and ten years old. Me and Dolan was a baby together. Me and him nursed the same time. Then their father remarried and took them back. We cried all that day. They were just like brothers to us. It was like pulling eyeteeth.

My daddy had 570-some acres of land there on them mountains towards Badin. Most of it in timber. We lived in a log house. The logs was as wide as that table and daubed with mud and sealed. I'm telling you there weren't no wind got in that thing. It was warm.

It was a good life, but we didn't know it then. We didn't think we had *nothing*. You know, we didn't have rugs on the floor. People didn't have things like that. We had our cows, we had our horses, we had our plows, we had our wagons.

And I didn't get nothing. I was under age and my husband sold it to the rest of them. The only reason we got a house I reckon. But he sold it for mighty near nothing. Now it's hard to tell that. That man has told me to keep my mouth shut. You see I was under age and didn't know that Neil had been put in as my guardian, but he had. My mother turned it over to him when we got married. I didn't have no say-so in it. I was almost seventeen and he was on towards thirty—about twelve years older than me.

I think people should marry near their own age. I learned that. People with too much difference in age don't see alike. One's got to take and give in and the other one's got to and they don't see things alike every time.

But I don't know as Daddy and Momma ever had any trouble. If they did, they kept it away from us. But he'd pout. He'd just sit down and not speak. It was just the way he had. You'd never know what it was all about, but he'd pout in spite of creation. And she would worry. She didn't know what was the matter, nor nobody else. And he didn't have no right to pout at her. But that's the worst thing I ever known him to do.

My sister did the same. One time I went up there and some of them said something about her pouting. I said, "Lola, you don't do that, do you?"

She said, "Yes, I do too."

I said, "Well, what are you pouting at?"

She said, "I don't know."

I reckon she got it from him. But boy, I never did pout. I'd talk about them or something like that, but I didn't pout.

We used to have a covered wagon we'd go to Grandma's in. They'd put us on the back of that wagon, spread a quilt over it, and us younguns had the best ride. It'd take just about half a day to go over there. They had a flat over there on the Yadkin River, and they'd drive in on that thing. They had cables up a wire, that carried you across. I was scared to death that them horses would get scared on there. Daddy'd get out and hold them.

Well, sometimes I think I'd love to be back in them days. I'd love to be back if I knowed what I know now, dodge a lot of trouble I've had.

We'd go on over to Grandma's and you could smell the coffee and ham cooking. Smelled better than it did at home. But they had open coffee pots then. These here percolators don't make good coffee.

Grandma was the talkingest woman I ever heard in my life. Sort of growl and groan with it. She sure could talk. They'd get together, you'd think they hadn't seen one another in ten years. That's the way they was, all the grannies talking at one time.

My daddy worked in a tanyard, grinding tanbark. He'd get his clothes and hands stained up. He couldn't get it off. Once a drummer come there at the store and looked at him and said, "You're the dirtiest man I ever saw."

And Daddy said, "Thank God it's all on the outside."

Daddy read his Bible every morning until breakfast was ready. And he conducted prayer meeting every Wednesday night for years down there at the Methodist church. There was two Methodist churches and a Primitive Baptist and a Missionary Baptist over there. They all got along together.

Everybody had their own church and their own meetings. But when they had a revival, everybody would go to the other fellow's church. It ain't the building. It's what you got in here, what you are. The church anyhow is God's people. The church is what He's going to rapture when He comes.

Me and my sister used to go to singing schools. I can't call up a hog now. They'd hold them at a church several days every summer. Charlie Cranford, a preacher, taught us the seven shapes of notes and what they was, the lines and the spaces, the flats and the sharps. I knew all that but I just never could keep time like I wanted to with it. I couldn't get the hang of it.

They had all-day dinners at the Methodists', and the Baptists would come and bring a basket. When they'd have it at the Baptists', the Methodists would come. The most I ever remember about the Primitive Baptists, you'd go to their meeting and be hungry. They'd just keep a-calling up another preacher to preach at dinner. Sometimes it'd be five or six that would speak. "Elder so-and-so is going to speak next," and it looked to me like they never would quit talking.

When we used to go to church up there, women and men didn't sit together. All of the women sat on the right-hand side and all the men sat on the left. When I first began to see a man sit beside a woman in church I thought it was awful. I'd never known nothing else but that, never heard it explained, nor don't know why they done it.

The children had to sit in front and wouldn't dare look back. I wouldn't no more look back if anybody come in or nothing like that. And, before or after service, we weren't allowed to get up in that pulpit and run over that church. We had to respect that place and other people's children did too. We knowed when we went in we was going to have to sit down, be still and be quiet.

We played ball on Saturday and we played tag and dropping the handker-chief behind. But we didn't play no ball on Sunday and there weren't no stores open on Sunday. We never was allowed to go nowhere much and if we went anywhere, we was timed. If you didn't come home at a certain time, she'd come after you with a hickory.

They believed in children minding and respecting their parents. They made us respect them. I loved my momma better than anything in the world and she's whipped me many a time. And when she promised us a whipping, we got it. She'd wait a few days and we dreaded that worse than we did taking it.

She never missed. And she didn't hit us with a strop, she didn't hit us with a board, and she didn't slap us with her hands. She had a peach tree right at the edge of the porch and it had keen little branches. She would get one of them off and burn your legs up. When I learned to jump rope at school and got so that I jumped that switch, she'd put my head between her legs and whip me.

And do you know what? Today I blame a lot of this way children are doing with the parents at home. You got to start them in the cradle. Let them know what's right and what's wrong. They're born, they don't know. They don't know if you don't tell them. But if you've ever taught them and ground it into them the right thing, they won't depart from it when they get older. It'll stay in them. I've raised eleven children and there ain't a one of them that I'd be afraid if you set your pocketbook down and went through here it'd never be bothered. I know them, they wouldn't touch it. And I'm not bragging. But you've got to teach a child, and you have to start at the cradle. Now I've had people come here and bring their children and the first thing that you know, they'd be in this drawer and that drawer, they'd be in my sewing machine. I never would allow nothing like that.

We had to "Mister" and "Miss" everybody and "Uncle" and "Aunt" the niggers. There weren't but two colored families around there. An old man and his wife lived down on the Uwharrie River. And there come the biggest— I reckon you call it an April freshet—these rains in the spring. That river would get up. One time it got up so high some of them went down there to see about them. It'd done gone up into their house. If they hadn't got them out, they'd a drowned in it. Cause they was real old.

I got a lot of whippings. I was full of mischief when I was little.

We had company one night. My sister had been gone for about a week helping a woman up above there do something. And there come a little calf there while she was gone. The very day she come home, we had company that night. I went out, the moon was a-shining, and I got that calf and brought him in the house and booed him at her. Momma gave me a whipping for that.

A preacher would come from way off to the Baptist church for a week. They'd go to our house and stay all night. My mammy fed more preachers than you could shake a stick at.

We had a corn shucking one time when Avery Hill was the preacher. And it came time to sit down at the table. Well, the children didn't eat until the older people eat.

They put Avery at the table right between me and my sister and asked him to ask the blessing. And when he prayed, he sung. He sung the prayer. He didn't say it like everybody else. My sister and I got tickled—if you think of getting tickled where you can't laugh. And I was punching her with my foot.

Afterwards I told her, "Didn't you notice it when I punched you?"

She said, "You never punched me."

It was *his* feet I was punching. I hated that.

Preachers expected to be fed. They thought they needed better. But they are just servants of God that's all. But they did eat at our house a lot.

One time they said—now this was before I knowed anything about it. They had the preacher there for dinner. One of the first children, little boys, that was by the first wife, said he got over behind the stove while they ate (they made him wait). And the preacher got done and started to slip his chair back and they told him to go ahead and eat some more. He said, "I've had a plenty." That youngun spoke and said, "Well, I think you ought to have."

When we was little they give us a toddy every morning before breakfast. They believed it was good for your stomach.

I had a half brother, Charlie, and he did drink bad. Drank himself to death. And he give me some one time and got me drunk. Now this ain't no lie. I'm ashamed of it but I don't feel guilty about it because I was little. My mammy seen him give me some and she told me if I took another drop what she'd do for me.

She went on about her business. I knowed she'd wear me out. I don't know why I done it. But she said the next thing she knowed I was standing out there just a-dancing and a-laughing. Just acting a fool. She give me a round about that too.

We had one a one-room school, one teacher. And she had each grade in a class. I couldn't hardly wait for dinner time to come, and recess. I just never could stand to be penned up.

The school had a stove and the tin stovepipe went up through the ceiling and out through the loft. The boys had to keep fire in that stove. That old schoolhouse would catch afire around that pipe. I'd see it, but I wouldn't say anything. I hoped it would burn down. I wanted to see that thing burn down. I knew then I wouldn't have to go.

It weren't compulsory, we didn't have to go. They didn't get on you then. But my half brother wanted us to go. He just stayed on our back all the time.

I'd stay out at home a lot of times when I didn't want to go bad enough, but I went more than my sister did. But we went enough. We got around to about the seventh grade. I thought that was the awfulest thing, every day, to have to get ready and get to that schoolhouse and sit there. I never could stand to be bound in like that much.

My sister never did talk so much as I did. You'd never hear of her doing nothing in school, and I had somebody laughing all the time. But I never did get a whipping in school, it's a wonder I hadn't.

One day—there was a boy who went there, well, he was ugly. To tell you the truth, he was just naturally ugly. And his sister was about our age. Well, I was determined to make my sister laugh. You couldn't get her to laugh nor talk nor nothing in school. She wouldn't do nothing. I wrote down on a piece of paper, "Sam Brewer looks like a booger," and give it to her. Instead of throwing it away she put it in her school book.

Well, I think it was that night that Mr. Brewer's folks come to sit till bedtime. We was looking at our lessons and everything, and Jenny his sister come across that and read it and I thought I'd die.

Back one time they said there was a bear that had been seen in the woods around where we lived. And we had a neighbor, Barley Halton, who bragged so much that he weren't afraid of it, he didn't care if one was out. How brave he was. And I heard him. I got tired of it. I thought I'd just see whether he was afraid or not.

They kept their cow in our pasture and he had to come through down at the edge of the field. I knowed at about what time that he'd go get her, every evening. So I went and slipped off down there and got down there behind an old tree before he come back by. After he passed me where I knowed he wouldn't look right at me and see me, I just gave a great big growl. And he stopped. He stopped that cow and he listened. When he did, I give another growl. He said, "Come up Lish." He lit out through the woods and went home and didn't stop till he got there. Like to scared him to death. They was talking about it around there. That he had heard that bear. But I don't think my mammy knowed when she was hearing that that I done it.

I remember Halley's comet. We'd go in the morning, I believe it was about four o'clock, to the kitchen porch and look out thataway and you could see it. I'd about forgot that thing. The tail went up. You'd think it'd come down.

Well they got out up there one time, you know people like that seeing— they don't know what's going to happen. Got out up there one time that the tail was going to drag the ground a certain day. Some of them got scared so bad they didn't know what to do. And I reckon I was scared too, I didn't know.

"My Mammy Weren't Much Afraid"

My momma delivered about three hundred babies. They called her a midwife, but she weren't only a midwife. She didn't even pretend to stop at nothing like that. And I never knowed her to lose a case that she worked with. She done everything there was to be done everywhere. Set bones and doctored people's newborn, or anything. If she seen that there was anything she couldn't control, she'd have them to go get a doctor. Nobody ever knowed what going to a hospital was. I never did either.

She said the first time, when she knowed she had talent to help anything— a chicken broke his leg and she set it. Said you wouldn't have ever known it.

And this done her so much good that from then on, if anything got wrong she wanted to try her hand on it. She learned by reading her doctor books. And then she just had a nature. It was her talent. She went to school when she was a child, but she never went to no college. She just naturally had talent.

She had some sort of license she got from Raleigh. When I was a baby she turned them back in. I asked her one time why she give them up and she said it was cause I come there. She figured she couldn't tend to me and everybody else. But people wouldn't let her alone. They asked her just as much as they ever would. They'd come and bring a buggy and get her and bring her back. My daddy'd say, "Well, if she can help anybody, I want her to help them." But I never did believe he was hardly satisfied with her being gone so much. Sometimes I have known us to meet her on the road and somebody else'd get her before she ever got home. Now that's how they used her up there. Cause that doctor had moved away from there. And she was good.

Sometimes when she'd go anywhere, they'd pay her eight or ten dollars when they come after her. Sometimes she didn't get nothing. She worked like a man. Went out in the cold all the time.

John Henderson's last wife got sick with pneumonia and the doctor couldn't get it broke up. He just gave her up. John knowed about my momma—what she could do. She had raised his two children after his first wife died. He knowed how she was and he went and got her.

She went down there and when she went in the house she thought the heat would burn her face up. She didn't open the windows where the wind was coming in but she opened up the opposite side. So the air could go in and out. Got that room cooled off, and then she went to work on her. That got to breaking loose. She got to spitting up that, and back then they spit in—we called them chambers, they was enamel. Said you could actually hear it when it hit. Momma just told John, "Don't clean none of that out. Just set it somewheres." Said, "You ought to send it to that doctor."

Fanny begin to get better. John called that doctor to come back. He asked her, said, "How did you do it? That's what I was trying to get up all the time."

And them babies. I've seen them bring more than one baby there that looked like they were just about dead. Babies that was little and sick and blue. They'd look blue and whine. They wouldn't nurse. If the weather was cold, she'd just sit down (this way) and lay that baby on her lap (like this) afore the fireplace and rub him. Then she'd take a razor and cut a split in that thick place between the shoulder blades. She work it and rub that baby until she got four or five drops of blood out. Their blood weren't circulating. She'd always get some blood out. Just a few drops was all she wanted. I believe she put a little of the blood in a little milk and give it back to the baby. Best I remember. I thought that was awful gross, but anyhow, them babies got well.

She showed me where to cut them babies if I ever had one like that, but I never did have to do it. I wouldn't a-done it. I might a-carried it to a doctor and had him do it, but I wouldn't try it.

We went to church one night and a baby kept whining, it weren't crying. People carried their babies to church back then. We went home and she said, "I don't know whose baby that was tonight but it ain't going to live." And it didn't. After a few days they heard about this baby was dead, and it was the one they had at the church.

She knowed a lot of herbs that she could pick up and make tea. She'd take this red oak, with thick bark. You get the rough bark off and there's a bark under there you pull up and it's red. She made a tea out of that that'd cure any kind of sore mouth. And she'd make a fine medicine out of green peach tree leaves, make a tea. She used a plant they called lion's heart, but I forgot what it was for. You know the Bible said that herbs was the healer of the nation. God prepared these things if somebody just knowed how to use them.

Every spring we had to take a round of castor oil. In the spring you're backed up, the cold settles in you. And we used to take a little bit of quinine. It was good for your liver. About once a year we'd take quinine for three days, then wait three and take a little more for three days.

People would come get for their animals too. One time somebody had a cow all swelled up and thought she was going to die. A cow meant something to people back then. They sent after my mammy to come. They had fed the cow something they had no business to feed her or she got hold of something. Momma just reached in her pocket and got her knife, just give her a punch, let that air out of her. She wasn't afraid to tackle nothing.

I had thought about being a nurse, but I didn't see no chance of ever being, cause we was just penned up there at that wide place in the road. Troy was the biggest town next to us and there weren't no getting nothing there. I believe I would've enjoyed that. I reckon I got that much after her. She would've made a good one, if she'd had the training. But people back then didn't have the chance of all these things. I wouldn't have never thought of ever going anywhere and train for a nurse. I wouldn't a-knowed where I'd a-went. Might have been Raleigh if it'd been anywhere. I bet it would have been that far off.

We had some school books and her doctor books and we had more than one Bible. We got a paper in the mail once a week from Troy, the *Montgomery*

Herald I believe was the name of it. That's where we got all our news. Didn't have no radio, television, nothing like that. No phone. They read the Bible aloud and prayed every night. And we went to prayer meeting every Wednesday. Most of the time my daddy conducted the prayer meeting.

We had two lamps—that's one of them there. That's her old lamp. We'd take two lamps to the church. I've wondered many times, it's a wonder they hadn't a-fell down with them. And maybe somebody else would bring one. They thought the church was pretty well lit up. They hadn't been used to nothing else. They'd sing and have prayer and then he'd get up and make a talk. And if anybody wanted to say anything, they'd have a chance to do that. I think Mrs. Thare did and people accused her of being a hypocrite.

Mrs. Thare didn't want her children to play with nobody else cause she was the cock of the walk. Her husband run the store. She had too much pride. And pride goes before the fall.

She was better than anybody else. She'd come into church and have on silk and she just rattled as she walked, just rattling. She just had better than anybody else. She had a rug on the floor.

She claimed to be a good Christian, but she didn't have nothing to do with nobody. And she didn't want her younguns with nobody else's. That's not Christianity, that's not the right kind of heart to have. And I ain't judging her nor nothing like that, I'm not talking about her. But that's just what happened, I'm just telling you what happened.

But you let one of her children get sick, and boy, she was glad for my mammy to come down there and us go with her. She couldn't get my mammy there quick enough.

Mrs. Thare had this baby and her niece come over to help look after it. The house was high off the ground like this one across the street, and it had brick laid down below it. That girl had that baby out on the front porch, toting it on a pillow, and let it roll off on that brick. Well it just like to have killed the little old thing. It weren't but five or six weeks old.

Mrs. Thare rode them up there to get my mother. Momma went down and said the blood was knocked out of its nose, its hip was broke, its legs, its back was just about broke up. She worked that baby over and tied it, fixed it up to a board so it couldn't move. She'd go down there two or three times a day and take it off and change it for Mrs. Thare. And it got well, you'd never notice a thing the matter with it.

When old man Thare was taken sick, they come and got her. She was living by herself then, me and Lola had left and married. He got sick down there one night and they come after her. He was bad off.

My mammy said she weren't much afraid but there was animals in them woods down there. Some called them catamounts. They had been known to jump out of trees. She weren't so afraid, but she just didn't feel right to go by herself much. But she got ready. They went along back down there to him. She said as she went along that hilly washed path a light followed her feet. I don't believe she'd lie. She said she seen every step she took in that road. I've heard her tell that more than one time. A higher power had to lead her path. She said she seen every step she took in that road. She said when she got there it left. He didn't live but a little bit.

She never stayed all night unless she had to. But a lot of times she didn't get no sleep. And maybe go there and back in one night and have to start her day's work. She really held out good to go through all she did.

Dipped her snuff. That's how come to use it. I thought it looked like it was the best stuff I ever seen in my life. Me and some of the girls ran there and got to stealing it and carrying it to school. They didn't know we dipped it. We'd go out at recess in the woods and dip our snuff. I don't know when she ever caught up with it, but she didn't say too much about it. She'd done it before me anyhow. You can't say much when you do it before anyone.

My daddy chewed tobacco. I'd go with him out to the woodpile and he'd slip me a little twist. He knowed how bad I wanted it. But she'd whip me if she caught me chewing tobacco.

Passing the Time in Eldorado

Daddy had these vats for tanning cow and sheep skins. He'd have lime water in the first vat. He'd put the skins in there raw and let them stay till after it'd eat their hair. Then he'd take them out and he had a block that was slanted. He'd rake every bit of that water off them. Then he'd put them over in the branch water to soak again. I've forgot how many days he'd let them soak. People killed a lot of beef back then. That's all the meat they had. There was a lot of hides up there.

When he'd take them out of the branch water, he had a mill under that shelter and he had a mule that'd grind red oak bark. He put that bark in the next vat full of water. He'd throw the skins in that tan water and let them soak so many days. Then he'd rinse them again and dry them. He'd roll those skins up and carry them up to old man Thare's store. Uncle Lee Harris would make some good shoes out of them. They weren't so pretty, but we thought they was. Had a brass tip on the toe to keep from stumping rocks. We wouldn't have none without that.

Uncle Lee was a Baptist preacher. Green Harris run the shoe shop and half-soled shoes and Uncle Lee made shoes. There was several things going there one time, but they sure has thinned out.

My daddy worked for Old Man Thare. He didn't have to do that. He had plenty to do with, if he'd got rid of some of that timber and stuff. And when he died they divided that up. Oh, that lumber was really bringing something. They was just buying new cars. Neal sold my part to them. I didn't get nothing.

Corn shuckings and wheat thrashings—well we just had the time of our life then cause that was about all the things we had to go to besides church. We'd haul all the corn up and just put it in a long pile. Just usually crooked it around. I don't know why they crooked it that way unless they'd throw the corn in that hollow and it'd be right at the crib door. Everybody would come that had corn. Then everybody would go to their house and shuck theirs. They'd always have a big supper. Apple pies, pumpkin custards.

They'd just get all around that pile and everybody would just shuck it and throw the shucks behind. Then we had all of them shucks to do away with. Put a lot of them in the cow stables where it was muddy.

We'd stack the hay, the straw, and put sweet potatoes back under that straw and pack it in there. They'd keep in the winter. You can put a watermelon down in your wheat bin, keep it till Christmas.

They'd thrash the wheat and then sack it and take it to the mill and swap it for flour or either they'd grind it while you're there. One time they was all busy and sent me to the mill. I took the horse and buggy. The horse didn't run away with me but I pulled her lines and made the singletree hit her heels. She trotted to get out of the way and as she went the buggy kept a-going and she got to loping. When she did, I jumped out. She come right up on the hitching stall at the mill like she always did. I came along after while walking.

When we was thrashing wheat or shucking corn, we'd have dances every night. My daddy and mammy'd go to somebody's house and Uncle Jim would pick the banjo. And boy they could do that Virginia Reel too. I think that's what you called it when they go around and get hold of their hands.

Them Harrises up there was full of music. All of them was good at music. They'd go to different ones' houses every once in a while and have a dance like that. They didn't think it was no harm, said nothing about it. But now some people think something like that's awful. Well, some of them is awful, but like they was a-doing, it weren't bad. It was right smart of fun. Just pass time. Weren't nothing else up there.

Sometimes some old man come through with some kind of a little old show, and it weren't nothing but everybody'd walk to it to see. And when them there Bunker men come to that mine in that little old car, everybody was at their front door when they heard them coming away up through the woods. You could hear it a mile. It looked like a buggy with two eyes. We hadn't never seen nothing like that.

And the thrashing machine. It had a smokestack and the smoke would just pop. When we heard that thing coming up the hill we knowed it was coming to our house and our heart'd just flutter. We just loved to see that thing come. We just never seen no motor things running like that back then.

"Just Me and My Mother and Lola"

When I was going on sixteen, my daddy died. I found him dead in the yard. He had been swelled up pretty bad and was under a doctor's care. He thought he was getting better and naturally I did too. I don't know what my mammy thought about it, she might have known.

But one Saturday he ate dinner and went out on the front porch and sat down. Me and my sister was washing dishes. He got up after a bit and come back through the hall, going to the back. I went out there to the shelf to wash my hands and seen him laying in the grass. I run to him and he was red black. He had swelled till a button had busted off his shirt, just that quick. I guess he had a heart attack. Back then you didn't know what they had.

When they died you put them on a board on two chairs. You didn't have no undertaker.

We went to the burying in a wagon. They took him in one wagon and the family in the wagon behind them. I don't know what the funeral preaching was about. You know we children didn't pay much attention to things. I hated he was dead, but I wasn't studying what they said. I did love my daddy though. He never hit me in my life. There was no finer than him.

He died in 1916. He was seventy-three. Just me and my mother and Lola was living at home then. Neil was boarding there. He boarded at our house two year before we married. My half-brother, Lin, had married and moved out. He lived right there below us and would do our plowing.

My mother took as many as thirteen boarders at Eldorado, several families did. When they opened that mine, there just weren't nowhere for them to live. They worked two shifts. When one'd come in, they'd take the beds and the other would go out. Some of them would go home on the weekend. They had to live that way until the mine finally built some houses. She charged twelve and a half dollars a month if she didn't do the washing. If she done the washing and ironing, it was thirteen.

We had a mineral spring up there, and that was good water. And we had a big spring we could use water out of. It never did go dry, right under the hill. That was the best water. We had our wash pot and tubs down there. It took a lot of washing to keep up something like that.

There was a big crawfish lived in the spring. They wouldn't let us fool with him. They said he kept the vein open. I was scared of it.

And we'd tote water about a half-mile up the hill from the spring. All that cooking to do and washing vegetables and bathing. And washing dishes. I hated that job worse than anything I ever done. If water gave out at the house, you had to go to the spring at night.

And burned wood in the cookstove. That was the best cooking you ever had. We had our chickens. Sometimes she'd fry them and make gravy, but most of the time she'd cook chicken pies. (I go around and try to buy chicken pie sometime and they got that chicken chipped up in it. I can't hardly stand that way.) She'd boil the chicken then lay it out over a pan, put dough on it and then lay another row of chicken and put more dough on it and butter and salt and pepper. Then put that juice in there, put a top on it and sit in the stove.

We had beef. Somebody'd engage a cow and we'd just get so many pounds when they killed it. We killed our own hogs. Had ham, middling meat, shoulder, and made sausage. Middling meat was the side meat with a streak of lean left in it. Now they pull all that out.

Momma could salt meat better than anybody I've ever seen. She didn't put too much on it. Neil just covered it up and let it melt. His was too salty.

We'd save our hams and shoulders and about Easter we'd cut the first one. It'd be just about right. And we'd dye Easter eggs. You couldn't buy no dye, but Mama'd get broom straw and cedar limbs and boil them. Dyed pretty eggs. They'd look tan and spotted. Looked sort of like a guinea egg. And we had eggs. I don't know what she done that with. It was enough color to know you had your Easter egg dyed.

We set our rabbit gums. I used to love rabbits. You'd go along by the rail fence down below the field below the house and see where they made their path. They'd gnaw the rail. Set your gums and right near to morning you'd have a rabbit.

She used to boil squirrels and rabbits before she'd fry them. Make squirrel stew. I reckon she might've fried a rabbit sometimes, but she usually boiled it. She didn't fry it raw like chicken.

There were plenty of deer up there in them woods and some people did kill them, but we never did. We had turkeys. We had guineas. We had some kind of meat all the time. Guineas are harder to cook than a chicken. But they're pretty ain't they? I love to hear them holler. I was outdoors here the other day in the garden and I heard the turtle doves. I said, "It's time to plant corn." We always done that.

We had several kinds of apples for pies and for eating. Yellow, red, sour, sweet. And peaches. And cherry trees. We had about four or five stands of bees. My mammy would go out there and rob them to get honey with comb in it. She wouldn't let us go about them.

We'd can all kinds of vegetables—beets, beans, English peas. Anything out of the garden that we could save. She had that old smokehouse lined.

We made kraut in a wooden barrel. Back in that time you could buy barrels, but you never hardly ever seen a pasteboard box. Nor a paper sack, nor nothing like that. But she had her kraut barrel and she had a hoe. That's what everybody used. You straightened out the hoe and sharpened it real sharp, cut the cabbage and just kept cutting it and putting it in the barrel. And add salt. She didn't put no water, unless there wasn't enough brine to cover it, then she'd add a little water.

We'd take big cabbage leaves and wash them and put them on top. Then put on something big enough to cover that, like a plate. And then she had a big white rock she kept washed to lay on that plate so the brine wouldn't get off. It kept that plate mashed down. And tie a cloth over the top. It wouldn't do to leave it open. The flies would ruin it.

You'd eat kraut with fried meat, or fry it in a little grease. I still love kraut. But I don't like that's cut up in strings. I like the chopped kraut. We ate it with our sausage at home.

She'd make her own yeast to make light bread and loaf bread. She'd take some corn meal and mash in some Irish potatoes to get it started. The older it got the more like yeast it was. You could just smell them loaves cooking all over the place.

We used to make sassafras tea and drink it at the table. Set it in the milk box and get it cold. Didn't have no ice. We had a milk box in the ground, had it lined.

And make locust beer. You get these locusts, get good ones out of the woods off a locust tree. Put straw in the bottom of your jar and put corn meal and a layer of locusts. And water. In a few days it would get to sparkling.

Me and my sister Lola carried lunches to the miners that boarded with us. We'd carry them every day. You've seen these gallon buckets with lids on them. They had a ring around the groove like a can and had a lid fit down on it like a pot, and a handle. We'd take two sticks and hang them buckets on them sticks and one would get forward and the other get behind and we'd take them to the Russell mine first, come back, and then she'd fix more and we'd take them to the Dark Springs mine. There where the water washed gold down the hill. About an hour and a half of walking. Go through the pasture of cows to come home. They never did bother us though.

When we had them boarders the post office was way down below us. The mailman would come up the road going up towards Denton every day. One time Momma had a letter or something she wanted to mail, and she sent me down there to wait for him. He was supposed to come along at three o'clock. I didn't want to sit there that long. I got tired of waiting so I slipped in the house and turned the clock hand up.

That night after them boarders ate dinner they were sitting around the fire. They hadn't been around there long till eight o'clock come. They knowed that something was wrong. And my mammy kept going on, she didn't know what changed the clock like that. And she would ask me and I'd say, "I never turned that clock up."

And she said, "Now you know if you lie to me you know what you'll get."

I said, "I know it, but I didn't do it." I didn't turn the clock up, I turned that hand up.

I finally told her. I don't think she whipped me for that though. I think she thought that was funny. She never did whip us and abuse us, but now, she would whip you with a hickory and you didn't have to have but one to behave awhile either.

"I Wanted to Get Away from up There"

Neil—Cornelius—boarded at our house about two years. And he said if he hadn't boarded there and known who he was marrying, he wouldn't-a never married. He said he done set his head he'd never marry. But he said he knowed what I was and who I was. He was there enough to know everybody that knowed me and knowed where I was raised.

He was from Chatham County, down towards Sanford. His daddy died when he was little. They had typhoid fever down in there. His aunt, his daddy's sister, come over there and she had a baby and she was taken down sick and Neil's daddy was taken down sick. They got the doctor. Neil's mother, Mrs. Dennis, said—she married a Dennis last time—she said Neil was let out to play and he come in and crawled over to his daddy on the bed to lay with him. And first thing she knowed, she said he was sick. They all had the typhoid fever.

Neil's daddy and his sister and that baby died. That's three corpses at one time. There was so much fever there they had to break up the family. Aunt Lucy Beal took Neil, I don't know where Zeke stayed, but they divided them

Ethel and Neil Hilliard, Cumnock, N.C., ca. 1921. Neil is holding C
(Cornelius, Jr.) and Ethel holds Blanche. (Courtesy of the Hilliard family)

out. That left her with two children to raise. She come up here to that woolen
mill at Snow Camp and raised them there. Then Neil left home and went
around to Spencer and different places and worked. He met someone who
offered him a job at the mine near where we lived. Then the boss man come
to see if my mammy was boarding. She didn't have no room, but he [the boss]
was her cousin. She told him she'd take Neil and try him. If he could stand it
that we could, I reckon.

He just stayed on there for near about two years. And he really loved her
cooking. Hers was the only chicken he'd eat.

When Daddy died I was between sixteen and seventeen. It was about a
year before I married. I ought to have had my throat cut. I don't think nobody
ought to marry under twenty-five or thirty year old. They don't know what

they're doing. I wanted to get away from up there, that's one thing. I thought I'd get out somewhere and be in a town where they had stuff.

People didn't have clothes then as much as they do now. We had about two everyday dresses and one Sunday dress. We knowed to take care of them too. You could get cloth, if they ever got any, but you had to get it when they got some in. I know a woman give Mammy enough cloth to make me a dress one time. It liked to tickled me to death.

I just wanted to get out and get in a home of my own. I wanted to have something. Get out of that hole up there. You couldn't never get nowhere up there. There just weren't nothing to do.

We used to pick cotton for people. That's the only way you had of making money. You picked a great big sack for twenty-five cents. It looked like you never get the thing filled up. That and bind wheat, pull corn, things like that.

There was a time when there just weren't no mills back then. When they got to hiring women, they were just tickled to death to make a little money. My sister went to Albemarle and worked awhile. She never would let me go. Thought I was too young. To tell the truth, I suppose if I'd had any way to work, I'd never have married. But I did. I didn't think nothing of getting married that young. But I believe he was the only person I ever seen I would a-married. Ain't nobody got along no better than me and him did for a few years after we were married.

I wanted to get out where the people had something. I know now I had more than some of them in town had. But I thought you'd just see more and more people. We used to visit Neil's momma after we married and I'd sit on the front porch and watch the people come out from work and just love to see them pass. Back home there weren't much people and there weren't much traveling on the road. It was a dirt road.

Now a lot of times, people'd come from over towards the river somewhere going down to Eldorado or down to Uwharrie, and then walk. They'd stop at somebody's house and stay all night. They don't think nothing about them coming in and staying all night. And when we went to Grandma's, I remember one time, we went over there and we stopped at somebody's house they knowed and they fixed dinner for us on the road.

That's the way people used to live. Help each other and enjoy seeing each other. People don't get the joy out of life they ought to have.

I've never had enough to make me big-headed towards a neighbor or cared what he had, or jealous of what he had. Now a lot of people is, but that don't bother me. It never did bother me.

We married at home with a magistrate and I always did hate that. Oh, that don't make no difference. Who fixes the paper don't make no difference. You make your vows in the sight of God. They never had no church weddings around there when I growed up, I never heard tell of none.

I was married in September, 1916, and I was seventeen in November. We married in the front room. My sister tried to fix it up. We had a big fireplace, dead black. She went out in the woods and got cedar. Then she made something like a flour or lime paste and mixed it with water and dipped the cedar. Then she put it in the fireplace where it was black, and filled all that over with white and I laughed at it. I laughed at her a-doing it. That's when she ought to have picked me up and whipped me. And I weren't none too big to take it either.

The way Neil proposed was he said he never envied the married till he met me. He'd done made up his mind he'd never marry nobody. But he boarded at our house two year, and he said he knowed what I was.

He said he didn't trust women. Why, I don't know. Running around, I reckon, before I ever knowed him.

He was the only person I ever seen that . . . I don't know why I married him. I didn't have to marry him. I knowed that, and he did, too. But I just thought a lot of him. Whatever I did have with him, though, he killed it. And that's the dead level. You can kill your love.

Public Work

It was dangerous working in the mines. There'd be accidents all along.

One time—you see they drawed this muck out of the mines. Somebody was back here with a machine and had a tipple and pulled that skip up full of mud out of there. Then they'd dump that mud and wash it, for gold. The miners could ride that skip out of the mine, but it was dangerous. It was liable to dump whether it was time or not. It was tricky.

That day, it was payday, and they wanted to go home quick. And all of them but this one man rode that skip and everyone got killed. One man climbed the ladder out and said he heard them as they come back by him, when it dumped. It killed four or five of them.

We stayed there in my daddy's house awhile, and then the mine went down and we had to leave. Neil knew this man, Buck. They used to work together and thought a lot of each other. They wrote to each other and Buck got to asking Neil to come up there and get a job. Work was good up there in them tire factories then, they was just beginning to make them.

So we left home and went to Akron, Ohio, on the train. That's the first time I rode a train. I weren't a bit afraid of it though. And I worked at the Miller and he worked at the Goodyear. That's the first public work I ever done. Neil made five dollars a day, I believe. That was good money back then. I don't believe I drawed that much. He was retreading tires.

I trimmed rubber shoe heels. When they pressed them, it left a little thin thing around all the edge. I had a crooked pair of scissors. I'd take the scissors and run them around the edge. That was my job. I made so much according to what I done. You really could get so you could do that fast. Turn out a lot of work—if I could have got to stay there and work long enough.

I liked that job. But it made my hands so sore they had to do my hands up, using the scissors so much. Skinned up.

We lived at Buck's house and he treated us nice. But his wife was awful. She thought, I reckon because we was from the South, we didn't have no sense. She'd throw off sometimes but I don't remember what she'd say. But I knowed that's what she was wanting to do.

This here woman and her was right thick buddies. One night she said they was going to town after supper to just look and shop around. Did I want to go with them? I said, "Well, I wouldn't mind it." Anyhow, it would be a way of passing off the time.

We went up there and stayed till way after dark. Then when they come home, instead of coming down where it was lit up, they come away out around town on an old back road and was telling me about somebody getting killed in there. They was doing it to scare me. I got the picture, but I didn't say nothing. I just took it.

And she had a sister who lived there, May, who'd walk with me to work every morning. She worked at Miller's too. She hadn't ever been married. We walked a right smart piece to work. We lived on Miller Street. I'll never forget the name of that street. I just wonder how it looks up there now.

May would tell me as we were going to work that she was sorry for me. She said, "I go through the same thing you do." She knowed her sister had a mean principle.

Me and this woman didn't fuss or nothing like that. She was just hateful, aggravating. You just wanted to be away from her when you could.

She would not put enough to eat on the table. Neil would come in, come through the kitchen side at night and get in her bread and stuff and bring me a sandwich upstairs. Make her so mad. He said he knowed I didn't get enough supper. He could get his supper out some. She'd make light bread— she could make it good too—and he'd come in there and slice two great big slices off it, put apple butter on it and bring it upstairs to me.

You know, nobody up there dipped snuff. But I'd have my momma to send me some and I'd get in the room, slip around and dip it.

I was at her house. I couldn't tell her what I thought. But if I had it to do over, I expect I'd get in the road and tell her when I left.

She's dead now though, and I hope she's at rest.

We stayed one winter in Akron. It snowed every day. We just kept thinking we'd get enough to get us a house to ourself. But we could not get ahead. And we didn't neither one have nothing when we married.

Finally Neil said, "I know you're homesick and I know it looks like we ain't getting nowhere. We'll just have to save up enough to get you home, then I'll save up and I'll come home."

When Neil took me to the depot to get the train, Buck came with us. He told me, "I hate to see you leave."

I said, "Well, I'd love to stay if we could get a start here, but we can't stay like this."

He said, "I know it," and he handed me a dollar to get something to eat on the train. I bet she never did know he gave me that dollar.

I got on the train and came on. I had one of these short coats with a pocket here. I stuck my money in there and put it under me and sat down. I was afraid I'd go to sleep.

The railroad come down by some river a long ways and we just started jerking. The train stopped and we just stood and stood and stood. I didn't know what was the matter. I didn't know nobody in there, didn't talk to nobody, strangers. And I was so sleepy I could not stand it.

The train had run off the rail. It hadn't run off the crossties, but it run off the rail. They had to send and get a wrecker to come and put it back on.

He sent me home in time to get to his momma's before midnight. I was supposed to get to Greensboro before twelve o'clock and go out to his mother's. She lived at Revolution. But we stood for two or three hours getting that thing back on the track. It throwed me way after midnight getting to Greensboro.

I fell asleep anyhow and didn't want to. The conductor was dying laughing when he got me awake to get off the train. I'd been talking in my sleep. I used to be bad at that. And I didn't know what I'd said—cause I was mad at that woman. I never had no words with her but I didn't like her.

When we got to Greensboro, the streetcars had quit running. I didn't intend to get a cab and go out there in the night. So I went in the station and took a seat to wait till morning.

I sat there in the depot all night and a cop'd pass that window. I just knowed he was watching me. I didn't know what I'd said to that conductor in my sleep. I thought sure he told that cop to watch me. And every little bit he'd make that round again, and I thought, "Now he sure is watching me."

I'd never been used to police or nothing like that. So, I wasn't going to get no cab out there, I knowed that. And the next morning when the streetcars started running, at six o'clock, I got on and that same cop got on with me. Then I knowed he was watching me. So I went on and he got off at White Oak and I went on up to Revolution and I was telling Neil's momma about it. She said, "Ethel, I know him. He lives out here. He was coming off his duty. He weren't after you." But you see when you're raised up where you never see nothing like that you don't know them things and you do get scared.

When I got to Mrs. Dennis's I was just simply dead to the world. She was ironing in a little room. She had a bed back there. It was quiet and she knowed when they come in to dinner from the mill they wouldn't bother me. She told me, "I'm going to move this ironing board out and you get in that bed and rest."

And I didn't know when they come to dinner from the mill. Mr. Dennis and Gussie, his daughter, worked down at the mill. That night I got up. He'd come in and built a fire. It weren't so cold but it was damp. I was sitting there this side of the fireplace.

He looked at me and said, "Ethel, what's the matter with you?" That scared me.

He said, "Your face is red as a beet." They got to looking at me and finally decided I had the measles. That's one reason I felt so bad. She made me go to bed and stay there. I had to stay a week or two before I could go on home.

Neil, he was still up at Akron. He was going to save money enough to come home. He wrote me a letter and said he had smallpox. They put him in the pesthouse.

Me down here and him up there. It just looked like we just didn't have no way of getting started. But, in about a month and a half, when he got out, he come on home. That's when he got in touch with Billy Hill.

Billy had moved to Cumnock, right this side of Sanford. He was married to Neil's cousin. He came from England and was the superintendent of that Coggins mine in Cumnock. Billy knowed Neil and wanted to give him a job. So Neil went on back down there at the coal mine. That's how come us to go down there.

When we lived at Cumnock, when the mine opened up, there weren't no houses but they had some shanties down in the bend of the Deep River. They used to keep cattle in them, but they fixed it up so that families could move in there until they could get some houses built. We lived there. They called it Frogtown.

I reckon my momma came down to Frogtown to deliver C, my oldest. He was born in April 1918. I never went to the hospital. Blanche was born in Cumnock in 1920 and I believe there was a colored woman at Goldston, Aunt Esther, who delivered her. She'd deliver babies and stay about two weeks, for thirty dollars. She was smart. I don't know what her last name was. All we ever called her was Aunt Esther.

Having a baby didn't scare me. I heard tell of so much of it and seen Momma come in so many times and tell about it. I never thought much of it. We was tickled to death because it was a boy. After we moved to Burlington, I'd have the doctors come, but I never did go to the hospital.

Now Neil bought that piano when I was twenty-one years old. He wanted me to have one. We weren't really able to do that. We hadn't been married that long to go and put out money like that. I never knowed what it was to get up on a cold floor. He'd warm my shoes every morning. But after he had that flu, he just couldn't—it really affected him somehow.

He was scared to death of a doctor. If we had to have one here for the younguns, he didn't say anything about him. Just scared him. He didn't want to hear it. He told me one time he just felt like he ought to go talk to a psychiatrist. I said, "If you feel that way about it, why don't you?" But he never did go. I wished he had. That flu done something to him. He never did get right.

I think it was not too long after Blanche was born that Neil had that bad flu. They used to call it influenza back then. And he like to have died. The whole neighborhood had it the first round [1918] and we didn't none of us have it. I'd cook and he'd carry food to them. They was glad to get anything when they began to get well.

Neil never took the flu that round when they had it so bad. But after, when it come around again, he got it. I didn't have it either time. There'd always be one in the family that didn't get down with it.

I got to Neil that night and he looked like he was going to climb the walls. He was out of his head. I was there with myself and them babies. And foggy, the fog was just as thick.

John Henry Barley had an automobile, first one to have bought a car down in there. I went and got the lantern and lit it, and found his house, got him up and asked him if he'd go and get the doctor. It was about midnight. He took that car and went and got him.

The doctor sat there all night till seven o'clock the next morning. I knowed Neil was bad off, I knowed that, but I didn't know he was as near dead as that doctor thought he was. His fever just dropped like that. He sweated that mattress till the springs rusted. And me young, never knowed nothing about death. I don't know what I'd have done.

When my husband got up, he looked like Abraham Lincoln. You couldn't shave him. He had a beard, and his cheeks was just all—but he never did feel right, he never was right after that. It done something to him. It done something to his nerves. Later, when we come here, we all had to take a— well everybody had to take a TB test. And they said he had scars on his lungs as big as quarters. He never did know when that happened, but I imagine that flu done it, I don't know.

While we were still living down there [1925], this Coal Glen mine across the Deep River from us exploded and killed sixty people. Folks went over there and helped get them all out. Then, not long after that, the Cumnock mine exploded and some more was killed. My husband had just come from work, he worked on the third shift. His job was sitting in the bottom of that mine just to keep that fan from touching, hitting, cause there was so much gas in there. He just got home and got in the bed when that happened. If he hadn't come home when he did, he'd a-been killed. We was living in Goldston then. But we built a house up there. Neil'd go backwards and forwards to work in his car.

Some of our neighbors was killed. That's kind of hard too, when you see your neighbors like that. It ain't too good to be in things like that much.

We was living in Cumnock when they was dividing up that land. My daddy had all that land up there towards Badin. I'd never known nothing else only my daddy had all that land. I never thought about what we'd ever get. There were nine of us—Daddy's first wife had seven and his last wife had two.

Then when me and Neil got married, my momma turned it over to him. I never thought nothing about it cause I'd always known that land was ours.

But then Neil sold it, sold my share of it, to my brother-in-law (my half sister's husband) for three hundred dollars. We never had no trouble when we married till then. Before he sold it to him I told him, "We ought not to get rid of that. We've got a family started and we'll need it one day." And he got mad at me. That's the first time he ever hit me. He kicked me. Then he said he didn't know what made him do that.

I said, "Well, I don't know what made you do it, either." I didn't like it, but I took it. And I took it a long time.

My half brother told him not to sell that land, especially at that price. But Neil wouldn't listen.

I don't know how many acres I would have got, but boy, I can tell you one thing, when they finally sold all of that land it was during the Depression. They was a-buying new automobiles, a-paying for them. And we was sitting here, couldn't get a living, and them just a-splurging on what they'd got up there. And I didn't like it but I took it, because I knowed there was nothing I could do about it.

When we came here and bought this lot and built this house, he wouldn't put my name on the deed. Now this is kind of private. I don't talk this stuff much. It was dirty. And he said he didn't intend to put it on there. But you see, he had my money tied up in it. But I could do without that all right if—I never did want so much from him. I really made my way, I know that. The land is gone and I've just forgot about it and let it go.

But after I come to Burlington, I sent up to Troy. I sent a lawyer up there and told him to look into my daddy's land to see what he had and what had happened. He's the one that told me that she had made him my guardian and that my daddy really had more land than I thought he had.

If it was so I could get it, I was going to get it, cause we needed it in that Depression with all these younguns. But he said there weren't but one thing I could do and I wouldn't want to do that, and I never even asked him nothing else. I knowed what that was.

The mine worked awhile after them people got blowed up but it didn't last too long. I don't know whether they got so they didn't find gold or the ore weren't no account or what. I never did know why it shut down.

Neil's momma lived out here in Burlington and knowed about this lot. She had him to buy it. We left Goldston in 1927, come here and built this ourselves—him and another man built it.

Neil's mother lived right up there in that white house. That's how come us here. When she moved out there that's when the Burlington Mills was coming in. She and Mr. Dennis bought a lot there. They bought that house, then she wrote and told us about this lot. Neil come up here and looked at it. We got it for a hundred dollars. There was only two left, and he wanted to get close to her. We bought it from Mr. Dan Long. He tried his best to get me to buy the one that adjoined this one. He said I could have it for a hundred dollars and just pay it like I wanted to. Raise chickens or anything to pay for it. And I was a fool for not doing it. But back then a dollar didn't come that easy and I was afraid of getting in something—I was always afraid, that was my trouble.

Neil's daddy had died with typhoid fever when he was little. His mother had raised them two boys. She married again. Her and Mr. Dennis met at some association or something. He lived at Revolution in Greensboro, worked in the mill there. She worked at Snow Camp in the woolen mills, but when she married him, she went to Greensboro.

Then they moved here. They had a few cows and sold milk and butter. People on the new mill hill that were working for the Burlington Mill would buy it.

I loved that woman as good as I did my own momma.

I stayed down at Goldston while Neil and Billy Thompson came up here and built the house. We moved in it in 1927, September. It's never leaked a drop. And it's got the same roof we put on it. Neil said if it was going to storm or cyclone, he'd rather be here than anywhere. I don't reckon there's a knot in none of this lumber. It's just the real stuff.

We moved in as soon as we could. We hadn't yet sealed it upstairs. The upstairs was empty and it just roared. That's another trick I played.

Neil would brag about how he weren't scared of things. I had a basket that his mother had given me. She made them out of reeds, and they'd dry. I kept it hanging up in the kitchen on a nail. I told the children one night, I said, "Now, supper I'm going to have some fun. Don't you all say a word." And I got that basket down and tied a long string to it. I took it upstairs and set it up on something.

Neil ate on this side of the table and I ate on this side and the children was all around the table. We was sitting there eating and I gave that string a little tug and you could hear that basket fall. He stopped and said, "What was that?"

I said, "Something upstairs."

When he started back to eating, I'd go to rolling it around my finger again, pulling it across the floor up there. Making the awfullest fuss you ever heard. He jumped up from the table, brave you know, and went up them stair steps. When he did, I come down with that thing and it come by him.

He said, "Where is that basket a-lying?"

I said, "It's sitting over there about that table." I'd stuck it back under the table. I wished I'd hung it back on that nail.

Don't tell me he weren't scared now. He said, "I would swear that thing passed me on them stairs."

I said, "Well, I know it's sitting right there." That's when the younguns got tickled. They had held in pretty good till then. It's the only way he caught me.

It was just like that boy bragging about not being scared of that bear. I was going to find out, and boy he run too. I never was scared of nothing like that.

When we first come here, the old man who built this fireplace was putting in that hearth and he said to my husband, "You may build here but you won't stay here." And Neil asked him why. He said, "This place here is haunted." George Garrison, who lived down the street, said the same thing. Neil was brave, you know. He never was afraid of nothing, to hear him talk.

And this old colored woman on the hill had dug and dug in them woods. She had dug holes as deep as that chair, hunting something. People just hunting for something in there.

But there is something to be heard here: I've heard it. But it don't scare me.

I stayed with a crippled girl here once when Frankie was working. And Zeke was at work, and I'd come home and sit in there and eat my supper. It'd sound just like somebody was walking in heavy boots. I'd go up there and there wouldn't be a thing moving. Neil heard it. He wouldn't own it, but he'd talk about it when there weren't nobody here. And we would find Indian arrowheads when we cleaned up there behind the house.

This sure had the name of being haunted, but I said I hadn't never done nobody no harm and weren't afraid of it. I talked to Neil's momma about it. She was pretty sensible. She read her Bible a lot. She said she didn't know, but she always heard it was unrestful spirits. There was something they wanted, somebody to speak to them, ask them what they wanted. But I never got there in time to speak. If I had I would. Every time I'd get there there weren't nothing. They'd be gone, I reckon.

There's been a couple of times I've heard that toilet flush and nobody about there at all. One of the neighbors got to teasing me about that toilet flushing, telling such tales. And I said, "Well I know it did," and "I heard it."

He said, "It must be that old man who rattles around, that old haint."

I said, "I guess that was him."

But me and Blanche was sitting in there one night looking at the paper. And something went through that hall just like a dry bush, just like it'd fill the whole thing. The awfullest whoosh you ever heard.

And one night we was all in the beds and all at once it sounded like the kitchen door fell on the floor and every dish and knife and fork with it. We thought somebody had got in the house. Neil got up and said, "There ain't nothing done . . . there ain't nothing moved in there." And there weren't. That biggest boy of ours come downstairs and asked us what it was. He said it sounded to him like pouring pinto beans in a tin pan.

I heard that. That did happen and I wouldn't lie about it. But it didn't scare me. Cause if you ain't done nobody no harm, you ain't afraid of them being after you.

One night Neil went to church and carried the children. I don't know how come I'd stayed home but I was sitting there in the dining room listening to the radio and Orson Welles come on and said there was little green men falling. He said there was little green men a-landing up there in—was in Virginia or Pennsylvania?—well, wherever it was. Little green men coming down, landing.

I heard that that night, and I got scared but I stayed still. They said people was just falling down the stairs and breaking their arms. He liked to scared people to death with that thing.

I was sitting in there by myself and when Neil come home I told him about it. And he said, "Did you hear that?"

I said, "Yeah, they sure told it on radio."

We found out though that it was only his pranks. I heard him talking not long ago about that and I thought, "Old fellow, I remember that night too, and you scared me." Cause you don't never know when it comes out on the air like that what is the truth. What he knowed something you didn't know. I think he kind of hated that after he found out people got their arms broke and everything. I was so glad Neil come home that night with them younguns.

Some people think there ain't nothing to these flying saucers, but I believe there is. Now I don't think there's anything to that little green men business, but my children was coming home from work one evening and they seen something hanging in the west. Said it looked like it was just hanging down, so long. And they stopped and they looked at it. And it just got gone. And since these flying saucers come in they think now that's what they seen. This here was when Russia put up that Sputnik.

Another time I was laying in there in that room and I had turned my face down to the window. And I seen the light a-coming way back in yonder. I jumped up and called C. He was upstairs. I said, "That Sputnik thing's coming over yonder." We both run outdoors to see it. He didn't even put on his clothes. He was in his pajamas.

And he got up to them and said, "That ain't anything in the world but a blame airplane."

I thought sure it was that thing coming through. But I do believe, cause I've heard people on the television that was honest about what they told about them things. There's too many tales how they do, that's the reason I believe it's so. And I just bet you, if that Bible was searched right, you could find it too.

When we come here we didn't have no inside water. I'd have my washing outdoors, wash on a board. Boiled my clothes in a pot.

And milked the cow. I've got up in the morning and put on my breakfast and go milk the cow and get them all ready to go to school and get myself to work at seven o'clock.

There was a long time we didn't have no well, but they'd took up a tree out there at the end of the porch and dug a well down there. And that was the best, coldest water. But little red worms come in it, and somebody told Neil to put a spoon or two full of salt in it and that would do away with them. He went up there and bought about a five- or ten-pound bag and poured it down, and we never could use it anymore. You could not wash in it. You couldn't do nothing. But I'd fix my butter and everything and put it in the well bucket. We didn't have no Frigidaires nor nothing like that then—and put it down in there where it was cold, and when that come up there that butter was just as hard and solid.

I started working in the spinning room out here at the Burlington Mill— Piedmont Heights they called it—in 1927. That was the first of it. They was still building this up when we come here. People was moving in.

They had started the spinning and I didn't have no trouble getting a job. I was winding on quills off a thread to go in the looms. But I didn't stay there long enough to learn much about it, because I couldn't take it. It was hard to get on to and get used to.

I just hadn't ever been in nothing like that. It works on your nerves. I just got balled up. I don't know how to tell you I felt but I didn't like that kind of work.

One thing I remember. I coughed the whole time I was in there. There was too much hot lint in it. And the machines was noisy running, and just a-flying. I couldn't take it. I might have worked a month or two in there. Then they started making bedspreads and put in that sewing room in the mill and I got on there. And boy, I enjoyed it. I boxed, I, I scalloped bedspreads, I hemmed tablecloths and napkins, hemmed bedspreads, swept the floor. When we first went in the sewing room, the women had to clean up before they left.

I enjoyed scalloping bedspreads. We used electric Singer sewing machines. You didn't have to pedal them. They was good little ol' machines. You'd just sit there and sew and scallop and they'd fall in a basket.

Your hand motion makes the right size scallop. It was big scallops the same every time. You have to learn to do that and turn the corner right and go back up the side. You could just turn them out like that. Talking about my talent, that's one thing was my talent, was working at something like that.

To do them tablecloths, now, the machines had a hemmer on them. You could zip them through there and do a whole lot in a ten- or eleven-hour day. I used to love to see how much I could get done.

I believe we was paid by the hundred. I don't know. I made about thirty dollars a week. People didn't make much back then. Spencer Love come in there now and then at Christmas. He was giving spreads to his friends and had me to box them and fix them up. I never did talk to him none or nothing like that but he seemed like a nice man what you did say to him.

At first, Neil worked at Burlington Mill somewhere. I've forgotten what he did. Then he quit.

He'd go out and pretend to be a-looking for jobs and then he'd come back and say he didn't care whether he got one or not. You'd just be let down a lot.

Well, I don't reckon he could get one job. Now they weren't easy jobs. But he guarded over at the Fairchild plant a long time and he guarded over here at the King Cotton Mill a long time, and he guarded up at Glen Raven.

But during the Depression he was mostly sitting on the front porch. Sometimes, when we used to have a garden, he'd have somebody plow it and we'd get it in the ground. From then on, I had it. I reckon he might have hoed some. I don't know.

"Every Time the Moon Changed"

Let's see now. Blanche was born in 1920, Zeke in 1922, Hazel in '24, Bertie in '26, Bill in '28, Lola in 1930. And Blanche weren't hardly ten years old when I weren't a bit afraid of leaving them babies with her while I worked. She could tend to a little bitty baby as good as I could. I don't know what I'd done without her. Blanche was just a regular momma to them when she was here and could be here.

I could walk home from work when the whistle blew at dinner. We'd come home and eat and I'd look to see if the children was all right. Then it'd blow again and we'd be back at work.

When Neil was sitting around here, I'd leave them youngsters here with him. He couldn't do nothing but see that they didn't get killed. That was about all.

I know one time when I was working in the sewing room, one of the neighbor children turned Melvin over in a red wagon and he split his head. Neil was sitting out on the porch reading the paper. He sent somebody up to get me at the mill. (I just lived in fear of something like that.) I had to come home and take Melvin to the doctor, have his head sewed up. The doctor showed me his skull.

I had all that to look after. He wouldn't take no responsibility on himself like that. I don't know what makes me tell all this, but I just know there's a lot nobody don't know nothing about.

And when them spells weren't on him, there weren't a better person that ever lived in the world, better-hearted. But he loved that dollar. I know he did grow up and didn't have nothing, but he had as much as I did.

I think one thing was just having one youngun after another. I think that got on his nerves. You know a parent like that's got a responsibility on them. And some people can't take it. But I worked mine out, I didn't worry about it. I worked at that sewing room and milked the cow and cooked and churned of a night, and washed of a night, and ironed of a night, go back the next day and get up and cook breakfast for these children so they could get off to school. And I don't know, the Lord just give me strength to go through with it, I don't know how in the world I ever done it, but I didn't get no sleep. Just about took day and night to keep this house going and working. But he didn't get no job, somebody had to do something. And he said one time, he didn't care whether he got one or not.

He didn't go with nobody much. But if anybody come, you would just think he loved them to death. Before they'd get out of the yard, he was talking about them. And that's not right. He'd say, "I wonder what they was nosing in to find out."

But I didn't fuss at him at all. There can't nobody say I ever had fusses with him. I never fussed at nobody that way. I never had a fuss with my neighbors. I've never toted a tale between my neighbors, told one what the other one said. I just don't like things like that. That's not my way.

But one time he kind of stalled around and said, "Ethel, I'd just give anything in the world if I was like you."

I said, "Well you wouldn't be much if you was but you could try." And he laughed. I don't think a lot of things he's done, he really meant to do it. When he'd have them ill spells he'd look just as blue. Just blue, ashy looking. When he had that flu so bad, coming at that time, I know that done something to his nerves. You have to bear with people like that when something happens.

He never would go to a doctor. I tried to get him to go. He was bothered with that angina. But he was scared to death of doctors.

He come over to the hospital twice when I was having my stomach removed and later he said, "Ethel, I know I didn't go there every day. I couldn't stand it. I just couldn't stand going to that place."

During the Depression I had a calf that my mammy give me. I'd sell milk and butter, and they'd deliver it. People on the new mill hill was working at the Burlington Mill and they would buy it. That's where a whole lot of what we eat come from.

They was good to me at that Burlington Mill. I'll tell you one thing, that was a good place to work. Now I don't know how other people have fared, but I wouldn't want no better place to work. When I worked at the sewing room, I'd have to work when I could and stop awhile. They'd always take me back. I'd stop when a baby was going to be born and then when they got old enough, I'd go back. Usually I'd stay out a couple of months.

The last time I worked before one of them children was born, I couldn't quit. There just weren't nothing coming in here. Bill Higgins was the boss man and I never will forget him. He's dead now. He came and talked to me one day and said, "I know you're embarrassed being here in the daytime, but I ain't going to tell you to quit. I know you need it. If you want me to, I'll get somebody to swap with you and put you on the second shift. You just work until you have to leave. Then just put a note in your pay slip and I'll understand all about it. You can come back when you get ready." He done everything he could for me not to lose no time.

Now one reason I worked as much as I did was because he was setting right here with nothing to do, and somebody needed to be a-working here. And I was determined that every youngun would get something to eat somehow or another. I don't believe in begging, and I wouldn't go to the welfare. I know the welfare's good if somebody can't do no better, but I never have done it, and I hope and pray to the Lord I'll never have to.

I know one time they come to me and wanted me to join a union, at the sewing room. In the 1930s. I'd never been in a union or around none nor heard much talk of one. And I told them then, if I don't know anything about anything I just ain't going to fool with it. They never did get that organized up there, they ain't got no union. They ain't never had one. But they sure did try to get one up there.

I still don't understand them. I know people are going to have to stick up for theirself, I know that. But I don't believe in too much confusion about nothing. And that does cause a lot of rioting. It's a help though if the company don't do you right, it's a help. I know that too. But I just didn't know about it. I didn't understand it and I just didn't have nothing to do with it. But they didn't get it nohow. But they really had a mess going up there at that street one time trying to keep them in or out one.

Every time I went back to work, I could always get on. I rested on that. I knowed when I was out, if I needed anything I could just go back over and go to work. They'd find something. Off and on, I reckon for twenty-some years, in and out.

I never have been nobody to be sick. I've had the pleurisy and I've had deep bad colds. I did have that ulcerated stomach but I think that come from a lot of nervous tension. Too many—just too many children. Trying to wait on all of them.

During that Depression, my sister and them up there in Eldorado was in the same fix. No work at all up there. Three of hers come down here to get a job and they lived here. You can imagine what I cooked for. I had nine or ten of my own and them three. I'd cook and I don't know how in the world I ever done it, but I just guess God just gave me strength. And I had that strength till here awhile back and these shingles hit me. I'd heard tell of shingles, and never thought much about them. Didn't know they hurt like that, just going like that.

Most of the other women didn't have so many children, or either they had done raised them. I don't remember nobody stopping to have one but me, and that was about every time that the moon changed.

Law, we never did know nothing about all that mess. Never heard tell of it [contraception]. There ain't none here that God don't intend to be here nohow. They're all for a purpose, whatever it is.

Everybody didn't have as many as I did. I reckon it just weren't intended, I don't know. But they sure weren't going through what they're going through now. I wouldn't be guilty of that. And I'll tell you, if people don't repent. . . . Now you can't tell me that ain't pure unadulterated murder. If there's ever a life there's got to be a murder if that life's killed. I don't care how big it is. I don't believe in it and I'm so proud that I never had no notion of nothing like that. Nor taking something, law me.

There was people that would do it. I knowed these people come there and my own mammy tell them what to take. They would have took anything. She'd tell them to get some tincture of iron and take so much.

And they could not get rid of one if they took that. It didn't make no difference what they'd take after that, they had to go on. She'd just fix them right. They had to go on with it.

Most everybody had children, but I don't know as they had as many as we had.

And every child ain't alike. You've got to treat every child a little different. Some way or another you've got to learn them. Some can take some things, some can't. They watch your actions, how you feel towards them, when you ain't thinking about it. And you just have to learn them and learn to treat them their way.

When my son's last baby was borned over there, the biggest child, she was sweet as she could be, but I told them, "You'd better watch. When that baby comes there, if you don't mind it, she'll change. She'll get to noticing how you take on to it, and she'll feel down. It'll cramp her." And you just have to watch them things so they'll still keep their ego up. Because they'll notice everything like that, and you don't think a child is noticing it, but they are. And when you have ten, you've got a lot of thinking to do, dealing with them.

I whipped my children. I made them mind me. I'd try to talk to them and do everything else but that, but if it come to that I'd do it. But Neil'd just fly mad at any time and just hit anybody uncalled for. And I don't like to see anybody hit a child. If they go to correct them, if they have to do anything, you can give them a little cane hickory or something. But I don't believe in taking razor strops and your fist and nothing like that. I just ain't got no use for nothing like that.

He'd just love these babies to death, till they got up big enough to pick at. He would make them sass, and then he'd whip them.

He'd just pick at them to make them sass him back and tease them and get them mad. They was little and just talked back, you know. But when they got big enough to whip, he'd do it, too. And if I said anything, he'd whip them to spite me. I had to keep my mouth shut when he would be beating on them.

He'd whip them with anything he could get his hands on. Law, I oughtn't to tell all this. It's all over and all past.

His momma was out here one night. We had a laundry heater there in that kitchen, and one of the children got up and went between the heater and him. That heater was hot. And he knocked him across that heater, and I grabbed him and I told him, "You ought not to never do a thing like that." He had a razor strop hanging on the wall in there, and he jumped up and he got that to hit me with. And his momma stood up and says, "Don't you hit her. If you want to hit anybody, you hit me. You didn't have no business knocking that child across that heater."

Just because he walked between him and the heater. Lord, what I went through. I couldn't even think of what I have went through with him. And a life like that's worrisome.

What made him thataway, I don't know. I think it was the responsibility of having a family to keep up. I think that was one trouble of it. I tried to help all I could. I'd go to work, and do my own work here, till they got big enough to work. Blanche was the first one of the children that went to work, and she went to work under age over here at the McEwen Hosiery Mill. He hired her under age, but I think some of the neighbors had talked to him about the condition of things here. Neil just would not buy enough to eat.

I just don't think he could feel responsible. He didn't want the responsibility. I think he loved them, when they was little babies, as much as anybody I ever seen in my life. He loved a little old baby. But I think it was the responsibility that he felt on him that made him like he was.

He didn't drink. I told him one time I'd rather put up with a drunkard than the way his temper was. He just had a temper.

Have you ever been nervous? Well, you know nothing don't seem right, does it? He'd just look like he'd just get full and wanted to do something. I still believe it was his nerves. But I always did wish he'd go see a doctor. I wished I'd let that one down yonder get him and have him examined. Might have done him a lot of good, but I was afraid. I was scared to death to do it.

I'll just tell you, he wanted to be a bigger person than he really was. That was it. It was just pride, and pitiful with it. Anybody ought to come to their senses that they're just what they are, and they're going to be what they are, and then they can act what they are, and not try to get above it.

Yes, I know he was hitting me, and I've seen him cry about it and tell me he didn't know what made him do it. He'd say, "I don't know what made me do that." That showed there was something wrong. He'd whip these younguns. He whipped C one day there in the hall. He was mad at me about something then. He wanted to take spite out on me. That's what it was. And he whipped him, and I knowed if I said anything that he'd beat him that much worse to spite me. And the woman down on the street that went to the Holiness Church over yonder—she was a good old woman—she come up the steps, and he quit whipping him.

The next day I was in the kitchen, and I heard C say, "Papa, what did you whip me for yesterday? What did I do?"

And he said, "Nothing. I just wanted to whip you."

He just wanted to fight it out. And then he'd empty out, he was all right. And that's just the way it worked, too. And he didn't care what he took it out on, either.

I don't know. It's all a mystery, but one day it'll come out. And yet he had a good momma. She was good, but he hadn't spoke to her in three days when she died. And she was old. She stayed out here every night, and I'd go out there every morning and build her fire and let her house warm up, and then she'd go home in the daytime. He had a spell at her. That's what it was. Beat anything I ever seen. It weren't because I did not try to help him get along, either. Now anybody'd tell you that. I worked like a dog trying to help him make it with his family.

"I Lived Like an Underdog"

C started to work at Burlington Mill, oiling that machinery, before he was old enough, because we needed the money. He was under age. I don't believe C finished school. I think they took him because they knowed we needed work. Neil didn't have no work to do.

And C oiled that machinery and climbed over them looms. I thought about that a lot of times. I don't reckon they really wanted to work a child like that, but they just done it to help out, I reckon. I know it was dangerous for him to be up there.

I think they had to be about sixteen to get a job. I believe Blanche went to work when she was fifteen. She got hired at the hosiery mill in Graham. They learnt her over there and she made them a good hand. She was a looper.

Before she got hired, I don't know how many times she had walked to Graham to try to get on down there at Graber. She would walk down there and back, trying to get a job. Then Dora, that lived over here and was good friends to us and knowed the circumstances here, told me one day that Blanche should go over there where she worked and see if Mr. McLendon would give her a job. So Blanche decided she would.

Dora told me, "Now if she goes, you get her to wear a long pair of stockings. Don't let her go without hose, or he won't hire her. And you go with her. He'll hire her a lot quicker if you're with her." He was strict.

She didn't have no stockings, and I didn't either. A woman out here on the corner had one pair and she let Blanche have them to wear. I went with her.

I went with her and he sit down a-diddling with a pencil. He never did look up and he didn't ask me no questions. He knowed she was under age but he knowed the circumstances. Finally, the only thing, he just asked me if he'd learn her, did I think she would stay with him. I said, "Yes, I believe she would because she's smart at home. But she ain't never worked out none." And he give her a job.

There was a woman . . . I oughtn't to tell this, but she had a girl, too, that run with Blanche all the time. She was going to do the same thing and get on, but he wouldn't hire her. She come back by and I said, "Well, did you have any luck?" I was in hopes that girl got a job, because they was always together.

And she said, "No. Before I'd go over there and tell a lie about her age, she wouldn't get no job."

I said, "Well, he didn't ask me Blanche's age. The only thing he said to me was did I think she would stay."

That woman got mad about that, but I couldn't help that. But her family was *all* working. They didn't need it. I knowed then that Blanche was just sure to lose her job because this woman told them they were working her under age.

When she come home I asked her, "Did they say anything to you today about being under age?"

She said, "No." She said she noticed they had watched her all day. Said the floor lady over there was just setting by her and a-learning her all day long, and he had come by to see how she was doing.

They kept her, and she worked there for years. She made a good hand. But stuff like that, though, is trouble. I don't want nobody a-thinking hard.

She's worked ever since. She worked there until she went to P. Lorillard. She's been there ever since, at the tobacco factory in Greensboro. I had four working there. Hazel died, and Zeke and C and Blanche still works up there. They've been there for years.

Now I'd rather work up there at that sewing room than work in a hosiery mill. It ain't as tedious. The work ain't as nerve-racking. Hosiery mill is close, tight work, like seaming them toes and all. But them old bedspreads, you can just handle them any old way, you're freer working, if you don't make quite as much. I mean you had to do them right, but they weren't tedious.

If I hadn't had all them low sugar spells, I'd go back up there and work yet. I like to had one this evening when I went and got that ice water. I don't reckon you've ever been bothered with it. Our doctor said taking out my stomach is what caused it. Did you see me setting here sweating?

Well, that's what it is. I get goosey. The first I ever had one of them things, I was down there watering the garden. I didn't know what was the matter. Just buckets and buckets. There's just knots in my. . . I ain't got no arm no more, it shrivelled up. But there's knots in my veins, ruptured veins, from carrying so much water. There's one. It took a lot of water to keep this house up, cooking, bathing children, washing clothes. I tell you. And it was two great big buckets, one turned right after another. I don't know how I ever got through with it.

I don't remember Neil ever carrying water. He might have sometime. He just didn't want people to see him at it. He was too proud, I reckon. If he ever washed any dishes, I never heard nothing about it. I know one time he decided he'd do the washing while I was at work, and I had to wash them over. He thought things like that looked sissy for a man. Well, I think if a man and woman both works, nothing don't look sissy for neither of them. I mean they ought to both take hold and do what they could and enjoy it instead of resenting what the other one's a-getting out of it.

I was cooking, but he was handling it. He'd get what he wanted me to cook, and that ain't right. If I've got to cook, I ought to go and get what I need.

It would make him so mad if he went and got groceries and one of the neighbors walked in while he was laying them out on the table. That made him mad as fire. He didn't want them to see how little he got. He didn't want nothing to show up on him.

What money he didn't save, he bought nice suits.

But he told me over yonder when he was sick before he died, "Well, Ethel, I ate the same thing I put on the table for the children." You know, that was on his conscience. We had enough, but I'll tell you, you can just eat too much gravy and biscuit and stuff like that.

But I don't feel guilty. I didn't do nothing to cause him to do that. I didn't do nothing I'd have cared for him a-knowing. And he was just a jealous person. He was jealous of your friends. He was jealous of what you had on. He didn't want me to have a dress unless he bought it.

When these children was coming up, when we first married, if I had to have a dress, he had to pick it out. And when he did get one, it was just an old straight thing with a band on each side you tied behind. He didn't want me to look like nothing. Shoot. He thought I was pretty, and he thought everybody else thought it. And I didn't look like nothing. He was just a jealous-hearted person.

Burlington Mill paid off in an envelope. He'd get it from me. Sometimes he'd grab it and say I'd never worked. I knowed I couldn't keep it and have no peace. I never had nothing to do with it after he got it. If I dared even get a cold drink, there'd be a fuss about it.

I lived like an underdog and done it to keep peace. I just lived under a . . . I don't know what you call it. It's a wonder I got good sense, and I ain't got much.

It was all a pitiful affair. But as I was a-telling, I married him, and I married him to live with for better or worse, and I took what I got, and that was it.

We went to his momma's one time at the fair at Greensboro. And after the children got big enough to get them a car, they'd carry us up to the mountains a time or two. No, we never did get off nowhere like that. I went twelve year and didn't go to see my momma but one time. I didn't have no way up there.

Sitting on the front porch, talking, looking at the traffic is all we did. We never did go nowhere. In fact, I was afraid to ride with him. He'd go through a red light. He'd just go right on through it.

We went to town one time and got a cab back, and he opened the door to spit. The cab driver stopped and told him, "Now, Sir, if you want to spit, you just tell me and I'll stop."

I've seen him cry and tell me he didn't know why he hit me.

I was there cooking out lard one day. The man over here at the store would

Ethel Hilliard, ca. 1951. (Courtesy of the Hilliard family)

buy hogs and meat and he'd give some of the neighbors half of the lard to cook it out for him. I was glad to get it, because it was hard to get anything. So I cleaned up everything on Friday so I could cook that lard one Saturday. You had to watch it.

And I was in there a-cooking that lard on the stove. I had a warming cloth on top of the range and the big pot of hot grease, lard, there a-cooking it. And he got up and come through there and was standing there in the door and looking. We hadn't even spoke. There hadn't been a cross word between us. But he looked right purple.

He was always taking soda. And he come around behind me to that cabinet, and I thought he was going to get a dose of soda. And the first thing I knowed, I was knocked up against the range. He hit me back of the head and I was blind as a bat. Turned around and started out the door and he hit me there.

After a few days my head begun to hurt, but I never thought much about it. But it got so bad I had to go to the doctor with it. His momma sent me to the doctor. She was a good woman. I loved that woman. And she hated it as bad as I did. He was as jealous of me and her as he could be. He didn't want her to think nothing of me.

And I went to the doctor and the doctor was gone, but he had another doctor in his place. He looked at it and said, "I wouldn't touch that thing with a ten-foot pole."

I said, "If my blood's that bad, I want something for it."

He said, "It's not the blood, it's a bruise." And they told me to keep hot towels to it that night and come back the next morning. And the doctor lanced it and got seven pulls out of it.

And then's when he run them two oldest girls off. He tried to run them all off. But one of them sat down there in the kitchen and said she wasn't going to leave me, not with him. And the other two went over yonder with some girls they worked with, and they took them in their apartment, but they wouldn't come home when he was here.

He'd sit out on the porch and read, and I'd be out in the garden, maybe, and he'd say, "Now don't you cook supper till after Douglas Edwards goes off of that news." Well, I didn't want to wait that late. I wanted to get over with my supper.

One evening I was a-working. When I come in, I didn't even look to see what time it was, never thought about the time. I was cooking supper and I heard him a-coming.

I'd fried out some meat—I bet the grease was *that* deep. I heard him a-coming and I looked out and he was going through that hall door by the porch and he had his fist balled up. He come in and says, "I told you not to cook till that news went off."

And I said, "I never even looked at the clock. I didn't know what time it was when I come out of the garden."

That pan had a long handle and I picked up that grease and he stopped and looked at me and said, "What are you going to do?"

I said, "I've took off of you. I've seen these children beat and I've took my last lick off of you. And if you hit me, I'll pour this all over you."

He said, "Well, Ethel, I don't believe you'd do it." He knowed I wouldn't do it. He knowed me and he knowed I wouldn't even fuss with him. And looked right purple that day.

He stepped back to that door by the porch, and he watched me all the time I was cooking supper. He said, "I believe you meant that."

I said, "I did, and if you ever hit me again, I'll get you if I have to pour it on you in the bed when you're asleep. I'm going to get you."

And you know, he never did offer to hit me no more after that. His momma told me a long time before that, if I'd buck up for myself, he'd quit it. Said he weren't nothing but a coward. He wouldn't hit nothing but a woman and a child. She said he had been thataway all his life, and she was afraid he would die thataway.

It was just one day of living at a time, and I can't hardly remember much about it. But I know one thing. I look back, and I don't know how in the world I ever got through. I know of people who've had a hard time as much as I have, but there weren't no need of a lot of it. I'll tell you, you've got to work together. One can't just set down and . . . And I'll tell you one thing about it. I wasn't leaving my younguns with—I was going to stick to them. They didn't ask to be here. And I tell you, they stuck to me, too. But there can't nobody say I ever fussed with him. I never fuss with nobody. I never had a fuss with one of my neighbors in my life, and I ain't a-going to.

And if anybody does me wrong, I just take it and swallow it and go on. There's no need of me doing something to feel guilty about.

He was just simply going to have his way about everything, or he wanted to boss. He wanted somebody under his . . .

God made Adam first, and then he made Eve for a helpmate. And when you leave that Bible, you've just left it all. Now I believe every word of it.

God made Eve for Adam's helpmate, and He didn't aim for her to go over his head. A man ought to be head of the house. He's supposed to provide for his family. I believe in women being treated right. I don't believe a man ought to mistreat his wife. I believe she ought to be free, free to speak if she wants to, but not take man's business in her hands. They're not supposed to be head of a home. The man's supposed to be head of the household. The Bible teaches it. And that's the reason I believe it, because the Bible teaches it.

Yes, you could separate, but people didn't believe in it. And I never did want nothing like that.

There ain't but one thing that the Lord gives you, that the Bible gives you, a right to separate, and that there is adultery. And there weren't none of that in our family. I knowed I had got into it and just as well tough it out.

I did leave one time. I left and took all of them little younguns up home

[Eldorado], and my mother sent me back. She couldn't put up with all me and them children. Blanche was old enough to drive a car, because she had bought a car, and she took us. And all of us went. But I come back with them. I thought it weren't her place to put up with all that crowd of children. I didn't aim to put that on her.

This was as much my home as it was his. He didn't have nothing when I married, and I didn't either. We'd had our table on a big old square wooden box where they'd ship stuff at the store. Put a cloth over it, and that was our eating table. We didn't have nothing to start with, and I knowed I'd put as much in this thing as he had ever put in it. And he knowed it, too. But he just didn't intend for my name to be on that deed.

He said he didn't aim for any damned man to ever get it when he was gone. I said, "You needn't worry. You've made me sick of all of them. You needn't worry."

I had news for him. He'd done cooked me of marrying. And I ain't never had no idea of ever marrying another man.

I love to fool with sewing, thread, and things like that. And I like music, I always did like music. But if I hadn't ever married, I would have been a nurse. Because I went around a lot when neighbors had the flu and they'd be down to the bed. I'd go and comb their hair, and if their shoulders weren't right I could feel it. I could feel their head weren't resting under here.

I knowed this woman, she was just breathing for dear life. I just reached over and picked her up and raised her up a little and pulled her pillow down under her shoulders. And her shoulders dropped down. You can just about tell, how you would feel. I got her awake a little bit. She wanted me to make her some soup. But she was so dead asleep, I couldn't hardly talk to her. I made her some nice potato soup, and I got it just as fine as I could so she could drink it through a straw. Next day I made her chicken soup and I went down there to carry it to her and I couldn't hardly get her awake. I did get her awake, and I said, "Ain't you got pills in you that you're sleeping like this?"

She said, "Yeah."

I said, "You just better let them things alone. They'll kill you." I think she had them in her when she died too. That woman breathed the hardest. Just before anybody dies, they breathe some hard breaths. I knowed when I went in there she weren't rested. I knowed she weren't a-laying comfortable.

I would've been a nurse if I hadn't married. And if I hadn't married as young as I did, I wouldn't have married. But I never seen nobody else I would marry but the one I did marry and I wouldn't have nobody else. Now that's the way I feel. I've never seen nobody since nor never even paid no thought about nobody else.

That never crossed my mind, ever marrying again or going with anybody. I felt like I had these children and there's nobody coming in over them to start again. And I didn't want one there no way. And I made it just fine too.

I don't think if anybody's mate dies and they want to marry again, it's any sin. But this here marrying, leaving your wife, marrying, having two and three and four wives and husbands and living together—that won't do. It's against the Bible, it's against God's will. There's been enough gospel in this world preached for people to know such as that.

I prayed all the time. I mean I prayed *all* the time, walking and a-working. And boy, God was with me, too, and I didn't know then what it was to be saved. I belonged to church, but I know you've got to be borned again. People might think that ain't nothing but turning over a new leaf, but it is. When you repent, now, you're going to get something that makes a joy. You're just going to have a peace that you never had before in your life.

I think the devil was a-fighting me about trying to get what I wanted there, too. And I knowed I lacked something. I went to church one Sunday, and Preacher Swinney preached on being borned again.[2] You know, the Baptists preaches that. I'd always went to the Primitive Baptists and Methodists and Missionary Baptists. We just went to all the churches up there. I never gave being borned again much of a thought, but I know I'd read it in the Bible a lot. I just thought it was changing your mind, that you knowed you was going to do the right thing about everything. I was baptized and dipped and everything, but I still weren't satisfied. And I think the devil fought me to keep me from trying to get whatever I was seeking. I didn't know what it was.

And one day Preacher Swinney was a-preaching, and he preached on that, and said people might think there weren't nothing to it, but said if you pray through something until you hit the rock, the fire will fly. That just got on me, and something did happen. And I was ashamed to talk to people about it because they thought I was a Christian. And I was. I was trying to live right. Did better then than I do now, because I'm going to talk.

Reverend Swinney baptized me and then Benny Howard baptized me, after I really got satisfied. I'd done joined the church and been baptized. But after that I played piano for a church up here at West Burlington a long time. I couldn't play by note, but boy, they all enjoyed it. Then I couldn't get away from them.

I was telling that preacher—he was a good person—about the way I felt, that I had never had no real change when I was baptized, and I just won-

Ethel Hilliard and her children, ca. 1967. *Front row, left to right*: William, Melvin, Cornelius, Jr., Ethel, Fitch. *Back row, left to right*: Jeannette Spillman (C's daughter), Bertie, Zeke, Lola, Blanche, Frankie, Hazel. (Courtesy of the Hilliard family)

dered. "Well," he said, "the Bible said do your first work over." And he said, "If you want to be baptized, next time I baptize I'll baptize you again." And I did feel better, and I've been baptized twice and sprinkled once. I ought to go to heaven.

That was that Free Will Holiness. And I didn't know nothing about Holiness churches, because we didn't have one up there. But I knowed they was good people. I always thought they was. I enjoyed helping them out. And when they washed feet, I washed with them. The first thing I knowed, they had my name up there on the book, and I hadn't never pulled out from Glen Hope. I didn't aim to leave Glen Hope. I love that church, always have.

But there's something more, talking about being borned again, there's a peace that you get you never had before. I'll tell you, the devil was a-fighting me about that, though. And my husband didn't want to hear about it. He didn't want it. He was too stubborn. I think it got on his conscience that I'd talk about it. And I think that was the main trouble that got on him, too. I think it was the devil, through him, working on me. The devil's got the next power to God.

I was afraid of him. There ain't no doubt about that. There was just something the matter with him. It was just something happened. I don't know what it was. I didn't know much about these things then, but I think he was demon-possessed. You ever hear tell of that? I believe that was what it was. If I'd knowed about that when he was living, I'd have said something to him about that. But I never was brought up with nothing like that, and I didn't know nothing about it, but since then I have learnt people is.

"If I Miss the Next World"

I kept a-hurting, and I just kept a-getting worse and worse, and I went to Duke Hospital. Blanche and Hazel carried me down there. Blanche had got her a car. And they checked me. They finally told me that I had an ulcerated stomach and put me on a diet. But I never have had the questions as much in my life. And everybody in there asked a row of questions. But they warned me about taking care of it and all like that. But finally they took out over three-fourths of it. But it was the making of me. I felt like a new person.

It was in fifty-something, I believe, that I had that done. While I was down there, they come in one day and told me there was a man who wanted to talk to me. I didn't think about a psychiatrist or nothing like that. But I know now that's what it was. And he questioned and talked and everything, and I held back a lot, and I reckon he knowed I did. But he wanted to send the sheriff to pick Neil up. He said, "He needs treatment."

He knowed that was what was the matter with my stomach, what I was going through with. He could read it, too. And I told him, "Buddy, you better not pick him up and ever turn loose of him. It wouldn't never do." I said, "You just don't know him."

He wanted to send up there to Graham and have the sheriff pick him up and have him treated. That wouldn't have never done. Whew! He was determined. I believe he would have died or had his way. I honestly believe that.

When my momma got old, she was just wore out. I'd keep her three months and my sister'd keep her three, when she broke up housekeeping. She weren't sick but she was just mighty near helpless.

She was just like a child. I'd get her in the bathtub. She never had nothing like that at home. I had a chair just about come even with the bath. A slat chair. I'd set her in that and drag her to the tub and put her feet over in the tub and I'd straddle the tub and get her under the arms and get her over in the tub. She was a big woman. How I ever done it, I don't know in the world. I'd get her in there and have it full of hot soapy water and she'd say, "I'm going under. I'm going under." When she was slick I couldn't hold her. And aggravate me like that. And I said, "If you do, you'll drown."

Then when I was getting ready to get her off, I'd have to really get her dry so I could hold her, and get her set back up on the tub. And get her back in the chair.

She'd do things like that just to tease me. But I thought about it a lot of times though, and it was a wonder that she hadn't drowned. The tub was long and she could've went down in it.

Momma died when she was eighty-four, in 1952. And she didn't have no disease when she died. She just wore out.

When she left here and went back up to my sister's, my sister was working and left a woman with her. She just let her lay in the bed. You've got to help anybody, or see they're turned over or take them up or something to keep them ticking.

I'd been in the hospital with my stomach and Momma had to go to my sister's. When I came out to see her, she died while I was up there. I believe she had pneumonia from not being turned like she ought to be.

Now when she was here, she was in bed a lot but I took her and put her in a chair. And we got her a wheelchair. I rented one from Mr. Loud, the undertaker. We'd put her in that wheelchair and roll her in here. She hated that television, she just didn't like them a little bit. And she didn't want no electricity in her house, said they weren't going to string that fire through her house. She come down here and I'd take her in the kitchen where I was busy. Take her out on the front porch and let her sit out there. I think she enjoyed being here but she just wanted to be back up home. My sister lives now in her house where she lived, but they worked it over and put electricity in it and everything.

Neil was sixty-five when he retired. He was a watchman over here at King Cotton Mill. He had to be a certain age. Then he was seventy-two or seventy-three when he died, in 1957.

When he worked, he worked. But during that Depression, I know there was part of the time he couldn't get work. A lot of people didn't. But he hated to work. Now he didn't deny that. I don't know what happened. Something happened. Something got wrong.

Ethel Hilliard, 1986. Photo by Tom Rankin.

He wouldn't go to a doctor. But that night he was taken sick with a heart attack, he was begging me to get one. I knowed right then he was bound to be sick, that he was really suffering.

I was trying to get hold of Dr. Field—he weren't in the office—trying to get in touch with him. Neil would walk out here and he'd say, "Ethel, hurry." Well, I couldn't hurry no faster than I was hurrying. They was trying to get in touch with him and let him know to call over here. Finally, Dr. Field came.

Neil had never put my name on the deed for this place here. But you know, when he died every youngun and in-law signed it over to me. There's about eighteen of them, all together.

That lawyer had told me, "Now have you ever thought about the in-laws? You look how many are going to have to sign that."

I said, "They'll every one do it." I hadn't asked them. I knowed they'd do it.

And when he got that thing fixed, that back of that envelope was about that long, plumb full of names. He said he had been in law a long time, but he had never seen nothing like it. He said, "Somebody always kicks."

I'd love to live my life over if I knowed some things. I wouldn't want to live it over like I have lived it. But boy, if I miss the next world, I'll miss it all. No doubt about that. These children don't like me to tell about things like that.

Lord, I don't know what I put on that tape. You cut out some of that because if some of them younguns ever read that book, it'll be too bad. They're ashamed of it.

Well, it's the truth, if it is on there it's the truth. And just a lot of things I can't even think of. Day after day.

· 7 ·

Brown Lung Blues

Grover and Alice Hardin

During 1980 I visited several times with retired mill workers Grover and Alice Hardin at their home in Greenville, South Carolina. I had heard about the Hardins from members of the Greenville Brown Lung Association, an organization of current and former textile-mill workers seeking to promote public awareness, legislative remedy, and legal redress for victims of byssinosis, a debilitating and life-threatening disease associated with the daily breathing in of cotton-fiber dust. Grover Hardin, whose working life was first made intolerable, then brought to an end, by brown lung disease, was seeking compensation from an industry that refused to acknowledge byssinosis as an occupational illness.

On two of my visits in the Hardin household I brought a tape recorder and interviewed Grover and Alice about their lives and work. This chapter consists entirely of edited excerpts from these interviews.[1]

The interview format seemed the best way to present the Hardins' life histories for several reasons. Their unassuming and understated manner of speaking, as well as Grover Hardin's need to marshal every breath, seldom led them into long, extended narratives in the manner of Ethel Hilliard or Lora League Wright. Yet, from their first words with me, I sensed their desire to tell about their lives, and I felt that all they said engaged the central issues of the Carolina Piedmont's industrialization. "There's so much I wanted to tell you," Alice Hardin said, lapsing into a long pause only minutes after beginning her first recollections, "and now I can't think of none of it." Her comment, and her evident disappointment, seemed to signal permission for my persistence.

Whether it is done unwittingly or with deliberation, the production of "works" of oral history often resembles the accelerated doffing of cheeses on

Lora League Wright's set of Barber-Colman automatic spoolers. Intent on an authoritative skein of facts and a well-seamed argument, the historian-manufacturer reaches for the inventory of spooled talk, spun by a workforce of narrators, and selects an affirming anecdote, then quickly ties on to another life for another illustration. Delimited in this way, lives as lived in a historical time and place become the fragmented parts of someone else's narrative.

The cumulative effect of the short, rather minimalist comments of Grover and Alice Hardin is a narrative read and sensed not as the compilation of so many facts, but as lived evidence with which the Hardins reassess their lives of unrelenting labor. Grover entered the cotton mills at age ten, Alice when she was fifteen. Their memories speak directly to the history of the region's working class: the migration from farm to factory; family work and domestic life; sexual division of labor; unionization; on-the-job relations with other workers and with bosses; the entrapment of mill routine and its debilitating consequences; and the mill workers' hope of something better for their children. Although Grover is heard here more than Alice, their presence together in these interviews is emblematic of the mutual support that sustained their lives amid industry's habits.

Brown Lung Victim Gets Settlement

After a 2½ year battle with Dan River Inc., brown lung victim Grover Hardin of Greenville, S.C., has reportedly been given a workers compensation award of $12,000. The Brown Lung Association said the settlement calls for Dan River to pay Hardin $10,000 awarded him by the state Industrial Commission and $2,000 for past and future medical expenses. Dan River spokesman Tom George said a "reasonable settlement" had been reached but declined to disclose the amount.

Hardin filed for workers compensation in 1978 and was diagnosed by three doctors as being totally disabled by byssinosis, or brown lung disease. Although the Industrial Commission twice awarded Hardin benefits, Dan River declined to make the payments.[2]

Alice Grogan Hardin: I was born in Greenville County, South Carolina, in 1911. My daddy was a farmer. He had eight children, five boys and three girls. I was the oldest girl.

I went to work helping my mother around the house when I was five years old. Then when I got old enough to pick cotton, I went to the field and picked cotton. And we'd pick cotton all day, and we'd come in and have an hour for dinner. And during blackberry time, we'd pick blackberries during that hour. And if it wasn't blackberry time, we'd sing. I'd play the organ, and we'd sing. And we sung the old-timey songs like "When the Roll Is Called Up Yonder" and "Bringing in the Sheaves" and "Down at the Cross," just old-timey songs like that.

My mother was a good singer. My daddy played the violin, and this neighbor of ours played the violin, and I played the organ. We'd go around and have parties and play for people. Then we'd play for square dances.

As we grew up and got older, the family would all work. The boys and the sisters, too, as they got old enough to work. I had four brothers older than I am. One was younger than me. My daddy thrashed his own wheat most of the time. The thrashers would come and thrash wheat all day long. My mother and whoever she could get to help her fix dinner would cook dinner for all the workers.

When we got older, we moved closer in the country to Greenville, and we still farmed while we was there. All of us children went to school. We canned everything we ate. Daddy raised everything he ate. He raised his hogs. He raised his cattle. And we canned vegetables, and we canned fruits, dried applies, dried peaches, and just had everything at home. Times would get hard sometimes, but we still had our food at home.

We didn't have water close to the house. We'd carry it from a spring. We'd bring several pails full of water, enough to do till the next morning. That was the children's jobs, to go get water the next morning before we went to the field to work. And we'd go then to the field and work till dinnertime. Then, if my mother was out of water we had to bring up enough to do her then till night.

Sometimes in the evening she'd come to the field and help us. If she didn't have time, she'd stay at home. And she had a big job at home. Because there was eight of us children, and my grandmother stayed with us. And, most of the time, my daddy had a man that lived with us and helped him on the farm.

Then we moved to another place, and we lived there for about two or three years, and then we moved to the Woodside Cotton Mill. Daddy had about five or six hands to go to work in the mill at one time.

We lived at the cotton mill until my daddy got sick, and he died.

In about three years, my mother died.

Then Grover and me took the three children, and we raised them until they got married.

Then after they got married, me and Grover bought a house. We never was able to buy one until our families was married off, because we raised three families.

I met Grover in a cafe. I didn't speak to him, but I knew I loved him.

We didn't see each other any more for about three months. I was working in the mill. So was he. And he would come and lay in the window that I looked out of where I was working.

So in three months we got married.

We had three children. I've got a little boy dead, and I've got two girls living. We've got a wonderful family. We've got a happy family. And I've got five grandchildren. I have a lot of people dead in my family, but let's don't talk about that.

There's so much I wanted to tell you, and now I can't think of none of it.

Tullos: What were your mother and father's names?

Alice Hardin: Charlie Grogan and Lydia Jane (Janie) Grogan.

Tullos: How big a farm did you have at first?

Alice Hardin: I don't remember. It was pretty good size. We didn't buy our farm ourself. We rented.

Tullos: Do you remember what kind of arrangements you'd work out to rent?

Alice Hardin: Generally he had to pay a third of everything he made on the farm.

Tullos: Did he have his own tools and mules?

Alice Hardin: Yes, he had his own mules and plows and hoes and everything he worked with.

Tullos: And the cash crop was cotton?

Alice Hardin: Yes. Cotton and corn.

Tullos: You also grew some wheat?

Alice Hardin: Oh, yes, we grew our bread. And we'd take our corn to the mill and have it ground for meal.

My grandfather stayed with us some. He was a furniture maker. He made chairs and swings and all kind of outdoor furniture. And indoor, too, if anybody wanted it.

Tullos: How did he get started in that?

Alice Hardin: I don't remember, but I do know that uptown here, on the rich people's porches, you could see his work sitting on their porch. It was very pretty work.

Tullos: Do you know where your grandparents said the family had originally come from or how they got into this part of the country?

Alice Hardin: We are partly Dutch. I don't know where they originally come from, but most of my daddy's people lived on down below Union and down in that part of the country, from my remembrance.

Tullos: Would your mother work in the field?

Alice Hardin: Oh, yes.

Tullos: Would she plow?

Alice Hardin: No, she would hoe and pick cotton. That's what the girls did, and the boys done the plowing.

My mother had her children at home. They didn't go to the hospital to have children then. They had them at home.

Tullos: Did she have someone to help deliver?

Alice Hardin: Oh, yes, doctors. Doctors and midwives, they call them. Back when I was little, they kept things a secret from you more so than they do now in that line. You didn't know as much what was going on till after it had done happened.

Tullos: They wouldn't ever talk about . . . ?

Alice Hardin: They wouldn't talk about raising children. Now if they was planning on another one coming, they wouldn't tell it like they do now. It was just kept a secret, all that stuff. And if we had company, us children had to go out and play. We didn't get to stay where our parents was to hear what was said, like they do today. You know, children today hear everything that's said, and back then you didn't.

Tullos: I've heard people say that when babies were being delivered, sometimes the children would be taken somewhere else.

Alice Hardin: I was the oldest girl, and when I was about thirteen, why, I'd take them out, maybe off to play or off to the barn somewhere and stay all day long. You know, if it took that long. But we didn't get to stick our head in that door while nothing was going on.

Tullos: And it was never ever explained to you, any of these matters about birth control or anything like that?

Alice Hardin: No. They thought it was a crime to talk about that in front of a child then. But now it's different.

Tullos: What would happen to women who had children and were not married who lived in those rural communities back then?

Alice Hardin: I knew a girl that went to school with me that wasn't married, and I didn't even know anything about her baby or anything. But one morning I was getting ready to go to school, and her daddy come to Mother's house for her. Her baby had been born, and she had put it in the dresser drawer and killed it. Her mother was dead, and she was about fifteen years old. If she was as ignorant and as green as I was, she didn't know what to do with it, so that's what she did with it. And so he come for my mother, but it was a long time before I ever knew what had happened. She wouldn't tell it, see.

Tullos: Did she stay in the community, or did she have to leave the community?

Alice Hardin: No, her daddy kept her.

Tullos: And she went right on . . . ?

Alice Hardin: Yes.

Tullos: How far did you go in school?

Alice Hardin: I was promoted to the eleventh grade. And my mother wanted me to go. I'd have finished in the eleventh. Back then there wasn't a twelfth grade. And I didn't. I quit.

Tullos: You stopped when you all moved to Greenville?

Alice Hardin: Yes. I went to work. I'd been used to work, and I wanted to work. [Laughs]

Tullos: What about your brothers and sisters?

Alice Hardin: My oldest brother went a long time, but he never did make his grade. He went as long as I did, just about, but I think he just got through the fifth grade. I think my other brother, Horace, went through about the eighth grade, and I think the others was about the same.

Tullos: How old were you when you all moved to the Woodside Cotton Mill?

Alice Hardin: I was fifteen.

Tullos: Was that when you started to work?

Alice Hardin: Yes, I went to work, and my three oldest brothers went to work, and Daddy went to work. Then Mother went to work through dinner hours.

Tullos: What would she do during the dinner hours?

Alice Hardin: She filled batteries in the weave shop.

Tullos: And she would do that every day?

Alice Hardin: Yes, every day.

Tullos: From twelve to one?

Alice Hardin: From eleven to one. They worked two hours. See, they'd start going out in the mill at different times, and she'd go on different sets of batteries to relieve the ones that was going off for their lunch.

Tullos: When you went into the mill, had you ever been in a mill before?

Alice Hardin: Hadn't ever been in it in my life.

Tullos: Can you remember that first . . . ?

Alice Hardin: I remember the first day I went in that mill. Spinning was what I went to work at, in the spinning room. And I put up an end on the

Poster announcing a performance by Fiddlin' John Carson at Parker High School, Greenville, S.C., mid-1920s. (Courtesy of the Greenville County Library)

spinning frame, the first time I ever went in the mill. So I knew that's what I wanted to do, and that's what I did. My daddy worked in the weave shop, and I had two brothers that worked in the carding department, and I had another brother that worked in the weave shop.

Tullos: Had your father ever done mill work before?

Alice Hardin: No, not before then. Didn't any of us had done any before then.

Tullos: How was it that he got this job for you all, or how did he find out about it?

Alice Hardin: We lived right around, not too far from Greenville, all of our life. Things had got tough in the country the way they started doing, so he just went and asked for a job, and they give us a job and a house. Back then I think they charged two dollars a week for a house, as well as I remember.

Tullos: Do you remember that it was any kind of harder work or different hours you had to get adjusted to, or anything different about working in the mill from working on the farm?

Alice Hardin: Us children liked the mill work better, because when we worked our hours, we was off. And we had our chores to do on the farm.

Tullos: So it seemed a little easier work in the mill?

Alice Hardin: Yes, we thought it was easier. We had more time to do what we wanted to.

Tullos: Do you remember any other incidents from the very first times that you all went into the mill, anything that your brothers or your father might have said, or how they reacted to it at first?

Alice Hardin: I don't think my father liked it at all, because he had rather be on the farm. But I think my brothers might have liked it all right. They never did say too much about it.

Tullos: So the reason that you all came in . . .

Alice Hardin: Farming, where you rented, was getting difficult to make a living. That's the reason we moved to the mill.

Tullos: Do you ever remember people having this disease called pellagra?[3]

Alice Hardin: I had it when I was a child.

Tullos: How do you know that that's what it was?

Alice Hardin: They told me it was, and I was in the St. Francis Hospital and the General Hospital. When I took it, I was a child about eleven years old. I was fair-complected, and my mother thought I was sunburned, because I was red on my arms. She carried me to the doctor, and he told her that that's what it was.

Tullos: What time of the year did you get it?

Alice Hardin: It was worse in the spring and the fall than any other time. Mother carried me to old Dr. Jackson at Greer when I was a child. Somebody told her that he could cure it.

Tullos: That's when you first noticed it?

Alice Hardin: Yes.

Tullos: You were living out on the farm?

Alice Hardin: Yes. He just drove it inside, a lot of other doctors told me. He just hid it, to say. I looked like I was well. When I married, I thought I was well. But when my first baby was born, I broke out with it again. And then I had it for about three years, I guess.

Tullos: What did you come to believe was the cause of that?

Alice Hardin: The doctors claimed there wasn't enough iodine in the food that we was getting. So they gave me black iodine when I had it.

Tullos: Did that do any good?

Alice Hardin: Yes.

Grover

Tullos: Maybe you could start by talking about your childhood a little bit, where you grew up and any memories you have of that.

Grover Hardin: Well, I was born in the mountain parts of Tennessee, Unicoi County, in 1909. I didn't grow up over there. We moved down here in 1916 to the mill. I went to work in 1919.

Tullos: What was your job?

Grover Hardin: I went into the carding department, all the way through, the opening room—that all goes together—picker room, opening room, and carding. And I guess I've learned every job in the carding department, from opening the bales of cotton on up.

Tullos: What about your parents?

Grover Hardin: My mother was a card room woman. She was a frame tender in the card room until she remarried again, then she quit the mill.

Tullos: What about your father?

Grover Hardin: He died when I was very small. I know very little about him.

Tullos: You were living in Tennessee on a farm?

Grover Hardin: Yes, sir. He died and my mother couldn't make it on the farm. That's why we came to South Carolina. We had a friend that lived here, and he wrote and told my mother that if she'd come down she could get a job and make a living for us.

We came on down, and as quick as I got big enough to go to work, then I went to work in order to help her with the other two children. There were three of us. At that time, she'd had a pretty hard struggle. I've been working ever since.

I worked in the mill from 1919 to 1962. November the fourteenth, '62, I came out and I haven't worked any since.

Worked in the Woodside Mills. It one time belonged to the Woodside brothers. I was practically raised at the Woodside Village.

Tullos: How long do you think your mother tried to keep on farming?

Grover Hardin: She tried it a couple of years. Almost two years, and she just couldn't make it. She'd have to hoe corn two or three days for somebody to get them to plow for her one. She just couldn't make it.

She'd do washing for people over in the mountains and work all day for maybe twenty-five or thirty cents. She just couldn't make the going. That's the reason we came down here.

Tullos: Do you remember being up there in the mountains?

Grover Hardin: Yes, sir, some. I guess I was seven or eight years old when I came down here, and I was the oldest child. I had a brother that was four months old when my daddy died. So she was left in a pretty tough shape there, in the mountains with a small baby like that. So when we come down here, why I looked after the children the best I could. Well, we done the best we could do, until we got up big enough, kind of, to go on our own. We've been left alone, what you might say, all of our entire lives, until our marriage.

Tullos: How did your father die?

Grover Hardin: I think he was much older than my mother. I think he died from an old rupture that had set up and got some way or another. I don't know any details. I just heard them say that he had a rupture to come out, and they couldn't get it.

Tullos: Do you remember your grandparents at all?

Grover Hardin: I remember Grandmother, because they moved down here in the early twenties, sometime in the early twenties they come down here and stayed a while, my grandmother on my mother's side. They were farmers in North Carolina and Tennessee. My grandmother lived in Tennessee, and her last husband, he was a North Carolina man.

Tullos: And so they came down here after you all had already been here?

Grover Hardin: Yes. We were the first in the family to come down, my mother was.

We had a friend that used to live there at Flag Pond, and he moved his family down here and they would go out and work at Monaghan Mill. He wrote and told my mother that if she'd come down here, why, she could get a job in the mill and make a living for us. We did come on down.

Tullos: Where did she go to work?

Grover Hardin: She went to work at Monaghan Mill. Later it became a J. P. Stevens mill. She worked there a while and at two or three other mills and finally wound up at Woodside. She stayed there a good while. She worked at Dunean Mill. That was a J. P. Stevens plant later, too. She worked with them about nine years. I know I went to work at Woodside, and we lived at Dunean for a while, and I would go back and forth home, from Woodside. I stayed at Woodside all the time.

Tullos: How long did your mother keep working?

Grover Hardin: She worked until she married. I just don't know what year that was that she married the second time. She married a W. O. Jones. He was a streetcar motorman. And she didn't work in the mill after she married.

Tullos: How old do you reckon she was when she stopped working in the mill?

Grover Hardin: I guess she was in her forties.

Tullos: Do you remember her talking about what conditions were like in the mill when she was working there?

Grover Hardin: Well, "hard work" is all she'd say, just "hard work." I worked right in the room with her for a long time. She was running a different job from the one I was at the time. Because I started from the brooms and went up. I come out of the mill in '62 running the same job my mother was, a frame tender. That was about the best paying job there. You'd work up.

Tullos: Did she work her way up, too, in Monaghan Mill?

Grover Hardin: I don't know what she done to start with. I imagine she had to because you don't learn a frame tender overnight, you know. It takes time to learn to make a good frame tender. And then they used to have doffers, and all like that. Had a lot of jobs behind, before you, that you don't have now, see.

Tullos: So she worked there at Monaghan for a while and then she worked at two or three other places and then went to Woodside. And that's when you first entered the mill, when she was working at Woodside?

Grover Hardin: Yes, sir.

Tullos: And did she find out about a job, and help you get that first job?

Grover Hardin: Yes, she got that first job for me.

Tullos: How would she have done that? Would she have talked to the overseer?

Grover Hardin: She'd talk to the overseer in the mill. You just talked to some overseer on the outside of the mill and got a job. If they needed you, why, they'd put you right on.

Tullos: As a child, had you gone into the mill before you started work?

Grover Hardin: Yes, sir. I had been in the mill, in and out, you know, just in and out.

Tullos: Why would you have done that?

Grover Hardin: Just to see.

Tullos: What did [your mother] do about fixing dinner for the children, or coming home for dinner while she was working, before you started?

Grover Hardin: Well, she would tell me what to do, and then I would carry it out the best I could till she got there. She'd make the bread after she come home. At that time, we worked ten hours a day. She'd fix the beans, and she'd tell me when to put a fire in the stove—we had a wood stove. A lot of times she'd put the water in them and what she wanted to do. Anyhow, she'd tell me and I done the best I could do. We got by.

Tullos: You were the oldest boy, and you had two younger brothers?

Grover Hardin: A younger brother and a sister. I have a sister living now in Greenville.

Tullos: So you were staying home, looking out for your brother and sister. Did you get to school very much?

Grover Hardin: I went to school some. I had the best chance in the world to play hookey because when she'd go to work, why, I got very little schooling.

We was just left alone, what you might say, and that's the reason I say I didn't go to school only just when I had to. I know a time or two they had mother on the carpet about me staying out so much and her not even know that I was staying out of schooling.

Tullos: She would tell you, then, things to do while she was at work?

Grover Hardin: She'd always tell me what to do. At lot of times I'd see her coming and then run and start doing, just like I was working all day, but she knowed that.

Tullos: What sort of a house did you all live in? Did you have a house by yourselves or did you have to share a house?

Grover Hardin: Yes, sir. We had a house. At that time the mill company owned the houses and they'd . . . rent it to you. A very cheap rent. . . .

Well, we usually had a three- or four-room house. We didn't have very much furniture, just a couple of beds. We didn't have the furniture that we have today. Just enough to get by on, is about all we had.

Tullos: Did you all have a garden in any of these places?

Grover Hardin: Yeah, we had a garden anytime we'd get a place where we could. If we had enough room, well, we'd put in a garden. Where they'd allow you, you know, to have a garden.

Tullos: And whose job was that to keep the garden up?

Grover Hardin: Well, we all pitched in. My mother was the head of it. She helped do what little she could and I did what I could.

Tullos: Was [your mother] able to come home any during the working hours, to check on you all, other than time off for dinner?

Grover Hardin: No. But they did get an hour at dinner and she'd come home at dinner, then go back. You had to be back at one. She laid her orders down to me and they had to do until six o'clock that night. She would give her orders in the morning, what to do and how to do, and like I said, why, when she got done I was in charge and I done the best I—Well, we got by. And she had a tough time, I'll put it like that.

Tullos: Did you all have any kind of entertainment much?

Grover Hardin: No entertainment, no. We didn't go to shows. We didn't have that kind of money. We'd just play around the house.

Tullos: Did you ever get to go back up to Tennessee to visit any of your relatives or friends up there?

Grover Hardin: I got to go maybe one time, until I got up big enough on my own. Somebody from here taken us up, I think, just for a short visit. All I remember going back was just the one time, until I got on my own.

Tullos: Did your mother ever think of going back there at all?

Grover Hardin: No, she couldn't. She couldn't think about it because she couldn't make it there.

Tullos: Did she write letters to people back up there?

Grover Hardin: Oh, yes. She'd keep in touch. Our people then got to coming down, more and more. She had a brother and a sister that moved to Greenville, you know, later on in the twenties. More 'n likely she was partly the cause of them coming down. I had one uncle to come down and he didn't stay long—four or five years—and he goes back. He didn't like the cotton mill.

Tullos: Do you remember the people that would go back like that—would they say anything about why they didn't like the cotton mill?

Grover Hardin: Well, I had an aunt, my mother's sister. She has told me since she went back. She moved back to Asheville, North Carolina, her husband did. Every time she'd see me she'd say, "Honey, why don't you get out of that cotton mill? You haven't got a color of blood about you. It's going to kill you."

Tullos: She said you hadn't got what?

Grover Hardin: She said, "You haven't got a color of blood about you." [Laughs] You know, looking at my face, I reckon. She said, "You ought to get out of the mill." Well, I didn't have no choice but to stay with the mill.

Tullos: Did the other relatives get jobs in the same mill that you all were working at?

Grover Hardin: Well, one time my mother had a brother-in-law and a brother. Her sister and them, they had a big family at that time. That's how come Uncle Starling moved down here. He had a big family and they had a hold of it and I think maybe my mother got her to move down here. I think at one time they had six hands in the mill, from one family. They're glad to get them big families. Then they can scatter them out, over the mill, and most of that time the children would have to stay, you know, till they got up big enough to get out on their own. Whether they liked the mill or not, why they'd have to stay.

Tullos: Do you remember the mills ever trying to bring people in or send recruiters out into the mountains at all, to try to get people to come in?

Grover Hardin: Well, just hearing the hands talk about it. I know one fellow at Woodside—I don't know how come they moved down—but he told me one day, "I'm going back to the farm. I don't like this."

And I asked him why.

He said, "Well, I work all day and I can look back and I can't see a thing I've done." [Laughs]

At the time he was laying up roping and they'd take it down about as fast as he'd lay it up. He didn't like that. So he didn't stay long. In about a couple of weeks, he was gone, sure enough. He didn't like it.

Tullos: Does it seem like there was a pretty fast turnover? Or did people come in, get jobs, and kind of stay on?

Grover Hardin: Well, like I said a while ago, if they'd get the big families here, well, they'd usually stay, because they had a home to live in. And they'd usually stay with them pretty good, and that's the reason they'd like to get big families, or two or three in a family anyway. It was a better showing for the company, about them staying. A lot of single people wouldn't stay, you know, if they [coughs]—when they'd get tired of working, they'd take off and get something else. Especially if they had enough education to get a better job.

Tullos: Well, Mr. Hardin, about how many grades of schooling did you get to finish?

Grover Hardin: I finished the second grade. I got promoted to the third but I never did go in it. And I went to night school a little bit along after I married.

Tullos: What about your brother and sister?

Grover Hardin: My sister got a better education. I think maybe she had—I don't know what grade she got—six or eight, I don't know, I guess, before she dropped out. My brother, he didn't get much. He didn't get over a third grade, I'm pretty sure. Like myself, he was a very poor writer and speller. He had a good chance to play out.

We was brought up to go to church. I was brought up a Baptist. I went to church a whole lot more regular when I was a child than I did after I got up on my own. My mother was a Baptist, and we were Baptists on my side. My wife's father was a Methodist. Her mother was a Baptist. She joined the

Methodist after they married. After Alice and me married, why, then she joined the Baptist church instead of the Methodist.

Tullos: Which church did you all go to?

Grover Hardin: We went to the Woodside Baptist Church. We were members. I go very little now. Last two or three times I went to church, when I'd get in a crowd, why, they would eat up my oxygen and I couldn't breathe and I'd either have to go out or use these things [respirator] and I'd make a racket.

I talked to the doctor about it and he said the crowd was what was doing it and for me to stay out of the big crowd. So I just quit going.

We get a tape every week from a Baptist church. We play it and mail it right back. My wife goes all alone up here to the Baptist. Our children belong up there, and she goes up there all alone, every chance she gets. But I usually don't go.

Tullos: When you moved here to Greenville, did your mother take you all every Sunday or every other Sunday, or not too much when she was having to work?

Grover Hardin: No. When we first moved to Greenville, she seen that we went to church. She didn't take us. She sent us. When we first moved to Monaghan Mill, I would go to the Methodist church, and the Presbyterian church, and the Baptist church. I would do that as long as we lived in the village, just wherever I wanted to go. But I did have to go to church.

Tullos: Did you go to Sunday school?

Grover Hardin: Sunday school and preaching.

Tullos: Did you go every week?

Grover Hardin: Yes, I'd go every week. I know one time, why, I was trying to get released from it, and she said no, I had to go on, I might miss something. Sure enough, when I went, my Sunday school teacher gave me a little Bible. I remember mighty well she said, "I told you you'd get a blessing if you'd go on."

Tullos: Let's talk a bit about your going to work. You started out sweeping. Can you remember much about that?

Grover Hardin: Yeah. I started out in the mill, the main reason, to help my mother. She wanted me to go to school until I got in the fifth grade at least, and I told her, I said, "You need help worse than I need the education, because I can get it later on, or I can do without it." And so I went to work just as quick as I possibly could. I started in as a sweeper.

Tullos: In the card room?

Grover Hardin: In the carding department. Naturally all the extra time I had, I tried to work on a job that paid a little more. So I learned as fast as I could and I'd get the next-best-paying job that I could get a-hold of.

Tullos: About how much do you think she was making back then?

Grover Hardin: My mother was making between seven and nine dollars [a week], somewheres in between that. The frame tenders got paid by the hank. Piece work, you know. That's the reason it would vary.

Tullos: And she would be going to work from about six in the morning?

Grover Hardin: From seven in the morning until six at night. With an hour off for dinner.

Tullos: Would they blow a whistle?

Grover Hardin: Yes, they'd blow a whistle.

Tullos: What time would it blow every day?

Grover Hardin: They'd blow a whistle at five-thirty in the morning. At a quarter till seven, they'd blow another, then at seven o'clock they'd blow the work whistle. That'd be it. If you wasn't there when the last whistle blowed, why you was kept out.

Tullos: What would happen during the last lunch hour, would they shut the machines down that she was working on?

Grover Hardin: At times they would shut them down. Then I have known them run right through dinner. But you'd either double up, whenever they run through the dinner hour, and then, say, all the spare hands were off that day. They'd have to come in and work from eleven until one. And they'd start letting them out at eleven o'clock for dinner, as many as they could, and everybody'd pitch in and run their job until they got back. Usually, a lot of time they would stop a full hour for dinner. Everything'd close down at dinner and start back up again.

Tullos: How long did you work as a sweeper before you were able to move up to the next job?

Grover Hardin: Well that depends on whether they would need you on the other job or not. As quick as they found out that you could run the next job in line, why then, when they needed you, they would take you off your sweeping job—'cause anybody could sweep—and put you on this job, and maybe you could run this job, and then drop back on your sweeping job. That would be your job, see, whatever you started off on first, well that would be your job until they'd give you another job.

I have run maybe the same job a year, and not run my job, but run other jobs, because I would know them and they would need a hand, but my job would drop right back to the sweeping job, whenever it come down to whose job it was, why this would be mine—the sweeping job. And maybe I'd run—

maybe two or three weeks—a job where somebody'd be out or off, or not
have nobody for that job. Maybe they'd hire a man, a card job, and maybe I'd
been running it two weeks. They'd hire a man for the card job and put me
back to the sweeping, see, and he'd be on the cards, you see.

Tullos: Could you describe what you'd do in a day's work as a sweeper?

Grover Hardin: Well, as a sweeper, you'd sweep between the cards, push
the lint over in a back alley, they call it. Then you'd sweep the straight alleys,
then you'd push all this up to the spare floor, what they call a spare floor at the
end of the machines. You did it all the way across the mill.

You'd sweep between the cards, then run up the alleys and with a couple of
brooms, push it up to the spare floor. Then you'd get burlap sacks and put
these sweepings in them. Then you'd push them burlap sacks over to the
shop and they'd pick them up and carry them to the waste house.

Then they finally got—at Woodside Mill—a cable that run from the mill
window to the waste house out here. We'd still have to sack up the sweepings
and carry them over to the window over here, then somebody'd put them on
this pulley and they'd go right down to the waste house. That took a lot of
work off us, from sacking these up and taking them down to the door and
then them hauling them over to the waste house, because it was a distance
from the mill.

On these cards now, when I'd run the cards, we'd have to take the fly waste
out from under the card. This was part of the card tender's job. This cylinder
that the cotton run through, underneath is galvanized ribs across with open-
ings, and this cotton and dust drops down and piles up. I took this fly waste
that'd drop down under the card. I'd take this from under the cards with a
long stick. They had sticks made the size of broom handles that were long
enough to go under this card that was about eight foot. You'd get, I'd say,
from a half a pound to a pound or more out from under each card. You'd go
down your line of cards on this side. The back end of them come together.
You'd pull this out. You'd come up on the other side in the same alley full,
because this was the first droppings from the card. We'd pull this out and
then we'd have to sweep this up, like I said, to the spare floor. The card hands
would do this, now. They sacked it up—when they got time they'd have to
run the job, but this had to be done at every shift. They'd have to pull these
out from under the cards 'cause it would build up under here. I guess it's
from a foot to two foot underneath, and I have seen them build up underneath to where it would catch back in the cylinder on the card clothing and
pull and choke the card down and tie it up. That's what would have to be got
out.

Tullos: Was this a straight stick you had?

Grover Hardin: Just like a broom handle, only they'd make them down in the shop for us, to where they would reach. They were longer than a broom handle. We'd pull this out and sack it up and it had to be done the same way as the sweepings did. Carry it over to the window and drag it up and send it down.

But the bad part about it: this was dust. I mean, solid dust. Because you're handling it, you're pulling it out, and picking it up by hand and putting it in this bag.

I was what you might call a "all-the-way-around-hand." They could use me on anything and they wouldn't have to train a man for the job. And I have been changed a lot of times. I have had a few of the people tell me that I was a valuable hand to them, because they wouldn't have to hire somebody for the job that I could run. They would change me a lot.

When Alice and I got married, in 1928, I was running cards, fifty-five hours a week for eight dollars and eighty cents. Plus, I'd do anything else that they needed me on. If they needed me on another job, why they'd take me off the cards. But the pay would run about the same. The sweeping didn't pay quite as much as the cards, and the drawings didn't pay quite as much as the cards. I think the cards was the next highest paid on the jobs, what they called the high jobs.

Tullos: What would have been the highest?

Grover Hardin: Frames. And they had a hank clock on it.

Tullos: Now the people who were fixers, they were paid by the hour?

Grover Hardin: Yeah, everything got paid hourly except the frames. That's all that had the hank clock on it.

Tullos: Did you ever think about leaving the card room and going to another department?

Grover Hardin: No, I didn't. I been borrowed one time, from the card room to the spinning room. That's not much better. It's some better, but not much.

Tullos: Would it be true that people would usually work in one department for most of their work life?

Grover Hardin: Yeah, that's it. You see, mighty few people change from one department to the other because the money running the top jobs in the card room run about the same as the top jobs in the weave room and the spinning room.

Tullos: When they changed you from one job to the other, did they change your pay at the same time, or would they still pay you at the better rate?

Grover Hardin: In the early part, why they'd pay you for whatever job you was running, and I have run a cheaper job off of my job. I'd have to run a cheaper one because I could do it, and I would do it for them, you know. I

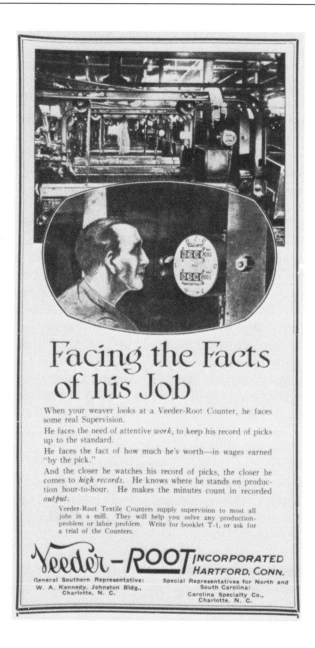

Advertisement for a Veeder-Root pick clock. (Reproduced from the *Southern Textile Bulletin*, 6 December 1928)

never did try to work aggravating the company I worked for. I always done the best I could.

Tullos: And there was no kind of organization, or even a feeling among the people that were working that this shouldn't go on?

Grover Hardin: It was that or else. You done what you was told to do, or else you didn't have a job. And that's what would make it hard on the younger people. They couldn't say, "Well, I'll quit. I'll go somewheres else." Because their parents was there. They had that to look after. Besides under the company's jurisdiction, you was under your parents. And you was obligated to obey them, and they just wouldn't listen. It was either you do or that's it. And you couldn't do nothing but go ahead and do it.

Tullos: During the day, if you were sweeping, did you have to do that all the time, or would you get caught up with that and get to rest a while?

Grover Hardin: Well, you'd catch up, but by the time you got around, sometimes you'd have a minute, but if they caught you, caught up, you could do something else. They'd have you help the other men, or do this, or do that.

There wasn't nothing you could do about it, only do it. Like I said, do it. And you'd get your job caught up to where you'd think you had a few minutes, why then maybe the overseer'd see you. Used to be one time, everybody was your bossman, from the fixer on up. They had a fixer and a second hand, and an overseer. If the fixer wanted you to do something, why, he could come and tell you to do something. And you'd quit your job and do it. Like I said, they'd report you and let you go for it. One time at Woodside Mill, I've known them to have that much authority. They'd just come and change the hands and tell you what to do.

Tullos: Would this have been back in the earlier times?

Grover Hardin: Yes, in the twenties. It was that way to a certain extent in the thirties. He wasn't a bossman, but even the fixer could tell you what to do and you'd almost have to do it. Like taking orders in the armed forces. If he's over you, he's over you.

Tullos: Did that make it harder to be friends with the fixers?

Grover Hardin: You was kind of under a fear, see. Because there was nobody you could take your troubles to. You couldn't carry it high. Because his word went above yours, regardless. Then if it went to the second hand, you'd better not buck a second hand, 'cause he had authority to fire you.

Tullos: Do you know much about the other departments in the mill? Was it pretty much the same? Or would some workers have a little more say about how things went in their department, or were able to get rid of an overseer, or a second hand who was trying to boss them too much?

Grover Hardin: No. Like I said, it was pretty well all the way down the line.

You didn't have means enough. I say, if you weren't financially able or have guts enough to tell them yourself, well, that was about it, because you just had to take it, or, like I said, lose your job, or something like that.

They didn't go around trying to pull stuff. I never had it happen to me, not pull stuff on me. But I have had to do things, that I was told to do, by the fixer, that didn't have no authority. Well, he did have an authority at the time. But I was afraid to even carry it higher, nobody to tell it to. All I could have carried it to would've been the next man in line, the bossman, and there's just no way you're going to do that, because you got your job there to look at.

Tullos: Do you remember any time, back in the twenties and thirties, when anyone tried to come in and organize unions in the textile mills here?

Grover Hardin: Yeah. Yeah, I do. They made, I remember, two or three attempts, but that was a sin to the hands, you know. They weren't supposed to mess with anything like that.

I know'd for a while, some of the hands would join the union secretly. It was like belonging to a secret order or something, and you had to slip. As quick as they found out, boy, they'd get down, you know.

One time, they was organizing Woodside Mill. And for a while it was organized. While they was organized they had the whole mills in South Carolina to fight, because they was all against us. If we got a little raise, why, all the other mills would raise first and then Woodside. Anything good happened happened to all the rest of them, then to Woodside. Woodside was always a leader in everything back in the olden time, until they got organized. They had a contract over there a pretty good while.

Tullos: Is it possible to remember when that was?

Grover Hardin: [coughs] It was in the forties. It was after World War II. I didn't belong to the union. I wasn't for it nor against it, see. Until one time I heard a man speaking on the radio and he said, "Suppose you go into the mill tomorrow to do your job, and they tell you they didn't need you anymore? Who'd you turn to?" So I got to thinking about that. The next morning I asked one of the members for a card, and I signed the card. I went in, though I didn't take an active part in it, or against it, was just a member. They did call a strike over there. I think it was illegal. But because, according to the contract you're supposed to try these jobs out for so long, then do what you's going to do. But they made a change with the battery filters in the weave room and they said they wasn't going to take it, and they would strike, and did. I'd come out with them whenever they did come out. And I went back whenever they went back.

Tullos: That was after World War II?

Grover Hardin: Yeah, this was in the forties.

Tullos: What about the secret organization?

Grover Hardin: I didn't go to none of the meetings they would have, 'cause I had a wife to keep up. I had a job to look forward to. But like I said, they was so dead against it, and still are—whole South Carolina like it is, there ain't no other way.

Tullos: Where would they have their meetings?

Grover Hardin: Just anywhere.

Tullos: Houses? Cafés?

Grover Hardin: I have heard they have them [coughs] . . . at people's houses. Anywhere they could get out of the way and talk a little bit about it.

Alice Hardin: They had a union hall, before it was over.

Grover Hardin: That was before it was secret. They was organized then.

Tullos: Were any of the other mills around here ever organized that you know of?

Grover Hardin: No.

"Smothering to Death"

Tullos: Do you recall [during the 1920s, 1930s, 1940s] people being affected in any way by the dust, that they would recognize that was the problem?

Grover Hardin: [coughs] I didn't pay too much attention to it, see. There was a continuously fog of dust in the carding department at all times. Especially around the cards and drawings, see, 'cause that was this fine stuff coming every way from the cloth.

When you hit the mill on Monday morning, you'd have a tough time a-coughing. You'd cough, and sneeze, and cough, and fill your mouth full of tobacco and anything else to try to keep this dust from strangling you.

I noted my breathing was getting worse and worse in the fifties, sometime in the fifties. I would pay no attention to it, and I would doctor it more myself. Home remedies. And the coughing would get worser and I couldn't stop that with the kind of cough syrup that I would buy over the counter.

I took these coughs and I couldn't get over them and I'd go home and I'd cough and cough and cough. Some of the boys in the plant would go to the doctor, the ones that was able to go to a doctor, I'll put it like that. They would go to the doctor and the doctor would tell them, "Well, you've got a little touch of asthma."

And I would ask the boys, you know, that I'd know'd went to the doctor. I have, a couple or three of them at different times, "Well, what'd the doctor tell you about your breathing and coughing?"

He'd say, "Oh, I just had a little touch of asthma."

So I would go get over-the-counter stuff for asthma and it wouldn't do no good, and so the heck with it, maybe it is a little touch of asthma and it'll go away.

I ended up getting worser in the fifties, where to nothing at all would do, would help no way, shape, form, or fashion. I would try everything that I know'd.

I didn't go to a doctor with it now. I didn't go to a doctor about my breathing. I would take, like I said, the home remedies for asthma, all I know'd to do by asking the boys what the doctor would tell them. Didn't know what it was then. Didn't know the word of emphysema or byssinosis, or stuff like that. Never had heard those words mentioned.

I got to getting worse and worse, worse and worse, till my wife said I'd better go to a doctor. I said they wouldn't do nothing. Can't do nothing for asthma, only just relieve it. I said maybe I'd get better.

As the time passed on it'd get worse. On Mondays I'd go in and it sure enough would be worse by that night, it'd be real bad. Tuesday, Wednesday it'd get a little better. I guess I'd get my lungs plugged up good, and over the weekend you'd clear your lungs up pretty good, then Monday morning, it'd be the same thing. Could get no air in my lungs, and I slowed up. I was always active, but I got slowing down till I just didn't have any breath.

I got to where I had to push on the job just to stay up there in the mill. And when I'd get a spare minute I'd go over and lay in the windows and get all the air I could. Well, that got to getting worse and worse. And the second hand I was working for, why, he would be along and ask me how I was doing, and I'd tell him I was doing pretty well, and I'd say, "How you doing?"

And he'd say, "Smothering to death." Maybe I'd be laying in the window and he'd come lay in with me. I told my wife, "Whatever I got, Claude Staton's got it." Claude'd come over to see me—he's a close friend—and I would ask him, after I'd come out of the mill and was cut completely down, I'd ask Claude about quitting. He was trying so hard to make it until he was sixty-two years of age, but he didn't make it. They had to carry him out a few times, and he didn't last too long after he did come out. The doctor was telling him to come out and not to go in. So he just pushed it a little too far, like I did.

Tullos: Going back into the 1920s and '30s, can you see people now, who

Grover and Alice Hardin, 1980. Photo by Allen Tullos.

were working back then, who probably had brown lung disease, but might have called it something else: tuberculosis or pneumonia or some other thing?

Grover Hardin: Yeah, I can look back and there were two three guys that's dead now. They've gone on. They coughed and done the same thing we're doing today that has brown lung, and they would think they had TB. One man I know of, whose family thought he had TB, worked till they carried him to the TB sanatorium. They didn't admit him, because if he'd a-had TB they'd a-kept him in the sanatorium. This boy's dead now, but he was telling, before they did take him to the sanatorium, that he had consumption. That's what the older people used to call it. But he didn't have it. And without any doubt in my mind, why, they could have had the same thing we have.

Tullos: Do you remember people back in the twenties and thirties who might have gone to work in the card room for a while and who decided they just couldn't take it because of the dust?

Grover Hardin: I've heard of people doing it, but I didn't know them personally. But I did talk to one man—I've forgotten his name—who worked in Woodside a while. And he told me, he said, "Boy, I can't stand that dust! I just can't stand it." This was after he already quit. But he was a man who had a good education and could get a better job in the mill. I don't know just how long he worked there. I didn't get too well acquainted with him, enough to talk with him along.

It got on in '60. It was getting worse all along. I was slowing up on it. I was wonderfully blessed with health. I had a doctor in 1921. And I had a doctor in 1962. That's a wonderful record. I'm thankful for it.

So, I got so bad, I was off on Friday, on Saturday, on Sunday. And on Monday, I believe it was. I believe I'm right on this. This is whenever I come out of the mill. Anyway I had a three days' rest out of the mill, only it was on account of my breathing, and I told my wife that morning, I got up and I said, "Alice, I'm going in this morning. I can't breathe no better and I ain't no worse. Maybe if I go in there and get hot and get to working it'll get to where I can breathe better."

She said, "You better not go."

I said, "Yeah, I believe I will. I ain't getting no better."

So I went on and worked that day, and it was so hot, the frames ran good that day and I stood there. Every spare minute I had while my job was running, why I'd lay in those windows. At that time the windows in the carding department wasn't bricked up. Well, I'd have the window lays. Every second I could, I'd be in that window, and so when I come in that night from work—it was four o'clock, we had eight hours then—I told my wife, I said, "Get that insurance policy." We had mill insurance. "I'm going to the hospital. I've either got pneumonia or I've got heart trouble, one." I could breathe, seemed like, about that much. So she did.

She got everything ready and we went straight to the hospital, emergency. I went in as an emergency. My doctor was out of town and I knew it, but I called a doctor that doctored with him. He come and checked me and he wanted to know what the trouble was, you know, and how long I'd been that way. And I said I'd been this way since Friday, Thursday night. This was either Monday or Tuesday—I've really forgotten now whether it was Monday or Tuesday. So he said, "When did you see a doctor last?"

And I told him, "In 1921."

He said, "What was the trouble then?"

And I said, "Pneumonia."

He said, "You know what? You've got it now, and you're going to have to stay."

I said, "Why, I thought so."

So he admitted me to the hospital and so in about seven days I got to come home. They x-rayed me. They give me the works up there. I went home for about two or three weeks after I come out of the hospital. I was feeling good. Doctor still hadn't told me what the trouble was. It was undercover. And I didn't know. I said, "Doctor, I'm going to work. How 'bout me going back to work?"

He said, "Now what do you want to do that for?"

I said, "Man, I ain't worked a lick since November the fourteenth."

And he said, "You can't work now."

Then it went on. I was seeing him about two or three times a week. Like I said, I was feeling good, and I went out there and I told him, I said, "Doctor, how about me going back to work now?"

He said, "I don't know how strenuous your job is, but you'll last about one minute in the strenuous parts."

So I said, "Well, I feel good."

He said, "Yeah, but your breath won't let you." I still didn't know I was through, you know. He hadn't told me. He told me, "You can go in and try it, but you won't last over a minute in the strenuous parts."

And I told him, "Well, parts of it is strenuous, parts of it is not."

Well, I went on and I stayed up there that day. The job run good that day, and I stayed in the window. And like he said, about a minute on laying these flyers up on the back line—the job was bigger than I was—I had to go over to the window and lay down, until I got my air cleared up, and another minute on that—it didn't take too awful long to lay them up, but one time I stopped three times just laying the back line of flyers off. They weigh about five pound apiece and I had to tiptoe to put them on top of this front line. They had two lines of spinners with this flyer go around each bobbin. They'd have to be laid off of the spindle up on there in order to get the full roping off.

The next day I couldn't make it. I went back to the doctor and I told him. And he said, "You can't work." I went for a couple of weeks and asked him again. See, I had no income except drawing eighteen dollars a week from the insurance company and it only lasted for so much. I asked him again and he said I couldn't. And I told him, "I believe I could."

He said, "Well, you ain't going to make it." Well, I goes up there the second time. I goes to the mill. This was in January, '63. When I went in the bossman, the main boss, he went up by his office.

He had his hand on my shoulder and he said, "Grover, don't go out there now and cut yourself down like you did before." Which was about two weeks beforehand, I went out and worked one day. I didn't much more than get to my job, till they brought two overhaulers—what they call overhaul, just go on and overhaul on my machinery—from the other end of the mill. There's a carding room in the other end.

He brought them over there, the second hand did, and he told me, "These boys are going to help you today. You lay over there in the window."

And this boy that told me this has the same identical thing that I've got. So I stayed at the window. They run my job. I didn't think nothing, see. I thought they was proud to see me back, see? Then the next day, I went in, there was the overhaulers running my job. It looks like I would've had better work than that, 'cause it was a production job, see. And them putting two guys on it. So they run my job Monday and Tuesday and I got paid for it. Tuesday and Wednesday, maybe it was, I went in. By Wednesday and Thursday, I went in. And on Thursday night, this boy, this bossman told me, the second hand, he said, "Grover, now you going to try to make it tomorrow?"

I said, "Man, yeah. I ain't got two days work in."

And he said, "Well, I got to have the overhaulers a few hours in the morning to blow down and clean the picker room out." This was on Friday.

And I said, "Well, I'll be in."

Well, the next morning I couldn't make it. So I rode with a lady that lived directly in front of me and I got up and I went on. I went and got in her car and went over to the mill. I crawled up the steps almost. I sat down on a little bench that was setting there and the second hand came by. I told him, "Claude, I'm not going to be able to make it today." But I did tell him I'd come in the day before.

He said, "I done got you a leave of absence wrote out and put in my desk. You go on home and stay until you get able to run this job."

And so I gets back home and go to the doctor and I told him and he said, "Lay off." So that was the last work I done.

Tullos: Tell me about how the Brown Lung Association entered the picture.

Grover Hardin: My doctor diagnosed my case as emphysema and he treated me for that. I think he was honest. I don't think he know'd more than emphysema, because he become a close friend of mine.

Tullos: How did he think you had gotten that?

Grover Hardin: That he never told me. He never did talk about it. He never mentioned a cigarette to me. He doctored me from 1962 until he died in 1979. Now I noticed in his office, he had signs, "Thanks for Not Smoking," but Dr. Gregory never mentioned a cigarette to me in his life.

Tullos: Did you smoke?

Grover Hardin: I used to smoke, yes, sir. But I quit smoking in '62. But I wasn't a heavy smoker. I didn't smoke on the job. We could. They finally got it so they could smoke on the job. I used chewing tobacco. I didn't smoke because I was on a production job, like I said, and if I had a machine standing, I wasn't making no money. A lot of time you could be in the water house smoking and losing money at the same time. So I didn't smoke on the job and at night I had to do all my work else I couldn't go round. Another thing, I was never financially able to be a chain smoker. 'Course at times, smoke a little more than others, on the weekend, but I never was a heavy smoker.

In 1977 some fellow gave me a call over the telephone and asked me did I have a breathing problem. I didn't know who it was. I told him, "Yes, I did."

And he said, "Do you care if I come over and talk to you?"

I told him no, to come on, I'd be glad to have him to come. He come over and he explained the brown lung to me, and what they were doing. That they would find out that cotton dust was the cause of the brown lung. He asked me did I think I could have it.

I said, "No, I've got bronchitis, emphysema."

He said, "Well, sometimes the doctors call it that, but they do find out that cotton-mill workers pick this brown lung up from cotton dust."

They invited me over to their meetings, having the meetings around in the churches at that time, wherever they'd let them have it. I went to a few of the meetings and learning, you know, all that I could about it. A lot of times they'd have a meeting and invite me and I wouldn't go because I wasn't able to stay at all with it. But other times I'd go, learning all I could. And I noticed each time I'd go, it seemed like they'd be more people in there and I got to looking around. And I'm seeing a lot of old friends and all of them like myself, fighting for breath. So I got interested in it.

Later on, you know, I went to Duke Hospital, and I stayed up there all day, and a doctor went through some questions. And he said that it was cotton dust, and it was brown lung, byssinosis—I ain't speaking that right. He said it was caused from cotton dust. I got that statement right here in the drawer.

Tullos: And this was the first one you know of complaining against Dan River Mills?

Grover Hardin: It might not be the first complaint, but it's the first award. And, as far as I know, it's the first award in this county. Without a doubt, they'll fight it to the finished extent. Not me, altogether, but the organization.

After I stopped working in 1962, we had a tough time to start with, but we was wonderfully blessed, too. We had no income whatsoever and it took six long months to get social security started. And it started out at a hundred and nine dollars after six months. Then we was just on the mercy of the people in Woodside community, plus our family. Plus everybody was good to us. We didn't go lacking for no needs. Our needs was taken care of. So, it was a pretty tough struggle till we got the hundred and nine dollars. But a hundred and nine dollars didn't go far with a family, and renting a house, and paying doctor bills. My wife has been to three doctors. She's under three doctors right now. You don't get them cheap, I'll put it like that. But we've all been blessed.

And so, after they did find out that I had brown lung, why I went to work trying to collect my compensation. Because, you see, I worked at Woodside, and they started the pension since I come out, but I didn't get in on that. And I thought maybe if I could collect a little compensation it would help out a whole lot.

Just week before last I got this paper—about eight days ago, I guess—that they had awarded me. They had the hearing and they had awarded the ten thousand dollars plus medical expenses. See, in 1962 the limit was ten thousand dollars. That was as high as they [South Carolina workmen's compensation] would go. Even your life, at that time, was ten thousand dollars. Well, mine was based on that.

Grover and Alice

Grover Hardin: Remember when we met? My wife worked in the spinning room. We met, and it must have been love at first sight because it wasn't long after we met that we married.

She was a spinning-room person, and I would go, when I could, up to the spinning room, and we'd lay in the window. We'd court a little bit on the weekend. We decided then just to get married and we did.

Alice Hardin: We've raised three families: our family, and his brother and sister, and my two brothers and sister.

Grover Hardin: After my mother married the second time, my brother, why, he stayed with us until he went to live in Tennessee with one of my aunts. Then, when Alice's parents died, she had two brothers and a sister, and they stayed with us until they married. They are the same as our own children in their feelings. And we have two children.

Tullos: What about your children? Did either of them ever work in the mill?

Grover Hardin: No, they never did.

Alice Hardin: One of my daughters teaches and one of them's a secretary.

Tullos: So they both went to high school?

Grover Hardin: Yes.

Tullos: Did you all ever say anything to them about whether you wanted them to work in the mill, or you'd rather them not?

Alice Hardin: We didn't want them to work in the mill.

Grover Hardin: We wanted better than what we had.

Alice Hardin: We wanted their lives to be more comfortable than ours was.

Grover Hardin: They both went to high school. Our youngest daughter didn't finish school. She married in her last year. But she didn't ever have to go to the mill.

Alice Hardin: She was a secretary for a long time for this . . .

Grover Hardin: . . . grading.

Alice Hardin: Grading firm, you know, that picks yarns and things.

Epilogue:
The Industry of History

" A man will think a long time before he'll speak out when he's got nine
little children about his knees," Clyde Thompson, a Carolina Piedmont mill worker, told Federal Writers' Project interviewer Leonard
Rapport in 1939. "If some people knew the things I've thought, the things
that are in my mind, the bitterness I've felt—I'd been run out long before. In
the Parrish strike I fought right on down to a frazzle—until I didn't have a
decent bed to lay down on; we liked to perished to death."[1]

Thompson's situation, his anger and bitterness, were shared by many of
the South's cotton-mill workers during the 1920s and 1930s as they were
stretched out, speeded up, curtailed, and laid off. A younger generation of
manufacturers (men like J. Spencer Love) adopted methods of stringent cost
accounting and efficiency measurement that were first developed in other
regions and industries. Intensifying international and domestic market competition brought home a post–World War I textile depression that especially
affected the coarser lines of goods that Piedmont mills produced. The introduction of new, worker-eliminating machinery (such as the automatic spoolers and warpers that Lora League Wright remembers), uncontrolled production (mills fighting each other with gluts and price cutting), and a labor pool
swelled by the continuing collapse of farming led to a shakeout of older,
"inefficient" mills and "superfluous" employees.

"It was a time," recalled one Burlington textile worker, "when you had to
work awfully hard, because there was always somebody standing at the gate
waiting for a job. And it looked like every time you got to where you could
keep a job up, they'd just add a little bit more to it. And you was always in a
hole, trying to catch up. I don't know if you've ever been like that or not.
You'll think, 'Now I'll do this, and I'll be caught up. I'll just do this and I'll be
caught up. Now I'll do this, and I'll be caught up in just a minute.' But at the

Early twentieth-century postcard view of textile mill and portion of village at Kannapolis, N.C. (Courtesy of the North Carolina Collection, University of North Carolina)

end of your shift, you're just as far behind as you were to start with. I've seen the time, a lot of times I'd think, 'Oh I just can't take any more.'"[2]

As workers felt they had little left to lose, and as the legitimacy of the national political economy itself came into question after 1929, protest by the Piedmont's industrial labor force increased to an unprecedented level during the twenties and thirties. The postwar streetcar and textile strikes in Charlotte provided early signals of the beginning of an era of labor stirrings; the defeat of the 1934 General Strike signaled an end. In between stood a score of organized walkouts and so-called "leaderless strikes" across the region and a few sensational events such as the 1929 rising at Gastonia. Before they were overpowered by mill-owner tactics that ranged from appeals to the old bonds of paternalism, to evictions and blacklisting, to reliance upon National Guard troops, thousands of angry and desperate mill workers had shut down their frames and looms, marched and rallied in downtown streets, and weighed even more radical possibilities.[3] "I got fired from one job here because they said I was a communist," Clyde Thompson told interviewer Rapport. "I wasn't no communist. I asked them, 'Tell me what communism is—what is it, anyhow? Is it something that lies between the River Jordan and the Red Sea? Just tell me what it is.'

". . . The government ain't ever helped us textile workers. As soon as they pass something, the mill figures some way to get around it. I'm tending four machines now but they're so speeded up they do a whole lot more than they used to—they're faster than we can rightfully tend. And one of the reasons we're on part time is that the mill is getting its cloth from South Carolina where there's no union and they've got them tending eight machines.

"If I had my say I'd go through the mill and I'd slow the machines down. Then I'd call in the mill policeman with his little badge and send him home, and save his forty dollars a week. Then I'd lay off the front office and call in the twenty and thirty-five thousand dollar a year men and say, 'If you want to stay here you can, for five thousand dollars a year and live like other people.' Then we could share that money and make enough to live halfway decently."

"To Serve without Prompting"

The 1920s, decade of speedup and stretchout, was also the decade in which North Carolina overtook Massachusetts as the leading state in the nation in the value of its textile products. Since the 1880s, Southern mill owners, newspaper editors, and governors had come to measure the section's level of civilization by comparing its swelling spindledges with examples in the North. Duke Power Company's Piedmont Carolinas' campaign (discussed in chapter four) sought to harness this machinery of insecurity and self-advertisement even as it pitched for Yankee businessmen and manufacturers to move where "conditions favor stability of earnings" and where "old native stock are untouched by unrest and un-American ideas" such as labor unions.

If the Piedmont's rise depended upon native "go-getters" out-Yankeeing the Yankees, perhaps other of the region's institutions could profit from Northern example and stimulation. So it seemed natural enough, in 1920, for Massachusetts-born and New England-educated Harry Woodburn Chase to assume the presidency of the University of North Carolina. Chase, the urbane spokesman of what would soon become the most progressive university in the South, understood what the institution's trustees foresaw for the postwar era at Chapel Hill—a university that could produce trained professionals and managers for an industrializing state. "The whole vital problem which lies at the heart of the new industrial society," Chase observed in his inaugural address, is "whether the Southern civilization of the future is to center about the machine or about the man."[4]

This problem of rightly relating industrial efficiency to human freedom every developing industrial civilization has faced, but none has fully solved. And as now the South confronts it, she must needs bring to bear

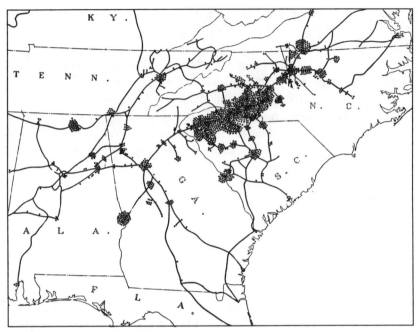

The textile industry in the area served by the Southern Railway System,
1925. This distribution represents 75 percent of the 17,359,420 cotton
spindles in the cotton-growing states. Each dot represents 10,000 spindles.
Note the concentration in the Carolina Piedmont. (Reproduced from
Potwin, *Cotton Mill People of the Piedmont*)

for its solution all her sturdy respect for human and for spiritual values.
To lose these is to buy industrial efficiency at too great a price. But
through them to transform industry into something more than a method
of making a living or of accumulating wealth, to make of it a great
instrument for achieving the ideals and the aspirations of democracy
itself—this is to write a chapter in Southern history that the whole world
will read.

By the decade's end, as Harry Chase left Chapel Hill to become the
president of the University of Illinois, manufacturers and mill workers of the
Appalachian foothills and the Carolina Piedmont were indeed writing a
chapter in Southern history that the whole world was reading. The pages in
this chapter told of the clashes at Elizabethton, Marion, Gastonia, Pineville,
Bessemer City, Charlotte, Pelzer, Anderson, and Greenville. Whether industry could be transformed into "something more than a method of making a

living or of accumulating wealth" seemed questionable to workers for whom industry had ceased to be even a means of making a living.

Chase's inaugural address posed the era's central question with an idealized rhetoric of public purpose that named neither the actors nor the unequal and undemocratic relations of power involved. The "problem" could not really be reduced to one of "man or machine" but actually centered upon the intentions of particular men who purchased and deployed particular machines, who set work assignments and profit margins, who hired and fired. The "problem" involved not only the competition of capitalists caught between each other and an international market, but also the aspirations of men, women, and children who ran the factory machines. These workers suffered the stretchouts and layoffs, the unhealthy working conditions, the lowest manufacturing wages and least unionization in the country, the constricted horizons of the mill village, and the separation by racist ideology from potential allies among the black working class. Could the state university acknowledge such a state?

One August day in 1922, E. C. Branson, professor of rural sociology at the University of North Carolina, replied to a letter he had recently received from writer Upton Sinclair:

> Referring to yours of the first instant, and the outline of your book on American Education:
> . . . To no extent whatsoever does special privilege control or attempt to control the University of North Carolina. I have seen no signs of it during my connection with this institution during the last eight years. The State University is far beyond the reach of organized big business and the politicians of the state. . . . We are free here to consider the foundational problems of life and livelihood in North Carolina, whether these concerns have to do with agriculture, manufacture, capital, labor, whatnot.
> . . . On the whole North Carolina is a free, unpurchasable, unterrified democracy.[5]

Despite the assurances that Professor Branson sent to Sinclair, the fortunes and prospects of the University of North Carolina were thoroughly intertwined with those of the state's financial, business, and manufacturing captains. In 1949 V. O. Key could write of a half-century of "economic oligarchy" in North Carolina. The oligarchs had emerged with the industrialization of the Carolina Piedmont. Politically, noted Key, "the effectiveness of the oligarchy's control has been achieved through the elevation to office of

The Southern Railway yard at Spencer Shops, N.C., ca. 1940. Photo by
Jim Torrence. (Courtesy of the North Carolina Collection, University of
North Carolina)

persons fundamentally in harmony with its viewpoint. Its interests, which are
often the interests of the state, are served without prompting."[6] The habits of
Industry had become the measure and definition of public interest.

At Chapel Hill, President Chase, intent upon "rightly relating industrial
efficiency to human freedom," oversaw a shifting of gears at his university
that coincided with the Carolina Piedmont's leading the way in the South in
the number of spinning, weaving, and knitting mills, in the manufacture of
tobacco and furniture, in the development of hydroelectric power, in bank
resources, in highway construction and sales of motor vehicles, in the number of chain stores and one-industry towns.[7] During the 1920s, the University of North Carolina developed departments of commerce, economics,
public welfare, sociology, journalism, and music. It began a scholarly press.
Its student enrollment increased from 1,200 men in 1920 to over 2,500 in
1924. In 1922 it joined the University of Virginia as the only Southern
institutions in the Association of American Universities. A school of engineering was established, according to the university's historian, "in response

to the demand for electrical engineers for the rapidly developing public utilities companies . . . and for highway engineers to aid in the extension of the North Carolina system provided for by the General Assembly of 1921 through the $50,000,000 bond issue."[8]

During the years of accelerating industrial change and crisis in the Piedmont, the sociological study of regionalism was in its heyday at the University of North Carolina. Its center was the newly established (1921) Institute for Research in Social Science, the creation of Rockefeller philanthropy, university aspiration, and the persuasiveness of a young social scientist (and Georgia native) named Howard Washington Odum. It was Professor Branson (also a native Georgian), the "intellectual godfather of the institute," and UNC President Harry W. Chase (like Odum, once a student at Clark University) who recruited the ambitious and industrious upstart—Odum—for Chapel Hill.[9] How would the new Institute, intended as a model laboratory for regional sociological investigation, engage what Chase called "the whole vital problem which lies at the heart of the new industrial society"? Could it uphold Branson's assurances to Upton Sinclair?

From the mid-1920s until World War II, the Chapel Hill regional sociologists under Howard Odum's direction claimed the name and sought to establish the boundaries of Southern regionalism. "In using the South as a term for the general living laboratory for regional research and development," wrote Odum's longtime coworker Katharine Jocher, "there is ample precedent and urge." Columbia University's sociology department had found its mission in New York City. University of Chicago social scientists were applying themselves to the study of their midwestern capitol. Surely Chapel Hill could assimilate the South.[10]

The Institute's outpourings began to appear in the mid-1920s with Odum's *Southern Pioneers in Social Interpretation* (1925), Odum and Guy Johnson's collections of black folksong, Odum's prose-poem trilogy on the day-laborer and wanderer he called Black Ulysses, Harriet Herring's investigations of welfare work in textile-mill villages, and Rupert Vance's work of cultural geography. There were books about cotton tenancy, civics, community planning, regionalism, folklife and race relations. Among the best were Vance's *Human Factors in Cotton Culture* (1929) and *Human Geography of the South* (1932), Guy Johnson's *John Henry* and *Folk Culture on St. Helena Island* (1930), Odum's *American Epoch* (1930), Arthur Raper's *Preface to Peasantry* (1936), Margaret Jarman Hagood's *Mothers of the South* (1939), and Arthur Raper and Ira De A. Reid's *Sharecroppers All* (1941). Even today, these pioneering works remain compelling.

Social science of any sort was new to the South of the 1920s, and Howard Odum's arrival only a few years out of graduate school in Massachusetts and New York was, on its face, enough to raise suspicions in some quarters. The willingness of Odum's journal, *Social Forces*, to print essays questioning some of the South's deepest articles of faith stirred rounds of protest and outrage from the Ku Klux Klan, the anti-evolutionists, and the most rabid of laissez-faire industrialists.[11] In their antimodern anxiety, the Agrarians of Vanderbilt University expressed strong doubts and misgivings. Donald Davidson, for instance, thought he detected, underneath Odum's oblique rhetorical cloak, the shapes of social scientists being secreted into positions of governmental planning authority. By means of a bureaucratic thwarting of democracy, Davidson felt that regionalism, no matter how well intentioned, would become an instrument of the expanding power of the State, the "Leviathan."[12]

Within the South, the Chapel Hill sociologists quickly established their liberal reputation. "And out of Chapel Hill," wrote W. J. Cash, "and all the lesser centers which followed Odum's lead, numbers of young men and women were going out through the schools of the South to hand on and expand the new attitude in ever-widening circles. By the end of the decade [the 1920s] even the high schools were beginning remotely to feel the influence, both of the new knowledge and of the new inquiry."[13]

Outside the South, Odum and company were cheered on by sociologists such as those at Chicago and Yale, who greeted them as equals in a young profession. H. L. Mencken offered praise and opened the pages of the *American Mercury* to their writings. Lewis Mumford, cofounder of the New York–based Regional Planning Association of America, felt that the University of North Carolina had become "the home of modern regionalism in America."[14]

Howard Odum described his coworkers at the Institute for Research in Social Science in 1926 as "a relatively enthusiastic and united group of social science folks working with more than average harmony and morale."[15] And the Institute apparently was a congenial place to work. Members shared opportunities and responsibilities; they undertook collaborative work. Unusual in any research organization during this time, a significant number of women figured prominently in all stages of Institute projects. Several sociology graduate assistants from the early years later became members of the Institute or the UNC faculty. There was a sense of loyalty, of duty, and of carrying on significant work. The good-spirited longevity of this research community stands, by itself, as an achievement.

The cumulative quantity and bulk of the studies by the Chapel Hill regional sociologists during the Odum years can weigh in confidently with

Howard W. Odum leads a discussion of regionalism at the University of
North Carolina, ca. 1938. (Courtesy of the Southern Historical Collection,
University of North Carolina)

those of any university research empire of that era. Yet, when one's eyes fall
from the scales and from the agrarian South that furnished the subjects for
the best of the Institute's work, one sees nothing to compare favorably with
Raper's incisive studies of sharecroppers or Hagood's portraiture of Southern white tenant farm women. Where are the critically engaged studies of the
industrial Piedmont? The books that realistically examine workers' living and
laboring conditions? The essays that challenge the self-promotional speechi-
fying of prominent and powerful manufacturers?

In conducting its few industrial studies, the Institute for Research in Social
Science exercised a gingerly care for the sensibilities of the region's mill
owners and businessmen. The history of the Carolina Piedmont's industrial
transformation, and the advocacy of regionalism itself, were harmonized with
a conflict-free interpretation of social change and an uncritical allegiance to
American nationalism. The Institute's disengaged and deferential posture
not only colored its research in the twenties and thirties, it also influenced the
choices and character of later projects and, perhaps more important, had

lasting effects upon both historical writing and popular depictions of the region's development.

For nearly twenty years, beginning in September 1925 when she joined the Institute, Harriet Herring was the only staff member working full time on industrialization research. Herring came to Chapel Hill from her job as personnel officer for the Carolina Woolen and Cotton Mills in Spray, North Carolina. She grew up in a "successful agricultural family in Lenoir County," was a graduate of Meredith College, held a master's degree from Radcliffe, and trained for a year in industrial relations at Bryn Mawr. "She was not an outsider," write Guion and Guy Johnson in their official history of the Institute, "but 'born here of the same folk,' and therefore Odum thought she would be an acceptable investigator to the mill owners."[16]

As her first task, Herring, in 1925, took a proposal for the study of the social and economic aspects of the Southern textile industry to the North Carolina Cotton Manufacturers Association for their approval and cooperation. Despite Herring's careful groundwork with several influential manufacturers, her project was rejected, thanks largely to the hostility and suspicions of the editor of the *Southern Textile Bulletin*, David Clark. Indeed, much of the reputation that the Institute enjoyed as an outpost for labor agitation sprang largely from the name-calling practiced by Clark, a man who held extreme views even by the baronial standards of Carolina manufacturers.[17]

Rather than proceed with the study without the approval of the Manufacturers Association, the Institute redirected Harriet Herring's work. In 1929 she completed *Welfare Work in Mill Villages*, a book built almost entirely upon interviews with textile executives. Upon its publication, UNC President Chase sent copies of *Welfare Work* to many of the state's leading industrialists to assure them they had nothing to fear from Chapel Hill's social scientists.[18]

Folkways and Technicways

Discussion of the Chapel Hill regionalists requires consideration of the formative influences upon Howard Odum's thought. For it was Odum, as director of the Institute, who hired the staff, raised its money, and set its goals. And it was Odum's benevolent tentativeness with the powers-that-were that eventually undermined the potential of his Institute and his species of regionalism.

Howard Washington Odum was born in 1884 in Bethlehem, Georgia. His father was a fundamentalist Protestant farmer, the son of a yeoman family. Odum's mother came from a planter family made land poor by the Civil War.

In *An American Epoch*, a partially autobiographical portrait of the South between 1875 and 1930, Odum presents the marriage of his parents across class lines in a manner symbolic of Odum's own desire for white, New South unity amidst "the ache of the past and the fear of the future." He writes that "in the intermarriage of these two families much of the older feeling of superiority and inferiority had been lost in the common struggle and a reasonable wholesome fellowship had developed in the rapidly growing, eager, and ambitious families."[19] Whether derived from his family's experience or projected back upon it, this is the face that Odum turned upon all manner of relations within Southern society and upon regional-national relations.

From several years of study, first at staunchly Methodist Emory College, then with G. Stanley Hall at Clark University (where he took a psychology Ph.D. in 1909), and with Franklin Giddings at Columbia (earning a sociology Ph.D. in 1910) Odum accumulated an undigested amalgam of psychological and social science theories, largely from an antiquated, organic worldview. He was strongly influenced by William Graham Sumner's concept of "folkways"—a near-fatalistic and frequently racist view of the slowness of cultural change. Folkways, even those that underwrote racial and gender-based prejudices, were not to be—indeed could not be—eliminated by stateways (such as statutory laws) until the folk themselves moved together to shape new folkways.[20]

As Michael O'Brien has observed, Odum took his "intellectual melange to the South. . . . Effecting a peculiar blend of pre–First World War sociology, he made no theoretical advances on it. As his theory grew older, he found little time or inclination for the fresh infusions of later years. Weber, Durkheim, Parato, Tönnies, adaptations of Marx, played no part in his intellectual biography."[21] Interlacing Odum's earnest, diffuse, obliging, liberal spirit, and holding it together, was an equivocating prose style, called Odumesque by his students and characterized by its ability to dodge oncoming points of view and to perch owlishly on the leading edge of the status quo. Consider this example:

> Folk society may abound in any stage of culture or civilization whenever the major conditioning factors are extra-organizational or when a synergy of conflicting forces and processes results in an integrated transitional society, the transition featuring change from one stage of culture to another; from individual and primary group development to social organization; or from the "paths of individual development" to the processes of cultural evolution.[22]

While at Clark University, Odum was stirred by G. Stanley Hall's vision that the leaders of the modern university should shape American society and that university builders should see themselves as social engineers. Through Hall, Odum also became aware of Patrick Geddes, the Scottish city planner, regionalist, and biologist. Geddes and Hall were good friends who had exchanged visits and correspondence for many years.[23] In Edinburgh, between 1892 and 1912, Geddes had charge of an old observatory that he transformed into "Outlook Tower," a workshop for the study of an expanding horizon of city, region, and world. Beginning with a view of Edinburgh seen from the top of the tower, a visitor descended through levels of the building devoted successively to the surrounding region, Scotland, the British Isles, and the world. Each floor contained books, charts, maps, models, and artifacts of ongoing research. "This regional Outlook Tower," said Patrick Geddes, "is thus itself a regional product; although its principle is easily adaptable to every region, as that of an encyclopedia may be used anywhere."[24] According to Lewis Mumford, the Outlook Tower significantly influenced Odum's plan for the regional workshop at Chapel Hill.[25]

From the first days of the Institute for Research in Social Science, Odum was anxious to show that his regionalism owed its primary allegiance to the national interest. Mindful of the legacy of Southern sectionalism, with its antagonistic posturings and embittered memories, he abandoned the use of the word *sectionalism* in any but a pejorative sense. "Regionalism," wrote Donald Davidson, recognizing Odum's tactic, did not have "the taint of war and confusion that hangs about the older words."[26]

In opting for a harmony of vocabulary, Odum questioned Frederick Jackson Turner's prophecy that sectionalism, far from dying, would become more important as America developed.[27] In 1922, the year that Odum founded the journal *Social Forces*, Turner wrote the essay "Sections and Nation" for the *Yale Review*. "We in America," observed Turner, "are in reality a federation of sections rather than of states. State sovereignty was never influential except as a constitutional shield for the section."

> We are so large and diversified a nation that it is almost impossible to see the situation except through sectional spectacles. The section either conceives itself as an aggrieved and oppressed minority, suffering from the injustice of the other sections of the nation, or it thinks of its own culture, its economic policies, and well-being as best for all the nation. It thinks, in other words, of the nation in terms of itself.[28]

As an explicit response to Turner, Odum published Edward A. Ross's essay "Sectionalism and Its Avoidance" in the 1924 issue of *Social Forces*.

Ross agreed that, for now, there were longstanding sectional differences in the United States, but he saw forces at work that would "nationalize" and "standardize" everything from clothes and house interiors to thinking and feeling. Such "unifying interests" as Ross found, he celebrated. "As negroes drift North," he wrote, "more northerners are able to get the southern white man's point of view on the race question." The rise of national magazines, mass advertising, motion pictures, and network radio would help insure "that in our time at least the nationalizing forces have the upperhand of the sectionalizing forces."[29]

In a 1934 *Social Forces* article, Odum contrasted his regionalism with Turner's vision and with earlier forms of "sectionalism." With the rhetoric of harmony, he sought to show how "balance" could be substituted for Turner's inevitable intersectional strife. Under the banner of balance, Odum adapted his regionalism into a nationalistic framework. "In the first place," he said, "regionalism envisages the Nation first, making the national culture and welfare the final arbiter. . . . For whatever else the Southern region may be, it is first of all a major part of the moving inventory of a powerful nation rebuilding its own fortunes and reconstructing its part in the world of nations."[30]

While Odum's anxiety over sectionalism led him to view the region always "in the perspective of the total national interest," other regionalists of that era—Lewis Mumford being perhaps the best known—saw nationalism as the mythology of a "war-state" and as "an attempt to make the laws and customs and beliefs of a single region or city do duty for the varied expressions of a multitude of other regions."[31] And while Odum wrote that "to set in motion forces which will turn the Southern potential into national power will constitute the supreme task of the next few generations," it was his sociologist colleague Rupert Vance who, in tracing the South's history as provider of natural resources, cheap labor, and unfinished manufactured goods to Northern businessmen and manufacturers, put forward the disharmonious term "colonial economy."[32]

What else might a regionalist in the South of that era have done? "I made a statement in 1929," recalls Myles Horton (b. 1905), cofounder in 1932 of the Tennessee activist-education school known today as the Highlander Center. "I said, 'We are going to have industrialization in Appalachia and in the South. It's going to come and we aren't going to be against it. But it's going to be exploitive unless we organize the people in the South to be ready to deal with it and demand their rights.' And I still believe that today. The reason industrialization has gotten out of hand is because we haven't had the organization to represent the people."[33]

Howard Odum offered no straightforward recognition of the crisis facing the Piedmont's farmers and factory workers. His adoption of William Graham Sumner's folkways concept and his own development of the idea of "technicways" as "the habits and customs that develop as adjustment to the innovations of science and technology" led to an amorphous and widely inclusive category of "folk" that lacked class and historical definition and to a view of technological development that failed to acknowledge real power relations in society.[34] His depiction of the folk as "a universal constant in a world of variables" allowed too easily for nostalgic projections and wishful harmony, leaving unacknowledged the influence of what V. O. Key called the "aggressive aristocracy of manufacturing and business."[35]

Technicways came, in Odum's view, like thundering providences, threatening to wash the folkways away. The mission of a social science institute like that at Chapel Hill was to monitor the process of disintegration and adjustment. Odum came to voice regret and concern at the rapidity of the changes even as he became identified with Progress. But he could not, or would not, call by name the visible hands and the intentions that brought the technicways. Technicways were understood to move as if they were natural forces, not the outcomes of contending human interests and unequal powers.

"I think," says Myles Horton (who knew well Odum, Vance, Herring, and other members of the Institute for Research in Social Science, and who drew upon their statistical findings whenever he could), "their whole concept of regionalism was to do things very step-by-stepish, not rock the boat; bring the whole state along, all the corporations, all the big farmers, all the other black and white people at the bottom, bring them all along. They had the fiction that everybody was in one class."[36]

In settling upon a false consensus in the Piedmont, Howard Odum and Harriet Herring placed themselves among proponents of the "industrial relations" approach to labor-management conflict. As Herring wrote in 1939 to textile-mill executive Luther Hodges, an old friend, former employer, and future governor of North Carolina, the New Deal industry codes, the eight-hour day, and minimum wage legislation "were a blessing in disguise" for manufacturers. "The stage was pretty well set," she observed, "for us here in the South to begin a period of labor warfare that would probably have been bloody and terrible; Southern workers are docile just so far and after that mighty headstrong and easily swung by an emotional leader on an issue that they feel keenly about; Southern employers are paternal—'father knows best'—and dictatorial because they had a long spell of running their business to suit themselves as far as the workers were concerned and because they have been so high in public esteem and workers so low in it."[37] Unacknowledged in Herring's analysis was the fact that textile industry leaders, having written the National Recovery Administration's Textile Code, and having crushed striking workers with guns and troops, had bestowed upon themselves and their fellow manufacturers both the blessing *and* the disguise of industrial peace.[38]

"Industrial relations," writes historian of technology David F. Noble, "aimed at improving the lot of workers in order to win their cooperation and loyalty" but represented neither lessening of control nor democratization of owner-worker arrangements.[39] In the Carolina Piedmont, industrial-relations strategies followed upon the heels of "welfare work" activities (the building of recreation facilities, libraries, and health clinics in mill villages) that had flourished in the boom years of World War I. During the textile depression of the 1920s, Piedmont mills cut back or eliminated many of their welfare activities, while industrial-relations advocates pressed for more formally structured, less paternalistic, work-centered methods of bonding worker loyalty.

A step beyond industrial relations lay the business strategy known as "human relations": "the catchword," observes Noble, "for transforming the stubborn 'human factor' of production into an efficient, adjusted part of the corporate mechanism."[40] In time, the outlook and the work of the Institute for Research in Social Science proved compatible with the mid-twentieth-century "human relations" approach. "Thirty years after the Institute began research in industrial and labor relations," write Guy and Guion Johnson, "the University of North Carolina Press published a composite study, *Human Relations in the Industrial Southeast* (1956). The book's author, Glenn Gilman, had 'never come under the personal influence' of the Institute but felt that he must 'give particular credit to Howard Odum, Harriet Herring and Rupert Vance . . . for the understanding their studies had given him of the special circumstances that surround living and working in a human fashion in the Southeastern United States.' "[41]

Although seldom read today, *Human Relations in the Industrial Southeast* synthesized a historical romance of the Piedmont's transformation that remains popular as the grist of newspaper feature stories, civic commemorations, advertising campaigns, and public history. Admitting no fundamental antagonisms between the interests of mill workers and mill owners, industrial-relations analyst Gilman saw problems of "communication" inherent in the industrial process. These problems were capable of adjustment by an enlightened management assisted by trade associations and governmental guidelines.[42] "The increasing complexity of organization for production,"

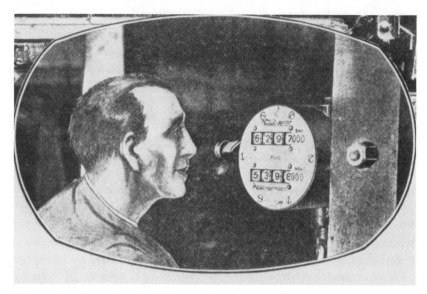

"Facing the Facts of his Job." Detail from an advertisement for Veeder-Root
pick clocks. (Reproduced from the *Southern Textile Bulletin*, 6 December
1928)

Gilman writes, "meant that what had formerly been left to follow its own
meandering path must now be deliberately planned for, that relationships
which in older days and simpler organizations could safely be left implicit
must now be explicitly spelled out, and that exchanges of information which
could be once accomplished by informal channels must now be supplemented, though not replaced, by formal means."[43]

Gilman approached the Piedmont with a "limited objective" in mind: "to
furnish the future supervisors, administrators, and executives of the southeastern cotton textile industry with an orientation toward industrial relations
that would enable them to maintain those relationships to the long-run
advantage of the industry, the region, and the nation."[44] To arrive at his
modest goal, Gilman relied especially on Odum's writings about folkways and
technicways. The folk, in Gilman's view, had adjusted well to industrialization, making the long transition from antebellum yeomanry to New South
mill-town culture while remaining quite in control of their common destiny.

Gilman's history unites Piedmont mill owner and mill worker in a shared
mission by insisting that they have always been *one* folk. "The folk built the
mills," Gilman proclaims, "and in the building of them they wove them into
the folkways. . . . The implicit controls to which southern mill managements

were thus submitted dwarfed in their power and inclusiveness the explicit and limited controls of legislation and ordinance. . . . They represented the natural, intuitive adjustments of a folk society to industrial technics which they themselves adopted and fashioned into an institution."[45]

That "the mill worker and his family had never stopped in for Sunday dinner with the local banker," should give no cause for worry. "Such things are not likely to happen in any society where there is sufficient differentiation of function to require some men to be bankers and others to be mill workers." "Differentiation of function" also required some men to acquire title to and oversee the running of particular mills or groups of mills. Yet, Gilman assures, "*title to and control of the institution of the manufacture of cotton textiles as a way of life for the Piedmont was retained by the folk*" (emphasis Gilman's). Because "Piedmont managements are themselves of the folk," workers are protected from arbitrary treatment by "the implicitly enforced set of community expectations." To maintain industrial peace, management need only formalize the unspoken consensus.[46] So Odum's folkways became Industry's habits.

Among the Chapel Hill regionalists, it was always Rupert Vance who urged Odum to be more straightforward, more candid. "I believe I must be wanting a more hardboiled view of social conflict," Vance wrote his friend and colleague in 1938 in a prepublication critique of Odum and Harry Estill Moore's *American Regionalism.* "Conflict," Vance continued, "we will always have with us. How does Regionalism take it out of the realm of hard knocks and place it in the realm of discussion and reasonable 'due process' of policy making? And what about class conflict? Is the resolution of Regional views an alternative to an increase of such conflict?"[47]

Odum left Vance's questions unanswered. With the coming of World War II, regionalism gave way to national mobilization and economic depression to boom times. If Odum's regionalism fared poorly in the postwar American empire, the Institute for Research in Social Science flourished, having, in the words of its historians, "entered into contracts with the Air Force for a series of studies of Soviet industrial capacities and a study of day-and-night populations of Soviet and American 'target cities,' and with the Public Health Service for studies of urbanization in connection with the building of the Savannah River atomic energy plant."[48] The vision of regional development incorporated the surveillance and planned destruction of regions. The desire to transform industry into "a great instrument for achieving the ideals and the aspirations of democracy itself" embraced a factory producing nuclear bombs and undisposable waste. In these pursuits university social science research itself took on the appearance of an industry thoroughly intertwined

Automobiles parked on the Duke University campus for the 1939 football
game between Duke and the University of North Carolina. Photo by
Marion Post, Odum Subregional Photographic Study. (Courtesy of the
Southern Historical Collection, University of North Carolina)

with the most irrational forces of the corporate state. Any alternative regionalist vision that might have sharpened criticism of the dominant "technicways" of the modern nation had fled in the face of the Institute's attraction to
the marketplace of ideas—a fascination intimated as early as 1927 when
Odum's friend, Professor Ernest Groves of Boston University, sent congratu-
lations to the young sociologist who had just received another Rockefeller
grant. "Odum, of North Carolina," wrote Groves, "has come to have a
meaning almost like a trademark in business."[49]

Quitting Time

"Many see in North Carolina," reported political scientist V. O. Key in the
late 1940s, "a closer approximation to national norms, or national expectations of performance, than they find elsewhere in the South. In any competition for national judgment they deem the state far more 'presentable' than its
southern neighbors."[50] What many saw and approved as familiarly "American" when they looked along the axis of the Carolina Piedmont, from Dan-

ville to Charlotte to Greenville, was a modern region now dominated by manufacturing and business, administered and ruled by a "progressive plutocracy" of white men. What also made the Piedmont look so American—and so un-Southern—were the supporting structures, institutions, services, and professions of a modern state: the network of railway tracks and electrical power lines; the public school and university systems; the web of paved roads, which led farmers to markets and mills and which supported the proliferation of freight-hauling trucks that connected manufacturing towns with each other and with the rest of the country; main street banks and businesses; radio towers; daily newspapers; and football-stadium parking lots filled on Saturday afternoons with the polished emblems of middle-class arrival.

That Carolina Piedmont manufacturers could become American manufacturers, no one could now doubt. Hadn't Buck Duke proved that the son of a Methodist yeoman farmer could become as wealthy, powerful, and philanthropic as a Rockefeller? Skeptics could be shown the mansions of families named Reynolds or Hanes, or taken to the "Pioneer Plant" in the Piedmont Heights section of the town of Burlington to see the mill from which the nation's largest textile company grew.

"They made their money out o' us," says a Piedmont mill worker named Marg in Myra Page's *Southern Cotton Mills and Labor* (1929). Marg is talking about the owners of the factory village where she lives and labors. "I look at their fine houses whin I go to town, 'n I thinks to myself, 'You made that out o' us. If we waran so poor, you'd not be so rich.' "[51]

Marg's observation, the simplest equation of the relationship between manufacturers and workers in the Piedmont, insists upon an understanding of the development of the Carolina Piedmont, not in terms of an inevitable, predictable result of "technicways" and autonomous "market forces," but as a contentious historical process in which the industrial fathers held a strong upper hand over desperate families who came to the mills already accustomed to long days and years of punishing physical work for little reward. By itself, hard work could establish little.

"In God's scheme of life," observed the Carolina Piedmont tobacco and hosiery manufacturer Julian Shakespeare Carr, "there is no place for the idler or hobos. At the fall the ground was cursed for man's sake, that in the sweat of toil he might be kept in health of body and mind and attain to true manhood."[52] The Piedmont's history is filled with the worn bodies of toil. Carr's motto, "Work as though you live forever, live as though you would die today," would have served equally well for D. A. Tompkins, Buck Duke, Simpson Tanner, J. Spencer Love, and other dynamos of the region's industrial regime whose single vision became an obsession. Only rarely and too late did any of them recognize, as Tompkins put it, that their driven lives of labor were "liable to lead to a sort of general break-down of the nervous system." Another way of life seemed intolerable, unimaginable. "The feeling of many a man," wrote Tompkins after his own collapse, "is that . . . he might as well continue the old way and die."

Old ways die hard. By the middle of the twentieth century, Piedmont manufacturers' assurance of having their way within the region, and their insistence on having their version of history publicly affirmed, had become venerable habits of Industry. In these pages I have sought to question industry's habits and Industry's assurance. It is long past quitting time.

Notes

Abbreviations Used in Notes

DATP   Daniel Augustus Tompkins Papers, SHC
ECBP   Eugene Cunningham Branson Papers, SHC
FWPP   Federal Writers' Project Papers, SHC
HLHP   Harriet Laura Herring Papers, SHC
JLLP   James Lee Love Papers, SHC
NA   National Archives, Washington, D.C.
NCSA   North Carolina State Archives, Raleigh, N.C.
PSC   Parker School District Scrapbook Collection, Greenville County
        Library, Greenville, S.C.
RBVP   Rupert Bayless Vance Papers, SHC
SHC   Southern Historical Collection, University of North Carolina,
        Chapel Hill

Preface

1. Bessie Buchanan interview, Durham, N.C.; Larson, " 'Miss Bessie.' "

2. Reed recorded, but probably did not compose, this popular song in 1927. Mainer's version followed by a few years. It's likely that Buchanan would have heard the recording of Mainer and his Mountaineers, who performed regularly on Charlotte radio station WBT and traveled throughout the Carolina Piedmont in the 1930s. Both Reed's and Mainer's versions include these verses:

> Why do you bob your hair, girls, you're doing mighty wrong;
> God says 'tis a glory and you should wear it long. . . .
>
> Why do you bob your hair, girls, it is an awful shame
> To rob the hair God gave you and bear the flapper's name.
> You're taking off your covering, it is an awful sin;
> Don't never bob your hair, girls, short hair belongs to men.

Why do you bob your hair, girls, it's not the thing to do.
Just wear it, always wear it, and to the Lord be true.
And when before the Judgment, you meet the Lord up there,
He'll say, "Well done for one thing, you never bobbed your hair."

For recorded versions, see Reed, *How Can a Poor Man Stand Such Times and Live*, and Mainer, *J. E. Mainer's Mountaineers*.

3. Organizing difficulties are summarized in Frederickson, " 'I Know Which Side I'm On.' "

4. See Liston Pope's discussion of the Loray strike in *Millhands and Preachers*, pp. 207–84. See also Hall, "Disorderly Women."

Introduction

1. On the topography of the Carolina Piedmont, see South Carolina Writers' Project, *South Carolina*, p. 11; Clay, Orr, and Stuart, *North Carolina Atlas*, p. 113; Vance, *Human Geography of the South*, p. 275.

2. Jonathan Daniels, "Tar Heels All," in Federal Writers' Project, *North Carolina*, p. 4.

3. Thomas Henderson, quoted in Lounsbury, "From Craft to Industry," p. 10.

4. Lillian Smith, "Two Men and a Bargain," in *Killers of the Dream*, pp. 154–69. On the concept of false consensus, see Gaventa, *Power and Powerlessness*, esp. pp. 29–30.

5. Chase, *State University and the New South*, pp. 60–61.

6. Fromm and Maccoby, *Social Character in a Mexican Village*, pp. 20–23.

7. Social character is discussed in Erich Fromm, *Escape from Freedom*, pp. 304–27, and Fromm and Maccoby, *Social Character in a Mexican Village*, pp. 16–23, 230–35.

8. Carl and Mary Thompson interview, Charlotte, N.C. The biblical reference is to Prov. 22:6.

9. Paul Cline interview, Greenville, S.C.

10. Lora League Wright interview, Greenville, S.C.

11. Geddes Dodson interview, Greenville, S.C.

12. Betty and Lloyd Davidson interview, Burlington, N.C.

13. Harry Lee Rogers interview, Burlington, N.C. Worker Icy Norman (see chapter three) also speaks of Copland as "just like a daddy" (Icy Norman interview, Burlington, N.C.).

14. "The economic changes of the postwar era," observed C. Vann Woodward, "the coming of the cotton mills, the heavy industry, the sharecropper system: those adjusted to the prevailing racial system" (Green, "Rewriting Southern History," pp. 90–91). Blacks in postbellum Piedmont industries are discussed in Northrup and Rowan, *Negro Employment in Southern Industry*; Stokes, "Black and White Labor"; Janiewski, *Sisterhood Denied*.

Mary Frederickson notes that, before 1940, fewer than 10 percent of Southern textile workers were black and 80 percent of these workers held laborer rather than production jobs. By the late 1970s, blacks accounted for 20 percent of all mill workers and held 25 percent of all operative jobs (Frederickson, "Four Decades of Change"). See also Starobin, *Industrial Slavery in the Old South*; Worthman and Green, "Black Workers in the New South"; Korstad, "Those Who Were Not Afraid"; Tilley, *Bright Tobacco Industry*.

15. Johnson, *Making of a Southern Industrialist*, pp. 50–54.

16. The image of the black worker as mule remained popular throughout the late nineteenth and early twentieth centuries, e.g.: "The freedman stands here present in the full enjoyment of his newly acquired freedom. As a laborer he has no equal for patient industry and mule-like endurance" (letter from Col. John Logan Black of Blacksburg, S.C., to *Manufacturers' Record*, 25 Oct. 1890, pp. 7–8).

17. Rodgers, *Work Ethic in Industrial America*, p. xii.

18. Lanier Rand, a former fieldworker with the Southern Oral History Program, told me this story, which she collected from an anonymous, retired Erwin Mill worker in Durham, N.C., in 1979.

Chapter One

1. George and Ethel Marshall Faucette interview, Burlington, N.C.

At the dinner table, the father traditionally sat at the head and the mother, after serving the food, sat at the foot. There "wasn't no fussing and quarreling during the meal," recalls retired mill worker Nannie Pharis of Burlington, N.C. "I don't remember that ever happening, but if it had my father would just tell us to be quiet. That meant that" (James and Nannie F. Pharis interview, Burlington, N.C.).

2. Paul and Don Faucette interview, Burlington, N.C.

3. A small but significant number of skilled textile machinists who migrated to the Carolina Piedmont from New England during the textile depression of the 1810s were also important in starting mills in the region and in training owners as well as workers (see my discussion of H. P. Hammett in chapter four). See also Beatty, "Lowells of the South."

4. Benson Lossing, quoted in Lounsbury, *Alamance County Architectural Heritage*, pp. 36–38.

5. Holt and his friend and fellow mill builder, Francis Fries, "cooperated by making alternate trips to the North where they investigated new improvements in machinery" and "ascertained marketing conditions" (Griffin and Standard, "Cotton Textile Industry in Ante-Bellum North Carolina, Part 2," p. 146).

6. Lounsbury, *Alamance County Architectural Heritage*, p. 33.

7. Lander, *Textile Industry in Antebellum South Carolina*, pp. 25–26, 100–101, 108; Griffin and Standard, "Cotton Textile Industry in Ante-Bellum North Carolina, Part 1."

8. See Wright, "Cheap Labor and Southern Textiles," and, as background, *Political Economy of the Cotton South*. See also Thomas J. Woofter's discussion of the Tobacco Piedmont and the Cotton Piedmont in "Subregions of the Southeast."

9. Lounsbury, *Alamance County Architectural Heritage*, pp. 48–53; Glass, "Southern Mill Hills," pp. 138–42; Pierpont, "Textile Industry in Alamance County, North Carolina," pp. 66, 72; Bresler, "Industrial Vernacular Architecture."

10. Pierpont, "Textile Industry in Alamance County, North Carolina," p. 68.

11. Ibid., pp. 27–31; Glass, "Southern Mill Hills," p. 139; Nathans, *Quest for Progress*, pp. 28–38.

12. An excellent study of a Piedmont mill town and its surroundings is DeNatale, "Bynum."

13. Charles and Zelma Murray interview, Burlington, N.C.

14. McLaurin, *Paternalism and Protest*, pp. 156–60 (for a discussion of the Knights of Labor in Alamance County, see pp. 79–83); see also McLaurin, "Knights of Labor in North Carolina Politics."

15. Swain, *Water-Power of the South Atlantic Watershed*, pp. 66, 98.

16. Ibid., p. 22. See also Rupert Vance's similar comments about the Piedmont in *Human Geography of the South*, pp. 276–77.

17. Mills, *Atlas of the State of South Carolina*.

18. Robert Roy Adams interview, Greenville, S.C.

19. John Montgomery Belk interview, Charlotte, N.C. Belk (b. 1920) is a former president of the Chamber of Commerce, a trustee of Davidson College, a former combat officer in World War II and Korea, and a former chairman of the National Retail Merchants Association (NRMA). A profile article appearing in the *New York Times* (13 Jan. 1974) upon Belk's election as NRMA chairman stated that the four hundred Belk stores in seventeen southeastern states generated $700 million annual volume and a 5 percent net profit on sales. Upon the death of his father in 1952, John Belk became coordinator of the Belk stores. Hospitalization for ulcers in 1958, said Belk, taught him the need for "a change in tempo when everything gets too much."

20. Milton Short interview, Charlotte, N.C.

21. Blythe, *William Henry Belk*, pp. 204–5.

22. John J. Parker, foreword to Blythe, *William Henry Belk*, pp. viii–ix.

23. "They call themselves Scotch-Irish in this section. . . . I understand they were pretty straight-out Scotch, and strong Presbyterians" (Henry Belk, quoted in Blythe, *William Henry Belk*, p. 14).

24. Meriwether, *Expansion of South Carolina*, pp. 137, 144; Blythe, *William Henry Belk*, pp. 18–19.

25. Howe, *Scotch-Irish and Their First Settlements*, p. 14.

26. Clark, "Andrew Jackson." I heard the tale of Jackson's father's last trip several times while doing field research in the Waxhaws.

27. U.S. Census, 1850, *Population, Free and Slave*, Lancaster District, S.C.; Lathan, *Lathan-Belk Families*, pp. 261–69; Robert N. McNelly, "Union County and the Old Waxhaw Settlement," in Lathan, *Lathan-Belk Families*, pp. 408–17; Blythe, *William Henry Belk*, p. 5; Ford, "Social Origins of a New South Carolina," pp. 30–31.

28. Blythe, *William Henry Belk*, pp. 179–82.

29. John Montgomery Belk interview. The 1860 census lists A. N. W. Belk, age twenty-seven, and Sarah Belk, age twenty-three. Abel is shown as a farmer with real estate valued at $2,500 and personal estate at $5,800. In that year, Abel Belk owned four slaves: three males and one female, ranging in age from fifteen to twenty-two (U.S. Census, 1860, *Population*, Lancaster County, S.C.).

30. With $1,100 in total wealth, Sarah Belk Simpson and her family ranked in the prosperous middle of Lancaster County's householders. Most common were listings from $100 to $300, with a handful of families showing from $5,000 to $15,000 in total wealth (U.S. Census, 1870, *Population*, Lancaster County, S.C.).

31. Howe, *Scotch-Irish and Their First Settlements*, p. 28.

32. Ervin, *William Henry Belk*, p. 9. Ervin's speech was delivered in 1958 at a Charlotte banquet given by the Newcomen Society (a group named in honor of the inventor of the deep-mine water pump). It was preceded by the introduction of Ervin by Irwin Belk, son of Henry and at that time president of Belk Enterprises. In his introduction, Irwin Belk offered Senator Ervin's credentials: "It is one of life's rarest treats to present to so distinguished an audience a man who, by his Scotch-Irish and Calvinistic inheritance, as well as by his long and distinguished career as lawyer, Solicitor, Superior Court Judge, Supreme Court Justice, Member of Congress and now of that august body, the U.S. Senate, is so intimately familiar with the people, the region, the religious and business environment in which my late father, William Henry Belk, grew and lived and served his fellow man" (p. 6).

33. See Janssen-Jurriet, *Sexism*, pp. 33–36.

34. Blythe, *William Henry Belk*, pp. 31–33.

35. Walden, *History of Union County*, p. 51.

36. Blythe, *William Henry Belk*, p. 174.

37. Ibid., p. 38.

38. William Henry Belk's brother John died in 1928 at the age of sixty-two. Like his brother, John Belk was an active Presbyterian elder who gave substantial time and money to the building of churches and Presbyterian hospitals. He, too, was a stockholder in several Piedmont cotton mills (*Raleigh News and Observer*, 22 Mar. 1928).

39. Bourne, "Puritan's Will to Power."

40. LeGette Blythe discusses Belk clerks and investments (*William Henry Belk*, pp. 85–95). See also Jean Cole Hatcher interview, Charlotte, N.C.; Stack and Beasley, *Sketches of Monroe and Union County*, pp. 81–83.

41. For an overview of economic conditions in the South's nonplantation areas during these turn-of-the-century decades, see Wright, *Old South, New South*, pp. 107–23. On the expansion of Belk stores, see Blythe, *William Henry Belk*, pp. 75–77, 92. Henry Belk usually offered one-third partnerships to those men he selected to start a new store in the Belk group. In 1974 there were five thousand part-owners embracing fifty families (*New York Times*, 13 Jan. 1974).

42. Blythe, *William Henry Belk*, p. 92.

43. The influence of the Presbyterian-founded Davidson College and the Presby-

terian-influenced University of North Carolina at Chapel Hill (both were white, male-only schools during the years covered in this study) on the fathers of the modern Piedmont must be reckoned as considerable.

44. Blythe, *William Henry Belk*, p. 193. Mary Irwin (1882–1968) was twenty years younger than Henry Belk (obituary, *Raleigh News and Observer*, 7 Feb. 1968).

45. Bourne, "Puritan's Will to Power," pp. 302, 305.

46. The following table is derived from Sitterson, "Business Leaders in Post–Civil War North Carolina," p. 119.

Church Membership of North Carolina Business Leaders

Denomination	Percentage	Number	% Dist. of Church Membership, 1890
Methodist	28.3	34	40.34
Baptist	5.8	7	45.37
Presbyterian	23.3	28	5.27
Episcopal	12.5	15	1.19
Roman Catholic	1.66	2	.39
Jewish	1.66	2	
Other Protestant	10.0	12	
Unknown	16.6	20	7.43
Total	99.82	120	99.99

47. Golden, in Ashmore, *Hearts and Minds*, pp. 100–108. "Charlotte's leading department stores," writes Ashmore, "all of which operated chain outlets throughout piedmont Carolina, bore the names of staunchly Protestant proprietors. Belks were Presbyterian, Effirds were Baptist, and Iveys were Methodist, so much so that patriarch, old George Ivey, ordered the shades drawn on his display windows on Sunday, and refused to stock playing cards, poker chips, or cocktail glasses—prompting Golden to inquire in the Israelite, 'Why beds?'" On Harry Golden, see "Harry Golden," *New York Times*, 3 Oct. 1981.

Chapter Two

1. Woodmason, *Carolina Backcountry*, pp. 16–17, 45.

2. Woodmason uses "Scots Irish" to identify settlers from Ulster (*Carolina Backcountry*, p. 23). For a history of the use of the term "Scotch-Irish," see Leyburn, *The*

Scotch-Irish, pp. 327–33; on Woodmason, see Klein, "Ordering the Backcountry," pp. 668–69.

3. Woodmason, *Carolina Backcountry*, p. 20.

4. Ibid., pp. 21–32, 52.

5. Lounsbury, "From Craft to Industry," pp. 27–28; my discussion in these paragraphs draws especially upon pp. 19–29 and upon Hilliard, *Atlas of Antebellum Southern Agriculture*, pp. 67–71.

6. In North Carolina, the term *backcountry* most commonly designated the areas west of the fall line (Klein, "Rise of the Planters," pp. 30–31, and "Ordering the Backcountry," pp. 662, 665; Crittenden, *Commerce of North Carolina*, p. 85. On the changing slave population, see Hilliard, *Atlas of Antebellum Southern Agriculture*, pp. 28–34.

7. See the discussion of the Cape Fear and Deep River Navigation Company in DeNatale, "Bynum," pp. 51–53.

8. Vance, *Human Geography of the South*, p. 276; Gilman, *Human Relations*, pp. 30–31; Clay, Orr, and Stuart, *North Carolina Atlas*, p. 112; South Carolina Writers' Project, *South Carolina*, p. 92.

9. Ford, "Social Origins of a New South Carolina," pp. 133–35.

10. See Kurath's map and the accompanying discussion in Eliason, *Tarheel Talk*, pp. 15–16. See also maps of speech areas in Morgan, "Status of /r/ among North Carolina Speakers," p. 173; McDavid, "Changing Patterns of Southern Dialects," pp. 206–28; and Williams, "Appalachian Speech."

11. Vance, *Human Geography of the South*, pp. 46–47; Woodward, *Mary Chesnut's Civil War*, pp. 420, 830–32; Tullos, "Great Hookworm Crusade," p. 41; Ettling, *Germ of Laziness*.

12. Hilliard, *Atlas of Antebellum Southern Agriculture*, pp. 7–9; Johnson, *Antebellum North Carolina*, pp. 5, 11.

13. Meriwether, *Expansion of South Carolina*, pp. 1, 113–15.

14. Dickson, *Ulster Emigration*, pp. 34, 59, 64; Leyburn, *The Scotch-Irish*, pp. 184–222.

15. Evans, "The Scotch-Irish," pp. 74–75. The interpretations of Forrest McDonald and Grady McWhiney seem to me romanticized, perilously ethnocentric, and historically static ("The South from Self-Sufficiency to Peonage"; in the same issue, see critical comments by Stanley L. Engerman and Thomas B. Alexander, pp. 1150–54, 1154–60, and the authors' reply, pp. 1160–63). See also McDonald and McWhiney, "Antebellum Southern Herdsmen"; McDonald and McDonald, "Ethnic Origins of the American People." For a critique of the McDonalds and McWhiney, see Berthoff, "Celtic Mist over the South." At times Bertram Wyatt-Brown shows a tendency to slip into the same mist (*Southern Honor*, pp. 36–38).

16. Hatley, "The Dividing Path," pp. 52–54, maps 3, 4; Clay, Orr, and Stuart, *North Carolina Atlas*. A Catawaba reservation was created during the colonial period. Today it is located between Rock Hill and Charlotte (Leyburn, *The Scotch-Irish*, p. 217). Cherokee history in North Carolina is discussed in Perdue, *Native Carolinians*, pp. 25–44, *Slavery and the Evolution of Cherokee Society*, and *Nations Remembered*.

17. Leyburn, *The Scotch-Irish*, pp. 219, 252; Meriwether, *Expansion of South Carolina*, pp. 241–61. See also Jean Stephenson, *Scotch-Irish Migration to South Carolina, 1772*.

18. Meriwether, *Expansion of South Carolina*, pp. 162–63.

19. Leyburn, *The Scotch-Irish*, pp. 293–95.

20. Klein, "Rise of the Planters," pp. 24, 32–35.

21. DeNatale, "Bynum," pp. 19–20. See also Ford, "Social Origins of a New South Carolina," pp. 83–84; Kenzer, "Portrait of a Southern Community," p. 6.

22. Leyburn, *The Scotch-Irish*, p. 213.

23. Meinig, *Shaping of America*, 1:292–93.

24. Dickson, *Ulster Emigration*, pp. 41, 76, 222–23; Metcalf, "Scotch-Irish."

25. Evans, "The Scotch-Irish," pp. 73–74, 78, 84. See also Metcalf, "Scotch-Irish"; Escott and Crow, "Social Order and Violent Disorder," p. 383.

26. Metcalf, "Scotch-Irish."

27. Quoted in Escott and Crow, "Social Order and Violent Disorder," p. 385.

28. Metcalf, "Scotch-Irish"; Evans, "The Scotch-Irish."

29. Leyburn, *The Scotch-Irish*, pp. 290–93, 321–22. Consider William Faulkner's North Mississippi Presbyterian character, Simon McEachern, in *Light in August*.

30. Metcalf, "Scotch-Irish," pp. 1092–93.

31. Stanza from "Missionary Song," in Walker, *Southern Harmony*, p. 197.

32. Bernheim, *History of the German Settlements*, p. 189.

33. Ibid., p. 148.

34. Ibid., pp. 153–54. See also Johnson, *Antebellum North Carolina*, p. 12; Leyburn, *The Scotch-Irish*, p. 216. The chronicles of Carolina Piedmont Moravians are found in Fries, *Records of the Moravians*. Two lengthy articles by Roger E. Sappington examine another German sect, the Dunkers, in the Piedmont's history ("Dunker Beginnings in North Carolina" and "Two Eighteenth-Century Dunker Congregations"; see also DeNatale, "Bynum," pp. 8–9). On the pattern of German settlement in that most typical of Piedmont counties, Gaston, see Brengle, *Architectural Heritage of Gaston County*, p. 3. See also Conzen, "Peasant Pioneers."

35. Bernheim, *History of the German Settlements*, p. 148.

36. Meriwether, *Expansion of South Carolina*, p. 114; Caruthers, *Interesting Revolutionary Incidents*, pp. 293–96.

37. Meriwether, *Expansion of South Carolina*, pp. 113–14. See also Vance, *Human Geography of the South*, pp. 88, 90; Trimble, *Man-Induced Soil Erosion*.

38. Sketch by James Mebane, in Caruthers, *Revolutionary Incidents and Sketches*, p. 359.

39. McCormick, *Scotch-Irish*, pp. 76–77.

40. Ibid., pp. 83–85.

41. Several studies by folklorists and historians have illuminated features of the yeoman culture and raised long-neglected regional perspectives. See Hahn, *Roots of Southern Populism*; Bruce, *And They All Sang Hallelujah*; Glassie, *Folk Housing in*

Middle Virginia; Fox-Genovese and Genovese, "Yeomen Farmers in a Slaveholders' Democracy." Rhys Isaac discusses the rise of evangelical religion in eighteenth-century Virginia in *Transformation of Virginia*; see also DeNatale, "Bynum"; Burton, *In My Father's House*; Watson, *An Independent People*.

42. See Stilgoe, *Common Landscape of America*, pp. 81–82, 211–12. See also the discussion of rural community in Faragher, "Open-Country Community."

43. Ford, "Social Origins of a New South Carolina," pp. 67, 95–97; Wright, *Political Economy of the Cotton South*, pp. 43–48.

44. Hahn, *Roots of Southern Populism*, p. 29.

45. Ford, "Social Origins of a New South Carolina," pp. 60–74.

46. DeNatale, "Bynum," pp. 22, 25–27, 31–46; Hahn, *Roots of Southern Populism*, pp. 26–32.

47. "Captain William Clarke," in Caruthers, *Revolutionary Incidents and Sketches*, p. 371. On the naming of churches and neighborhoods in the Carolina Piedmont, see DeNatale, "Bynum," pp. 11–12.

48. Interview by T. Pat Matthews, Varina, N.C., 25 Nov. 1938, FWPP, p. 8220.

49. Tench Coxe, *A View of the United States of America* (1794), quoted in Griffin and Standard, "Cotton Textile Industry in Ante-Bellum North Carolina, Part 1," p. 16.

50. Quoted in Johnson, *Antebellum North Carolina*, p. 88.

51. Bernheim, *History of the German Settlements*, pp. 184–85; see also Howe, *Scotch-Irish and Their First Settlements*, pp. 15–16.

52. Zug, *Turners and Burners*, p. 11. "Virtually all of the folk potters in North Carolina," writes folklorist Zug in his extensive history, "have resided in the Piedmont." On the Carolina Piedmont's Moravian potters of the eighteenth century, see Bivens, *Moravian Potters in North Carolina*; see also Burrison, *Brothers in Clay*.

53. The range of the handicraft tradition is glimpsed in Glassie, *Pattern in the Material Folk Culture*, pp. 75–109, 194–201, 234–41.

54. On the Piedmont's shape-note songsters, see Jackson, "'Singing Billy' Walker," pp. 55–69. For a discussion of the lives of two shape-note tunebook compilers, see Daniel W. Patterson's sketch of John Gordon McCurry, in Patterson and Garst, *Social Harp*, pp. xviii–xxi; and Patterson, "William Hauser's *Hesperian Harp* and *Olive Leaf*." The history and rudiments of one tradition of shape-note singing can be found in Cobb, *Sacred Harp*. On household frolics, see Glenn Hinson, album notes to *Eight-Hand Sets and Holy Steps*. On ballads, see Belden and Hudson, *Folk Ballads*.

55. My discussion of antebellum Carolina Piedmont housing draws especially upon Lounsbury, "From Craft to Industry," pp. 33–35. See also Whatley, *Architectural History of Randolph County*, pp. 21–24, 37–39.

56. Isaac, *Transformation of Virginia*, p. 93.

57. Harris, *Plain Folk and Gentry*, p. 119; Burton, *In My Father's House*, p. 29; DeNatale, "Bynum," pp. 13–15.

58. Hahn, *Roots of Southern Populism*, pp. 38–39; Kenzer, "Portrait of a Southern Community," pp. 53, 54.

59. Kenzer, "Portrait of a Southern Community," pp. 9, 14.

60. Johnson, *Antebellum North Carolina*, p. 30; Ford, "Social Origins of a New South Carolina," p. 103.

61. Isaac, *Transformation of Virginia*, pp. 164–68, 260–64. Isaac takes the evangelicals seriously and is most valuable for the richness of his descriptive detail (e.g., his discussion of the New Lights, pp. 147–50). Problems with Isaac's approach are discussed in Agnew, "History and Anthropology."

62. Weisberger, *They Gathered at the River*, p. 40.

63. Rev. Paul Henkel from Davidson County, quoted in Bernheim, *History of the German Settlements*, p. 353.

64. Bruce, *And They All Sang Hallelujah*, pp. 12–24, 34, 37–41; Boles, *Great Revival*, pp. x–xi, 8–9, 129; Agnew, "Methodism on the Frontier," pp. 494–505; Weisberger, *They Gathered at the River*, pp. 45–46; Sweet, *Religion on the American Frontier*, 3:42–50.

65. Johnson, *Antebellum North Carolina*, pp. 371–80. See also Johnson, "Camp Meeting in Ante-Bellum North Carolina"; Stokes, "North Carolina and the Great Revival"; Boles, *Great Revival*, p. 199. Donald Mathews, in pointing out that no other organization in America increased so rapidly, over so large an area, as did the Methodists between 1781 and 1840, is impressed primarily by those "professional organizers," the itinerants. "What made the Methodists so successful," he has suggested, "was not the intellectual content of their preaching, which was meager, but their ability to do what voluntary societies, state governments and even political parties would soon do—organize people" ("Second Great Awakening," p. 27).

66. Boles, *Great Revival*, pp. 94–98, 186; Gabriel, "Presbyterians."

67. Bernheim, *History of the German Settlements*, pp. 351–52.

68. Cleveland, *Great Revival in the West*, p. 30.

69. Sweet, *Religion on the American Frontier*, 2:88–89, 3:69.

70. Posey, *Frontier Mission*, p. 22; Boles, *Great Revival*, p. 17.

71. Johnson, "Frontier Camp Meeting," p. 95, and *Frontier Camp Meeting*, pp. 3–7.

72. Johnson, *Frontier Camp Meeting*, p. 209; Weisberger, *They Gathered at the River*, pp. 20–21.

73. Agnew, "Methodism on the Frontier."

74. Boles, *Great Revival*, p. 111. See also Boles, "Evangelical Protestantism in the Old South."

75. Boles, *Great Revival*, pp. 111, 121–23; Johnson, *Frontier Camp Meeting*, pp. 201–7; Bruce, *And They All Sang Hallelujah*, pp. 90–91.

76. This particular camp meeting spritual survives today in western North Carolina, where Madison County ballad singer Cas Wallin sang it for me in 1975 (Allen Tullos, ed., "Cas Wallin, Ballad Singer," 3d program in the radio series "North Carolina Folk Traditions," produced by the Curriculum in Folklore, University of North Carolina, 1976).

77. Bruce, *And They All Sang Hallelujah*, pp. 57–59; Posey, *Baptist Church in the Lower Mississippi Valley*, p. 89; Agnew, "Methodism on the Frontier," p. 522.

78. Harris, *Plain Folk and Gentry*, p. 101.

79. Stroupe, " 'Cite Them Both to Attend the Next Church Conference' "; Harris, *Plain Folk and Gentry*, pp. 101–2.

80. And see the discussion in Rodgers, *Work Ethic in Industrial America*, pp. 8–9.

81. This ballad was recorded in the summer of 1945 from Pat Frye of East Bend, Yadkin County, North Carolina. Frye, blind at the time, had been a tobacco farmer and miller. He was seventy-three years old and had lived in or near East Bend all his life (Belden and Hudson, *Folk Ballads from North Carolina*, pp. 247–48).

Recorded versions of this ballad include The Columbia Buddies, "A Lazy Farmer Boy" (Columbia 15702D 1930), reissued on *Ballads* (Folkways FA 2951); Seena Helms, "The Young Man Who Wouldn't Hoe Corn" or "Pioneer Courtship," field recordings in Union County, N.C., 1976–79, by Karen G. Helms and Otton Henry, on *Traditional Music of Union County, North Carolina*, vol. 1 of *Hand-Me-Down-Music: Old Songs, Old Friends* (Folkways FES 34151). Recorded versions from other yeoman areas include Vern Smelser, field recording in Paoli, Ind., 1964, by Pat Dunford, on *Fine Times at Our House: Traditional Music of Indiana* (Folkways FS 3809); and Edna and Jean Ritchie, field recordings in Viper, Ky., by Jean Ritchie and George Pickow, on *The Ritchie Family of Kentucky* (Folkways FA 2316). For more on this American ballad, see Laws, *Native American Balladry*, no. 13.

82. Erikson, *Everything in Its Path*, pp. 79–84.

83. Letter from Stephen Fox to Governor Spaight, 10 Sept. 1836, and record of pardon, 19 Sept. 1836, Governor's Letter Book, NCSA.

84. Erikson, *Everything in Its Path*, pp. 83–84.

85. Rorrer, *Rambling Blues*.

86. Materials on Frail Joines are taken from the ethnographic film *Being a Joines*, produced by Tom Davenport et al. Also see the booklet, *"Being a Joines": Background, Transcription, and Commentary*, which accompanies the film. The male ethos in the mountains is further considered in the audiotape documentary *Frail Joines: Brushy Mountain Storyteller*, produced by Allen Tullos. One need not adopt, whole hog, Bertram Wyatt-Brown's (*Southern Honor*) explanatory panoply erected around the "ethic of honor" in order to appreciate his many insights, observations, and overviews—such as the discussion of verbal insult (p. 43)—and his urging that regional historians not neglect the observation of longstanding cultural habits of thought and belief. For a more historically engaged view, see Gorn, " 'Gouge and Bite.' "

87. Cash, *Mind of the South*, pp. 59–60, 321.

88. Burke [Dargan], *Call Home the Heart*, pp. 159–68.

89. Hahn, *Roots of Southern Populism*, p. 31.

90. Ibid., pp. 17–18.

91. Wright, *Political Economy of the Cotton South*, p. 13; Ford, "Social Origins of a New South Carolina," pp. 10–11.

92. Ford, "Social Origins of a New South Carolina," p. 61.

93. David Ramsay, *The History of South Carolina* (1809), quoted in ibid., pp. 9–11.

94. Ibid., pp. 20–22.

95. Klein, "Rise of the Planters," pp. 294, 306. See also Hilliard, *Atlas of Antebellum Southern Agriculture*, pp. 32–37, 60–62.

96. Watson, "Conflict and Collaboration," p. 277.

97. Petition to Governor Richard Dobbs Spaight, Jr., 24 Apr. 1836, in Governors Papers, NCSA.

98. Trimble, *Man-Induced Soil Erosion*, pp. 49–68.

99. Ford, "Social Origins of a New South Carolina," p. 18; DeNatale, "Bynum," p. 71.

100. Stanley W. Trimble's observations are summarized in Cowdrey, *This Land, This South*, p. 76.

101. Trimble, *Man Induced Soil Erosion*, p. 1.

102. Cowdrey, *This Land, This South*, p. 76.

103. Lounsbury, "From Craft to Industry," pp. 30–31.

104. DeNatale, "Bynum," pp. 15–19.

105. Lounsbury, "From Craft to Industry," p. 33.

106. Cecil-Fronsman, "Common Whites," pp. 179–80; see also my discussion of the house of E. M. Holt in chapter one.

107. Ford, "Social Origins of a New South Carolina," pp. 313, 303; see also Ford's chapter five, "A New South in the Old?" pp. 269–368.

108. Ford, "Social Origins of a New South Carolina," pp. 170–71; Isaac, *Transformation of Virginia*, pp. 110–14.

109. Harris, *Plain Folk and Gentry*, p. 117. See also Harris's discussion of Alexander H. Stephens and the means through which the "existing elite deliberately infused itself with new blood" (pp. 117–19).

110. Ibid., pp. 104–8.

111. Johnson, *Antebellum North Carolina*, pp. 31–36, 76 (see pp. 31–36 for a discussion of antebellum sectionalism in North Carolina counties). The regional pattern of slaveholding can be seen in Clay, Orr, and Stuart, *North Carolina Atlas*, fig. 1.12, p. 26.

112. Kruman, *Parties and Politics in North Carolina*, pp. 46–50.

113. Fox-Genovese and Genovese, "Yeoman Farmers in a Slaveholders' Democracy," pp. 255–56.

114. Mary Rumbley (b. 1878), interview with Ida L. Moore, Glen Raven Cotton Mill, Burlington, N.C., 31 Oct. 1938, FWPP, p. 8837.

115. Clayton, *Close to the Land*, pp. 25–31.

116. Clay, Orr, and Stuart, *North Carolina Atlas*, p. 26.

117. Thomas, *Confederate Nation*, pp. 86–87; Sitterson, *Secession Movement in North Carolina*, pp. 218–29; Eaton, *History of the Southern Confederacy*, pp. 21–23, 42–43; Carlton, *Mill and Town*, p. 148; Otten, "Disloyalty in the Upper Districts of South Carolina"; Foner, *Politics and Ideology*.

118. Jonathan Worth, quoted in Briggs, "Mill Owners and Mill Workers," p. 74. See also Montgomery, *Beyond Equality*, pp. 52–55; Eaton, *History of the Southern Confederacy*, pp. 38–42.

Chapter Three

1. James Lee Love manuscript, 12 Jan. 1921, JLLP (hereafter Love manuscript); Love, "Some Recollections of Daniel Efird Rhyne," JLLP (hereafter "Daniel Efird Rhyne"). My discussion of Grier Love and James Lee Love draws especially upon these two sources and upon James Lee Love, *R. C. G. Love: A Builder of the New South.* Much material on the Loves and their contemporaries during the period of Gaston County's postbellum rise can be found in Ragan, *Pioneer Cotton Mills of Gaston County.*

2. Love, *R. C. G. Love*, pp. 7–9, 12; Love manuscript, 21 Jan. 1921, 12 Jan. 1921.

3. Love, *R. C. G. Love*, pp. 7–9.

4. Ibid., pp. 16–17. See Gen. 1:28; Ps. 8:6–8; Hos. 4:1–3.

5. Love, "Daniel Efird Rhyne," p. 2. James Lee Love writes that where the two tides of immigrants—Scotch-Irish Associate Reformed Presbyterians and German Lutherans—met, "textile industries grew up." He cites as proof both Gaston and Alamance counties.

6. Ibid., pp. 1–2. See also the discussion of one well-known shape-note composer in Patterson, "William Hauser's *Hesperian Harp* and *Olive Leaf.*"

7. Love manuscript, 12 Jan. 1921.

8. Love, *R. C. G. Love*, pp. 10–11; Love manuscript, 12, 21 Jan. 1921.

9. Love, *R. C. G. Love*, pp. 8–9, 14–15.

10. Love manuscript, 12 Jan. 1921.

11. Ibid., 18 Jan. 1921.

12. Love, *R. C. G. Love*, p. 8.

13. Patterson, "Upland North and South Carolina Stonecarvers."

14. Prov. 22:6.

15. Love manuscript, [n.d.] Jan. 1921.

16. Exod. 34:6–7. See Trible, *God and the Rhetoric of Sexuality*, pp. 1–2.

17. Love manuscript, 12 Jan. 1921.

18. Ibid., 6 Jan. 1940.

19. Ibid., 14 Feb. 1921.

20. Ibid., 12 Jan. 1921.

21. Love, *R. C. G. Love*, pp. 8–9, 14–16; Pope, *Millhands and Preachers*, p. 8n.

22. Love manuscript, 18 Jan. 1921.

23. Ibid., [n.d.] Jan. 1921.

24. Love, *R. C. G. Love*, p. 27.

25. Love manuscript, [n.d.] Jan. 1921; Love, "Daniel Efird Rhyne," pp. 3–4, 7; Love, *R. C. G. Love*, pp. 21–23, 34–35.

26. Love manuscript, 20 Jan. 1921; Love, *R. C. G. Love*, p. 21.

27. Love manuscript, [n.d.] Jan. 1921.

28. Ibid., 29 Jan. 1921.

29. In the 1877 credit reporting ledgers of R. G. Dun and Company, Baker Library, Harvard University, R. C. G. Love is described as "honest, sober and industrious . . . buys considerable cotton and is cautious. . . . Good for all he buys." Love's worth was

estimated at $6,000 to $8,000. My thanks to Bess Beatty for passing along the Dun notes on the Rhyne (later Love) store in Woodlawn.

30. Love, "Daniel Efird Rhyne," pp. 5–6. And see Clark, *Southern Country Store*, pp. 271–91.

31. Love, "Daniel Efird Rhyne," pp. 6–7.

32. Ibid., pp. 3–4.

33. Ibid., pp. 9–10.

34. Ibid.

35. Love manuscript, [n.d.] Jan. 1921.

36. Ibid., 1 Jan. 1921.

37. Ibid., 13 Jan. 1921.

38. Ibid., 6 Jan. 1940.

39. Ibid., 21 Jan. 1920.

40. Ibid., [n.d.] Jan., 21 Jan. 1921.

41. Ibid., 1 Jan. 1921. An annual North Carolina Threshers Reunion, held in Davidson County, remains as a contemporary celebration of threshing and steam machinery.

42. Ibid., 1 Jan. 1940.

43. Ibid., [n.d.] Jan. 1921.

44. Love, *R. C. G. Love*, pp. 28–29, 33–34.

45. Ibid., pp. 34, 37.

46. Ibid., pp. 39–41. The Gastonia Cotton Manufacturing Company was the first steam-powered mill in the county (see Young and Young, *Textile Leaders of the South*, pp. 79, 753). In *Millhands and Preachers* (p. 22), Liston Pope prints George Gray's tombstone inscription:

A CAPTAIN OF INDUSTRY—
A PIONEER OF PROSPERITY—
BY INDUSTRY AND HONESTY HE
ACHIEVED SUCCESS—BY JUSTICE
AND MAGNANIMITY HE WON THE
RESPECT AND LOVE OF HIS FELLOW
MEN—BY FAITH IN CHRIST HE
BUILT A CHRISTIAN CHARACTER.
"AND A MAN SHALL BE AS THE
SHADOW OF A GREAT ROCK IN A
WEARY LAND" ISA. 32:2.

47. Love, *R. C. G. Love*, p. 38.

48. Ibid., pp. 38–39.

49. Ibid., p. 42.

50. Ibid., pp. 44–46.

51. Manuscript of a speech prepared for the fiftieth anniversary of the class of 1884, University of North Carolina at Chapel Hill, 8–12 June 1934, JLLP. Love's

years at the University of North Carolina are recorded in Love, *'Tis Sixty Years Since*.

52. Love, *R. C. G. Love*, p. 37; James Lee Love to James B. Conant, 25 May 1939, and James Lee Love to K. D. Metcalf, 10 Mar. 1940, JLLP; *Burlington Daily News*, 23 Nov. 1923.

53. Cornelia Spencer Love interview, Greensboro, N.C. See also discussions of the rise of J. Spencer Love in Hall et al., *Like a Family*, and Murphy, "Burlington, North Carolina."

54. From a biographical sketch of Spencer Love by James Lee Love, 18 Jan. 1949, JLLP.

55. James Lee Love to Staley Cook, 10 May 1949, JLLP.

56. Pierpont, "Textile Industry in Alamance County, North Carolina," pp. 264–65.

57. James Lee Love, "Note on the Gastonia Manufacturing Company," [n.d.], JLLP; Pierpont, "Textile Industry in Alamance County, North Carolina," p. 265.

58. Reid Maynard interview, Burlington, N.C.

59. *Greensboro Daily News*, 3 Nov. 1923; Burlington Industries, *A Brief History*; *American Wool and Cotton Reporter*, 14 Dec. 1950; *Textile World*, 23 Jan. 1932, pp. 24–25.

60. Pierpont, "Textile Industry in Alamance County, North Carolina" pp. 265–66; Reid Maynard interview; Burlington Industries, *Burlington Mill Review—Thirty Years*. Additional material on Burlington Mills's history, including proxy statements and annual reports of various years, are located in the Burlington corporate offices, Greensboro, N.C. An early discussion of Southern rayon can be found in Rose, "Rayon Weaving in the South."

61. Pierpont, "Textile Industry in Alamance County, North Carolina," pp. 267–69.

62. Anonymous sketch of J. Spencer Love in *American Fabrics* (Summer 1953): 88–89. Part of clipping collection at Burlington corporate headquarters, Greensboro, N.C. (entire article pp. 86–89).

63. *Southern Textile Bulletin*, 31 Jan. 1929, pp. 25–26.

64. Burlington Industries, "Burlington—A Review," 1973. Part of clipping collection at Burlington corporate headquarters.

65. Gillespie, "Character Study of an Empire Builder."

66. Edward and Mary Harrington interview, Burlington, N.C.

67. Rogers's comments, made in 1968, are quoted in "Model Mill Issue: Burlington at 50," a June 1973 special issue of *Textile World* (pp. 18–19,).

68. J. S. Love to J. C. Cowan, 26 Nov. 1948, JLLP. See also Love, "We Have a Better Team Than Ever Before."

69. Gillespie, "Character Study of an Empire Builder."

70. Ibid.

71. L. Worth Harris interview, Charlotte, N.C.

72. Harry and Janie Adams interview, Burlington, N.C.

73. Gillespie, "Character Study of an Empire Builder."

74. Anonymous sketch of J. Spencer Love in *American Fabrics*.

75. Harry and Janie Adams interview.

76. At the pioneer plant of the Love chain—the mill he began in 1924 at Piedmont Heights in Burlington, North Carolina—Spencer Love would return now and then to visit and to chat for a few minutes with members of the first group of employees who had gone to work for him. Mildred Shoemaker Edmonds and Mattie Shoemaker, sisters who worked in the Piedmont Heights winding room, say of Love: "He was just one great man. He was a fine man. He came through that mill. He'd stop in there and he wasn't dressed a bit better than nobody working in that mill" (Mildred Shoemaker Edmonds and Mattie Shoemaker interview, Burlington, N.C.).

77. Icy Norman interview, Burlington, N.C. Icy Norman is also considered in Hall et al., *Like a Family*, especially pp. 264–69, 360–63. I am especially grateful to Mary Murphy for many in-the-field conversations about Burlington Mills and the Piedmont Heights community of Burlington.

Chapter Four

1. *Charlotte Observer*, 17 Aug. 1869.
2. Ibid., 24 Sept. 1869.
3. Ibid., 1 June 1869, editorial.
4. Ibid., 4 Nov. 1875.
5. Wright, *Old South, New South*, pp. 54–57, 75–76, 115–23, 118t; Street, *New Revolution in the Cotton Economy*, pp. 26–27; Federal Writers' Project, *North Carolina*, pp. 59, 61.
6. Woodward, *Origins of the New South*; McMath, *Populist Vanguard*; Daniel, *Breaking the Land*; Hahn, *Roots of Southern Populism*; Carlton, *Mill and Town*; Woodman, "Postbellum Social Change"; Ford, "Labor and Ideology in the South Carolina Upcountry" and "Rednecks and Merchants." Douglas DeNatale presents a detailed account of the post–Civil War transformation of the rural economy of Chatham County in the North Carolina Piedmont ("Bynum").
7. Carlton, *Mill and Town*, pp. 20–21.
8. This broad meaning of *Piedmont*—the plateau that extends from hinterland New York to northern Alabama—remains in modern usage (Vance, *Human Geography of the South*, p. 90). See "Piedmont," in Mathews, *Dictionary of Americanisms*; "Piedmont," in Challinor, *Dictionary of Geology*; Battisti and Alessio, *Dizionario Etimologico Italiano*.
9. Robert Mills, "Face of the Country, Soil, Health, etc.," in *Atlas of South Carolina*.
10. Wiley, *North Carolina Reader*, pp. 5, 50–53.
11. "Piedmont," in Mathews, *Dictionary of Americanisms*.
12. Stribling, *Black Ghost of the Rocky Branch*.
13. *Greenville Enterprise*, 24 June 1873. On immigrants, see Wright, *Old South, New South*, p. 76.
14. Stover, *Railroads of the South*, pp. 42, 57–61.
15. "Greenville as a Cotton Market," *Greenville Enterprise*, 11 Dec. 1872.
16. See *Charlotte Observer*, 14 Sept. 1869.

17. Ibid., 29 May 1873.

18. Ibid., 24 Sept. 1873, editorial.

19. Ibid., 30 Mar. 1873. For similar accounts, see issues for 2 Apr., 30 May, 26 Aug. 1873.

20. Ibid., 9 Aug. 1873; see also issues for 28 June, 8 July 1873.

21. Stover, *Railroads of the South*, pp. 107–21; Woodward, *Origins of the New South*, pp. 292–95.

22. *Charlotte Observer*, 3 Apr. 1873.

23. Quoted in ibid., 1 Feb. 1874., p. 1

24. W. L. Mauldin, in Crittenden, *Greenville Century Book*, p. 64.

25. *Greenville Enterprise*, 30 Apr. 1873.

26. Ibid., 19 Feb. 1873.

27. Jacobs, *The Pioneer*, pp. 71–72; Lander, *Textile Industry in Antebellum South Carolina*. More information on Bates can be found in the South Carolina Room of the Greenville County Library, in a vertical file labeled "Textile Mills—Greenville" and containing a collection of anonymous and generally undated newspaper clippings.

28. *Manufacturers' Record*, 1 Feb. 1883, cited in Mitchell, *Rise of Cotton Mills in the South*, p. 171.

29. Crittenden, *Greenville Century Book*, pp. 66–67; Andrews, "History of the Textile Industry," p. 55; Mitchell and Mitchell, *Industrial Revolution in the South*, p. 72.

30. Tompkins, *Cotton Mill Commercial Features*, pp. 188–89.

31. Crittenden, *Greenville Century Book*, pp. 65–67.

32. Tompkins is discussed in greater detail later in this chapter. See also Gaston, *New South Creed*; Clay, "Daniel Augustus Tompkins"; Winston, *Builder of the New South*; Billings, *Planters and the Making of a "New South."*

33. My discussion of the Reynolds family draws upon Tilley, *Reynolds Homestead.*

34. The Holts are discussed in chapter one, above. H. P. Hammett is one of the pioneers featured in Jacobs, *The Pioneer*; see also Lander, *Textile Industry in Antebellum South Carolina*; Andrews, "History of the Textile Industry"; Crittenden, *Greenville Century Book*; Carlton, *Mill and Town*. The Linebergers are the subjects of a number of newspaper and periodical clippings and excerpts from biographical dictionaries, all compiled in Ragan, *Pioneer Cotton Mills of Gaston County.*

35. Genovese, "Industrialists under the Slave Regime," p. 207.

36. For more on Smyth and Pelzer, see Carlton, *Mill and Town* and " 'Builders of a New State' "; Jacobs, *The Pioneer.*

37. The Dukes are discussed later in this chapter; see also Durden, *Dukes of Durham*. Biographical accounts of James Cannon can be found in Powell, *Dictionary of North Carolina Biography*, vol. 1; Jacobs, *The Pioneer*; and obituaries, *Southern Textile Bulletin*, 22 Dec. 1921. For information on George Gray, see Mitchell and Mitchell, *Industrial Revolution in the South*, and the collection of clippings found in Robert Allison Ragan's helpful volume, *Pioneer Cotton Mills of Gaston County*. On the Hanes family, see Linn, *People Named Hanes*. For an account of George Washington Ragan, see Ragan, *Pioneer Cotton Mills of Gaston County*; also Ashe, Weeks, and Van Noppen,

Biographical History of North Carolina, vol. 8. On the Stowe family, see Ragan, *Pioneer Cotton Mills of Gaston County*; Blythe, *Robert Lee Stowe*. The Belks are discussed in chapter one, above, and in Blythe, *William Henry Belk*. Two other useful general references are Young and Young, *Textile Leaders of the South*, and Sitterson, "Business Leaders in Post–Civil War North Carolina."

38. Cash, *Mind of the South*, pp. 210–11. Cash overemphasized the extent to which strictly planter progeny could be counted among the New South's captains of industry. Yet he also recognized the importance of the supply merchants and yeomanry—much more than does Dwight Billings in *Planters and the Making of a "New South."* The question of the degree of planter persistence versus the role of the "new men" needs to be asked from region to region within the South. The answer varies depending on whether one discusses the Delta, the Black Belt, or the Carolina Piedmont.

39. Fromm and Maccoby, *Social Character in a Mexican Village*, pp. 103–4, 117.

40. Ibid., pp. 17, 103–4, 233–34.

41. Ibid., p. 104. Fromm and Maccoby also acknowledge, as I do, the interrelationship of Protestantism and developing capitalism and have profited from Max Weber's *The Protestant Ethic and the Spirit of Capitalism*.

42. My discussion of Ragan draws upon the *Gastonia Gazette* of 4 April 1965, reprinted in R. A. Ragan's published clipping collection, *Pioneer Cotton Mills of Gaston County*; see also "George Washington Ragan," in Ashe, Weeks, and Van Noppen, *Biographical History of North Carolina*, pp. 429–34; obituary, *Charlotte Observer*, 10 June 1936.

43. From newspaper obituary for Lineberger (1948), collected in Ragan, *Pioneer Cotton Mills of Gaston County*.

44. From Jacobs, *The Pioneer*, p. 61.

45. From Mitchell and Mitchell, *Industrial Revolution in the South*, pp. 77–78.

46. Linn, *People Named Hanes*, pp. 54, 76–79.

47. Edmonds, "Biography of Daniel Augustus Tompkins."

48. Winston, *Builder of the New South*, p. 9.

49. Ibid., pp. 13–15.

50. Arthur S. Tompkins, unpublished sketch of Smyly family, [n.d.], DATP. In the 1830s Smyly, a strong Union man, had a falling-out with his cousin, John C. Calhoun, over the issue of nullification.

51. Ibid.

52. Winston, *Builder of the New South*, pp. 13–17.

53. Ibid., pp. 22–23. To LeConte (later of the University of California), Tompkins attributed the statement—of lasting influence upon his views of apprenticeship training and industrial education for Piedmont youth—that "Christian civilization is founded upon the fact that the white race can carry its training further than that of any other and maintain it longer" (pp. 277–78).

54. Eliza Mims to D. A. Tompkins, 8 May 1871, DATP.

55. Holley was a trustee of Rensselaer Polytechnic Institute. In 1875 he served as president of the American Institute of Mining Engineers (Winston, *Builder of the New*

South, p. 28). Also, on the matter of Gus's earning his college expenses, see D. A. Tompkins to A. S. Tompkins, 15 Aug. 1898, DATP.

56. See Noble, *America by Design*, p. 37.

57. Winston, *Builder of the New South*, pp. 33, 369.

58. D. A. Tompkins to Harriet Brigham, 21 Oct. 1974. Excerpts from Tompkins's letters to Brigham can be found in the Daniel Augustus Tompkins Papers, SHC. A fuller collection of the letters is located in the Tompkins materials at the Duke University Rare Manuscript Room. I am indebted to Sydney Nathans of Duke and to his student Richard Eichenbaum for calling my attention to Eichenbaum's unpublished seminar paper (Fall 1978) on the Tompkins-Brigham correspondence.

59. D. A. Tompkins to Harriet Brigham, 23 Nov. 1874, excerpted in Eichenbaum, unpublished paper.

60. Ibid., 6 Mar. 1883, DATP.

61. Ibid., 23 May 1883, excerpted in Eichenbaum, unpublished paper.

62. Clay, "Daniel Augustus Tompkins," p. 60.

63. D. A. Tompkins to Charles A. Gambril, 17 Apr. 1908, DATP; address to Boiler Makers' Convention, Atlanta, Ga., 9 Oct. 1907, DATP. Broadus Mitchell and George S. Mitchell suggest that Tompkins "was probably directly responsible for the building of more cotton mills than any other man" (*Industrial Revolution in the South*, p. 79).

64. Edmonds, "Biography of Daniel Augustus Tompkins."

65. Woodward, *Origins of the New South*, pp. 147–48; on Tompkins and New South ideology, see also Gaston, *New South Creed*, pp. 160–64. Next to nothing exists among Tompkins's books and letters, nor in biographical sketches and writings, about his religious beliefs and practices.

66. Winston, *Builder of the New South*, p. 350.

67. See articles on Tompkins in *Charlotte Observer*, 5, 13 July 1958; Clay, "Daniel Augustus Tompkins," pp. 183–84, 203, 218; Winston, *Builder of the New South*, pp. 219–23.

68. Winston, *Builder of the New South*, p. 142.

69. Ibid., pp. 276–77.

70. A. J. S. Thomas to D. A. Tompkins, 14 July 1906, DATP.

71. Clay, "Daniel Augustus Tompkins," p. 271.

72. D. A. Tompkins to A. S. Tompkins, 18 Feb. 1913, DATP.

73. Winston, *Builder of the New South*, pp. 195–99.

74. Ibid., p. 360.

75. H. E. C. Bryant to D. A. Tompkins, 1 Dec. 1910, DATP. On the China possibility, see D. A. Tompkins to Elliott Durand, 24 Jan. 1908; D. A. Tompkins to Wade Harris, 8 Feb. 1908; D. A. Tompkins to J. Elwood Cox, 9 Sept. 1908; Thomas Settle to D. A. Tompkins, 11, 15 Nov. 1908; D. A. Tompkins to Elwood Cox, 31 Dec. 1908; D. A. Tompkins to H. E. Miles, 12 Jan. 1909; D. A. Tompkins to Marion Butler, 1 Feb. 1909, all in DATP.

76. See letters written during the summer and autumn of 1909, DATP.

77. D. A. Tompkins to C. W. Pritchett, 28 Oct. 1912, DATP.

78. "Memorandum. Apr. 1, 1913," DATP.

79. Woodward, *Origins of the New South*, pp. 130–31, 308–9. On the history of the Duke family, see Durden, *Dukes of Durham*; a concise summary of the Dukes' rise is found in Nathans, *Quest for Progress*, pp. 20–27. See also Winkler, *Tobacco Tycoon*; Porter, "Advertising in the Early Cigarette Industry."

80. Durden, *Dukes of Durham*, pp. 182–83. There is at present no satisfactory history of Duke Power; a brief, celebratory book is Maynor, *Duke Power*.

81. Interview with Herman Wolf (b. 1896), veteran Duke Power electrical engineer, Charlotte, N.C.

82. Ibid.

83. Maynor, *Duke Power*, p. 28.

84. Durden, *Dukes of Durham*, p. 182.

85. Macy, "Power Supply of Southern Industry"; Tindall, *Emergence of the New South*, p. 72; Durden, *Dukes of Durham*, p. 185. Buck Duke and his brother B. N., along with W. S. Lee and Edgar Thompson, were, writes Robert Durden, "key figures" in the building—in the 1910s—of the electric Piedmont and Northern Railway, a passenger and freight line that connected several South Carolina Piedmont towns along a hundred-mile stretch and, on a separate division, also connected Charlotte and Gastonia.

86. Durden, *Dukes of Durham*, p. 83.

87. Ibid., p. 278.

88. My thanks to Catherine Peck for sharing Father Daniel Berrigan's comment. And see Cash, "Buck Duke's University."

89. Quotes from Freeman's speech are taken from "The Piedmont Carolinas' Movement," *Southern Textile Bulletin*, 1 Dec. 1927, pp. 32–33.

90. Tindall, *Emergence of the New South*, p. 409.

91. The quotations that follow are taken from Duke Power's Piedmont Carolinas advertisements in 1927–28 and from the Duke Power booklet, *Piedmont Carolinas: Where Wealth Awaits You*. Over the decades, Duke Power has often returned to the regional theme in its self-advertisements. See, for example, its booklets entitled *The Piedmont Carolinas*, published in 1960 and 1965. In its 1960 edition, Duke Power cited "Metropolis," a Ford Foundation study, in assessing the prospects of the "Piedmont Industrial Crescent"—"the core of the Piedmont Carolinas"—clusters of rapidly growing small cities strung along the familiar heart of the region: "These cities extend Crescent-like through sixteen counties in the Carolinas for about 275 miles . . . with housing and industrial tentacles already reaching from city to city. Some observers believe that in time the entire Crescent may become a linear city" (quoted in *The Piedmont Carolinas*, p. 3).

92. See Wright, *Old South, New South*, pp. 147–55, for an economic overview of the textile crisis of the 1920s. Efforts to unionize textile-mill workers in the Charlotte area by the United Textile Workers of America between 1918 and 1921 were broken by the power of employers with the assistance—when necessary—of municipal and state

police. In 1919, the Charlotte Chamber of Commerce and the Southern Power Company (owned by Duke interests—its president, W. L. Lee, was an influential member of the chamber's board of directors) set the tone for business-labor relations for years to come when they beat back a union organizing campaign by Charlotte's streetcar workers. The Southern Power Company, owners of the streetcar company, imported strikebreakers who ultimately provoked a riot, during which police killed five men and wounded more than a dozen. See Marshall, *Labor in the South*, pp. 82–85; Shaw, "A City in Conflict"; J. B. Ashe interview, Charlotte, N.C.; Loy Connelly Cloniger interview, Charlotte, N.C. See also George and Mamie Shue interview, Charlotte, N.C.

Chapter Five

1. *Southern Textile Bulletin*, 22 June 1922, pp. 10–12, and 6 July 1922, p. 14. The engineers were L. W. Roberts, J. E. Sirrine, and J. Norman Pease. (Pease, the only one of these men still alive in 1981, had no recollection of this contest.) Here is the complete text of League's entry:

The Prize Winning Article
by D. W. League, Greenville, S.C.

I would equip my mill to make medium and fine plain and fancy goods with colors to meet the demand of the trade.

My reason for making this class of goods is:

(a) The trade is being gradually educated to use the finer quality of merchandise, hence the growing demand for the best that the designer and manufacturer can put out is finding a ready market.

(b) The help of the South is being educated up to the place where a mill of this type can be both successfully and economically operated.

Building

I would build a reinforced concrete structure of two stories for the carding and spinning. The first floor should be of heavy concrete for the carding. The second floor should be of reinforced concrete for the spinning, spooling, cone winders, twisters, and warpers. I would build an ell to the south corner of this building of same construction as above, first floor for picker room, second floor for slasher room. I prefer this type of building because of the fine adjustments it is necessary to have on machines to make fine work, which cannot be obtained in the ordinary mill building.

The weave room should be built on the south side of carding and spinning mill of one story with saw-tooth type roof. These buildings should be arranged in this manner to take advantage of the natural atmospheric and temperature conditions which in a measure determine the running of the work in each department. All modern light features should be taken advantage of as far as practical. Opening room and cotton warehouse should be placed at west end of carding and spinning mill. Cloth room and cloth warehouse to west side of weave room and near enough to cotton warehouse to be accommodated by one switch track.

The power plant should be located at the southeast corner of the carding and spinning mill (if power is generated by steam). The village should be of modern type with special attention given to sanitary lighting, social and spiritual features.

Opening and Lapping Machinery

I would recommend a large opening room equipped with vertical opener, with at least two large bins to receive cotton when run through opener. The picker room should be equipped with automatic feed system. Three processes of Kitson pickers equipped with Atherton evener, feeding slow and light cleaned. The pickers should be equipped with individual drive. In this department as well as in carding and spinning I would resort to the plan laid down by Woodrow Wilson: "I would use all the brains I have and all I could borrow" of the active members of the S.T.A. [Southern Textile Association] and especially its foundation department.

Cards

Cards and ribbon lappers should be separated from other machines by fire wall. I would equip for light quick carding and use the best vacuum stripping system. I would equip these machines with group drive.

Combers and Drawing

I would equip with the best combers on the market, also two processes of drawing, with metallic rolls. If half the time and care is expended on metallic rolls that is required on leather rolls they will give much better results.

Roving Machinery

I would equip with slubbers, intermediates and speeders with jack frames to take care of the finer counts. Enough machines should be provided to avoid high speeds and long drafts. Each machine should be equipped with individual motor drive.

Spinning

I would install spinning frames with 224 tape driven spindles, with No. 1 flange rings. Filling frames with traverse to conform to quill used. Warp frames with filling wind and no separators. Frames equipped with individual motor drive.

Spoolers

Spoolers should be equipped to use filling wind stock.

Warpers

Warpers should be equipped with V type creel, also extra combs to take care of special colored work dyed by Franklin process.

Cone Winders

Cone winders should be of latest type. I would drive spoolers, warpers and cone winders with group drive.

Twisters

Twisters should be equipped for medium and fine work, with individual motor drive.

Slashers

Slashers should be equipped with size circulating system and automatic size temperature control. Size boxes and kettles should be lined with heavy copper inside and covered with asbestos on outside. All size pipes and pumps should be of brass. Slashers and pumps equipped with group drive.

Beaming Machinery

Instead of using beaming machinery for colored goods I would have my yarn dyed by Franklin process, which I consider more economical.

Weave Room

I would equip with 36- and 40-inch looms for plain, box and fancy dobby work, equipped with group drive from below, a line of shafting to each line of looms.

Cloth Room

I would equip with steam pipes for heating with automatic regulator. I would equip with the best humidifier on the market with automatic regulators in carding, spinning, weaving and cloth rooms. Section beams should be handled on overhead trolley from warpers to slasher room. I would use fibre boxes for handling roving and yarn.

2. *Southern Textile Bulletin*, 22 June 1922, p. 12.

3. My interpretation of the League family unfolds from several sources. First, while interviewing in Poe Mill village for the Piedmont Industrialization Project in the summer of 1979, I met Lora League Wright and her husband, Edward. Lora told me of her father and mother, D. W. and Mary League, and, in a brief interview, about her family's life and work in Poe Mill village.

Several months later, while paging through a collection of high school scrapbooks at the Greenville County Library, I kept being drawn to random newsclippings which, when taken together, sketched the story of Nigel League—D. W. and Mary's son. A systematic reading of the *Southern Textile Bulletin*, for the purpose of gaining manufacturers' perspectives during the years encompassed by this chapter, luckily turned up the mill-building contest. All these sources sent me back to Poe Mill village for extensive interviews with the Wrights (7 June, 11 November 1979), and to Simpsonville, South Carolina, for an interview with Lora and Nigel's sister, Shirley League Whitmire (13 July 1982). All quotations from Lora and Ed Wright and from Shirley Whitmire come from these interviews. For a general discussion of life in the Piedmont's mill villages, drawn from other interviews in the Piedmont Industrialization Project, see Hall et al., *Like a Family*.

4. For another eldest daughter's similar story, with the same result, see Betty Davidson interview, Burlington, N.C.

5. D. W. League diary, 19, 22 Aug. 1917 (diary is in the possession of the Wright family). Traditionally, thrash was treated by a healer who blew into the child's mouth and spoke a charm. "Thrash," says Shirley League Whitmire, "was sores, a breaking-out, in the mouth."

6. D. W. League diary, 1 Oct. 1917.

7. Information on the Parker School District is from the Parker Scrapbook Collection, Greenville County Library (PSC). The PSC contains a large newspaper clipping file. See also McAllister, *L. P. Hollis*; Albert Sanders interview, Greenville, S.C.

Parker District, observed a reporter in 1936, "is possibly the most exclusively Anglo-Saxon section in America. There are about 30,000 residents . . . and there are only two families of foreign parentage. There are about 300 Negroes in the area and these are families of teamsters, yard hands and others who work for the corporations" (Rogers, "Greenville Cotton Mills Maintain Educational System"). Parker District's black population lived in segregated settlements and attended segregated elementary schools; they had no high school.

The mill owners' prerogative to control and prescribe the appropriate education for workers and their children is reflected in obliging articles such as "What Industry Expects of the Public School," by E. H. Fish, published in September 1924 in the journal *Management and Administration*. Fish begins his essay, which immediately follows another article entitled "The Southern Industrial Labor Supply," with this sentence: "The continued existence of industry as now organized depends on the education of employees in two ways—to make them understand the problems of the owners and managers, and to give them expert knowledge of the various trades."

8. West, "Parker Mill District," in PSC.

9. Woolf, "Motivated Method of the Parker District," in PSC.

10. Nigel is not a name found in the Bible. That Lora thinks so testifies to the mighty role the Bible has assumed in mediating the "foreign" and the "familiar" in Southern folk cultures. The family pronunciation of the name rhymes with "vigil."

11. PSC.

12. Clippings from the *Greenville News*, May 1925, in PSC. Many children in the district dropped out of school at age fourteen (the compulsory limit in South Carolina, and also the age at which children could work full-time in the mills). A breakdown of Parker District enrollment for 1930 is as follows:

First grade	1,289
Second grade	1,118
Third grade	863
Fourth grade	719
Fifth grade	678
Sixth grade	438
High school	947
Total	5,950

See also Morland, "Educational and Occupational Aspirations."

13. *Greenville News*[?], 23 May 1925, in PSC.

14. PSC.

15. " 'Efficiency Systems' Cause Strikes in Southern Mills," *Greenville News*, 1 Apr. 1929; "Recent Textile Trouble in South Carolina Brought on by 'Stretch-Out' System," *Greenville News*, 12 Aug. 1929; "Piedmont Mill and Farm Ills Are Described," *Greenville News*, 16 Nov. 1929; and see discussion of strikes in Pope, *Millhands and Preachers*.

See also "Revolt of the Textile Workers," in Marshall, *Labor in the South*, pp. 101–20; also "When Southern Labor Stirred," in Tindall, *Emergence of the New South*, pp. 318–53. On textile workers' wages in the 1920s, Tindall writes:

> The collapse of textile unionism in 1921 left depression wage cuts in effect, although the rates never quite sank to prewar levels. A male loom fixer in the South (the aristocrat of cotton mill help) earned $32.88 for a full week's work in 1920 but only $21.41 in 1922 and $22.20 in 1928; the average for female weavers declined from $26.56 to $19.37. But full-time work was not always available, so that the loom fixer in 1928 actually averaged $18.38; the female weaver, $12.05; and five other standard occupations brought less than $10, only $6.76 in the case of male frame spinners. (p. 339)

16. "Strikes and Scripture," letter to the editor of the *Greenville News*, from T. T. Cromer, Greenwood, S.C., 8 Sept. 1929. The verse cited is 1 Pet. 2:18–19; other verses quoted in full by Cromer are Eph. 6:5–9; Col. 3:22, 4:11, 1 Tim. 6:1; Titus 2:9–10; Prov. 3:910; 1 Sam. 2:69; James 1:5.

17. Mill-worker protest should be considered through the insights of John Gaventa with regard to "hidden aspects of power" in company towns (see *Power and Powerlessness*, pp. 25–30). And see Pope, *Millhands and Preachers*, pp. 146–61. "Managerial authority over mill churches," writes Pope, "seldom needs to be made explicit, however, because it really inheres in the relations characteristic of mill villages" (p. 152). For a helpful overview of paternalistic structure in comparative perspective ("formal, familial, and fraternal" styles) for both North and South, see Scranton, "Varieties of Paternalism." With regard to the origins of post–Civil War paternalism in Southern mills, Scranton relies too heavily on Dwight Billings (*Planters and the Making of a "New South*," p. 247).

18. To "work a notice" was to give an employer a period of warning (usually two weeks to one month) before leaving a job, in order that a replacement might be found.

19. For a historical treatment of Southern political localism, see Key, *Southern Politics*, pp. 37, 135. Key's observations must be considered in the light of Gaventa's insightful chapter in *Power and Powerlessness* entitled "Voting and Vulnerability: Issues and Non-Issues in Local Politics" (pp. 137–64).

20. *Greenville News*, 23 Aug. 1932, PSC.

21. Ibid., 25 Aug. 1932.

22. Ibid., [n.d.] 1940 (column by Robert Quillen).

Although mill workers in Greenville produced no "Ballad of Nigel League," several families—one of whom I met—named children for Nigel. When I asked Ila Dodson where she had come up with the name Nigel for her youngest son, she responded: "Nigel League was running for the House of Representatives here in Greenville, and he was a very outstanding young man. He was a graduate from Parker High, an outstanding student.

"I read about him all the time in the paper because he was into everything over there. And I loved that name. He was a good-looking boy. He would have got it on the first go-around if he had lived to run.

"He was a good Christian boy, and the Lord didn't want him mixed up in this politics. He was up making a speech one night and dropped dead, Nigel League did. And I said, 'If this baby is a boy, he's going to be named Nigel' " (Ila Dodson interview, Greenville, S.C.).

23. The following pages draw upon my interviews with Ed and Lora Wright.

24. See Peterson, "Better Winding and Warping Machinery." Barber-Colman, an established textile machinery company with general offices and plant in Rockford, Illinois, installed the first of its new systems in the Pacific Mills of Dover, New Hampshire, in 1917. Within a couple of years, the company had also put the equipment into a handful of additional mills in the Midwest and South for purposes of testing and demonstration on different styles of yarns and cloths. See other discussions in the *Southern Textile Bulletin*, 26 Sept. 1929, p. 4, and 13 Mar. 1930, p. 31; and Peterson, "Automatic Spooler vs. High Speed Warper."

25. Stern, "Mechanical Changes in the Cotton-Textile Industry," pp. 4, 16.

26. Ibid., p. 17.

27. Ibid., pp. 16–17.

28. Peterson, "Better Winding and Warping Machinery."

29. Peterson, "Advantages of Automatic Spoolers," pp. 11–13; see also the editorial in the same issue.

30. Still, "Advantages of High Speed Spooling," p. 36.

31. Ibid.; J. H. Howarth, "Advantages of High Speed Winding and High Speed Warping," p. 48.

Chapter Six

1. This chapter draws primarily upon three interviews with Ethel Hilliard at her home in Burlington, North Carolina, on 29 March, 3 April, and 10 August 1979. During the five years following August 1979, I visited Mrs. Hilliard on several occasions, read with her the manuscript for the chapter as it took shape, and met members of her family. On 16 November 1982, I conducted another lengthy taped interview as we paged through the draft of her autobiography in essentially the form that it appears here. I am deeply grateful to Mrs. Hilliard, and to her children, for sharing their family history.

2. For a discussion of Rev. George Washington Swinney and the role of the Glen Hope Baptist Church in the Piedmont Heights community, see Hall et al., *Like a Family*, pp. 273–88.

Chapter Seven

1. The interviews excerpted here are those of 25 March and 2 May 1980. Complete tapes and transcripts of these interviews are archived with the Piedmont Industrialization Project collection, located in the Southern Historical Collection at the University of North Carolina at Chapel Hill.

Brown lung disease (byssinosis) in the Southern textile industry is discussed in Bouhuys, "Epidemiology of Chronic Lung Disease"; U.S. Senate, *Brown Lung*; Conway, *Rise Gonna Rise*; Judkins, "Occupational Health." On Greenville, South Carolina, see chapter five, above; see also Cliff Sloan and Bob Hall, "It's Good to Be Home in Greenville," in Miller, *Working Lives*, pp. 229–45. On present-day business control of South Carolina, see Walser, "Taking Care of Business."

More than any other retired mill workers whom I interviewed, those with brown lung disease spoke with evident anger about their sense of abandonment by textile companies when they could no longer "make production." Here are the comments of mill worker Paul Cline of Greenville:

"A big corporation, as much money as they have and as loyal workers as we was to the company that they treat us . . . When we come from the farm—I told you we farmed before we went—we had an old mule one time. It got old and got to where it couldn't pull a plow good. So my neighbor says, 'Why don't you send him to the glue factory?'

"My daddy said, 'That mule has made us a living for several years. I'm going to turn him out in the pasture and let him live the rest of his life in peace.'

"That's better than the mill will do. They'll turn you out with nothing. They don't even think that you're worth . . . think you're like cattle. They'll turn you out with nothing, won't take care of you. There's lot of people don't even have a pension. They just started this pension here a few years back. The only reason they done that was to keep the union away from them. But one of these days, they going to reap what they sow. Their past sins are going to find them out.

"Then, if you had a birthday coming round, bunch of them in the same month, they'd give you a little cup of coffee and a little cake with a candle on it, and the second hands sing 'Happy Birthday' to you. Instead of giving you money in your paycheck and giving you workmen's compensation when you sick, they do something like that.

"They pat you on the back as long as you're able to work. When you ain't able to work, they kick you out. That's a fact. It's been that way ever since there's been a cotton mill. If you don't produce, you don't stay in there.

"All the people that I know and everybody that you can find out is loyal to a company—stand up for them. But whenever you want them to stand up for you, they're not around. We got people running around here with J. P. Stevens stickers on, 'Stand Up for Stevens.' I got news for them people, I stood up with them for nearly forty years and look what I got—case of byssinosis and twenty-two dollars a month" (Paul Cline interview, Greenville, S.C.).

2. *Charlotte Observer*, 17 Feb. 1981.

3. As early as 1914, Joseph Goldberger of the U.S. Public Health Service concluded that the nutritionally deficient diets of tenant farmers, mill workers, and dependent populations in orphanages and asylums led to pellagra. Unrelenting meals (especially over the winter months) of grits, cornmeal, bleached white wheat flour, dried beans, "white meat" or "fat back" (salt pork fat), and sorghum or cane molasses would lead in several months to pellagra symptoms: weight loss, indigestion, nervousness, head and stomach aches. Advanced pellagra presented more obvious signs: red, sunburned-looking skin that became rough and scaly, eventually cracking and peeling; bilaterally symmetrical discoloration on the backs of hands, forearms and face; a sensation of burning or scalding in the mouth or on the tongue; and, in a small percentage of cases, temporary insanity. Pregnant women were particularly vulnerable.

Writing in 1924 amid the epidemic years of pellagra, Frank Tannenbaum wondered "whether another aspect of the excessive cultivation of cotton in the South is, in addition to tenancy, poverty, debt and intellectual stagnation, the ruination of the health of a considerable proportion of those who spend their lives in its production." Directly correlated with family income and variety in diet, the plague of pellagra singled out the South's most beleaguered population groups from 1900 until World War II.

See Terris, *Goldberger on Pellagra*. Many of the pellagra studies of Edgar Sydenstricker and Joseph Goldberger are reprinted in Kasius, *Challenge of Facts*. Also see Roe, *Plague of Corn*.

Epilogue

1. Interview with Clyde Thompson by Leonard Rapport, Durham, N.C., 10 May 1939, FWPP, pp. 9262–9269. The "Parrish" strike is apparently a name change made by Rapport.

2. Mrs. Howard K. Glenn interview, Burlington, N.C.

3. See not only the interviews in the North and South Carolina files of the Federal Writers' Project Papers, but also the remarkable collection of letters written by mill workers to President Franklin Roosevelt and National Recovery Administration director Hugh Johnson. These letters (discussed in Hall et al., *Like a Family*, pp. 289–363) are located in the records of the Cotton Textile National Industrial Relations Board and the Textile National Industrial Relations Board, Record Group 9, National Recovery Administration Records, NA. See also Pope, *Millhands and Preachers*, for a discussion of the Gastonia strike of 1929.

For dissenting and protesting voices of the 1920s and 1930s, see Haessly, "Mill Mother's Lament"; Tannenbaum, *Darker Phases of the South*; Tippett, *When Southern Labor Stirs*; Frederickson, "A Place to Speak Our Minds"; Dunbar, *Against the Grain*; Hall, "Disorderly Women."

4. Harry Chase's inaugural address is contained in a small volume published to commemorate the event (see *State University and the New South*, pp. 60–61).

5. Upton Sinclair to E. C. Branson, 1 July 1922, Branson to Sinclair, 17 Aug. 1922, Sinclair to Branson, 6 Sept. 1922, Branson to Sinclair, 15 Sept. 1922, ECBP. My thanks to Douglas DeNatale for bringing these letters to my attention. For a brief discussion of Branson, see Singal, *The War Within*, pp. 120, 389 (n. 10).

6. Key, *Southern Politics*, p. 211.

7. Hobbs, *North Carolina*, pp. 132–38; Lahne, *Cotton Mill Worker*, pp. 88–89; Triplette, "One-Industry Towns"; personal correspondence with Triplette, 24 Apr. 1981. Triplette defines a "one-industry town" as "a community dominated economically by a single manufacturing firm" ("One-Industry Towns," p. 24).

8. Wilson, *University of North Carolina*, p. 420; Henderson, *Campus of the First State University*, p. 478.

9. Johnson and Johnson, *Research in Service to Society*, pp. 8–18; Jocher and Johnson, "Howard W. Odum," p. vii; Odum, "From Community Studies to Regionalism," in Odum and Jocher, *In Search of the Regional Balance of America*, pp. 4–5; Brazil, "Howard W. Odum," pp. 73–74, 121–22. See also Odum, "G. Stanley Hall," pp. 139, 144–45, and "Patrick Geddes' Heritage," p. 279. For the first twenty-five years of its life, the Institute was primarily dependent on a variety of Rockefeller funds (see Johnson and Johnson, *Research in Service to Society*, pp. 101–18; O'Brien, *Idea of the American South*, pp. 70–71).

10. Jocher, "Regional Laboratory for Social Research and Planning," pp. 43–44. Among the contents of this volume is a list of all publications and manuscripts produced by the Institute for Research in Social Science from 1922 through 1944 (pp. 60–87).

For a fuller discussion of Odum and the IRSS, see "Folk, Region, and Society in the Carolina Piedmont," in Tullos, "Habits of Industry," pp. 412–58. For other views of Odum and his work, see Tindall, "Significance of Howard W. Odum"; Karanikas, "The Aesthetics of Regionalism," in *Tillers of a Myth*, chap. 6; Kantor, "Howard W. Odum"; Brazil, "Howard W. Odum"; Sosna, "The Silent South of Howard Odum," in *In Search of the Silent South*, chap. 3; O'Brien, *Idea of the American South*, chaps. 2–4; Johnson and Johnson, *Research in Service to Society*; King, *Southern Renaissance*; Singal, *The War Within*, chaps. 5, 10; and Rodgers, "Regionalism and the Burdens of Progress."

11. See Gatewood, "Embattled Scholar"; Johnson and Johnson, *Research in Service to Society*, pp. 38–43.

12. Davidson, *Attack on Leviathan*, pp. 52–55, 324–27.

13. Cash, *Mind of the South*, p. 333.

14. Hobson, "The 'New Southerners': The Social Critics and the South," chap. 5 of *Serpent in Eden*; Mumford, "Thought for the Growing South," p. 2. Mumford's regional planning issue of *Survey Graphic* (May 1925) was one of the first stirrings of the American regionalist movement. Although Mumford saluted the Chapel Hill group in print from time to time, he had little personal contact with them (Mumford, letter to author, 1 Sept. 1973). For a sample of the praise that greeted the emergence of the Chapel Hill group in the mid-1920s, see Mims, *Advancing South*, pp. 113–42.

15. Brazil, "Howard W. Odum," pp. 121–22; Guy Johnson interview, Chapel Hill, N.C.

16. Johnson and Johnson, *Research in Service to Society*, pp. 201–4. For a short time, Jennings J. Rhyne, a graduate student in sociology, also worked as a research associate in "industrial relations." Rhyne's *Some Southern Cotton Mill Workers and Their Villages* (1930) is a superficial assessment of the quality of mill-village life. Harry Douty, a graduate student in economics, produced "The North Carolina Industrial Worker, 1880–1930" (1936), an important dissertation that went further and more sympathetically into the state's labor history and conditions than any previous study. It, however, remains unpublished.

Across the Chapel Hill campus from the Institute for Research in Social Science, William T. Couch (director of the University of North Carolina Press) supervised the collection of over a thousand life histories of Southerners during the late 1930s as a part of the Federal Writers' Project (FWP). Although the collection ranges widely in quality and helpfulness to present-day scholars of industrialization, some of the best sketches of workers' lives that remain from the 1930s can be found in these life histories. Two published collections (Federal Writers' Project, *These Are Our Lives*, and Terrill and Hirsch, *Such as Us*) present only a small fraction of the life histories gathered by the FWP in the South. The complete collection can be found in the Southern Historical Collection. For more on Couch—and his relations with Odum—see Singal, *The War Within*, pp. 265–301.

17. Johnson and Johnson, *Research in Service to Society*, pp. 200–216, 233–34; Herring, *Welfare Work in Mill Villages*, p. 12. See Herring correspondence files for Sept., Oct., and Nov. 1925, and H. W. Chase to Harriet L. Herring, 2 Feb. 1929, HLHP; *Southern Textile Bulletin*, 3 Dec. 1925, p. 26. David Clark's attacks began in 1923 (see "Dangerous Tendencies," *Southern Textile Bulletin*, 20 Dec. 1923, p. 22). In the midst of Clark's assaults on the Institute and on other voices from the university, President Chase sent a remarkable, confidential memorandum to Odum, to Frank

Graham (then of the Department of History), and to the dean of the School of Commerce. Guy B. and Guion Griffis Johnson print a portion of this memo (*Research in Service to Society*, pp. 212–13), from which the following is excerpted:

> The question has been raised—What are proper and what improper activities for members of a university faculty in the field of the social sciences? . . . It should be clear that no principle having to do with the teaching of freedom is under discussion. . . .
>
> No faculty member has any right to allow his personal sympathies for any controversial cause to involve his colleagues and his institution in a situation that means general embarrassment, restricted educational opportunities for students and threatened careers for his colleagues. . . . If his sympathy for such a cause becomes sufficiently strong to raise in his mind a real conflict with his institutional loyalty, he should obviously sever his connection with the institution.
>
> To what causes does the above apply? . . . In North Carolina they certainly involve, for example, advocacy of particular forms of taxation, of the organization of labor, of social equality between the races, of a socialist regime, etc. (H. W. Chase to Howard Odum, D. D. Carroll, and Frank P. Graham, 6 Mar. 1928, University Papers, SHC)

18. "Book Tells of Mill Villages," *Southern Textile Bulletin*, 7 Feb. 1929, p. 33. And see the anonymous poem "An Idiossey," ibid., 18 Nov. 1926, p. 18.

19. Odum, *An American Epoch*, pp. 4–10.

20. Sumner's *Folkways: A Study of the Sociological Importance of Usages, Manners, Customs, Mores and Morals* was published in 1907.

21. O'Brien, *Idea of the American South*, pp. 36–37.

22. Odum, "Folk and Regional Conflict," p. 243.

23. Boardman, *Patrick Geddes*, pp. 109, 169, 216–17, 406–7; Mumford, "Disciple's Rebellion."

24. Zeublin, "World's First Sociological Laboratory"; Geddes, "Talks from Outlook Tower."

25. Lewis Mumford to author, 17 Feb. 1977. And see Howard Odum to W. T. Couch, 27 Jan., 6 Mar. 1943, in Press Authors files, SHC. Lewis Mumford suggested the University of North Carolina Press to Phillip Boardman as a publisher for Geddes's biography (Mumford to author, 7 Apr. 1977.) For more on the Odum-Mumford-Geddes connection with UNC, see Tullos, "Habits of Industry," pp. 426–27.

26. Davidson, *Attack on Leviathan*, p. 41.

27. See Turner's "Is Sectionalism Dying Away?" a paper read before the American Sociological Society, 28 Dec. 1907, and reprinted in Turner, *Significance of Sections in American History*, pp. 287–314.

28. Turner's *Yale Review* article is reprinted in *The Significance of Sections in American History*. This quotation is from pp. 321–26 of the latter.

29. Ross, "Sectionalism and Its Avoidance."

30. Odum, "Regionalism vs. Sectionalism."

31. Odum, "From Community Studies to Regionalism," p. 13; Mumford, *Culture of Cities*, p. 349; Lewis Mumford to author, 17 Feb. 1977. For accounts of Mumford's circle (the Regional Planning Association of America), see Lubove, *Community Planning in the 1920s*; Sussman, *Planning for the Fourth Migration*. For a statement on European regionalism, see Hintze, "Regionalism"; also Mumford, "Theory and Practice of Regionalism."

32. Odum, "A Southern Promise," p. 24; Vance, *Human Factors in Cotton Culture*, pp. 467–81. In an article for *Social Forces*, Vance points to several geographers who influenced his exploration of regionalism, including Mumford's mentors—Vidal de la Blache, Brunhes, and Patrick Geddes. He expresses the hope that, given time, American cultural geographers can "produce results equal to the best work of the French School" ("Concept of the Region"). Thanks to John Shelton Reed and Daniel Singal, the editors of *Regionalism and the South*, Vance's writing is again in circulation.

Throughout his long association with the University of North Carolina, Vance kept his habit of pointing out as many unpleasant facts as pleasing ones. And the textile industry kept up its habits as well. Consider the following letter, written in 1968 to William Friday, president of the university, from B. C. Trotter, an attorney from Leaksville, North Carolina:

My dear Bill,

Some of our textile friends who are friends of the University have called my attention to the March, 1968, issue of "The University of North Carolina News Letter" which contains an article "When Southern Labor Comes of Age" written by Rupert B. Vance, a university professor. They feel the article is detrimental to the textile industry and attributes the low per capita earnings of North Carolina citizens to the textile industry—that it is a warning to any textile manufacturer who might anticipate coming to North Carolina to establish a plant that he is not welcome—that North Carolina wants only industries which operate on the highest wage scales. Our friends are fearful that the University will be construed as hostile to the textile industry when as a matter of fact the University is accepting money from the industry to assist in the operation of the textile school in Raleigh.

I am afraid it puts the University in a bad light with the industry.

I am passing this information along to you for what it may be worth. (Trotter to Friday, 22 Apr. 1968, RBVP)

33. Myles Horton, interview by Allen Tullos, Highlander Center, New Market, Tenn., 13 July 1981. More about Horton, the Highlander Center, and some related organizations of the 1930s can be found in several sources: Dunbar, *Against the Grain*; Horton, "Highlander Folk School"; Thrasher, "Radical Education in the Thirties."

34. Rupert B. Vance, "Howard W. Odum and the Case of the South," address to the southeastern meeting of the American Studies Association, 11 Apr. 1970, RBVP.

35. Key, *Southern Politics*, p. 211.

36. Myles Horton interview, Highlander Center, New Market, Tenn.

37. Harriet Herring to Luther Hodges, 4 July 1939, HLHP.

38. See Hall et al., *Like a Family*, pp. 289–99; Hodges, *New Deal Labor Policy*, pp. 44–63.

39. Noble, *America by Design*, pp. 286–89.

40. Ibid., p. 289.

41. Johnson and Johnson, *Research in Service to Society*, p. 207.

42. Gilman, *Human Relations*, pp. v–vi, 239–42. For a contemporary version of Gilman's conventional wisdom, see the interview with businessman Milton Short, Charlotte, N.C.

43. Gilman, *Human Relations*, p. 242.

44. Ibid., pp. v–vi.

45. Ibid., pp. v, 44, 89.

46. Ibid., pp. 193, 104. And see pp. 39–45, 89. As for unions, "they were the antithesis of everything the folk society stood for" (see pp. 236, 239, 309, 312).

47. "Memorandum" from Rupert Vance to Howard Odum, 21 Jan. 1938, RBVP. My thanks to Jerrold Hirsch for calling this item to my attention. Daniel Singal also discusses this memo (*The War Within*, pp. 314–15).

48. Johnson and Johnson, *Research in Service to Society*, p. 121.

49. Ernest R. Groves to Howard Odum, 20 June 1927, University of North Carolina Research Files, Laura Spelman Rockefeller Memorial Archives, North Tarrytown, N.Y. In 1953, Odum received the O. Max Gardner Award (named for the millowner governor of North Carolina who had sent the National Guard to Gastonia in 1929 to protect the Loray Mill property) "as that member of the consolidated University of North Carolina who . . . has made the greatest contribution to the welfare of the human race." Among the members of the UNC Board of Trustees committee that presented the award were manufacturers Reid Maynard and J. Spencer Love. The citation to Odum read, in part: "Never one to evade issues or dodge the meaning of facts, he has maintained a balanced perspective on controversial issues, often to the dismay of militant radicals" (from the notice of Gardner Award and Citation, RBVP; see also Parramore, *Express Lanes and Country Roads*, pp. 35–36).

George B. Tindall has too hastily dismissed regionalism: "With interregional balance apparently approaching reality, the whole concept has somehow fallen into disuse. Regionalism has come to appear in perspective as a sort of way station on the road from Southern sectionalism toward integration into the national culture—and not as a permanent phenomenon" ("Significance of Howard W. Odum"). See also O'Brien, "Odum: The Failure of Regionalism," in *Idea of the American South*, chap. 4; Singal, *The War Within*, p. 152.

50. Key, *Southern Politics*, pp. 205–6.

51. Page, *Southern Cotton Mills and Labor*, pp. 22–24. Myra Page is the pen name of Dorothy Markey, a writer and organizer in the South during the 1920s and 1930s. For more on Page, see Frederickson, "Myra Page."

52. Sunday school lesson, Oct. 1909, by J. S. Carr, Julian Shakespeare Carr Papers, SHC; motto excerpted from a letter from Carr to E. C. Branson, 19 Sept. 1922, ECBP. Carr was the paragon of the militant Christian capitalist, capable of calculating the efficiency factor and cost per capita for Methodist missionaries to convert the world's heathen. On Carr, see also Webb, *Jule Carr*.

Guide to Sources

Interviews

A Note on the Piedmont Industrialization Project

Between September 1978 and September 1980, I served as research associate and project coordinator for the Southern Oral History Program at the University of North Carolina at Chapel Hill in its project "Perspectives on Industrialism: The Piedmont Crescent of Industry, 1880–1940" (supported by the National Endowment for the Humanities). The Piedmont Industrialization Project had as its major objective the creation of an archive of life-history interviews, primarily with first- and second-generation textile workers who experienced the transition of the Piedmont from a rural to an industrializing society. Altogether, our team of interviewers conducted interviews with nearly 350 people, evenly divided between men and women. More than thirty interviews were conducted in each of six "core communities": Burlington, Bynum, Charlotte, Durham, and Hickory-Conover, North Carolina, and Greenville, South Carolina. In addition, our collection includes approximately one hundred interviews from the industrial towns of Elizabethton, Tennessee, and Badin, Carrboro, Cramerton, Marion, Spencer Shops, and Winston-Salem, North Carolina.

Because blacks were excluded from most textile occupations, the interviewees who appear in this study are predominately white. A tabulation of the more than two hundred interviewees upon which *Habits of Industry* is based reveals the following profile. Interviewees fall mainly into three age groups: 26 percent were born between 1891 and 1900, 41 percent between 1900 and 1910, and 25 percent between 1911 and 1920. One-fourth of the interviewees began work before the age of fourteen. About half were the first in their families to enter factory work. By the post–World War II era, most of the children of these longtime workers did not work in textile mills but in other manufacturing and service employment. Also included among our interviewees are several manufacturers, industrial engineers, businessmen, and Piedmont townspeople who offer their perspectives on the habits of industry in the region. For additional discussion of the project, see Hall et al., *Like a Family*, preface. See also Cathy Abernathy, Lynn Hudson, and Alisa Blackmar, "Collective Profile of Interviewees," research report, Southern Oral History Program, University of North Carolina, 1981 and 1986.

In carrying out the interviews, fieldworkers received a set of guidelines suggesting topics to be pursued in the categories of family, work, and community history. We did not, however, attempt to follow a rigid schedule of questions. Instead we allowed people to narrate the story of their own lives, emphasizing topics and themes that seemed most important and meaningful to them. We guided subsequent conversation by asking for elaboration or clarification or by bringing up new topics, while trying to maintain an atmosphere in which unanticipated information could emerge.

To make the tapes of the interviews accessible, we indexed all of them topically and transcribed approximately half. They are now available to scholars and are located in the Southern Historical Collection at the University of North Carolina. The following interviews from the Piedmont Industrialization Project contributed significantly to *Habits of Industry*.

Burlington, North Carolina

Adams, Harry and Janie. Interview by Allen Tullos, 28 February, 20 March, 11 May 1979.

Adams, Lottie Jeanette. Interview by Mary Murphy, 23 March 1979.

Brooks, Jesse L. Interview by Cliff Kuhn, 20 July 1977.

Carden, Stella Foust. Interview by Mary Murphy, 25 April 1979.

Cates, Bertha. Interview by Mary Murphy, 13 June 1979.

Chapman, Ernest. Interview by Mary Murphy, 4 June 1979.

Crutchfield, Joseph. Interview by Allen Tullos, 26 June, 5 November 1979.

Davidson, Betty and Lloyd. Interview by Allen Tullos, 2, 15 February 1979.

Faucette, Ethel Marshall and George. Interview by Allen Tullos, 16 November 1978, 4 January 1979.

Faucette, Paul and Don. Interview by Allen Tullos, 7 January 1979.

Glenn, Mrs. Howard K. Interview by Cliff Kuhn, 27 June 1977.

Gordon, Staley. Interview by Allen Tullos, 3 May 1979.

Haithcock, Versa Vernon. Interview by Mary Murphy, 4 April 1979.

Harrington, Edward and Mary. Interview by Mary Murphy, 28 February 1979.

Hilliard, Ethel. Interview by Allen Tullos, 29 March, 3 April, 10 August 1979.

Johnson, Sallie, and Rena Capes. Interview by Mary Murphy, 20 March 1979.

Lupton, Carrol. Interview by Mary Murphy, 18 May 1979.

McBride, Gladys and Dewey. Interview by Mary Murphy, 16 May 1979.

Maynard, Grace Moore. Interview by Allen Tullos, 27 February, 30 March 1979.

Maynard, Reid. Interview by Allen Tullos, 6, 13 February, 3 April 1979.

Meacham, H. G. Interview by Cliff Kuhn, 26 July 1978.

Murray, Charles and Zelma. Interview by Brent Glass, 4 March 1976.

Newman, Lessie. Interview by Cliff Kuhn, 28 June 1977.

Norman, Icy A. Interview by Mary Murphy, 6, 30 April 1979.

Overman, Mildred Mae. Interview by Allen Tullos, 17 April 1979.

Pharis, James. Interview by Cliff Kuhn, 24 July 1977.

Pharis, James and Nannie F. Interview by Allen Tullos, 5 December 1978, 8, 30 January 1979, 27 March 1979.

Robertson, William and Margaret. Interview by Allen Tullos, 27 March 1979.

Robinette, J. M. Interview by Cliff Kuhn, July 1977.

Rogers, Harry Lee. Interview by Cliff Kuhn, 21 July 1977.

Rogers, Harry Lee. Interview by Allen Tullos, 2 February, 11 May 1979.

Shockley, Ethel Bowman. Interview by Cliff Kuhn, 24 June 1979.

Shoemaker, Mattie, and Mildred Edmonds. Interview by Mary Murphy, 23 March 1979.

Splawn, V. Baxter. Interview by Cliff Kuhn, 27 July 1977.

Stackhouse, Verna Cates. Interview by Cliff Kuhn, 19 July 1977.

Staley, Thomas Lee. Interview by Allen Tullos, 22, 29 May 1977.

Stout, Nettie Mae. Interview by Mary Murphy, 13 June 1979.

Swinney, Etta Gay. Interview by Mary Murphy, 24 April 1979.

Taylor, Hestor M. Interview by Mary Murphy, 4 April 1979.

Truitt, Herman N. Interview by Allen Tullos, 5 December 1978, 3, 19 January 1979.

Weaver, Christine. Interview by Cliff Kuhn, 25 July 1977.

Webster, Frank. Interview by Allen Tullos, 30 January, 29 May 1979.

Whitesell, Emma. Interview by Cliff Kuhn, 27 July 1977.

Wiles, Bennie Green. Interview by Allen Tullos, 15 February 1979.

Wrenn, Ina Lee. Interview by Allen Tullos, 23 March 1979.

Charlotte, North Carolina

Andrews, Mildred Gwin. Interview by Mary Murphy and Jim Leloudis, 15 June 1979.

Ashe, J. B. Interview by Allen Tullos, 13 June 1980.

Austin, Ralph C. Interview by Jim Leloudis, 14 June 1979.

Belk, John Montgomery. Interview by Allen Tullos, 14 July 1980.

Cloniger, Loy Connelly. Interview by Allen Tullos, 18 June 1980.

Dunn, John and Minnie. Interview by Allen Tullos, 31 January 1980.

Dunn, Minnie Lawrence. Interview by Jim Leloudis, 21 June 1979.

Dyer, George and Tessie. Interview by LuAnn Jones, 5 March 1980.

Evitt, Alice P. Interview by Jim Leloudis, 18 July 1979.

Hargett, Edna Y. Interview by Jim Leloudis, 19 July 1979.

Harris, L. Worth. Interview by Allen Tullos, 11 June 1980.

Hatcher, Jean Cole. Interview by Allen Tullos, 12 June 1980.

Hopkins, Eva Ballentine. Interview by LuAnn Jones, 5 March 1980.

Honnecutt, Willie Mae. Interview by Allen Tullos, 31 January 1980.

Kimbirl, Julius Edwin. Interview by Jim Leloudis, 10 July 1979.

Kirkpatrick, Laura M. Interview by Jim Leloudis, 21 June 1979.

Kiser, Coy M. Interview by Jim Leloudis, 11 July 1979.

McCorkle, Hoyle and Mamie. Interview by Jim Leloudis, 11 July 1979.

Martin, Benjamin V. Interview by Allen Tullos, 8, 9 June 1980.

Merritt, Baxter J. Interview by Allen Tullos, 1 February 1980.

Pitts, Viola. Interview by LuAnn Jones, 21 April 1980.

Sanders, Lila Mae. Interview by Jim Leloudis, 12 July 1979.

Short, Milton. Interview by Jim Leloudis and Carol Shaw, 6 June 1979.

Shue, George R. and Mamie. Interview by Jim Leloudis, 20 June 1979.

Shuping, Gertrude. Interview by LuAnn Jones, 29 February, 6 March 1980.

Shuping, Lloyd J. Interview by LuAnn Jones, 29 February 1980.

Strickland, Ralph. Interview by LuAnn Jones, 1 April 1980.

Thomas, Claude C. Interview by LuAnn Jones, 18 April 1980.

Thompson, Carl and Mary. Interview by Jim Leloudis, 19 July 1979.

Wilson, Ada Mae. Interview by Allen Tullos, 1 February 1980.

Wofford, Blaine H. Interview by Allen Tullos, 1 February 1980.

Wolf, Herman. Interview by Allen Tullos, 15 July 1980.

Durham, North Carolina

Allen, Sally. Interview by Lanier Rand, February 1977.

Arnold, Lellie. Interview by Mary Murphy, 11 July 1979.

Barbee, Annie Mack. Interview by Beverly Jones, 28 May 1979.

Brown, Maude. Interview by Beverly Jones, 3 August 1979.

Buchanan, Bessie. Interview by Lanier Rand, June 1977, 13 July 1977.

Burt, Thomas. Interview by Glenn Hinson, 6 February, 26 October, 3 November 1979.

Caesar, Hallie. Interview by Glenn Hinson, 21 May 1979.

Clark, Chester and Rosanna. Interview by Glenn Hinson, 5, 26 January, 8 June 1979.

Cooke, Elizabeth. Interview by Kenneth Kornblau, 17 April 1979.

Dove, Mary Magaline. Interview by Beverly Jones, 7 July 1979.

Dunn, Maude W. Interview by Kenneth Kornblau, 20 April 1979.

Ellington, Harvey (with Sam Pridgen). Interview by Allen Tullos, 1 March, 5 April 1979.

Glenn, Bessie. Interview by Mary Murphy, 12 July 1979.

Henry, Lovie (Mrs.). Interview by Lanier Rand, June 1977.

Hodges, Estelle. Interview by Glenn Hinson, 23 May 1979.

Latta, J. Ernest. Interview by Lanier Rand, 7 July 1977.

Lowery, Leota. Interview by Mary Murphy, 17 July 1979.

McCaughin, Mamie. Interview by Kenneth Kornblau, 19 April 1979.

McMillon, Salina. Interview by Glenn Hinson, 25 October 1976.

Mack, Charlie Necoda. Interview by Beverly Jones, 16 August 1979.

Marcom, Fannie. Interview by Mary Murphy, 17 July 1979.

Miller, Dora Scott. Interview by Beverly Jones, 6 June 1979.

Mitchner, Reginald. Interview by Glenn Hinson, 15 November, 7 December 1976, 7 February 1979.

Oakley, Maxie. Interview by Mary Murphy, 12 July 1979.

O'Neal, Reuben M. Interview by Beverly Jones, 16 August 1979.

Parks, George. Interview by Lanier Rand, 27 July 1977.

Phillips, E. S. Interview by Lanier Rand, February 1977.

Phillips, Edward. Interview by Kenneth Kornblau, 19 April 1979.

Pridgen, Samuel Lee. Interview by Allen Tullos, 16 February 1979.

Richmond, Ovie. Interview by Lanier Rand, July 1977.

Richmond, Ozzie. Interview by Lanier Rand, 16, 21 June 1977.

Riley, Luther. Interview by Lanier Rand, July 1977.

Russell, Charles. Interview by Glenn Hinson, 30 November 1976.

Saunders, Vernon (Mr. and Mrs.). Interview by Lanier Rand, 26 October 1976.

Saunders, Vernon. Interview by Allen Tullos, 24 May 1979.

Scott, Blanche. Interview by Beverly Jones, 11 July 1979.

Trice, Richard. Interview by Glenn Hinson, 16 February 1978, and 1 January 1979.

Tucker, James. Interview by Lanier Rand, 1 August 1977.

Winn, Lloyd. Interview by Lanier Rand, 21 July 1977.

Greenville, South Carolina

Adams, Robert Roy. Interview by Allen Tullos, 29 August, 19 October 1979.

Carter, Jessie Lee. Interview by Allen Tullos, 5 May 1980.

Cleveland, Myrtle. Interview by Allen Tullos, 22 October 1979.

Cline, Paul. Interview by Allen Tullos, 8 November 1979.

Dodson, Ila Hartsell. Interview by Allen Tullos, 23 May 1980.

Dodson, Geddes Elam. Interview by Allen Tullos, 26 May 1980.

Duncan, Mack. Interview by Allen Tullos, 7 June, 20 August 1979.

Duncan, Norvin (with Wilson Pace). Interview by Allen Tullos, 5, 7 May 1980.

Enlow, Curtis Lelon. Interview by Allen Tullos, 9 November 1979.

Gambrell, James and Dovie. Interview by Allen Tullos, 4 May 1980.

Gentry, Myrtle. Interview by Allen Tullos, 22 October 1979.

Griffith, Paul and Pauline. Interview by Allen Tullos, 24 March 1980.

Hardin, Alice. Interview by Allen Tullos, 2 May 1980.

Hardin, Grover. Interview by Allen Tullos, 25 March 1980.

Harvell, Evelyn. Interview by Allen Tullos, 27 May 1980.

Hickum, Ernest. Interview by Allen Tullos, 27 March 1980.

Holden, Mildred Virginia. Interview by Allen Tullos, 29 May 1980.

Lowe, Martin E. Interview by Allen Tullos, 19, 21 October 1979.

Osteen, Letha Ann Sloan. Interview by Allen Tullos, 8 June 1979.

Padgett, Everette and Mary. Interview by Allen Tullos, 28 May 1980.

Sanders, Albert. Interview by Allen Tullos, 30 May 1980.

Soderberg, Walter. Interview by Allen Tullos and Billy Mass, 15 February 1980.

Trammel, Naomi Sizemore. Interview by Allen Tullos, 25 March 1980.
Wright, Lora League. Interview by Allen Tullos, 7 June, 11 November 1979.
Wrigley, Georgia. Interview by Allen Tullos, 27 August 1979.

Additional Interviews

Hinson, Glenn. Interview by Allen Tullos, Durham, N.C., 25 July 1980.
Johnson, Guy. Interview by Archie Green, Chapel Hill, N.C., 15 November 1979.
Love, Cornelia Spencer. Interview by Lee Kessler, Greensboro, N.C., 26 January 1975.
Melton, (Mrs. Ollie). Interview by Doug DeNatale, East Rockingham, N.C., 19 December 1979.
Moore, Musker Semple. Interview by Allen Tullos, Raleigh, N.C., 17 May 1979.
Outlaw, John Thomas. Interview by Allen Tullos, Raleigh, N.C., 5 June 1980.
Porter, Joseph A. Interview by Allen Tullos, Raleigh, N.C., 25 June 1979.
Smith, E. L. Interview by Margaret Lee, Greensboro, N.C., July 1979.
Tate, Flicka. Interview by Stephen Lamb, Pacolet Mills, S.C., Fall 1978.
Tate, Grace. Interview by Stephen Lamb, Pacolet Mills, S.C., Fall 1978.
Whitmire, Shirley League. Interview by Allen Tullos, Simpsonville, S.C., 13 July 1982.

Manuscripts

Cambridge, Massachusetts

Baker Library, Harvard University
    Credit Reporting Ledgers, R. G. Dun and Company

Chapel Hill, North Carolina

North Carolina Collection, University of North Carolina
    Harriet L. Herring Clipping Collection, 1927–37. Microfilm.
Southern Historical Collection, University of North Carolina
    Eugene Cunningham Branson Papers
    Burlington Dynamite Case Files
    Julian Shakespeare Carr Papers
    William T. Couch Papers
    Federal Writers' Project Papers
    Harriet Laura Herring Papers
    Edwin Michael Holt Papers
    K. P. Lewis Papers
    James Lee Love Papers
        James Lee Love Manuscript

Love, James Lee. "Some Recollections of Daniel Efird Rhyne"
James Spencer Love Papers
McBee Family Papers
Howard Washington Odum Papers
Daniel Augustus Tompkins Papers
University Papers
Rupert Bayless Vance Papers
James Webb Papers

Durham, North Carolina

Manuscript Collection, Perkins Library, Duke University
  Papers of Mary Cowper

Greenville, South Carolina

Greenville County Library
  Parker School District Scrapbook Collection
  Monaghan Mill Collection
Textile Hall
  Gilkerson, Yancy S. "Textile Hall's First Sixty Years." 1975. Typescript.
  Textile Exposition Collection

North Tarrytown, New York

Laura Spelman Rockefeller Memorial Archives, Rockefeller Archive Center
  University of North Carolina Research Files

Raleigh, North Carolina

North Carolina State Archives
  Nell Battle Lewis Papers
  Governors' Papers
    Letterbook of Governor Richard Spaight
  Patterson Family Papers

Washington, D.C.

National Archives
  National Recovery Administration Records

State and Federal Records

Hand-Book of North Carolina. Raleigh, N.C.: P. M. Hale, 1886.

Massachusetts Department of Labor and Industries. *Report of Special Investigation into Conditions in the Textile Industry in Massachusetts and the Southern States, 1923*. Boston: Arkwright Club, n.d.

North Carolina Board of Agriculture. *Handbook of North Carolina*. Raleigh, N.C.: Ashe and Gatling, 1883.

————. *Handbook of North Carolina*. Raleigh, N.C.: Edwards and Broughton, 1893.

North Carolina Bureau of Labor and Printing. *Annual Reports*, 1887–1908.

Polk, L. L. *Handbook of North Carolina*. Raleigh, N.C.: Raleigh News Steam Book and Job Printing, 1879.

South Carolina Department of Agriculture, Commerce, and Immigration. *Handbook of South Carolina*. Columbia, S.C.: n.p., 1907.

————. *Year Book of South Carolina, 1914*. Columbia, S.C.: Gonzales and Bryan, 1915.

————. Labor Division. *Annual Reports*, 1909–20.

U.S. Congress. Senate. *Brown Lung: Hearing before a Subcommittee of the Committee on Appropriations*. 95th Cong., 1st sess. Washington: Government Printing Office, 1978.

————. *Working Conditions of the Textile Industry in North Carolina, South Carolina and Tennessee: Hearings before the Committee on Manufacturing*. 71st Cong., 1st sess., 8, 9, and 20 May 1929.

U.S. Department of Agriculture. *The Story of Soil Conservation in the South Carolina Piedmont, 1800–1860*. By Arthur C. Hall. Miscellaneous Publication No. 407. Washington, D.C.: Government Printing Office, 1940.

————. *Value of Small Plot of Ground to Laboring Man*. By W. C. Funk. Bulletin No. 602. Washington, D.C.: Government Printing Office, 1918.

U.S. Department of Commerce. *Commercial Survey of the Southeast*. By John M. Hager. Washington, D.C.: Government Printing Office, 1927.

U.S. Department of Labor. *Job Descriptions for the Cotton Textile Industry*. Washington, D.C.: Government Printing Office, 1939.

U.S. Department of Labor. Bureau of Labor Statistics. *Labor in the South*. Bulletin No. 898. Washington, D.C.: Government Printing Office, 1947.

————. *Wages and Hours in Cotton-Goods Manufacturing, 1910–1928*. Bulletin No. 492. Washington, D.C.: Government Printing Office, 1928.

U.S. Department of Labor. Employment Service. *Job Specifications for the Cotton Textile Industry*. Washington, D.C.: Government Printing Office, 1935.

U.S. Department of Labor. Women's Bureau. *Hours, Earnings, and Employment in Cotton Mills*. Bulletin No. 111. Washington, D.C.: Government Printing Office, 1933.

————. *Lost Time and Labor Turnover in Cotton Mills: Study of Cause and Extent*. Bulletin No. 52. Washington, D.C.: Government Printing Office, 1926.

Newspapers and Trade Publications

American Fabrics
American Wool and Cotton Reporter
Burlington Daily News
Charlotte Observer
Clark's Directory of Southern Cotton Mills. Charlotte, N.C.: Clark Publishing Co.,
    1912.
Davison's Textile "Blue Book." New York: Davison Publishing Co., 1888.
Gastonia Gazette
Greensboro Daily News
Greenville Civic and Commercial Journal. Vol. 1, *1921–22*; vol. 2, *1922–23*; vol. 3,
    1922–23; vol. 4, *1924–25*; vol. 5, *1925–26.*
Greenville Enterprise and Mountaineer
Greenville News
Greenville Piedmont
Manufacturers' Record (Baltimore, Md.)
Southern Textile Bulletin (Charlotte, N.C.)
Textile World

Secondary Sources

Agee, James, and Walker Evans. *Let Us Now Praise Famous Men.* Boston: Houghton
    Mifflin, 1941.
Agnew, Jean-Christophe. "History and Anthropology: Scenes from a Marriage." Pa-
    per presented at the Shelby Cullom Davis Center for Historical Studies, Prince-
    ton University, 24 October 1986.
Agnew, Theodore L. "Methodism on the Frontier." In *The History of American
    Methodism,* edited by Emory Bucke. 1:488–545. Nashville, Tenn.: Abingdon,
    1964.
Allen, Rutillas Harrison. *Part-time Farming in the Southeast.* Washington, D.C.: Gov-
    ernment Printing Office, 1937.
American Conference of Governmental Industrial Hygienists. *Cotton Dust: Proceed-
    ings of a Topical Symposium, 12–13 November 1974.* Cincinnati, Ohio: ACGIH,
    1975.
Andrews, Mildred Gwin. *The Men and the Mills: A History of the Southern Textile In-
    dustry.* Macon, Ga.: Mercer University Press, 1988.
Ashe, Samuel A., Stephen B. Weeks, and Charles L. Van Noppen. *Biographical His-
    tory of North Carolina.* 8 vols. Greensboro, N.C.: Van Noppen, 1905–17.
Ashmore, Harry S. *Hearts and Minds: The Anatomy of Racism from Roosevelt to Reagan.*
    New York: McGraw-Hill, 1982.
Auman, Dorothy Cole, and Charles G. Zug III, "Nine Generations of Potters: The

Cole Family." *Southern Exposure* 5, nos. 2–3 (1977): 166–74. Special issue, *Long Journey Home: Folklife in the South*, edited by Allen Tullos.

Ayer, Hartwell M. *The Resources and Manufacturing Industries of the State of South Carolina*. Charleston, S.C.: Lucas and Richardson Co., 1895.

Badger, Anthony J. *North Carolina and the New Deal*. Raleigh: North Carolina Department of Cultural Resources, 1981.

Baker, Robert A. "The Contributions of South Carolina Baptists to the Rise and Development of the Southern Baptist Convention." *Baptist History Heritage* 17 (July 1982): 2–9, 19.

Barnwell, Mildred Gwin. *Faces We See*. Gastonia, N.C.: Southern Combed Yarn Spinners Association, 1939.

Bastin, Bruce. *Crying for the Carolines*. London: November Books, 1971.

———. *Red River Blues: The Blues Tradition in the Southeast*. Urbana: University of Illinois Press, 1986.

Bateman, Fred, and Thomas Weiss. *A Deplorable Scarcity: The Failure of Industrialization in the Slave Economy*. Chapel Hill: University of North Carolina Press, 1981.

Battisti, Carlo, and Giovanni Alessio, eds. *Dizionario Etimologico Italiano*. Firenze: G. Barbera Editore, 1954.

Beal, Fred E. *Proletarian Journey*. New York: Hillman-Curl, 1937.

Beatty, Bess. "The Edwin Holt Family: Southern Capitalists." Paper presented at the annual meeting of the Southern Historical Association, Charleston, S.C., November 1983.

———. "Lowells of the South: Northern Influence on the Nineteenth-Century North Carolina Textile Industry, 1830–1890." *Journal of Southern History* 53 (February 1987): 37–62.

Belden, Henry M., and Arthur Palmer Hudson, eds. *Folk Ballads from North Carolina*. Vol. 3 of *The Frank C. Brown Collection of North Carolina Folklore*, edited by Newman Ivey White. Durham, N.C.: Duke University Press, 1952.

Bell, John L., Jr., *Hard Times: Beginnings of the Great Depression in North Carolina, 1929–1933*. Raleigh: North Carolina Division of Archives and History, 1982.

Benjamin, Walter. *Illuminations*. New York: Schocken, 1969.

Berglund, Abraham, George T. Starnes, and Frank T. DeVyver. *Labor in the Industrial South; A Survey of Wages and Living Conditions in Three Major Industries of the New Industrial South*. Charlottesville: Institute for Research in Social Science, University of Virginia, 1930.

Bernheim, Gotthardt Dellmann. *History of the German Settlements and of the Lutheran Church in North and South Carolina*. Philadelphia: Lutheran Book Store, 1872. Reprint. Spartanburg, S.C.: The Reprint Co., 1972.

Bertelson, David. *The Lazy South*. New York: Oxford University Press, 1967.

Berthoff, Rowland. "Celtic Mist over the South." *Journal of Southern History* 52 (November 1986): 523–46.

Billings, Dwight. *Planters and the Making of a "New South": Class, Politics, and Development in North Carolina, 1865–1900.* Chapel Hill: University of North Carolina Press, 1979.

Billings, Dwight, Kathleen Blee Billings, and Louis Swanson. "Culture, Family, and Community in Preindustrial Appalachia." *Appalachian Journal* 13 (Winter 1986): 154–70.

"Bishops and Other Ministers Tell Why They Did or Didn't Sign the Letter about Cotton Mill Villages." *Manufacturers' Record* (28 April 1927): 61–68.

Bivins, John, Jr. *Longrifles of North Carolina.* York, Pa.: George Shumway, 1968.

———. *The Moravian Potters in North Carolina.* Chapel Hill: University of North Carolina Press, 1972.

Blanshard, Paul. *Labor in Southern Cotton Mills.* New York: New Republic, 1927.

Blethen, Tyler, and Curtis Wood, Jr. *From Ulster to Carolina: The Migration of the Scotch Irish to Southwestern North Carolina.* Cullowhee, N.C.: Mountain Heritage Center, Western Carolina University, 1983.

Blicksilver, Jack. *Cotton Manufacturing in the Southeast: An Historical Analysis.* Studies in Business and Economics, bulletin no. 5. Atlanta: Georgia State College of Business Administration, 1959.

Blythe, LeGette. *Robert Lee Stowe: Pioneer in Textiles.* Charlotte, N.C.: Heritage Printers, 1965.

———. *William Henry Belk: Merchant of the South.* Chapel Hill: University of North Carolina Press, 1950.

Boardman, Philip. *Patrick Geddes: Maker of the Future.* Chapel Hill: University of North Carolina Press, 1944.

Boles, John. "Evangelical Protestantism in the Old South: From Religious Dissent to Cultural Dominance." In *Religion in the South*, edited by Charles Reagan Wilson, pp. 13–34. Jackson: University Press of Mississippi, 1985.

———. *The Great Revival, 1787–1805.* Lexington: University Press of Kentucky, 1972.

Botsch, Robert Emil. *We Shall Not Overcome: Populism and Southern Blue-Collar Workers.* Chapel Hill: University of North Carolina Press, 1980.

Bouhuys, A. "Epidemiology of Chronic Lung Disease in a Cotton Mill Community." *Lung* 154 (December 1977): 167–86.

Bourne, Randolph. "The Puritan's Will to Power." In *The Radical Will: Randolph Bourne, Selected Writings, 1911–1918*, edited by Olaf Hansen, pp. 301–6. New York: Urizen, 1977.

Bowman, Isaiah. *Forest Physiography of the United States.* New York: Wiley, 1911.

Boyd, William Kenneth. *The Story of Durham.* Durham, N.C.: Duke University Press, 1925.

Boyte, Harry. "The Textile Industry, Keel of Southern Industrialization." *Radical America* 6, no. 2 (March/April 1972): 4–49.

Braverman, Harry. *Labor and Monopoly Capital: The Degradation of Work in the Twen-*

tieth Century. New York: Monthly Review Press, 1974.

Brazil, Wayne Douglas. "Howard W. Odum: The Building Years, 1884–1930." Ph.D. diss., Harvard University, 1975.

Brengle, Kim Withers. *The Architectural Heritage of Gaston County, North Carolina.* Gastonia, N.C.: Commercial Printers, 1982.

Bresler, Helen. "Industrial Vernacular Architecture: The Mill Villages of Glencoe and Bynum." Seminar paper, University of North Carolina, 1979.

Briggs, Martha Tune. "Mill Owners and Mill Workers in an Antebellum North Carolina County." Master's thesis, University of North Carolina, 1975.

Britten, Rollo Herbert. *The Health of Workers in a Textile Plant.* Washington, D.C.: Government Printing Office, 1933.

Brody, David. *Workers in Industrial America: Essays on the Twentieth-Century Struggle.* New York: Oxford University Press, 1980.

Brown, Douglas. *A City without Cobwebs: A History of Rock Hill, S.C.* Columbia: University of South Carolina Press, 1953.

Bruce, Dickson D., Jr. *And They All Sang Hallelujah: Plain Folk Camp Meeting Religion, 1880–1845.* Knoxville: University of Tennessee Press, 1974.

Burgess, Allen Edward. "Tar Heel Blacks and the New South Dream: The Coleman Manufacturing Company, 1896–1904." Ph.D. diss., Duke University, 1977.

Burke, Fielding [Olive Tilford Dargan, pseud.]. *Call Home the Heart.* Old Westbury, N.Y.: Feminist Press, 1982.

Burlington Industries. *A Brief History.* Greensboro, N.C.: Burlington Industries, 1979.

———. *Burlington Mill Review—Thirty Years.* Greensboro, N.C.: Burlington Industries, 1953.

Burton, Orville Vernon. *In My Father's House Are Many Mansions: Family and Community in Edgefield, South Carolina.* Chapel Hill: University of North Carolina Press, 1985.

Byerly, Victoria. *Hard Times Cotton Mill Girls: Personal Histories of Womanhood and Poverty in the South.* Ithaca, N.Y.: ILR Press, 1986.

Byington, Robert H. *Working Americans: Contemporary Approaches to Occupational Folklife.* Los Angeles: California Folklore Society, 1978.

Camack, D. E. *Human Gold from Southern Hills.* Greer, S.C.: privately printed, 1960.

Campbell, John C. *The Southern Highlander and His Homeland.* Chapel Hill: University of North Carolina Press, 1921. Reprint. Spartanburg, S.C.: The Reprint Co., 1973.

Carlson, James A. "The Iron Horse in Court: Thomas Ruffin and the Development of North Carolina Railroad Law." Ph.D. diss., University of North Carolina, 1972.

Carlton, David L. " 'Builders of a New State': The Town Classes and Early Industrialization of South Carolina, 1880–1907." In *From the Old South to the New: Essay on the Transitional South*, edited by Walter J. Fraser, Jr., and Winifred B. Moore, Jr., pp. 43–62. Westport, Conn.: Greenwood Press, 1981.

_____. *Mill and Town in South Carolina, 1880–1920.* Baton Rouge: Louisiana State University Press, 1982.

Carolina Population Center. *County Population Trends, North Carolina, 1790–1960.* Chapel Hill, N.C.: CPC, 1969.

Caruthers, E. W. *Interesting Revolutionary Incidents and Sketches of Character Chiefly in the Old North State.* Philadelphia: Hayes and Zell, 1856.

Cash, Wilbur J. "Buck Duke's University." *American Mercury* 30 (September 1933): 102–10.

_____. *The Mind of the South.* New York: Knopf, 1941.

Cathay, Cornelius O. *Agricultural Developments in North Carolina, 1783–1860.* Chapel Hill: University of North Carolina Press, 1956.

Cecil-Fronsman, Bill. "The Common Whites: Class and Culture in Antebellum North Carolina." Ph.D. diss., University of North Carolina, 1983.

Chandler, Alfred D., Jr. *The Visible Hand: The Management Revolution in American Business.* Cambridge, Mass.: Harvard University Press, 1977.

Chartier, Barbara. "Weaverton: A Study of Culture and Personality in a Southern Mill Town." Master's thesis, University of North Carolina, 1949.

Chase, Harry. *The State University and the New South.* Chapel Hill: University of North Carolina, 1920.

Clark, David. "Dangerous Tendencies." *Southern Textile Bulletin* (20 December 1923): 22.

Clark, Thomas D. "Andrew Jackson." In *The Reader's Encyclopedia of the American West*, edited by Howard R. Lamar, p. 583. New York: Crowell, 1977.

_____. "The Piedmont South in Historical Perspective." *Mississippi Quarterly* 24 (Winter 1970–71): 1–17.

_____. *Pills, Petticoats, and Plows: The Southern Country Store, 1865–1900.* Norman: University of Oklahoma Press, 1964.

Clay, Howard Bunyan. "Daniel Augustus Tompkins: An American Bourbon." Ph.D. diss., University of North Carolina, 1950.

Clay, James W., and Douglas M. Orr, Jr. *Metrolina Atlas.* Chapel Hill: University of North Carolina Press, 1972.

Clay, James W., Douglas M. Orr, Jr., and Alfred W. Stuart. *North Carolina Atlas.* Chapel Hill: University of North Carolina Press, 1975.

Clayton, J. Glen. "South Carolina Shapers of Southern Baptists." *Baptist History Heritage* 17 (July 1982): 10–19.

Clayton, Thomas H. *Close to the Land: The Way We Lived in North Carolina, 1820–1870.* Chapel Hill: University of North Carolina Press, 1983.

Cleveland, Catherine. *The Great Revival in the West, 1797–1805.* Chicago: University of Chicago Press, 1916.

Cobb, Buell. *The Sacred Harp: A Tradition and Its Music*. Athens: University of Georgia Press, 1978.

Cobb, James C. *Industrialization and Southern Society, 1877–1984*. Lexington: University Press of Kentucky, 1984.

Collins, Camilla Anne. "Twenty-four to a Dozen: Occupational Folklore in a Virginia Hosiery Mill." Ph.D. diss., Indiana University, 1978.

Conway, Cecilia. "The Afro-American Traditions of the Folk Banjo." Ph.D. diss., University of North Carolina, 1980.

Conway, Mimi. *Rise Gonna Rise: A Portrait of Southern Textile Workers*. Photographs by Earl Dotter. Garden City, N.Y.: Anchor, 1979.

Conzen, Kathleen Neils. "Peasant Pioneers: Generational Succession among German Farmers in Frontier Minnesota." In *The Countryside in the Age of Capitalist Transformation*, edited by Steven Hahn and Jonathan Prude, pp. 259–92. Chapel Hill: University of North Carolina Press, 1985.

Cook, John Harrison. *A Study of the Mill Schools of North Carolina*. Columbia University Contributions to Education, no. 178. New York: AMS Press, 1972.

Couch, William T. *Culture in the South*. Chapel Hill: University of North Carolina Press, 1935.

Cowdrey, Albert E. *This Land, This South: An Environmental History*. Lexington: University Press of Kentucky, 1983.

Coxe, Tench. *A View of the United States of America*. Philadelphia: U.S. Census Bureau, 1794.

Cramer, Stuart Warren. *Useful Information for Cotton Manufacturers*. 2d ed. 4 vols. Charlotte, N.C.: Queen City Printing and Paper Co., 1904–9.

Crittenden, Charles Christopher. *The Commerce of North Carolina, 1763–1789*. New Haven, Conn.: Yale University Press, 1936.

Crittenden, S. S. *The Greenville Century Book*. Greenville, S.C.: Press of the Greenville News, 1903.

Daniel, Pete. *Breaking the Land: The Transformation of Cotton, Tobacco, and Rice Cultures since 1880*. Urbana: University of Illinois Press, 1985.

———. *The Shadow of Slavery: Peonage in the South, 1901–1969*. New York: Oxford University Press, 1973.

Davenport, Tom, Joyce Joines Newman, Daniel W. Patterson, and Allen Tullos, producers. *Being a Joines: A Life in the Brushy Mountains*. American Traditional Culture Series. Delaplane, Va.: Davenport Films and Curriculum in Folklore, University of North Carolina, 1980.

David, Charles Alexander. "Greenville of Old." *Greenville News*, 1926–31. Series of articles published under one title.

Davidson, Donald. *The Attack on Leviathan: Regionalism and Nationalism in the United States*. Chapel Hill: University of North Carolina Press, 1938.

Davidson, Elizabeth H. *Child Labor Legislation in the Southern Textile States*. Chapel Hill: University of North Carolina Press, 1939.

Davis, Burke. *War Bird: The Life and Times of Elliott White Springs*. Chapel Hill: University of North Carolina Press, 1987.

Dawley, Alan. *Class and Community: The Industrial Revolution in Lynn*. Cambridge, Mass.: Harvard University Press, 1976.

Deetz, James. *In Small Things Forgotten: The Archaeology of Early American Life*. Garden City, N.Y.: Anchor, 1977.

De Graffenreid, Claire. "The Georgia Cracker in the Cotton Mill." *Century* 41 (February 1891): 483–98.

DeNatale, Douglas. "Bynum: The Coming of Mill Village Life to a North Carolina County." Ph.D. diss., University of Pennsylvania, 1985.

———. "Traditional Culture and Community in a Piedmont Textile Mill Village." Master's thesis, University of North Carolina, 1980.

Dickson, R. J. *Ulster Emigration to Colonial America, 1718–1775*. London: Routledge and Kegan Paul, 1966.

Dombrowski, James A. "From a Mill-Town Jail." *New Republic* 60 (October 1929): 171–72.

Douty, Harry. "The North Carolina Industrial Worker, 1880–1930." Ph.D. diss., University of North Carolina, 1936.

Dowd, Jerome. "Cheap Labor in the South." *Gunton's Magazine* 19 (February 1900): 113–21 [reply by editor, pp. 121–30].

———. "Strikes and Lockouts in North Carolina." *Gunton's Magazine* 20 (February 1901): 136–40.

Drake, Joseph Turpin. "The Negro in Greenville, South Carolina." Master's thesis, University of North Carolina, 1940.

Dublin, Thomas. *Women at Work: The Transformation of Work and Community in Lowell, Massachusetts, 1826–1860*. New York: Columbia University Press, 1979.

Duke Power Company. *Piedmont Carolinas: Where Wealth Awaits You*. Charlotte, N.C.: Duke Power Co., 1927.

———. *The Piedmont Carolinas*. Charlotte, N.C.: Duke Power Co., 1960, 1965.

Dunbar, Anthony P. *Against the Grain: Southern Radicals and Prophets, 1929–1959*. Charlottesville: University Press of Virginia, 1981.

Durden, Robert F. *The Dukes of Durham, 1865–1929*. Durham, N.C.: Duke University Press, 1975.

Durrill, Wayne K. "Producing Poverty: Local Government and Economic Development in a New South County, 1874–1884." *Journal of American History* 71 (March 1985): 764–81.

Earle, John R., Dean D. Knudsen, and Donald W. Shriver, Jr. *Spindles and Spires*. Atlanta, Ga.: John Knox Press, 1976.

Eaton, Clement. *A History of the Southern Confederacy*. New York: Free Press, 1954.

Ebert, Charles H. V. "High Point's Evolution as a Furniture Town." Master's thesis, University of North Carolina, 1953.

Edmonds, R. H. "Biography of Daniel Augustus Tompkins." *Daily Bulletin of the*

Manufacturers' Record, 30 April 1912.

Eichenbaum, Richard. Untitled seminar paper on D. A. Tompkins, Duke University, Fall 1978.

Eliason, Norman E. *Tarheel Talk: An Historical Study of the English Language in North Carolina to 1860*. Chapel Hill: University of North Carolina Press, 1956.

Eller, Ronald D. *Miners, Millhands, and Mountaineers: The Modernization of the Appalachian South, 1880–1930*. Knoxville: University of Tennessee Press, 1982.

Emory, S. T. "Topography and Towns of the Carolina Piedmont." *Economic Geography* 12 (January 1936): 91–97.

Erikson, Kai. *Everything in Its Path: Destruction of Community in the Buffalo Creek Flood*. New York: Simon and Schuster, 1976.

Ervin, Samuel James, Jr. *Humor of a Country Lawyer*. Chapel Hill: University of North Carolina Press, 1983.

———. *William Henry Belk: Merchant of the South*. New York: Newcomen Society of North America, 1958.

Escott, Paul D. *Many Excellent People: Power and Privilege in North Carolina, 1850–1900*. Chapel Hill: University of North Carolina Press, 1985.

Escott, Paul D., and Jeffrey J. Crow. "The Social Order and Violent Disorder: An Analysis of North Carolina in the Revolution and the Civil War." *Journal of Southern History* 52 (August 1986): 373–402.

Etheridge, Elizabeth W. *The Butterfly Caste: A Social History of Pellagra in the South*. Westport, Conn.: Greenwood Press, 1972.

Ettling, John. *The Germ of Laziness*. Cambridge, Mass.: Harvard University Press, 1981.

Evans, E. Estyn. "The Scotch-Irish: Their Cultural Adaptation and Heritage in the American Old West." In *Essays in Scotch-Irish History*, edited by E. R. R. Green, pp. 73–84. London: Routledge and Kegan Paul, 1969.

"Factory Labor in the South." *Gunton's Magazine* 14 (April 1898): 217–28.

Faragher, John Mack. "Open-Country Community: Sugar Creek, Illinois, 1820–1850." In *The Countryside in the Age of Capitalist Transformation*, edited by Steven Hahn and Jonathan Prude, pp. 233–58. Chapel Hill: University of North Carolina Press, 1985.

Faulkner, Ronnie. "North Carolina Democrats and Silver Fusion Politics, 1892–1896." *North Carolina Historical Review* 59 (July 1982): 230–51.

Faulkner, William. *Light in August*. New York: Harrison Smith and Robert Haas, 1932.

Federal Writers' Project. *North Carolina: A Guide to the Old North State*. Chapel Hill: University of North Carolina Press, 1939.

———. *A History of Spartanburg County*. Spartanburg, S.C.: Bond and White, 1940.

———. *These Are Our Lives*. Chapel Hill: University of North Carolina Press, 1939.

Fink, Leon. *Workingmen's Democracy: The Knights of Labor and American Politics*. Urbana: University of Illinois Press, 1983.

Fish, E. H. "What Industry Expects of the Public School." *Management and Administration* 8 (September 1924): 257–59.

Flynt, J. Wayne. "The Impact of Social Factors on Southern Baptist Expansion, 1800–1914." *Baptist Historical Heritage* 17 (July 1982): 20–31.

Foner, Eric. *Politics and Ideology in the Age of the Civil War.* New York: Oxford University Press, 1980.

Ford, Lacy K. "Labor and Ideology in the South Carolina Upcountry: The Transition to Free-Labor Agriculture." In *The Southern Enigma: Essays on Race, Class, and Folk Culture,* edited by Walter J. Fraser, Jr., and Winifred B. Moore, Jr., pp. 22–41. Westport, Conn.: Greenwood Press, 1983.

———. "Rednecks and Merchants: Economic Development and Social Tensions in the South Carolina Upcountry, 1865–1900." *Journal of American History* 71 (September 1984): 294–318.

———. "Social Origins of a New South Carolina: The Upcountry in the Nineteenth Century." Ph.D. diss., University of South Carolina, 1983.

Foust, James D. "The Yeoman Farmer in the Westward Expansion of U.S. Cotton Production." Ph.D. diss., University of North Carolina, 1967.

Fox-Genovese, Elizabeth, and Eugene D. Genovese. "Yeoman Farmers in a Slaveholders' Democracy." In *Fruits of Merchant Capital: Slavery and Bourgeois Property in the Rise and Expansion of Capitalism,* pp. 249–64. New York: Oxford University Press, 1983.

Frederickson, Mary. "Four Decades of Change: Black Workers in Southern Textiles, 1941–1981." Paper presented at the Conference on Recent Black American History, Boston College, 27 February 1982.

———. " 'I Know Which Side I'm On': Southern Women in the Labor Movement in the Twentieth Century." In *Women, Work, and Protest: A Century of U.S. Women's Labor History,* edited by Ruth Milkman, pp. 157–62. Boston: Routledge and Kegan Paul, 1985.

———. "Myra Page: Daughter of the South, Worker for Change." *Southern Changes* 5, no. 1 (January/February 1983): 10–15.

———. "A Place to Speak Our Minds: The Southern Summer School for Women Workers." Ph.D. diss., University of North Carolina, 1981.

Freeze, Gary Richard. "Agricultural Origins of Piedmont Cotton Mill Families, 1880–1900: The Case of the Forest Hill Community, Concord, North Carolina." Seminar paper, University of North Carolina, 1981.

———. "Master Mill Man: John Milton Odell and Industrial Development in Concord, North Carolina, 1877–1907." Master's thesis, University of North Carolina, 1980.

Fries, Adelaide L., ed. *Records of the Moravians in North Carolina.* 11 vols. Raleigh: North Carolina Division of Archives and History, 1922–69.

Fromm, Erich. *The Anatomy of Human Destructiveness.* New York: Holt, Rinehart and Winston, 1973.

_____. *Escape from Freedom*. New York: Holt, Rinehart and Winston, 1941.

Fromm, Erich, and Michael Maccoby. *Social Character in a Mexican Village*. Englewood Cliffs, N.J.: Prentice-Hall, 1970.

Gabriel, Ralph H. "Presbyterians." In *The Reader's Encyclopedia of the American West*,
edited by Howard R. Lamar, pp. 962–64. New York: Crowell, 1977.

Gallman, Robert E. "Influences on the Distribution of Landholdings in Early Colonial North Carolina." *Journal of Economic History* 42 (September 1982): 549–75.

_____. "Slavery and Southern Economic Growth." *Southern Economic Journal* 45
(1979): 1007–22.

Gaston, Paul M. *The New South Creed: A Study in Southern Mythmaking*. New York:
Knopf, 1970.

Gatewood, Willard B., Jr. "Embattled Scholar: Howard W. Odum and the Funda-
mentalists, 1925–1927." *Journal of Southern History* 31 (November 1965): 375–92.

_____. *Preachers, Pedagogues, and Politicians: The Evolution Controversy in North
Carolina, 1920–1927*. Chapel Hill: University of North Carolina Press, 1966.

Gaventa, John. *Power and Powerlessness: Quiescence and Rebellion in an Appalachian
Valley*. Urbana: University of Illinois Press, 1980.

Geddes, Patrick. "Talks from Outlook Tower," *Survey*, 1 Feb., 1 Apr., 1 June, 1 July,
1 Aug., 1 Sept. 1925.

Genovese, Eugene. "The Industrialists under the Slave Regime." In *The Political
Economy of Slavery*, pp. 180–220. New York: Random House, 1961.

Gilbert, John, and Grady Jefferys. *Crossties through Carolina: The Story of North Carolina's Early Day Railroads*. Raleigh, N.C.: Helios Press, 1969.

Gillespie, David E. "Character Study of an Empire Builder." *Charlotte Observer*,
[n.d.] 1962. Part of a clipping collection at the corporate offices of Burlington
Mills, Greensboro, N.C.

Gilman, Glenn. *Human Relations in the Industrial Southeast: A Study of the Textile Industry*. Chapel Hill: University of North Carolina Press, 1956.

Glass, Brent D. "King Midas and Old Rip: The Gold Mining District of North
Carolina." Ph.D. diss., University of North Carolina, 1980.

_____. "Southern Mill Hills: Design in a 'Public' Place." In *Carolina Dwelling: To-
wards Preservation of Place: In Celebration of the North Carolina Vernacular Landscape*,
edited by Doug Swaim, pp. 138–49. Raleigh: School of Design, North Carolina
State University, 1978.

Glass, Brent D., and Pat Dickinson. *Badin, a Town at the Narrows: An Historical and
Architectural Survey*. Albermarle, N.C.: Stanly County Historic Properties Commission, 1982.

Glassie, Henry. *Folk Housing in Middle Virginia: A Structural Analysis of Historic Artifacts*. Knoxville: University of Tennessee Press, 1975.

_____. *Pattern in the Material Folk Culture of the Eastern United States*. Philadelphia:
University of Pennsylvania Press, 1968.

Goodwyn, Lawrence. *Democratic Promise: The Populist Moment in America*. New York:

Oxford University Press, 1976.

Gordon, David M., Richard Edwards, and Michael Reich. *Segmented Work, Divided Workers: The Historical Transformation of Labor in the United States.* New York: Cambridge University Press, 1982.

Gorn, Elliott J. " 'Gouge and Bite, Pull Hair and Scratch': The Social Significance of Fighting in the Southern Backcountry." *American Historical Review* 90 (February 1985): 18–43.

Grantham, Dewey W. *Southern Progressivism: The Reconciliation of Progress and Tradition.* Knoxville: University of Tennessee Press, 1983.

Gray, Lewis Cecil. *A History of Agriculture in the Southern United States.* 2 vols. Washington: Carnegie Institute of Washington, 1933.

Green, Archie. "Born on Picketlines, Textile Workers' Songs Are Woven into History." *Textile Labor* 22 (April 1961).

———. "Industrial Lore: A Bibliographic-Semantic Query." In *Working Americans: Contemporary Approaches to Occupational Folklife,* edited by Robert H. Byington, pp. 71–102. Smithsonian Folklife Studies, no. 3. Los Angeles: California Folklore Society, 1978.

———. "Interpreting Folklore Ideologically." In *Handbook of American Folklore,* edited by Richard M. Dorson, pp. 351–58. Bloomington: Indiana University Press, 1983.

———. *Only a Miner: Studies in Recorded Coal-Mining Songs.* Urbana: University of Illinois Press, 1972.

Green, James. "Rewriting Southern History: An Interview with C. Vann Woodward." *Southern Exposure* 12, no. 6 (November/December 1984): 87–92.

Griffin, Richard W. "Poor White Laborers in Southern Cotton Factories." *South Carolina Historical Magazine* 61 (January 1960).

———. "Reconstruction of the North Carolina Textile Industry, 1865–1885." *North Carolina Historical Review* 41 (January 1964): 34–53.

Griffin, Richard W., and Diffie W. Standard. "The Cotton Textile Industry in Ante-Bellum North Carolina, Part 1: Origin and Growth to 1830." *North Carolina Historical Review* 34 (January 1957): 15–35.

———. "The Cotton Textile Industry in Ante-Bellum North Carolina, Part 2: An Era of Boom and Consolidation, 1830–1860." *North Carolina Historical Review* 34 (April 1957): 131–64.

Gullick, Guy A. *Greenville County: Economic and Social.* Bulletin of the University of South Carolina, no. 102. Columbia: University of South Carolina and Greenville Chamber of Commerce, 1921.

Gutman, Herbert G. *Work, Culture, and Society in Industrializing America.* New York: Knopf, 1976.

Haessly, Lynn. "Mill Mother's Lament: Ella May, Working Women's Militancy, and the 1929 Gaston County Strikes." Master's thesis, University of North Carolina, 1987.

Hagood, Margaret Jarman. *Mothers of the South: Portraiture of the White Tenant Farm Woman*. Chapel Hill: University of North Carolina Press, 1939. Reprint. New York: Norton, 1977.

Hahn, Steven H. *The Roots of Southern Populism: Yeoman Farmers and the Transformation of the Georgia Upcountry, 1850–1890*. New York: Oxford University Press, 1983.

Hahn, Steven H., and Jonathan Prude, eds. *The Countryside in the Age of Capitalist Transformation: Essays in the Social History of Rural America*. Chapel Hill: University of North Carolina Press, 1985.

Hall, Jacquelyn Dowd. "Disorderly Women: Gender and Labor Militancy in the Appalachian South." *Journal of American History* 73 (September 1986): 354–82.
_____. "An Oral History of Industrialization: Learning by Listening." *Institute for Research in Social Science Newsletter* 66 (April 1981): 5–9.

Hall, Jacquelyn Dowd, James Leloudis, Robert Korstad, Mary Murphy, Lu Ann Jones, and Christopher B. Daly. *Like a Family: The Making of a Southern Cotton Mill World*. Chapel Hill: University of North Carolina Press, 1987.

Hammond, Harry. *South Carolina: Resources and Population, Institution and Industries*. Charleston, S.C.: Walker, Evans and Cogswell, 1883.

Hareven, Tamara K. *Family Time and Industrial Time*. Cambridge: Cambridge University Press, 1982.

Hareven, Tamara K., and Ralph Langenbach. *Amoskeag: Life and Work in an American Factory City*. New York: Random House, 1978.

Harris, J. William. *Plain Folk and Gentry in a Slave Society: White Liberty and Black Slavery in Augusta's Hinterlands*. Middletown, Conn.: Wesleyan University Press, 1985.

Hatley, Tom. "The Dividing Path: The Direction of Cherokee Life in the Eighteenth Century." Master's thesis, University of North Carolina, 1977.

Hauser, William. *The Olive Leaf: A Collection of Beautiful Tunes, New and Old*. Philadelphia: n.p., 1878.

Heer, Clarence. *Income and Wages in the South*. Chapel Hill: University of North Carolina Press, 1930.

Helper, Hinton Rowan. *The Impending Crisis of the South: How to Meet It*. New York: Burdick Bros., 1857.

Henderson, Archibald. *The Campus of the First State University*. Chapel Hill: University of North Carolina Press, 1949.

Henretta, James A. "Families and Farms: *Mentalité* in Pre-Industrial America." *William and Mary Quarterly* 35 (1978): 3–32.

Herring, Harriet L. " 'The Clement Attachment'—an Episode of Reconstruction Industrial History." *Journal of Southern History* 4 (May 1938): 185–98.
_____. "Early Industrial Development in the South." *Annals of the American Academy of Political and Social Science* 153 (January 1931): 1–10. Special issue, *The Coming of Industry in the South*, edited by William J. Carson.
_____. "The South Goes to the Bindery." *Social Forces* 9 (March 1931): 427–31.

————. *Southern Industry and Regional Development*. Chapel Hill: University of North Carolina Press, 1949.

————. *Welfare Work in Mill Villages: The Story of Extra-Mill Activities in North Carolina*. Chapel Hill: University of North Carolina Press, 1929.

Hilliard, Sam Bowers. *Atlas of Antebellum Southern Agriculture*. Baton Rouge: Louisiana State University Press, 1984.

Hinson, Glenn, prod. *Eight-Hand Sets and Holy Steps: Traditional Black Music of North Carolina*. Crossroads C-101.

Hintze, Hedwig. "Regionalism." In *Encyclopedia of the Social Sciences*, 13:208–18. New York: Macmillan, 1934.

Hirsch, Jerrold Maury. "Culture on Relief: The Federal Writers' Project in North Carolina, 1935–42." Master's thesis, University of North Carolina, 1973.

————. "Folklore in the Making: B. A. Botkin." *Journal of American Folklore* 100 (January 1987): 3–38.

————. "Portrait of America: The Federal Writers' Project in an Intellectual and Cultural Context." Ph.D. diss., University of North Carolina, 1984.

History of the J. E. Sirrine Textile Foundation, Inc. Columbia, S.C.: R. L. Bryan Co., 1961.

Hobbs, Peter Burke. "Plantation to Factory: Tradition and Industrialization in Durham, N.C., 1880–1890." Master's thesis, Duke University, 1971.

Hobbs, Samuel Huntington, Jr. *North Carolina: Economic and Social*. Chapel Hill: University of North Carolina Press, 1930.

Hobsbawm, Eric J. *Primitive Rebels: Studies in Archaic Forms of Social Movements in the Nineteenth and Twentieth Centuries*. New York: Norton, 1965.

Hobson, Fred C., Jr. *Serpent in Eden: H. L. Mencken and the South*. Chapel Hill: University of North Carolina Press, 1974.

————. *Tell about the South: The Southern Rage to Explain*. Baton Rouge: Louisiana State University Press, 1983.

————, ed. *South-Watching: Selected Essays by Gerald W. Johnson*. Chapel Hill: University of North Carolina Press, 1983.

Hodges, James A. *New Deal Labor Policy and the Southern Cotton Textile Industry, 1933–1941*. Knoxville: University of Tennessee Press, 1986.

Hood, Robin. "The Loray Strike." Master's thesis, University of North Carolina, 1932.

Horton, Aimee. "The Highlander Folk School: A History of the Development of Its Major Programs Related to Social Movements in the South, 1932–1961." Ph.D. diss., University of Chicago, 1971.

Horton, Laurel McKay. "Economic Influences on German Scotch-Irish Quilts in Antebellum Rowan County, North Carolina." Master's thesis, University of North Carolina, 1979.

Howarth, J. H. "Advantages of High Speed Winding and High Speed Warping." *Southern Textile Bulletin*, 3 November 1927, pp. 48–50.

Howe, George. *The Scotch-Irish and Their First Settlements on the Tyger River*. Columbia, S.C.: Southern Guardian Steam-Power Press, 1861.

Institute for Research in Social Science. "A Survey of the Catawba Valley: A Study Made by the Institute for Research in Social Science for the Tennessee Valley Authority." Typescript, University of North Carolina, 1935.

Isaac, Rhys. *The Transformation of Virginia, 1740–1790*. Chapel Hill: University of North Carolina Press, 1982.

Jackson, George Pullen. " 'Singing Billy' Walker and his 'Southern Harmony.' " Chapter 6 of *White Spirituals in the Southern Uplands*. Chapel Hill: University of North Carolina Press, 1933.

Jacobs, Thornwell. *Step Down, Dr. Jacobs: The Autobiography of an Autocrat*. Atlanta, Ga.: The Westminster Publishers, 1945.

———, ed. *Diary of William Plummer Jacobs*. Atlanta, Ga.: Oglethorpe University Press, 1937.

Jacobs, William Plummer. *The Pioneer*. Clinton, S.C.: Jacobs and Co., 1934.

———. *Problems of the Cotton Manufacturer in South Carolina*. Clinton, S.C.: Jacobs and Co., 1932.

Janiewski, Dolores. *Sisterhood Denied: Race, Gender, and Class in a New South Community*. Philadelphia: Temple University Press, 1985.

Janssen-Jurriet, Marielouise. *Sexism: The Male Monopoly on History and Thought*. New York: Farrar, Straus and Giroux, 1982.

Jay, Martin. *The Dialectical Imagination: A History of the Frankfurt School and the Institute of Social Research, 1923–1950*. Boston: Little, Brown, 1973.

Jocher, Katharine. "The Regional Laboratory for Social Research and Planning." In *In Search of the Regional Balance of America*, edited by Howard Odum and Katharine Jocher, pp. 43–48. Chapel Hill: University of North Carolina Press, 1945.

Jocher, Katharine, and Guy B. Johnson. "Howard W. Odum." In *Folk, Region, and Society: Selected Papers of Howard W. Odum*, edited by Katharine Jocher and Guy B. Johnson. Chapel Hill: University of North Carolina Press, 1964.

Johnson, Charles A. "The Camp Meeting in Ante-Bellum North Carolina." *North Carolina Historical Review* 10 (April 1933): 95–110.

———. *The Frontier Camp Meeting*. Dallas, Tex.: Southern Methodist University Press, 1955.

———. "The Frontier Camp Meeting: Contemporary and Historical Appraisals." *Mississippi Valley Historical Review* 37 (1950/51): 91–110.

Johnson, Gerald W. *The Making of a Southern Industrialist: A Biographical Study of Simpson Bobo Tanner*. Chapel Hill: University of North Carolina Press, 1952.

Johnson, Guion Griffis. *Antebellum North Carolina: A Social History*. Chapel Hill: University of North Carolina Press, 1937.

———. "The Camp Meeting in Antebellum North Carolina." *North Carolina Historical Review* 10 (April 1933): 108.

Johnson, Guy B., and Guion G. Johnson. *Research in Service to Society: The First Fifty Years of the Institute for Research in Social Science at the University of North Carolina*.

Chapel Hill: University of North Carolina Press, 1980.

Jolley, Harley E. "The Labor Movement in North Carolina: 1880–1922." *North Carolina Historical Review* 30 (July 1953).

Joyner, Charles W. "Up in Old Loray: Folkways and Violence in the Gastonia Strike." *North Carolina Folklore* 12, no. 2 (December 1964): 30–34.

Judkins, Bennett M. "Occupational Health and the Developing Class Consciousness of Southern Textile Workers: The Case of the Brown Lung Association." *Maryland Historian* 13 (Spring/Summer 1982): 55–71.

———. *We Offer Ourselves as Evidence: Toward Workers' Control of Occupational Health.* Westport, Conn: Greenwood Press, 1986.

Kantor, Harvey A. "Howard W. Odum: The Implications of Folk, Planning, and Regionalism." *American Journal of Sociology* 79 (September 1973): 278–95.

Kaplan, Peter B. *The Historic Architecture of Cabarrus County, North Carolina.* Charlotte, N.C.: Craftsman Printing Co., 1981.

Karanikas, Alexander. *Tillers of a Myth: Southern Agrarians as Social and Literary Critics.* Madison: University of Wisconsin Press, 1966.

Kasius, Richard V. *The Challenge of Facts.* New York: Milbank Memorial Fund, 1974.

Kasson, John. *Civilizing the Machine: Technology and Republican Values in America, 1776–1900.* New York: Grossman, 1976.

Keil, Charles. "The Concept of 'the Folk.'" *Journal of the Folklore Institute* 16 (September/December 1979): 209–10.

———. "Who Needs 'the Folk'?" *Journal of the American Folklore Institute* 15 (September/December 1979): 209–10.

Kenzer, Robert Charles. "Portrait of a Southern Community, 1849–1881: Family, Kinship, and Neighborhood in Orange County, North Carolina." Ph.D. diss., Harvard University, 1982.

Key, V. O., Jr. *Southern Politics.* New York: Knopf, 1949.

King, Richard H. *A Southern Renaissance.* New York: Oxford University Press, 1980.

Klein, Rachel. "Ordering the Backcountry: The South Carolina Regulation." *William and Mary Quarterly* 38 (October 1981): 661–80.

———. "The Rise of the Planters in the South Carolina Backcountry, 1767–1808." Ph.D. diss., Yale University, 1979.

Klontz, Harold E. "An Economic Study of the Southern Furniture Manufacturing Industry." Ph.D. diss., University of North Carolina, 1948.

Kniffen, Fred. "Folk Housing: Key to Diffusion." *Annals of the Association of American Geographers* 55 (1965): 549–77.

Kohn, August. *The Cotton Mills of South Carolina.* Columbia: South Carolina Department of Agriculture, Commerce, and Immigration, 1907. Reprint. Spartanburg, S.C.: The Reprint Co., 1975.

———. *The Water Powers of South Carolina.* South Carolina Department of Agriculture, Commerce and Immigration. Charleston, S.C.: Walker, Evans and Cogswell, 1911.

Korstad, Robert. "Those Who Were Not Afraid: Winston-Salem, 1943." In *Working*

Lives: The Southern Exposure History of Labor in the South, edited by Marc S. Miller, pp. 184–99. New York: Pantheon, 1980.

Kruger, Barbara. *We Won't Play Nature to Your Culture*. London: Institute of Contemporary Arts, 1983. Exhibition Catalog.

Kruman, Marc W. *Parties and Politics in North Carolina, 1836–1865*. Baton Rouge: Louisiana State University Press, 1983.

Lacy, Dan Mabry. "The Beginnings of Industrialism in North Carolina." Master's thesis, University of North Carolina, 1935.

Lahne, Herbert J. *The Cotton Mill Worker*. New York: Farrar and Rinehart, 1944.

Lander, Ernest McPherson, Jr. *A History of South Carolina, 1865–1960*. 2d ed. Columbia: University of South Carolina Press, 1970.

⸺. *The Textile Industry in Antebellum South Carolina*. Baton Rouge: Louisiana State University Press, 1969.

Larkin, Margaret. "Ella May's Songs." *The Nation* 129 (9 October 1929): 382–83.

Larson, Susan. " 'Miss Bessie' to See Students at Homecoming." *Durham Sun*, 24 April 1976.

Lathan, B. M. *The Lathan-Belk Families and In-Laws, 1710–1979*. Monroe, N.C.: privately printed, 1980.

Laws, G. Malcolm, Jr. *American Balladry from British Broadsides*. Philadelphia: American Folklore Society, 1950.

⸺. *Native American Balladry*. Philadelphia: American Folklore Society, 1950.

Ledgerwood, Mikle Dave. "Ethnic Groups on the Frontier in Rowan County, North Carolina, 1750–1778." Master's thesis, Vanderbilt University, 1977.

Lefler, Hugh Talmadge, and Albert Ray Newsome. *North Carolina: The History of a Southern State*. 3d ed. Chapel Hill: University of North Carolina Press, 1973.

Leifermann, Henry P. *Crystal Lee: A Woman of Inheritance*. New York: Macmillan, 1975.

Leiss, William. *The Domination of Nature*. New York: George Braziller, 1972.

Lemert, Ben F. *The Cotton Textile Industry of the Southern Appalachian Piedmont*. Chapel Hill: University of North Carolina Press, 1933.

⸺. "The Furniture Industry in the Southern States." *Economic Geography* 10 (April 1934): 183–99.

⸺. "The Knit-Goods Industry in the Southern States." *Economic Geography* 11 (October 1935): 368–88.

Levine, Lawrence W. *Black Culture and Black Consciousness: Afro-American Folk Thought from Slavery to Freedom*. New York: Oxford University Press, 1977.

Lewis, Sinclair. *Cheap and Contented Labor*. New York: United Features Syndicate, 1929.

⸺. "Sinclair Lewis on North Carolina's Labor War." *Literary Digest* 103 (9 November 1929): 36, 43–48.

Leyburn, James G. *The Scotch-Irish: A Social History*. Chapel Hill: University of North Carolina Press, 1962.

Limon, José E. "Western Marxism and Folklore: A Critical Introduction." *Journal of American Folklore* 96 (January/March 1983): 34–52.

Linn, Jo White. *People Named Hanes*. Salisbury, N.C.: Privately printed for the Hanes family, 1980.

Little-Stokes, Ruth. *An Inventory of Historic Architecture: Caswell County, North Carolina*. Yanceyville, N.C.: Caswell County Historical Association and North Carolina Division of Archives and History, 1979.

————. *An Inventory of Historic Architecture: Iredell County, North Carolina.* Statesville, N.C.: Iredell Properties Commission, 1978.

Lounsbury, Carl Reavis. *Alamance County Architectural Heritage*. Graham, N.C.: Alamance County Historical Properties Commission, 1980.

————. "From Craft to Industry: The Building Process in North Carolina in the Nineteenth Century." Ph.D. diss., George Washington University, 1983.

Love, J. Spencer. "We Have a Better Team Than Ever Before." *Burlington Mill Review* 3 (May/June 1952): 1.

Love, James Lee. *R. C. G. Love: A Builder of the New South*. Chapel Hill: University of North Carolina Press, 1949.

————. *'Tis Sixty Years Since*. Chapel Hill: University of North Carolina Press, 1945.

Lubove, Roy. *Community Planning in the 1920s: The Contribution of the Regional Planning Association of America*. Pittsburgh, Pa.: University of Pittsburgh Press, 1963.

McAllister, Jim. *L. P. Hollis: Greenville's Greatest Public Educator*. Greenville, S.C.: Greenville County Foundation, 1975.

McCormick, Andrew Phelps. *The Scotch-Irish in Ireland and in America*. New Orleans: privately printed, 1897.

McDavid, Raven Ioor. "Changing Patterns of Southern Dialects." In *Essays in Honor of Claude M. Wise*, edited by Arthur J. Bronstein, pp. 206–28. Hannibal, Mo.: Standard Printing Co., 1970.

————, ed. *Linguistic Atlas of the Middle and South Atlantic States*. Chicago: University of Chicago Press, 1979.

McDonald, Forrest, and Ellen S. McDonald. "The Ethnic Origins of the American People, 1790." *William and Mary Quarterly* 37 (April 1980): 177–99.

McDonald, Forrest, and Grady McWhiney. "The South from Self-Sufficiency to Peonage: An Interpretation." *American Historical Review* 85 (December 1980): 1095–1118.

————. "The Antebellum Southern Herdsmen: A Reinterpretation." *Journal of Southern History* 41 (May 1975): 147–66.

MacDonald, Lois. *Southern Mill Hills: A Study of Social and Economic Forces in Certain Textile Mill Villages*. New York: Alex L. Hillman, 1928.

McKelway, Alexander J. "Child Labor in the Carolinas." *Charities and the Commons* 21 (1909): 743–57.

McLaurin, Melton Alonza. "The Knights of Labor in North Carolina Politics." *North Carolina Historical Review* 49 (July 1972): 298–315.

_____. *Paternalism and Protest: Southern Cotton Mill Workers and Organized Labor, 1875–1905*. Westport, Conn.: Greenwood Press, 1971.

McLendon, Paula. "Time and Time Again: The Workers, the Union, and the Vanity Factory." *Southern Changes* 6, no. 5 (October/November 1984): 8–17.

McMath, Robert C. *Populist Vanguard: A History of the Southern Farmers' Alliance*. Chapel Hill: University of North Carolina Press, 1975.

Macy, Ralph G. "The Piedmont Section of the Carolinas." Pt. 1, "The Southward Trend of Manufacturing"; pt. 2, "The Power Supply of Southern Industry"; pt. 3, "The Construction and Costs of Southern Cotton Mills and Equipment"; pt. 4, "The Southern Industrial Labor Supply." *Management and Administration* 7, 8 (May, June, July, September 1924): 517–22, 663–68, 47–52, 253–57.

Mainer, J. E. *J. E. Mainer's Mountaineers, Volume 1*. Old Timey LP106.

Marshall, F. Ray. *Labor in the South*. Cambridge, Mass.: Harvard University Press, 1967.

Mathews, Donald G. *Religion in the Old South*. Chicago: University of Chicago Press, 1977.

_____. "The Second Great Awakening as an Organizing Process, 1780–1830." *American Quarterly* 21 (Spring 1969): 23–43.

"Maynard of Tower Hosiery." *North Carolina* 28 (August 1970).

Maynor, Joe. *Duke Power: The First Seventy-Five Years*. Charlotte, N.C.: Duke Power Co., 1979.

Meinig, Donald W. "The Mormon Culture Region." *Annals of the Association of American Geographers* 55 (June 1965): 191–220.

_____. *The Shaping of America*. Vol. 1, *Atlantic America, 1492–1800*. New Haven, Conn.: Yale University Press, 1986.

Mendenhall, Marjorie S. "A History of Agriculture in South Carolina, 1790–1860." Ph.D. diss., University of North Carolina, 1940.

Meriwether, Robert L. *The Expansion of South Carolina, 1729–1765*. Kingsport, Tenn: Southern Publishers, 1940.

Messenger, Betty. *Picking Up the Linen Threads: A Study of Industrial Folklore*. Austin: University of Texas Press, 1978.

Metcalf, P. Richard. "Scotch-Irish." In *The Reader's Encyclopedia of the American West*, edited by Howard R. Lamar, pp. 1092–93. New York: Crowell, 1977.

Miller, Marc S., ed. *Working Lives: The Southern Exposure History of Labor in the South*. New York: Pantheon, 1980.

Millett, Kate. *Sexual Politics*. New York: Doubleday, 1969.

Mills, Robert. *Atlas of the State of South Carolina*. Charleston: State of South Carolina, 1825.

Mims, Edwin. *The Advancing South*. New York: Doubleday, Page and Co., 1926.

Mintz, Sidney. "The Rural Proletariat and the Problem of Rural Proletarian Consciousness." *Journal of Peasant Studies* 1 (April 1974): 291–323.

Mitchell, Broadus. "Growth of Manufacturers in the South." *Annals of the American*

Academy of Political and Social Science 153 (January 1931). Special issue, *The Coming of Industry to the South*, edited by William J. Carson.

———. *The Rise of Cotton Mills in the South*. Baltimore, Md.: Johns Hopkins University Press, 1921. Reprint. Gloucester, Mass.: Peter Smith, 1966.

———. *William Gregg: Factory Master of the Old South*. Chapel Hill: University of North Carolina Press, 1928.

Mitchell, Broadus, and George Sinclair Mitchell. *The Industrial Revolution in the South*. Baltimore, Md.: Johns Hopkins University Press, 1930.

Mitchell, George Sinclair. *Textile Unionism and the South*. Chapel Hill: University of North Carolina Press, 1931.

Montgomery, David. *Beyond Equality: Labor and the Radical Republicans, 1862–1872*. Urbana: University of Illinois Press, 1981.

———. *Worker's Control in America: Studies in the History of Work, Technology, and Labor Struggles*. Cambridge: Cambridge University Press, 1979.

Morgan, Lucia C. "The Status of /r/ among North Carolina Speakers." In *Essays in Honor of Claude M. Wise*, edited by Arthur J. Bronstein, pp. 167–86. Hannibal, Mo.: Standard Printing Co., 1970.

Morland, John Kenneth. "Educational and Occupational Aspirations of Mill and Town School Children in a Southern Community." *Social Forces* 39 (1960): 169–75.

———. "Kent Revisited: Blue Collar Aspirations and Achievements." In *Blue Collar World: Studies of the American Worker*, edited by Arthur B. Shostak and William Goldberg, pp. 134–43. Englewood Cliffs, N.J.: Prentice-Hall, 1964.

———. *Millways of Kent*. Chapel Hill: University of North Carolina Press, 1958.

Mumford, Lewis. *The Culture of Cities*. New York: Harcourt Brace Jovanovich, 1938.

———. "The Disciple's Rebellion." *Encounter* 27 (September 1966): 11–21.

———. *The Myth of the Machine*. 2 vols. New York: Harcourt Brace Jovanovich, 1967, 1970.

———. *Technics and Civilization*. New York: Harcourt, Brace and World, 1934.

———. "The Theory and Practice of Regionalism." *Sociological Review* 20 (April 1928): 131–41.

———. "A Thought for the Growing South." *The Southern Packet* 5 (April 1949): 1–5.

Murphy, Mary. "Burlington, North Carolina." Working paper, Southern Oral History Program, University of North Carolina, 1980.

Myerson, Michael. *Nothing Could Be Finer*. New York: International Publishers, 1978.

Myrdal, Gunnar. *An American Dilemma: The Negro Problem and Modern Democracy*. New York: Harper and Row, 1944.

Nathans, Sydney. *The Quest for Progress: The Way We Lived in North Carolina, 1870–1920*. Chapel Hill: University of North Carolina Press, 1983.

Newman, Dale. "The Myth of the 'Contented' Southern Mill Worker." In *Perspec-*

tives on the American South, edited by Merle Black and John Shelton Reed, 1:187–204. New York: Gordon and Breach Science Publishers, 1981.

————. "Work and Community Life in a Southern Textile Town." *Labor History* 19 (Spring 1978): 204–25.

Newman, Joyce Joines. "Humorous Local Character Stories from Wilkes County, North Carolina: An Individual Storytelling Tradition." Master's thesis, University of North Carolina, 1978.

Nichols, Jeanette Paddock. "Does the Mill Village Foster a Social Type?" *Social Forces* 2 (March 1924): 350–57.

Nickerson, Bruce. "Is There a Folk in the Factory?" *Journal of American Folklore* 7 (1974): 133–39.

Noble, David F. *America by Design: Science, Technology, and the Rise of Corporate Capitalism*. New York: Oxford University Press, 1979.

Nolan, Dennis, and David Jonas. "Textile Unionism in the Piedmont, 1901–1932." In *Essays in Southern Labor History*, edited by Gary Fink and Merle Reed. Westport, Conn.: Greenwood Press, 1977.

Northrup, Herbert R., and Richard L. Rowan. *Negro Employment in Southern Industry*. Philadelphia: University of Pennsylvania, Wharton School of Finance and Commerce, 1970.

Oates, Mary Josephine. *The Role of the Cotton Textile Industry in the Economic Development of the American Southeast: 1900–1940*. Dissertations in American Economic History. New York: Arno Press, 1975.

O'Brien, Gail Williams. *The Legal Fraternity and the Making of a New South Community, 1848–1882*. Athens: University of Georgia Press, 1986.

————. "Power and Influence in Mecklenburg County, 1850–1880." *North Carolina Historical Review* 54 (April 1977): 120–44.

————. "War and Social Change: An Analysis of Community Power Structure, Guilford County, North Carolina, 1848–1882." Ph.D. diss., University of North Carolina, 1975.

O'Brien, Michael. *The Idea of the American South*. Baltimore. Md.: Johns Hopkins University Press, 1979.

O'Conner, Flannery. *The Complete Stories*. New York: Farrar, Straus and Giroux, 1971.

Odum, Howard W. *An American Epoch: Southern Portraiture in the National Picture*. New York: Henry Holt, 1930.

————. "Folk and Regional Conflict as a Field of Sociological Study." Presidential address read before the American Sociological Society, December 1930. *Publication of the American Sociological Society* 25 (May 1931): 1–17. Reprinted in *Folk, Region, and Society: Selected Papers of Howard W. Odum*, edited by Katharine Jocher and Guy B. Johnson, pp. 239–55. Chapel Hill: University of North Carolina Press, 1964.

————. "From Community Studies to Regionalism." In *In Search of the Regional Bal-*

ance of America, edited by Howard W. Odum and Katharine Jocher. Chapel Hill: University of North Carolina Press, 1945.

———. "G. Stanley Hall." *Social Forces* 3 (November 1924): 139, 144–45.

———. "Patrick Geddes' Heritage to 'The Making of the Future.'" *Social Forces* 22 (March 1944).

———. "The Promise of Regionalism." In *Regionalism in America*, edited by Merrill Jensen. Madison: University of Wisconsin Press, 1951.

———. "Regionalism vs. Sectionalism in the South's Place in the National Economy." *Social Forces* 12 (March 1934): 338–42.

———. *Social and Mental Traits of the Negro*. Studies in History, Economics, and Public Law, no. 37. New York: Columbia University Press, 1920.

———. "A Southern Promise." Introduction to *Southern Pioneers in Social Interpretation*. Chapel Hill: University of North Carolina Press, 1925.

———. *The Way of the South*. New York: Macmillan, 1947.

Odum, Howard W., and Katharine Jocher, eds. *In Search of the Regional Balance of America*. Chapel Hill: University of North Carolina Press, 1945.

Olsen, Tillie. *Silences*. New York: Delacorte, 1978.

———. *Yonnondia: From the Thirties*. New York: Laurel, 1974.

Opper, Peter Kent. "North Carolina Quakers: Reluctant Slaveholders." *North Carolina Historical Review* 52 (January 1975): 37–58.

Otten, James T. "Disloyalty in the Upper Districts of South Carolina during the Civil War." *South Carolina Historical Magazine* 75 (April 1974): 95–109.

Owsley, Frank Lawrence. *Plain Folk in the Old South*. Baton Rouge: Louisiana State University Press, 1949.

Page, Myra. *Southern Cotton Mills and Labor*. New York: Workers Library, 1929.

Palmer, Bruce. *"Man over Money": The Southern Populist Critique of American Capitalism*. Chapel Hill: University of North Carolina Press, 1980.

Parker, Thomas Fleming. "How the Sunday School Can Assist in Village Welfare Work." *Bulletin of the University of South Carolina* (April 1911): n.p.

———. "Some Educational and Legislative Needs of South Carolina Mill Villages." *Bulletin of the University of South Carolina* (January 1911): n.p.

———. "The South Carolina Cotton Mill: A Manufacturer's View." *South Atlantic Quarterly* 8 (1909): 328–37.

———. "The South Carolina Cotton Mill Village—a Manufacturer's View." Address at Benefactor's Day, Trinity College, Durham, N.C., 3 October 1910. Reprinted in *South Atlantic Quarterly* 9 (1910): 349–57.

Parramore, Thomas C. *Express Lanes and Country Roads: The Way We Lived in North Carolina, 1920–1970*. Chapel Hill: University of North Carolina Press, 1983.

Patterson, Daniel W. "Upland North and South Carolina Stonecarvers: A Report on Research in Progress." *Newsletter for Gravestone Studies* 6, no. 3 (September 1982): 3–4. Special issue on southern tombstones, edited by Ruth Little-Stokes.

———. "William Hauser's *Hesperian Harp* and *Olive Leaf*: Shape-note Tunebooks as Emblems of Social Change and Progress." *Journal of American Folklore* 101 (January/March 1988): 23–36.

Patterson, Daniel W., and John F. Garst. Introduction to facsimile edition of *The Social Harp*, by John G. McCurry [1855], vii–xxv. Athens: University of Georgia Press, 1973.

Perdue, Theda. *Nations Remembered: An Oral History of the Five Civilized Tribes, 1865–1907*. Westport, Conn.: Greenwood Press, 1980.

———. *Native Carolinians: The Indians of North Carolina*. Raleigh: Division of Archives and History, North Carolina Department of Cultural Resources, 1985.

———. *Slavery and the Evolution of Cherokee Society, 1540–1866*. Knoxville: University of Tennessee Press, 1979.

Peterson, B. A. "Advantages of Automatic Spoolers and High Speed Warpers." *Southern Textile Bulletin*, 17 July 1924, pp. 11–13.

———. "Automatic Spooler vs. High Speed Warper." *Southern Textile Bulletin*, 16 Apr. 1931, p. 15.

———. "Better Winding and Warping Machinery." *Southern Textile Bulletin*, 14 July 1912, p. 10.

Pickard, Walter. *Burlington Dynamite Plot*. New York: International Labor Defense, 1935[?].

Pierpont, Andrew W. "Development of the Textile Industry in Alamance County, North Carolina." Ph.D. diss., University of North Carolina, 1953.

Pope, Liston. *Millhands and Preachers: A Study of Gastonia*. New Haven, Conn.: Yale University Press, 1942.

Porter, Patrick G. "Advertising in the Early Cigarette Industry: W. Duke and Company of Durham." *North Carolina Historical Review* 48 (January 1971): 31–43.

Posey, Walter B. *The Baptist Church in the Lower Mississippi Valley, 1776–1845*. Lexington: University Press of Kentucky, 1957.

———. *The Development of Methodism in the Old Southwest*. Tuscaloosa, Ala.: Weatherford Printing Co., 1933.

———. *Frontier Mission: A History of Religion West of the Southern Appalachians to 1861*. Lexington: University Press of Kentucky, 1966.

———. *The Presbyterian Church in the Old Southwest, 1777–1838*. Richmond, Va.: John Knox Press, 1952.

Potwin, Marjorie A. *Cotton Mill People of the Piedmont*. New York: Columbia University Press, 1927.

Powell, William S. *Dictionary of North Carolina Biography*. Vol. 1, *A–C*; vol. 2, *D–G*; vol. 3, *H–K*. Chapel Hill: University of North Carolina Press, 1979–88.

Prince, Richard E. *Steam Locomotives and Boots: Southern Railway System*. Green River, Mo.: Richard E. Prince, 1965.

Prude, Jonathan. *The Coming of Industrial Order: Town and Factory Life in Rural Massachusetts, 1810–1860*. New York: Cambridge University Press, 1983.

Ragan, Robert Allison. *The Pioneer Cotton Mills of Gaston County, N.C.* Charlotte, N.C.: R. A. Ragan, 1973.

Ramsey, Robert W. *Carolina Cradle: Settlement of the Northwest Carolina Frontier, 1747–1762*. Chapel Hill: University of North Carolina Press, 1964.

Rand, H. Lanier. " 'I Had to Like It': A Study of a Durham Textile Community." Honors essay, University of North Carolina, 1977.

Ransom, Roger L., and Richard Sutch. *One Kind of Freedom: The Economic Consequences of Emancipation*. Cambridge: Cambridge University Press, 1977.

Raper, Arthur F. *Preface to Peasantry: A Tale of Two Black Belt Counties*. Chapel Hill: University of North Carolina Press, 1936.

Reed, Alfred. *How Can a Poor Man Stand Such Times and Live: The Songs of Blind Alfred Reed*. Rounder 1001.

Reed, John Shelton, and Daniel Singal, eds. *Regionalism and the South: Selected Papers of Rupert Vance*. Chapel Hill: University of North Carolina Press, 1982.

Rhyne, Jennings J. "Studies of Mill Village Population in North Carolina." Ph.D. diss., University of North Carolina, 1927.

————. *Some Southern Cotton Mill Workers and Their Villages*. Chapel Hill: University of North Carolina Press, 1930.

Richardson, James M. *History of Greenville, South Carolina*. Atlanta, Ga.: A. H. Crawford Co., 1930.

Robertson, Ben. *Red Hills and Cotton: An Upcountry Memory*. New York: Knopf, 1942.

Robinson, F. H., and Ward C. Jensen. *An Agricultural Production, Consumption, and Marketing Study in the Greenville, South Carolina, Trade Area*. South Carolina Experiment Station Bulletin No. 240. Clemson, S.C.: Clemson Agricultural College, 1927.

Rocky Mount Mills: A Case History of Industrial Development, 1818–1943. Rocky Mount, N.C.: Rocky Mount Mills, 1943.

Rodgers, Daniel T. "Regionalism and the Burdens of Progress." In *Region, Race, and Reconstruction*, edited by J. Morgan Kousser and James McPherson, pp. 3–26. New York: Oxford University Press, 1982.

————. *The Work Ethic in Industrial America, 1850–1920*. Chicago: University of Chicago Press, 1978.

Roe, Daphne. *A Plague of Corn: The Social History of Pellagra*. Ithaca, N.Y.: Cornell University Press, 1973.

Rogers, Manuel J. "Greenville Cotton Mills Maintain Educational System Unique in U.S." *Journal of Commerce* (1936). Clipping in the Parker School District Scrapbook Collection, Greenville County Library, Greenville, S.C.

Rorrer, Kinney. *Rambling Blues: The Life and Songs of Charlie Poole*. London: Old Time Music, 1982.

Rose, H. W. "Rayon Weaving in the South." *Cotton* 96, nos. 9, 10 (September, October 1932): 17–19, 64–66.

Rosengarten, Theodore. *All God's Dangers: The Life of Nate Shaw*. New York: Knopf, 1975.

Ross, Edward A. "Sectionalism and Its Avoidance." *Social Forces* 2 (May 1924): 484–87.

Ross, James. *They Don't Dance Much*. New York: Houghton Mifflin, 1940. Reprint. Carbondale, Ill.: Southern Illinois University Press, 1975.

Rothstein, Morton. "The Ante-Bellum South as a Dual Economy: A Tentative Hypothesis." *Agricultural History* 41 (October 1967): 373–82.

Ruffin, Edmund. *Sketches of Lower North Carolina*. Raleigh, N.C.: Institution for the Deaf and Dumb and the Blind, 1861.

Sappington, Roger E. "Dunker Beginnings in North Carolina in the Eighteenth Century." *North Carolina Historical Review* 46 (July 1969): 214–39.

_____. "Two Eighteenth-Century Dunker Congregations in North Carolina." *North Carolina Historical Review* 47 (April 1970): 176–204.

Saville, Thorndike. "The Power Situation in the Southern Power Province." *Annals of the American Academy of Political and Social Science* 153 (1931).

Schwenning, G. T. "Prospects of Southern Textile Unionism." *Journal of Political Economy* 39 (December 1931): 783–810.

_____, ed. *Management Problems with Special Reference to the Textile Industry*. Chapel Hill: University of North Carolina Press, 1930.

Scranton, Philip. "Varieties of Paternalism: Industrial Relations and the Social Relations of Production in American Textiles." *American Quarterly* 36 (Summer 1984): 235–57.

Seeman, Ernest. *American Gold*. New York: Dial Press, 1978.

Separk, Joseph H., ed. *Gastonia and Gaston County*. Gastonia, N.C.: Joseph H. Separk, 1936.

Sharp, Cecil J. *English Folk Songs from the Southern Appalachians*. Edited by Maud Karpeles. 1918. Reprint. 2 vols. London: Oxford University Press, 1932.

Shaw, Carol. "A City in Conflict: The 1919 Charlotte Streetcar Strike." Honors essay, University of North Carolina, 1980.

Shaw, Martha. "Textile Industry in Greenville County." *Greenville News*, 29 December 1928, 7 April 1935, 19 June 1956, 11 December 1958, 26 June 1962; *Greenville Piedmont*, 15 October 1929, 29 July 1938.

_____. "The Textile Industry in Greenville County, South Carolina." Master's thesis, University of Tennessee, 1964.

Shore, Laurence. "Daniel Augustus Tompkins and Blacks: The New South Faces the Race Question." Honors essay, University of North Carolina, 1977.

_____. *Southern Capitalists: The Ideological Leadership of an Elite, 1832–1885*. Chapel Hill: University of North Carolina Press, 1986.

Simkins, Francis Butler. *Pitchfork Ben Tillman: South Carolinian*. Baton Rouge: Louisiana State University Press, 1944.

Simpson, William Hays. *Life in Mill Communities*. Clinton, S.C.: P. C. Publishing Co., 1943.

_____. *Southern Textile Communities*. Durham, N.C.: American Cotton Manufacturers Association, 1948.

Singal, Daniel Joseph. *The War Within: From Victorian to Modernist Thought in the South, 1919–1945*. Chapel Hill: University of North Carolina Press, 1982.

Sitterson, Joseph Carlyle. "Business Leaders in Post–Civil War North Carolina,
    1865–1900." In *Studies in Southern History*, edited by J. C. Sitterson, pp. 111–21.
    James Sprunt Studies in History and Political Science, vol. 39. Chapel Hill: Uni-
    versity of North Carolina Press, 1957.
———. *The Secession Movement in North Carolina.* James Sprunt Studies in History
    and Political Science, vol. 23, no. 2. Chapel Hill: University of North Carolina
    Press, 1939.
Sketches of Monroe and Union County. Charlotte, N.C.: News and Times Printing
    Co., 1902.
Sloan, Clifford Myer. "The J. P. Stevens Dispute: An Episode in Southern Labor
    History." Honors essay, Harvard University, 1979.
Smith, Fenelon DeVere. "The Economic Development of the Textile Industry in the
    Columbia, South Carolina, Area from 1790 through 1916." Ph.D. diss., Univer-
    sity of Kentucky, 1952.
Smith, Lillian. *Killers of the Dream.* New York: Anchor, 1963.
Smith, Robert Sidney. *Mill on the Dan: A History of Dan River Mills, 1882–1950.*
    Durham, N.C.: Duke University Press, 1960.
Sosna, Morton. *In Search of the Silent South.* New York: Columbia University Press, 1977.
South Carolina in 1884: A View of the Industrial Life of the State. Charleston: News
    and Courier, 1884.
South Carolina Writers' Project. *South Carolina: A Guide to the Palmetto State.* New
    York: Oxford University Press, 1941.
Springs, Katherine Wooten. *The Squires of Springfield.* Charlotte, N.C.: William
    Lofton, 1956.
Starobin, Robert S. *Industrial Slavery in the Old South.* New York: Oxford University
    Press, 1970.
Stein, Maurice. *The Eclipse of Community.* Princeton, N.J.: Princeton University
    Press, 1960.
Stephenson, Jean. *Scotch-Irish Migration to South Carolina, 1772.* Washington, D.C.:
    Shenandoah Publishing House, 1971.
Stern, Boris. *Mechanical Changes in the Cotton-Textile Industry, 1910 to 1936.* Wash-
    ington, D.C.: Bureau of Labor Statistics, 1937.
Stevens, William. *Anvil of Adversity: Biography of a Furniture Pioneer.* New York:
    Popular Library, 1968.
Stilgoe, John R. *Common Landscape of America, 1580–1845.* New Haven, Conn.: Yale
    University Press, 1982.
Still, Fred. "Advantages of High Speed Spooling and Warping." *Southern Textile Bul-
    letin* (3 November 1927): 36, 48.
Stokes, Allen Heath, Jr. "Black and White Labor and the Development of the
    Southern Textile Industry, 1880–1920." Ph.D. diss., University of South Caro-
    lina, 1977.
Stokes, Durward T. *Company Shops: The Town Built by a Railroad.* Winston-Salem,
    N.C.: John F. Blair, 1981.

_____. "North Carolina and the Great Revival of 1800." *North Carolina Historical Review* 43 (October 1966): 401–12.

Stott, William. *Documentary Expression in the Thirties America*. New York: Oxford University Press, 1973.

Stover, John F. *The Railroads of the South, 1865–1900*. Chapel Hill: University of North Carolina Press, 1955.

Street, James H. *The New Revolution in the Cotton Economy: Mechanization and Its Consequences*. Chapel Hill: University of North Carolina Press, 1957.

Stribling, J. C. *The Black Ghost of the Rocky Branch, or the Slave-Time Possum Hunter*. Pendleton County, S.C.: Pendleton Farmers Society, 1908.

Stroupe, Henry S. " 'Cite Them Both to Attend the Next Church Conference': Social Control by North Carolina Baptist Churches, 1772–1908." *North Carolina Historical Review* 52 (April 1975): 156–70.

Strout, Cushing. *The Veracious Imagination: Essays on American History, Literature, and Biography*. Middletown, Conn.: Wesleyan University Press, 1981.

Sussman, Carl. *Planning for the Fourth Migration: The Neglected Vision of the Regional Planning Asssociation of America*. Cambridge, Mass.: MIT Press, 1976.

Swaim, Doug. "North Carolina Folk Housing." *Carolina Dwelling* 26 (1978): 28–45.

Swain, George F. *Report on the Water-Power of the South Atlantic Watershed*. Washington, D.C.: Government Printing Office, 1885.

Sweet, William W. *Religion on the American Frontier*. Vol 2, *The Presbyterians*; vol. 3, *The Methodists*. Chicago: University of Chicago Press, 1946.

Tamburro, Frances. "The Factory Girl Song." *Southern Exposure* 2 (1974): 42–51.

Tannenbaum, Frank. *Darker Phases of the South*. New York: G. P. Putnam's Sons, 1924.

Taylor, Caroline H. "A Yankee in the Piedmont." *South Atlantic Quarterly* 8 (July 1909): 215–21.

Terrill, Tom E. "Eager Hands: Labor for Southern Textiles, 1850–1860." *Journal of Economic History* 36 (March 1976): 84–99.

_____. "Murder in Graniteville." In *Toward a New South?: Studies in Post–Civil War Southern Communities*, edited by Orville V. Burton and Robert C. McMath. Westport, Conn.: Greenwood Press, 1982.

Terrill, Tom E., and Jerrold Hirsch, eds. *Such as Us: Southern Voices of the Thirties*. Chapel Hill: University of North Carolina Press, 1978.

"This Is the Piedmont Carolinas." *Charlotte News*, 29 July 1947. Special edition.

Thomas, David Nolan. "Early History of the North Carolina Furniture Industry." Ph.D. diss., University of North Carolina, 1964.

_____. *Foundation of the North Carolina Furniture Industry*. Raleigh: School of Forestry, North Carolina State University, 1967.

_____. "Getting Started in High Point." Extract from *Forest History* 11, no. 2 (July 1967): 22–32.

_____. "A History of Southern Furniture." *Furniture South* 46, no. 10 (October 1967): 13–15.

Thomas, Emory. M. *The Confederate Nation: 1861–1865*. New York: Harper and Row, 1979.

Thompson, E. P. "Eighteenth-Century English Society: Class Struggle without Class?" *Social History* 3 (May 1978): 136–65.

———. *The Making of the English Working Class*. New York: Vintage, 1963.

———. "Time, Work-Discipline, and Industrial Capitalism." *Past and Present* 38 (December 1967): 56–97.

Thompson, Ernest Trice. *Presbyterians in the South*. 3 vols. Richmond: John Knox Press, 1963.

Thompson, Holland. "The Civil War and Social and Economic Changes." *Annals of the American Academy of Political and Social Science* 153 (January 1931): 11–20. Special issue, *The Coming of Industry to the South*, edited by William J. Carson.

———. *From Cottonfield to Cotton Mill*. New York: Macmillan, 1906.

———. *The New South*. New Haven, Conn.: Yale University Press, 1921.

Thompson, William W., Jr. "A Managerial History of a Cotton Textile Firm: Spartan Mills, 1888–1958." Ph.D. diss., University of Alabama, Tuscaloosa, 1962.

Thrasher, Sue. "Radical Education in the Thirties." *Southern Exposure* 1, nos. 3–4 (Winter 1974): 204–10.

Tilley, Nannie May. *The Bright Tobacco Industry, 1860–1929*. Chapel Hill: University of North Carolina Press, 1948.

———. *The R. J. Reynolds Tobacco Company*. Chapel Hill: University of North Carolina Press, 1985.

———. *Reynolds Homestead, 1814–1970*. Richmond, Va.: Robert Kline and Co., 1970.

Tindall, George Brown. *The Emergence of the New South, 1913–1945*. Baton Rouge: Louisiana State University Press, 1948.

———. "The Significance of Howard W. Odum to Southern History: A Preliminary Estimate." *Journal of Southern History* 24 (August 1958): 285–307.

Tippett, Tom. *When Southern Labor Stirs*. New York: Jonathan Cape and Harrison Smith, 1931.

Tompkins, D. A. *Cotton Mill Commercial Features: A Textbook for the Use of Textile Schools and Investors*. Charlotte, N.C.: privately printed, 1899.

———. *Cotton Values in Textile Fabrics*. Charlotte, N.C.: privately printed, 1900.

———. *History of Mecklenburg County*. Charlotte, N.C.: Observer Printing House, 1903.

Trible, Phyllis. *God and the Rhetoric of Sexuality*. Overtures to Biblical Theology Series, no. 20. Philadelphia: Fortress Press, 1978.

Trimble, Stanley, W. *Man-Induced Soil Erosion on the Southern Piedmont, 1700–1970*. Ankeny, Iowa: Soil Conservation Society of America, 1974.

Triplette, Ralph R., Jr. "One-Industry Towns: Their Location, Development, and Economic Character." Ph.D. diss., University of North Carolina, 1974.

Tuan, Yi-Fu. *Topophilia*. Englewood Cliffs, N.J.: Prentice-Hall, 1974.

Tullos, Allen. "The Great Hookworm Crusade." *Southern Exposure* 6, no. 2 (Summer 1978): 40–49.

_____. "The Habits of Industry: A Study of White Culture, Protestant Temperament, and the Emergence of the Carolina Piedmont." Ph.D. diss., Yale University, 1985.

_____, ed. *Long Journey Home: Folklife in the South*. Special issue, *Southern Exposure* 5, nos. 2–3, 1977.

_____ (producer). *Frail Joines: Brushy Mountain Storyteller*. Audiotape documentary in the series North Carolina Traditions. Chapel Hill: Cece Conway and Curriculum in Folklore, University of North Carolina, 1988.

Turner, Frederick Jackson. *The Significance of Sections in American History*. New York: Henry Holt and Co., 1932.

Tuttle, Marcia Lee. "The Location of North Carolina's Nineteenth-Century Textile Industry." Master's thesis, University of North Carolina, 1974.

Vance, Rupert B. *All These People: The Nation's Human Resources in the South*. Chapel Hill: University of North Carolina Press, 1945.

_____. "The Concept of the Region." *Social Forces* 8 (December 1929): 108–28.

_____. "Howard W. Odum and the Case of the South." Address to the Southeastern Meeting of the American Studies Association, 11 April 1970.

_____. *Human Factors in Cotton Culture*. Chapel Hill: University of North Carolina Press, 1929.

_____. *Human Geography of the South: A Study in Regional Resources and Human Adequacy*. Chapel Hill: University of North Carolina Press, 1932.

Vance, Rupert B., and Nicholas J. Demerath, eds. *The Urban South*. Chapel Hill: University of North Carolina Press, 1954.

Van Osdell, John Garrett. "Cotton Mills, Labor, and the Southern Mind: 1800–1930." Ph.D. diss., Tulane University, 1966.

Van Vorst, Bessie, and Marie Van Vorst. *The Woman Who Toils*. New York: Doubleday, Page and Co., 1903.

Van Vorst, Marie. *Amanda of the Mill*. New York: Dodd, Mead and Company, 1905.

Vorse, Mary Heaton. *Strike!* New York: Liverwright, 1930.

Walden, H. Nelson. *History of Union County*. Charlotte, N.C.: Heritage Printers, 1964.

Walker, William. *The Southern Harmony and Musical Companion*. Philadelphia: E. W. Miller, 1854.

Wallace, David Duncan. *The History of South Carolina*. 4 vols. New York: American Historical Society, 1934.

_____. *South Carolina: A Short History, 1520–1948*. Chapel Hill: University of North Carolina Press, 1951.

Walser, Jim. "Taking Care of Business: Government in South Carolina." *Southern Changes* 6, no. 3 (June/July 1984): 3–13.

Watson, Harry L. "Conflict and Collaboration: Yeomen, Slaveholders, and Politics in the Antebellum South." *Social History* 10 (October 1985): 273–98.

_____. *An Independent People: The Way We Lived in North Carolina, 1770–1820*. Chapel Hill: University of North Carolina Press, 1983.

Weare, Walter B. *Black Business in the New South*. Urbana: University of Illinois Press, 1973.

Webb, Mena. *Jule Carr: General without an Army*. Chapel Hill: University of North Carolina Press, 1987.

Weber, Max. *The Protestant Ethic and the Spirit of Capitalism*. New York: Scribner, 1958.

Weisberger, Bernard. *They Gathered at the River*. Boston: Little, Brown, 1958.

West, Don L. "Parker Mill District Is Fully Alert to Need for Education of the Youth." *Greenville News*[?], June 1926[?]. Clipping in the Parker School District Scrapbook Collection, Greenville County Library, Greenville, S.C.

West, James Lemuel Willis. "Early Backwoods Humor in the Greenville *Mountaineer*, 1826–1840." *Mississippi Quarterly* 25 (Winter 1971): 69–82.

Whatley, Lowell McKay, Jr. *The Architectural History of Randolph County, North Carolina*. Asheboro: North Carolina Division of Archives and History, 1985.

Whisnant, David E. *All That Is Native and Fine: The Politics of Culture in an American Region*. Chapel Hill: University of North Carolina Press, 1983.

White, Benjamin F., and E. J. King. *The Sacred Harp*. Philadelphia: S. S. Collins, 1860.

White, Burton Kirke. "Cotton Mills and Organized Labor: Danville, Virginia, 1930–1931." Master's thesis, University of North Carolina, 1971.

White, Newman Ivey, gen. ed. *The Frank C. Brown Collection of North Carolina Folklore*. 7 vols. Durham: Duke University Press, 1952–64.

Wickenden, William. *Report of the Investigation for the Promotion of Engineering Education*. Pittsburgh, Pa.: Society for the Promotion of Engineering Education, 1930.

Wiener, Jonathan. *Social Origins of the New South: Alabama, 1860–1885*. Baton Rouge: Louisiana State University Press, 1978.

Wiggins, Gene. *Fiddlin' Georgia Crazy: Fiddlin' John Carson, His Real World, and the World of His Songs*. Urbana: University of Illinois Press, 1987.

Wiley, C. H. *The North Carolina Reader*. Philadelphia: Lippincott, Grambo and Co., 1851.

Williams, Cratis. "Appalachian Speech." *North Carolina Historical Review* 55 (April 1978): 174–76.

Williams, John A. "Radicalism and Professionalism in Folklore Studies: A Comparative Perspective." *Journal of the Folklore Institute* 11 (1975): 211–39.

Williams, Raymond. *The Country and the City*. New York: Oxford University Press, 1973.

———. *Culture and Society*. New York: Columbia University Press, 1958.

———. *Key Words: A Vocabulary of Culture and Society*. New York: Oxford University Press, 1976.

———. *Marxism and Literature*. New York: Oxford University Press, 1977.

———. *The Sociology of Culture*. New York: Schocken, 1982.

Williamson, Gustavus G., Jr. "Cotton Manufacturing in South Carolina: 1865–1892." Ph.D. diss., Johns Hopkins University, 1954.

Wilson, Louis R. *The University of North Carolina, 1900–1930: The Making of a Modern University*. Chapel Hill: University of North Carolina Press, 1957.

Winkler, John K. *Tobacco Tycoon: The Story of James Buchanan Duke*. New York: Random House, 1942.

Winston, George Taylor. *A Builder of the New South: Being the Story of the Life Work of Daniel Augustus Tompkins*. New York: Doubleday, Page and Co., 1920.

Wolfe, Thomas. "The Crisis in Industry." Worth Prize thesis, University of North Carolina, 1919.

Woodman, Harold D. *King Cotton and His Retainers: Financing and Marketing of the Cotton Crop of the South, 1800–1925*. Lexington: University Press of Kentucky, 1968.

———. "Postbellum Social Change and Its Effects on Marketing the South's Cotton Crop." *Agricultural History* 56 (January 1982): 215–30.

Woodmason, Charles. *The Carolina Backcountry on the Eve of the Revolution*. Edited by Richard J. Hooker. Chapel Hill: University of North Carolina Press, 1953.

Woodward, C. Vann. *American Counterpoint: Slavery and Racism in the North-South Dialogue*. Boston: Little, Brown, 1971.

———. *Origins of the New South*. Baton Rouge: Louisiana State University Press, 1951.

———. *Thinking Back: The Perils of Writing History*. Baton Rouge: Louisiana State University Press, 1986.

———, ed. *Mary Chesnut's Civil War*. New Haven, Conn.: Yale University Press, 1981.

Woodward, W. E. *The Gift of Life*. New York: E. P. Dutton, 1947.

———. *The Way Our People Lived*. New York: Liverwright, 1944.

Woofter, Thomas J., Jr. "The Subregions of the Southeast." *Social Forces* 13 (October 1934): 43–50.

Woofter, Thomas J., Jr., Rupert Vance, Harriet Herring, and J. H. Johnson. "A Survey of the Catawba Valley, 1935." Unpublished study by the Institute for Research in Social Science, University of North Carolina, made for the Tennessee Valley Authority, 1935.

Woolf, Douglas G. "The Motivated Method of the Parker District." *Textile World* (March 1927[?]), reprinted in *Greenville News* [?], [n.d.]. Clipping in Parker School District Scrapbook Collection, Greenville County Library, Greenville, S.C.

World Leadership in Denims. Greensboro, N.C.: Proximity Manufacturing Co., 1925.

Worthman, Paul B., and James R. Green. "Black Workers in the New South, 1865–1915." In *Key Issues in Afro-American Experience*, edited by Nathan Huggins, Martin Kilson, and Daniel M. Fox, 2:47–69. New York: Harcourt Brace Jovanovich, 1971.

Wright, Gavin. "Cheap Labor and Southern Textiles before 1880." *Journal of Economic History* 39 (September 1979): 655–80.

_____. *Old South, New South: Revolutions in the Southern Economy since the Civil War.* New York: Basic Books, 1986.

_____. *The Political Economy of the Cotton South: Households, Markets, and Wealth in the Nineteenth Century.* New York: Norton, 1978.

Writers' Project Administration for the State of North Carolina. *Charlotte: A Guide to the Queen City of North Carolina.* Charlotte: News Printing House, 1939.

Wyatt-Brown, Bertram. *Southern Honor: Ethics and Behavior in the Old South.* New York: Oxford University Press, 1982.

York, Brantley. *The Autobiography of Brantley York.* Edited by W. K. Boyd. Durham: Seeman Printery, 1910.

Young, James R., and Marjorie W. Young. *Textile Leaders of the South.* Columbia, S.C.: R. L. Bryan Co., 1963.

Young, T. M. *The American Cotton Industry: A Study of the Work and Workers.* London: Metheum and Co. 1902.

Zeublin, Charles. "The World's First Sociological Laboratory." *American Journal of Sociology* 4 (March 1899): 577–92.

Zug, Charles G., III. "Pursuing Pots: On Writing a History of North Carolina Folk Pottery." *North Carolina Folklore Journal* 27 (1979): 34–55.

_____. *The Traditional Potters of North Carolina.* Chapel Hill, N.C.: Ackland Art Museum, 1981. Exhibition catalog.

_____. *Turners and Burners: The Folk Potters of North Carolina.* Chapel Hill: University of North Carolina Press, 1986.

Acknowledgments

M any people have guided, accompanied, and encouraged this historical foray into the Carolina Piedmont. Those of us who worked with the Southern Oral History Program's Piedmont Industrialization Project are especially indebted to the retired mill workers, engineers, and manufacturers who recalled their lives on the region's farms and in its emerging textile towns. Their names appear in the endnotes and are listed in the Guide to Sources. The collection of interviews, conducted between 1975 and 1980, is available to researchers at the Southern Historical Collection of the University of North Carolina at Chapel Hill.

Far north of the Carolina Piedmont, I found encouragement among the faculty and graduate students in American Studies at Yale University. I can imagine no more supportive adviser than Alabama native, Western historian, and comparative regional scholar Howard Lamar, who, amid his own teaching, writing, and administrative duties as dean of Yale College, regularly discussed and improved my drafts and revisions.

At every stage of the writing I benefited from the keen eye and critical counsel of Jean-Christophe Agnew, who always knew better than to leave well enough alone.

During C. Vann Woodward's final year of graduate seminars on the history of the South, I completed papers that form parts of two chapters in this book. Professor Woodward's attention then, and in later correspondence and discussions about the manuscript, have left me, among a large and excellent company, in his lien.

In New Haven, Bill Ferris offered a sustaining cheer in the difficult early going. Kai Erikson encouraged my joining of biography with an investigation of regional ethos. Charles F. Montgomery taught me to look more closely at a world of material objects and their makers. George Rosen and Arthur Viseltear oversaw a year-long exploration into southern public health history.

During my sojourns in and visits to Chapel Hill, Daniel W. Patterson, guiding spirit of the Curriculum in Folklore at the University of North Carolina, has stood, as only his students and colleagues can appreciate, as careful critic, painstaking reader, and generous friend.

In his investigations of power, technology, regionalism, and human development, explored in many books and across several decades, Lewis Mumford has ranged as chronicler and prophet of American studies. For many years I have been heartened by our correspondence and encouraged by visits with Lewis and Sophia Mumford at their farmhouse in Amenia, New York.

A very deep appreciation is owed to Candace Waid, who has talked cultural geography, gender, class, and race with me since those startling years at the University of Alabama at Tuscaloosa when the South was turned upside down. Candace's interpretive gifts have improved each of my revisions.

Doug DeNatale, also in pursuit of the Piedmont's meanings, shared thoughts, tunes, and hours of companionship over the region's highways and low roads, among the archives, bookshelves, and coffee cups.

There are many others to whom I am very much obliged, and who are not elsewhere acknowledged: Judith Babbitts, Tommie Bass, Bess Beatty, Cecelia Conway, Tom and Miriam Davenport, Deborah Ellis, Dan Ellison, Ruthie Ervin, Cary Fowler, Elliott Gorn, Susie Hamrick, Tom Hatley, Glenn Hinson, John E. and Blanche Joines, Harriet Jones, the Bertha Landis family, Roger Manley, William Mass, Joyce Joines Newman, Catherine Peck, Tom Rankin, Elizabeth Siceloff, Steve Suitts, Brett and Ellen Sutton, Tommy Thompson, and Terry Zug.

Fellowships from the National Endowment for the Arts and the National Museum Act enabled my graduate study at Yale. While I was in New Haven, a Margaret Giles Whiting Fellowship in the Humanities supported a full year of writing. A fellowship from the American Council of Learned Societies, a semester's leave, and a summer faculty grant from Emory University helped me to turn manuscript into book.

I also wish to thank the staffs of the North Carolina Collection and the Southern Historical Collection of the University of North Carolina at Chapel Hill, as well as to the librarians and archivists at the North Carolina Department of Archives and History, the Perkins Library at Duke University, the Greenville (South Carolina) Public Library, the Charlotte-Mecklenburg Library, and Greenville's Textile Hall.

Many people have given critical readings, encouragement, and various forms of occasional or singular assistance: Bruce Bastin, Roscoe Brooks, Will D. Campbell, Dan T. Carter, Mimi Conway, Arthur Dye, John Egerton, Henry Glassie, Archie Green, Steve Hahn, Suzanne Hall, Jerrold Hirsch, Laurel Horton, Chip Hughes, Si Kahn, Kip Lornell, Paige McCullough,

Robert Mitchell, David Montgomery, Dan Morrill, Barry O'Connell, Barry Poss, Jonathan Prude, Tom Schlesinger, Carol Shaw, Nick Spitzer, Lynn Stanley, Frances Tamburro, Tom E. Terrill, Sue Thrasher, Reba Vance, David E. Whisnant, Randall Williams, and Margaret Yocom.

I especially thank the Southern Oral History Program at the University of North Carolina at Chapel Hill, its director Jacquelyn Dowd Hall, and my coworkers in the Piedmont Industrialization Project: Hugh Brinton, Dorothy Casey, Della Coulter, Doug DeNatale, Patty Dilley, Bill Finger, Mary Frederickson, Brent Glass, Rosemarie Hester, Glenn Hinson, Jean Houston, Dolores Janiewski, Beverly Jones, Lu Ann Jones, Bob Korstad, Cliff Kuhn, Jim Leloudis, Mary Anne McDonald, Mary Murphy, Rachel Osborn, Valerie Quinney, Lanier Rand, Carol Shaw, and Pamela Upton. Elizabeth Fink and Frank Munger provided office space at the Institute for Research in Social Science. The National Endowment for the Humanities supported this remarkable project in oral history.

At the University of North Carolina Press I thank Iris Tillman Hill, Ed King, April Leidig-Higgins, and, especially, Pamela Upton, whose familiarity with the subject of this book complemented her industrious and meticulous eye.

Georgia and David Dreger typed, retyped, processed, and proofed several drafts of hundreds of pages, always managing to find, sort, shuffle, and reshuffle the many versions and revisions. For her thoughtful and careful indexing, which readers will quickly appreciate, I thank Deborah Beckel.

And I thank my parents, Rolf E. and Dorothy H. Tullos, for their steadfast love and support from the home region of deepest memory.

Index

A. T. and O. Railroad, 135
Abbeville, S.C. (city and county), 25, 48, 78
Abolitionism. *See* Antislavery
Abortion: Ethel Hilliard on, 239. *See also* Contraception
Adams, Harry, 121, 123
Adams, John, 27, 28
Adams, Robert Roy, 25, 27–29, 40; education, 25; Scottish and textile background, 25, 27; family work habits, 27; Sirrine engineer, 27; on early mills, 27–28; religion, 27–28; father as farmer, surveyor, mill builder and owner, and Presbyterian, 27–29; mother's household production, 29; on differences between backcountry and Low Country, 40
Advertising, 173; of Belk stores, 36; of Burlington Industries, 116, 118, 131–32; and agrarian myths, 134–35, 137–38; creation of Piedmont's industrial image, 134–35, 138–43, 157–60, 163, 166–71, 287–303; central to American Tobacco Company, 162; and Duke Power Company's promotion of Piedmont industrialization, 163, 166–71, 287; of Barber-Colman automatic and high-speed textile machinery, 199, 201–2; of Veeder-Root pick clocks, 273, 300. *See also* Capitalists; Publicists
Agrarians (Vanderbilt University), 292
Agriculture: last quarter of 19th century, xiv, 19, 34, 134–36, 143; commercialization, 34, 77–82, 94, 134–36, 143; Low Country, 42–43; Piedmont, 46, 49–50, 53; antebellum small farm, 57, 77–82. *See also* Corn; Cotton; Farm families; Farm work; Sharecropping and tenancy; Soil erosion; Tobacco; Wheat
Air-Line Railroad, 34, 138–39; built in 1870s, 138, 140; importance to Piedmont's industrialization, 138–39, 140–43; built with northern capital, 138–39, 142; promotion, 138–43; and growth of Piedmont towns and capitalists, 139–43; absorbed by Northern-owned Southern Railroad, 142
Airplanes, 206, 207
Alabama, 50, 65, 80
Alamance County, N.C.: textile mills, 19–20, 113–14; textile work force, 21, 114; unionization efforts, 24; Pennsylvania Dutch settlers, 52; Spencer Love moves mill to, 113–14. *See also* Burlington Industries; Haw River